ReadingsPLUS *with* WebLinks

Issues in
American Government
1999/2000

*Current and controversial readings
with links to relevant Web sites*

Readings and World Wide Web Sites
Edited and Selected by

James Brent, Ph.D.
San Jose State University

Morton Publishing Company
925 W. Kenyon Avenue, Unit 12
Englewood, CO 80110

800/348-3777

http://www.morton-pub.com

About the Editor: James Brent is assistant professor of political science at San Jose State University. He obtained bachelors degrees in political science and advertising from Southern Methodist University and a Ph.D. in political science from Ohio State University. He teaches courses relating to the American judiciary and Congress. His research interests include the relationships between the Supreme Court and lower courts. He attempts to motivate his students by emphasizing the importance of politics to their own lives. He also integrates the Internet into all of his courses. His home-page can be found at **http://www.sjsu.edu/depts/PoliSci/faculty/brent.html**.

Credits:
Interior Design: Joanne R. Saliger
Cover Design: Bob Schram, Bookends
Typography: Ash Street Typecrafters, Inc.
WebLinks Logo: Laura Patchkofsky

For Morton Publishing Company:

Douglas N. Morton, President and Publisher
Mimi Egan, Publisher, Series Publishing
Maureen Owen, Senior Editor, Series Publishing

ReadingsPLUS with WebLinks: Issues in American Government, 1999/2000
Copyright © 1999, Morton Publishing Company
925 W. Kenyon Avenue, Unit 12
Englewood, Colorado 80110
800/348-3777

ISBN: 0-89582-464-7

5   4   3   2   1

Printed in the United States of America.

WebAdvisory Board

Members of the WebAdvisory Board provide feedback on readings and World Wide Web sites, and generally advise the editor and the publishing staff. They are academics with a variety of specialties and teaching experiences. Because Morton Publishing Company also values the perspective students bring to course materials, student advisors are instrumental in shaping *ReadingsPLUS with WebLinks.*

David Aronson
Department of Political Science
University of South Dakota

MaryAnne Borrelli
Department of Government
Connecticut College

Scott McLean
Department of Political Science
Quinnipiac College

Kyran Owen-Mankovich
Student Advisor
University of Colorado-Boulder

Preface

Now is an interesting time to be studying political science. We have been faced with the extraordinary prospect of a president being removed from office. The Republican Party is ascendant at all levels of government for the first time in more than half a century. American politics is grappling with the fact that the country is becoming more diverse. And the Internet is changing the way we relate to each other and, consequently, the way politics is conducted.

ReadingsPLUS: Issues in American Government introduces you to some of the most important political controversies and cultural currents reflected in American government today. Although it is difficult to separate politics from politicians, the readings in this book were selected with a focus on issues (and currency) rather than on personalities. Therefore you will find no attacks on Kenneth Starr or discussions of the president's sex life. However, you will find readings on the Independent Counsel Act and on the office of the presidency. In addition, you will find readings on: the balance of power between the states and the federal government; campaign finance reform; the rights of women and minorities; the role of the media in politics; and conducting foreign policy in the post-Cold War era, to highlight but a few of the many readings.

Also, issues of particular importance or interest to college-age citizens have deliberately been included. For example, you will find selections on the use of tax money to build sports stadiums; how the Disney corporation is trying to establish a sense of community at a company-built town in Florida; the war on drugs; the regulation of sport-utility vehicles; and privacy rights in contemporary society.

In addition to the readings, there is a comprehensive, fully-annotated directory of 140 academically appropriate Web sites that directly correspond to the topics and issues raised in the readings. There are three selections in the Introduction that offer advice and guidelines for how to analyze a reading assignment (and get the most out of what you read) and on how to conduct research on the Web.

ReadingsPLUS is organized to complement traditional textbooks in undergraduate courses in American Government. The readings have been selected to present both liberal and conservative viewpoints as well as progressive opinions that do not fall neatly into those categories. Some of the selections are informational, others are controversial. All are designed to encourage critical thinking on issues in American Government, to provide a basis for class discussion or debate, to assist in research and writing assignments, and to enhance the experience of the course.

—James Brent

A Note from the Publisher

Welcome to *ReadingsPLUS!*

Alert and adventurous readers are important to us in keeping this volume up-to-date and accurate. So if you would like to recommend a timely reading on an important topic in American Government, or if you happen upon a great World Wide Web site with compelling resources, or even if you discover an error (it happens), we'd appreciate hearing from you. Our phone number is 1-800-348-3777. Or just drop us a line at:

✉ **Morton Publishing Company**
925 W. Kenyon Avenue, Unit 12
Englewood, Colorado 80110

Fax: 303-762-9923

✉ E-mail: morton@morton-pub.com

💻 Web address: http://www.morton-pub.com

What You Will Find in This Book

This book contains current and controversial readings on important topics in American government and politics. The readings are drawn from a mix of professional journals and popular, high-quality magazines and newsletters. The readings that are controversial carry the label *A Reading for Critical Thinking*. In addition, you will find:

Reading Review Form

(See Part 12 at the back of the book.) The Reading Review Form is designed to assist you as you reflect on the readings that have been assigned and to enhance your critical thinking skills. Use it for extra credit for assigned readings, for writing class papers or exercises, or to generate classroom discussion. You are encouraged to tear out the Reading Review Form and make photocopies of it and use it for each reading in whatever way works best for you.

Introduction: Critical Reading and Internet Research Skills

There are three readings at the front of the book that provide a thorough overview of student study skills and using the World Wide Web (what it is and how to use it as a resource). **Reading 1** is a general introduction to critical reading techniques. **Reading 2** is a set of basic guidelines you can use to evaluate Internet resources of any kind. **Reading 3** looks at search engines and how to use the Web for research.

WebLinks: A Directory of Annotated World Wide Web Sites

At the back of the book in **Part 12: Working with the World Wide Web**, you will find Web sites that contain information and resources relevant to the issues discussed in the readings. The Web addresses have been fully verified, and all the sites are briefly described. The Web sites are organized alphabetically by site name, and each site has been numbered for easy reference and referral. **The Quick Reference Guide to Topics/Readings/World Wide Web Sites** (which is described in detail below) will let you quickly match a reading with the Web sites that are relevant to it. However, please note that the Guide, while extensive, is not exhaustive in linking readings with Web sites, and you may want to explore sites on your own and make your own connections between readings and Web sites. The brief description of each Web site can also assist you in deciding which sites to consult.

Web Site Evaluation Form

In Part 12 at the back of the book you will find a Web Site Evaluation Form, which you can use in any of a number of ways: to evaluate Web sites that are assigned for extra credit, as a tool to assist you if you are preparing a research assignment, or simply for your own reference. Even if your instructor does not require you to use the Web Site Evaluation Form, we encourage you to photocopy it and use it to direct your work on the Web.

Web Journal

(See Part 12 at the back of the book.) Use these pages to make note of sites you have visited. You could record your reactions to a site, or briefly note what information you found there. Is the site worth a repeat visit in your opinion? Could you use it for personal reference? Could you use it for a research assignment? Who runs the site? Where is it located? You may want to develop the habit of evaluating both the content at a site and how well the site operates. Ask yourself, is the site easy to navigate? Are the graphics odd or are they appropriate? Are there any special features that you particularly like? How does the information at a site compare with what you have learned in a reading? If you write up your visit to a site, you will have a record of where you have been on the Web. Use these pages as you would any journal or lab manual. It is a place for you to make personal observations about your Web experiences, and to raise issues you would like to discuss in class about a site.

(Should you run out of Web Journal pages, you may photocopy the Web Journal for your own personal use.)

Quick Reference Guide to Topics/Readings/World Wide Web Sites

The Quick Reference Guide correlates topics in American government with the readings and World Wide Web sites found in the book. It can be used for easy reference to locate readings and Web sites. In addition, the Quick Reference Guide makes it possible to integrate readings and Web sites with any course syllabus or textbook. The Guide can also be used to make class assignments. Although it is not comprehensive in its scope (i.e., there may be topics addressed in the readings and Web sites that are not listed in the Quick Reference Guide), it can still serve as a convenient starting point.

Other Features

Updates to WebLinks (http://www.morton-pub.com/updates/updates.stml)

Using the Web as an academic resource is not without its frustrations and limitations! You type the complete address for a site into the Location bar and,

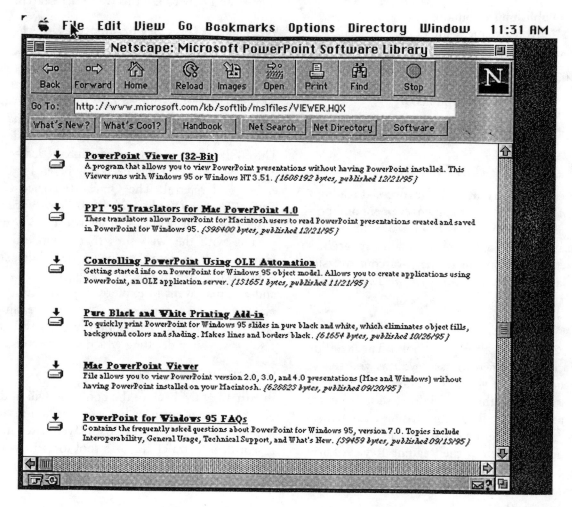

to your dismay, you don't get the results you are expecting. The site doesn't load, or it no longer exists, or the site has moved to a new location but no forwarding address or link has been provided. It is like going to the library to check out a book that is supposed to be on reserve for your course only to discover that it is not there. At our Morton Publishing Company Web site, we have developed a section dedicated to keeping you updated about the Web addresses listed in our books that we discover are no longer operational for one reason or another. Although we carefully verify all Web addresses just prior to a book's publication, and although the publishing staff and academic editor select reputable, stable sites that will in all likelihood exist for some time, Web addresses can change or go out of service. It's the nature of the technology. Should you be unable to access a site and think that the problem is not with the server, time of day, how you entered the address, etc., go to the **Updates to WebLinks** section of the Morton Web site (http://www.morton-pub.com/updates/updates.stml), scroll down to the title of the book you are using, and click on the *Update!* icon to see if we have recommended a replacement site or a new address.

You will also find an annotated table of contents at the front of the book, which highlights key sentences from the readings, and *ReadingsPLUS with WebLinks* is fully indexed.

Suggestions for Accessing a Web Site

WebLinks: A Directory of Annotated World Wide Web Sites contains sites that relate to the topics covered in the readings. You will see that each Web site has been assigned a descriptive heading and a number. For each site, the exact address, or Universal Resource Locator, is provided. Here is an example of a site's descriptive heading with its assigned number: *The U.S. Constitution Online*, No. 123. Its address or URL is http://www.usconstitution.net) To access a Web site, you will need to be at a computer that is hooked to the Internet and has a graphical browser— that is the software that allows you to access the World Wide Web. (The most popular browsers are Netscape's Navigator and Internet Explorer from Microsoft.) Once you have opened your browser, delete the address that appears in the Location bar. Then, *carefully* type the address or URL of the Web site into the Location bar (or Go To bar) on the screen and press the Enter key.

The screen may look something like the one page vi after you have typed in the address.

There are many ways to visit cyberspace, and the WebLinks Directory is designed to be a guide to academically appropriate Web sites on issues related to American Government. Use it for research for class assignments, or to follow your own interests.

A Word About Critical Thinking

ReadingsPLUS with WebLinks: Issues in American Government introduces you to a wide variety of current and controversial readings, and there are over 100 World Wide Web sites for you to consult as well. All the readings have been selected with care to provide you with a wide range of perspectives. The readings that are labeled "A Reading for Critical Thinking," however, are ones that are especially designed to encourage your critical thinking skills. To arrive at a thorough understanding of a topic, you will need to think critically about what you are reading (both in print and on screen). Critical thinking skills are increasingly important, particularly as the amount of information available to the average person keeps expanding. To be a critical thinker, you will need to learn how to ask questions, and to consider not only what is said (or written) but what is not said (or implied). You may want to consider taking a course in critical thinking. And we recommend the following print and online resources:

In Print

M. Neil Browne and Stuart M. Keeley, *Asking the Right Questions: A Guide to Critical Thinking*, 2nd ed. (Prentice-Hall, 1986).

Vicent Ryan Ruggiero, *Becoming a Critical Thinker*, 2nd ed. (Houghton Mifflin, 1996).

Glen Thomas and Gaye Smooth, "Critical Thinking: A Vital Work Skill," *Trust for Educational Leadership* (February/March 1994), pp. 34–38.

Online

Effective Learning: Study Skills/Critical Thinking

http://www.cdtl.nus.sg/UFM/Effect/Es4_3_7.html

The National University of Singapore has a portion of its Web site devoted to student study skills, including critical thinking skills. This address will take you to several lively pages that define critical thinking, explain the characteristics of a critical thinker and review fallacies to avoid. Although there are no links, the straightforward, practical text is well-designed and the guidelines are useful. (You might also want to check out the entire orientation section, which offers advice on how to make a smooth transition to higher education and on how to develop communication skills and time management skills, among other suggestions.)

The Critical Thinking Community

http://www.sonoma.edu/CThink/

This site is maintained by Sonoma State University's Center for Critical Thinking. Site provides educators, students, and the public with a wealth of information about the theory and practice of critical thinking, concepts and definitions, techniques for learning and teaching, and classroom exercises that implement the principles. Other features include weekly updates, an Educator's Resource Guide for integrating critical thinking into the curriculum, a collection of critical thinking articles, and a list of conferences. Links to online discussion groups. The site is directed by Richard Paul, Ph.D., and comments are invited through E-mail addresses provided. Also offers links to a sampling of critical thinking offices nationwide.

Mission: Critical

http://www.sjsu.edu:80/depts/itl/

This site is produced by the Institute for Teaching and Learning at San Jose State University. Its goal is to create a "virtual lab" capable of familiarizing users with the basic concepts of critical thinking in a self-paced, interactive environment. Comments and reactions are encouraged, and an E-mail address is provided. Site includes links to each step in the process plus exercises for the student to do. A good online way to become a critical thinker.

Your Thoughts Are Important to Us

Our mission in developing *ReadingsPLUS with WebLinks* is simple: to make the resources of the popular press and the World Wide Web accessible and usable within a course specific context. By carefully selecting current, academically appropriate readings from high-quality popular press sources, and by filtering and organizing World Wide Web sites, we can help you keep up-to-date and current, and we can assist you in incorporating new technology into your courses. We sincerely welcome your feedback, and please contact us with your suggestions and recommendations.

Contents

Preface..iv

A Note From the Publisher..v

Quick Reference Guide to Topics/Readings/WWW Sites.............xv

INTRODUCTION
Critical Reading and Internet Research Skills, 1

1 Critical Reading Strategies 2
Valerie Gray Hardcastle, Ph.D., *World Wide Web:*
>http://mind.phil.vt.edu/www/1204crs.html<
(July 8, 1995)

Here I present seven critical reading strategies that I have shamelessly stolen from someone else. These are strategies that you can learn readily and then apply not only to the reading selections in this class, but also to your other college reading.

2 Ten C's for Evaluating Internet Resources 4
Elizabeth B. Richmond, *World Wide Web:*
>http//www.uwec.edu/Admin/Library/10cs.html<
(November 20, 1996

How can you apply critical thinking skills, including previous knowledge and experience, to evaluate Internet resources?

3 Desperately Seeking Susan OR Suzie NOT Sushi............. 6
Matt Lake, *The New York Times* (September 3, 1998)

To search the Web successfully, pick the right engine and learn how to use it.

PART I   *The Constitution and American Democracy, 11*

4 Unsound Constitution: Oklamoma City and the Founding Fathers 12
George P. Fletcher, *The New Republic*
(June 23, 1997)

[M]cVeigh's notion of the Constitution, a notion that in his deranged mind led to terrorism, is far more influential than we commonly assume. And it is fundamentally wrong.

5 Has Democracy a Future? 16
Arthur Schlesinger, Jr., *Foreign Affairs*
(September/October 1997)

A majority of the world's inhabitants may be living under democracy . . . , but democratic hegemony is a mere flash in the long vistas of recorded history. One wonders how deeply democracy has sunk roots in previously nondemocratic countries in the years since the collapse of the totalitarian challenges. Now the democratic adventure must confront tremendous pent-up energies that threaten to blow it off course and even drive it onto the rocks.

6 Is Nothing Private?.............. 21
Jeffrey Rosen, *The New Yorker* (June 1, 1998)

As Starr prepares to submit his X-rated report to Congress, one virtue of his seemingly endless inquisition has been to remind Americans how little our legal system cares about privacy today. The subpoenas issued by Starr and Klayman are perfectly legel under current law, but a hundred years ago many of them would have been supressed as clear violations of the right to privacy.

Please note: Indicates a reading on a controversial topic, to encourage critical thinking.

PART 2 · *Federalism and Federal-State Relations, 27*

7 **Town-Building Is No Mickey Mouse Operation** **28**
Michael Pollan, *The New York Times Magazine* (December 14, 1997)

Disney occupies a special place in the American landscape and culture. Few companies are as skillful at making places, at shaping the physical environment to affect our behavior.. . . But Disney's expertise is in building theme parks for paying guests, not towns for citizens. A real community is messy, ever-changing and inevitably political — three adjectives that pretty much sum up everything the culture of Disney cannot abide.

8 **Grassroots Graft: Corruption in State Governments** **38**
John Hood, *Reason* (August/September 1998)

When it comes to corruption, state governments are second to none.

9 **The Disunited States** **42**
John D. Donahue, *The Atlantic Monthly* (May 1997)

"Devolution" — shifting power from Washington to the fifly states — is no cure for what ails American govermnent.

10 **The Stadium Trap** **46**
Charles Mahtesian, *Governing* (May 1998)

The message from the voters is clear: They don't want to pay for new professional sports stadiums. But that doesn't mean they don't want them.

11 **Power Grab** **50**
Eliza Newlin Carney, *National Journal* (April 11, 1998)

The "Devolution" revolution promised by congressional Republicans four years ago has mostly fizzled. Instead of handing over authority to state and local governments, they're taking it away.

PART 3 · *Civil Rights and Civil Liberties, 55*

12 **Is Affirmative Action on the Way Out? Should It Be?** **56**
Nathan Glazer, *Commentary* (March 1998)

Affirmative action has in part been a "hand up" to "people who have had a hard time," but its original design was so faulty that it soon became much more than that.

13 **Is the Drug War Racist?** **59**
Samuel G. Freedman, *Rolling Stone* (May 14, 1998)

America's war on drugs has ravished the inner cities it aspired to save. Without curbing drug traffic, the crusade has sent a generation of young black males into the criminal-justice system, which offers them not rehabilitation but firsthand instruction in violent crime.

14 **Who's Sorry Now?** **64**
Naomi Wolf, *George* (August 1998)

Why does an apology matter? Why is memorializing our slave past important for the present? These things matter because without them, both sides remain stuck.

15 **The Chador Hits Cyberspace** **66**
Wendy Kaminer, *The Nation* (March 9, 1998)

When feeling safe becomes as paramount a public concern for women as being safe, the drive for equality is sacrificed to demands for protection. Civil liberties and civil rights suffer.

16 **Life in the 90s: Rights and Responsibilities in an Individualistic Culture** **68**
Terry Golway, *America* (March 21,1998)

Yes, we all have a right to buy a gas-guzzling, sedan-smashing sport utility vehicle. The question, though, is this: What about our responsibilities? Do we not owe society a little less self-indulgence? If we can purchase a car that will use fewer of the planet's resources and pose less of a danger to society's members in good standing, shouldn't we?

17 **Ganging Up on Civil Liberties** **70**
Nina Siegal, *The Progressive* (October 1997)

Two of the most popular gang-fighting strategies today — employed widely in California and under consideration in other states — are gang-tracking databases and civil gang injunctions. Although police and prosecutors herald both tactics as effective methods of gang control, opponents say the measures infringe on the basic civil liberties of young people and are biased against minorities.

PART 4   *Public Opinion and Political Participation, 74*

18 The Sleeping Giant Awakes: A Portrait of the Latino Vote 75

Dale Maharidge, *Mother Jones* (January/February 1998)

For many years, the political cliche describing the Latino population was the "sleeping giant." If awakened, it would have a profound impact on America's political and social landscape. In many ways, Republicans and Democrats alike were happy that the giant slumbered. It made things easy.

19 Democracy in Texas: The Frontier Spirit 79

Editorial Staff at *The Economist*, *The Economist* (May 16, 1998)

Mr. Fishkin proposes to introduce to American politics the idea of "deliberative polling." This is a process that would draw together a representative group of ordinary people, have them listen to all sides of an issue, and then cast their considered votes on behalf of their fellow citizens.

20 Monica Lewinsky's Contribution to Political Science 81

John R. Zaller, *PS: Political Science & Politics* (June 1998)

The bounce in President Clinton's job ratings that occurred in the initial 10 days of the Lewinsky imbroglio may offer as much insight into the dynamics of public opinion as any single event in recent memory.

PART 5   *The Mass Media, 89*

21 Money Lust: How Pressure for Profit Is Perverting Journalism 90

Neil Hickey, Columbia Journalism Review (July/August 1998)

A new era has dawned in American journalism. A *New York Times* editor describes its hallmark: "A massively increased sensitivity to all things financial."

22 Network Failure 99

Brent H. Baker and Tim Graham, *National Review* (June 22, 1998)

Are the major media frivolous or biased? Some of each, find our reporters in the field.

23 Extra! The Press Is Liberal (So What?) 102

Richard M. Cohen, The Nation (May 26, 1997)

Still, we journalists are so busy resisting the liberal label that it hasn't occurred to us that it's no crime. The countervailing bias of our bosses is generally conservative. Corporate news managers do not rock the boat, and they are in charge. News executives care more about holding on to customers and increasing profits than challenging the establishment. The status quo seems safe.

PART 6   *Interest Groups and Political Parties, 104*

24 A Republic— If We Can Keep It 105

Joseph Lieberman, *The Atlantic Monthly* (July 1998)

The present corrupt system of financing elections, a U.S. senator argues, poses a serious threat to our democracy. The sad lesson of the recent campaign-finance scandals is not only that the laws are vaporous but also that politicians won't change their ways without public pressure.

25 The Business of Persuasion Thrives in Nation's Capital 108

Jill Abramson, *The New York Times* (September 29, 1998)

[M]r. Andrews and many lobbyists interviewed in recent months predicted that more would be spent on influencing the Federal Government this year than in 1997, when a record $1.2 billion was reportedly spent.

26 The Buying of the Bench 117

Sheila Kaplan and Zoë Davidson, *The Nation* (January 26, 1998)

The campaign fundraising scandal has drawn new attention to the way moneyed interests buy political favors in Washington. But far from the nation's capital, many of these same donors operate unchecked in a venue that may prove more disturbing than the Lincoln Bedroom: the state courts.

PART 7 — *Congress, 123*

27 Roll Out the Barrel: The Case Against the Case Against Pork 124

Jonathan Cohn, *The New Republic* (April 20, 1998)

Listen closely the next time some smug good-government type starts criticizing pork: it's an awful lot of fuss over what is, in fact, a very small amount of money.

28 75 Stars: How to Restore Democracy in the U.S. Senate (and End the Tyranny of Wyoming) 129

Michael Lind, *Mother Jones* (January/February 1998)

Because of our Senate — the least representative legislative body in the democratic world except for the British House of Lords — an ever shrinking minority of voters has the power to obstruct policies favored by an overwhelming majority of the American people. The Senate is the worst branch of government, and it's going to get even nastier in the century ahead.

29 The Senator's Dilemma 134

Joe Klein, *The New Yorker* (January 5, 1998)

In the fall of 1996, . . . Rick Santorum became — somewhat to his own surprise—the leader of the anti-partial-birth forces in the Senate. It was a role that placed him at the center of what soon became a very emotional and personal, maelstrom.

30 Congress and the Constitution 140

Gary Benoit, *The New American* (April 27, 1998)

If most members of Congress were to stand by their oath to "support and defend the Constitution of the United States against all enemies foreign and domestic" and to "bear true faith and allegiance to the same," big government would disappear.

31 Capitol Flight: Why Congressmen Are Never in Washington 146

Jennifer Bradley, *The New Republic* (April 7, 1997)

The result is a Congress that doesn't function properly because it simply isn't there often enough. Lawmaking may not be brain surgery, but it's not a no-brainer, either. It requires not merely representatives but legislators — people who spend enough time on the Hill to learn the substance and form of lawmaking.

PART 8 · *The Presidency, 148*

32 Unchecked and Unbalanced: Why the Independent Counsel Act Must Go..... 149

Cass R. Sunstein, *The American Prospect* (May/June 1998)

The Independent Counsel Act creates dangerous incentives not only for the independent counsel, but for members of Congress and the press as well. Investigations under the act deflect attention from serious public issues and focus the attention of Congress, the press, and citizens alike on scandals that are sometimes imaginary and that, even if real, may not deserve the prominence that the possible or actual appointment of an independent prosecutor gives them.

33 Stroke of His Pen Subverts the Law.......... 155

Keith Russell, *Insight on the News* (July 27, 1998)

The Founders would be shocked to learn presidents now make law by executive order. But for Bill Clinton and many of his predecessors, it has been a potent political tool.

34 There He Goes Again: The Alternating Political Style of Bill Clinton....... 159

Fred Greenstein, *PS: Political Science & Politics* (June 1998)

The tempest over whether Clinton was involved in a dalliance with a White House intern is a reminder of his tendency to oscillate between an uninhibited, anything-goes approach to leadership and a more measured operating mode in which he sets attainable goals and proceeds skillfully in his efforts to realize them.

PART 9 · *The Bureaucracy, 162*

35 The Fraud Fraud 163

Michael Walzer, *The New Republic* (November 3, 1997

Is it really true that there is more waste and crime in the public than the private sector? I doubt it. Waste and crime are significant costs for private business, but almost no one is doing the journalistic work (or the academic research) necessary to keep us informed about them.

36 Crimes on Paper: Filling Out the Wrong Government Form Could Cost You 165

James Bovard, *The American Spectator* (January 1998)

Each year, according to the Office of Management and Budget, citizens and businesses spend over 6.7 billion hours filling out forms for various federal agencies. These wasted hours are bad enough; more alarming, however, is the power government commandeers via endless reporting requirements.

37 Pandora's Box — American Style: Government as a Cause of Problems........ 167

Gerald F. Kreyche, *USA Today Magazine: A Publication of the Society for the Advancement of Education* (March 1997)

Few question the bureaucracy's good intentions in trying to help society, but the road to hell is paved with such, as virtue driven to excess becomes a vice. To illustrate, let's document some ills that have resulted from the government's involvement in "doing good."

38 What Made the Government Grow? 169

Bernard A. Weisberger, *American Heritage* (September 1997)

[I]n 1990 the national government was still huge and still growing, albeit at a slackened pace. The reason was that for all the growing dissatisfaction with expensive bureaucracies, people did not truly want government "off their backs."

PART 10   *The Judiciary, 180*

39 Unrestrained: The Supreme Court May Be More Conservative, But It's as Activist as Ever 181

Max Boot, *National Review* (June 1, 1998)

The principled position is to say that political judgments should be left to voters and their elected representatives. The attempt by a handful of black-robed old coots isolated in Washington to craft national resolutions to contentious issues will always be doomed to failure.

40 The Ten Commandments and the Constitution 184

Dennis Teti, *The Weekly Standard* (July 21, 1997)

The Supreme Court and Congress are on a collision course. Three times in the final week of its term, the high court struck down laws passed by overwhelming congressional majorities, championed by the president, and defended by the Justice Department. This is historically unprecedented.

41 We the 50 Peoples: State Constitutionalism Challenges the Federal Judicial Leviathan 188

Brian Doherty, *Reason* (March 1997)

When you think Constitution, you probably imagine the Supremes, those nine contentious, berobed guys and gals in their august Washington halls. But such brethren aren't just in D.C. Every state has its own set, interpreting its own constitution.

PART 11   *U. S. Foreign Policy, 191*

42 The Trade Weapon and Other Myths 192

Michael Ledeen, *The American Spectator* (February 1998)

Whenever the U. S. has a problem with another country it likes to impose trade sanctions on it. They're a great weapon to use against friends, but for all intents useless against regimes that hate us anyway. There's also a tendency to think that sanctions relieve us of the need to defend freedom in oppressed countries — or to assume that trade by itself can bring freedom.

43 Dollar Diplomacy Returns 198

Lawrence F. Kaplan, *Commentary* (February 1998)

It has long been a truism of international politics that the best guarantor of peace is democracy; whatever quarrels they may have with one another, democratic nations do not resort to war to resolve them. But this fundamental understanding has lately been undergoing a profound revision.

44 Bits, Bytes, and Diplomacy 201

Walter B. Wriston, *Foreign Affairs* (September/October 1997)

Information technology has demolished time and distance. Instead of validating Orwell's vision of Big Brother watching the citizen, the third revolution enables the citizen to watch Big Brother. And so the virus of freedom, for which there is no antidote, is spread by electronic networks to the four corners of the earth.

PART 12   *Working With the World Wide Web, 206*

WebLinks: A Directory of Annotated Web Sites 207

How to Cite a Web Site 218

Web Journal 219

Web Site Evaluation Form 221

Reading Review Form 225

Index 227

Quick Reference Guide to Topics/Readings/WWW Sites

For a complete description of the Web sites that appear in this Guide, please consult *WebLinks: A Directory of Annotated Web Sites,* which is located at the back of the book in **Part 12: Working With the World Wide Web.** There you will find in detail all the Web sites referred to in the Quick Reference Guide, and more.

Topic Area	Treated in: Readings	Treated in: Web Sites
Anti-Government Terrorism	4. Unsound Constitution	The Constitution of the United States (Annotated), No. 33 The Federalist Papers, No. 50 The Oklahoma City Bombing Trial Transcripts, No. 86
Bureaucracy	35. The Fraud Fraud	National Center for Policy Analysis/Privatization, No. 72 Social Security Privatization, No. 108 CAPWEB: The Internet Guide to the U.S. Congress, No. 16 The Federal Web Locator, No. 49 Houghton Mifflin Documents Collection/American Government, No. 56
	36. Crimes on Paper	The Federal Web Locator, No. 49 National Taxpayers Union, No. 81
	37. Pandora's Box	Affirmative Action Special Report, No. 1 Proposition 209, No. 97 Thomas/Legislative Information on the Internet, No. 117
	38. What Made the Government Grow	Directory of Federalism Links, No. 38
Censorship	15. The Chador Hits Cyberspace	Internet Public Library/Ready Reference, No. 61 National Organization for Women, No. 78
Civil Liberties	6. Is Nothing Private?	Electronic Privacy Information Center, No. 40 The Privacy Forum, No. 96
	16. Life in the 90s	Center for the Defense of Free Enterprise, No. 19 Sport Utility Vehicle Anti-Fan Club, No. 110
	17. Ganging Up on Civil Liberties	American Civil Liberties Union, No. 3 Federal Gang Violence Act, No. 47 School Violence and the Legal Rights of Students, No. 106
	36. Crimes on Paper	The Federal Web Locator, No. 49 National Taxpayers Union, No. 81
Civil Rights	12. Is Affirmative Action on the Way Out? Should It Be?	Affirmative Action Special Report, No. 1 Americans United for Affirmative Action, No. 7 Proposition 209, No. 97
	13. Is the Drug War Racist?	Families Against Mandatory Minimums, No. 44 National Institute on Drug Abuse, No. 76 War on Black People, No. 133
	14. Who's Sorry Now?	Apologizing for Slavery: History in the News, No. 9 The Civil Rights Project, No. 27 National Association for the Advancement of Colored People, No. 70
	15. The Chador Hits Cyberspace	Internet Public Library/Ready Reference, No. 61 National Organization for Women, No. 78
	37. Pandora's Box	Affirmative Action Special Report, No. 1 Proposition 209, No. 97 Thomas/Legislative Information on the Internet, No. 117

Topic Area	Treated in: Readings	Treated in: Web Sites
Clinton, Bill	33. Stroke of His Pen Subverts the Law	Federal Emergency Management Agency, No. 46 Search Executive Orders, No. 107 U. S. Constitution Online, No. 123
	34. There He Goes Again	APSANet, No. 10 The Committee to Impeach the President, No. 28 Democratic Leadership Council, No. 36
Community	7. Town-Building Is No Mickey Mouse Operation	Celebration: A Town Is Born, No. 18 Preservation, Mixed Use and Urban Vitality. No. 94
Congress	11. Power Grab	Contract with America, No. 34 National Conference of State Legislatures, No. 74 Reviewing the Revolution, No. 101 States News, No. 113 U. S. State Constitutions and Web Sites, No. 124
	27. Roll Out the Barrel	American Voter: Rate Your Rep, No. 5 Citizens Against Government Waste: The Pork Patrol, No. 25 House of Representatives, No. 57
	28. 75 Stars	The Constitution of the United States (Annotated), No. 33 United States Senate, No. 129
	29. The Senator's Dilemma	National Abortion and Reproductive Rights, No. 69 National Right to Life, No. 80 Thomas/Legislative Information on the Internet, No. 117
	30. Congress and the Constitution	The Articles of Confederation. No. 12 CAPWEB: The Internet Guide to the U. S. Congress, No. 16 The Federalist Papers, No. 50 The United States Constitution, No. 126
	31. Capitol Flight	C-Span, No. 35 Roll Call Online, No. 104
The Constitution	4. Unsound Constitution	Amendments Never Ratified, No. 2 The Constitution of the United States (Annotated), No. 33 The Federalist Papers, No. 50 Index to the Anti-Federalist Papers, No. 60 To Form a More Perfect Union, No. 118
	30. Congress and the Constitution	The Articles of Confederation, No. 12 CAPWEB: The Internet Guide to the U. S. Congress, No. 16 The Federalist Papers, No. 50 The United States Constitution, No. 126
Consumerism and Government Regulations	16. Life in the 90s	Center for the Defense of Free Enterprise, No. 19 The Roadhog Info Trough, No. 102 The Sport Utility Vehicle Anti-Fan Club, No. 110 Ultimate Guide to Sport Utility Vehicles, No. 120
Corruption in Government	8. Grassroots Graft	Citizens Against Government Waste, No. 24 Waste in Your State, No. 134
	24. A Republic—If We Can Keep It	Campaign Finance Information Center, No. 15 Common Cause, No. 29 *Congressional Quarterly*: Campaign Finance, No. 31 Ethics in the News, No. 42 National Voting Rights Institute, No. 82

Topic Area	Treated in: Readings	Treated in: Web Sites
	26. The Buying of the Bench	Common Cause, No. 29 Ethics in the News, No. 42 National Center for State Courts, No. 73 Voter's Guide to Judicial Elections, No. 131
Democracy	5. Has Democracy a Future?	The Economist OnLine, No. 39 The Federalist Papers, No. 50 The Guardian of Liberalism: America, Cigars, and Arthur M. Schlesinger, Jr., No. 55 National Voting Rights Institute, No. 82 Voting Rights Act Clarification, No. 132
	19. Democracy in Texas	Americans Talk Issues Foundation, No. 6 The Center for Deliberative Polling, No. 20 National Issues Convention, No. 77
	28. 75 Stars	The Constitution of the United States (Annotated), No. 33 United States Senate, No. 129
	44. Bits, Bytes, and Diplomacy	U. S. Department of State, No. 125 United Nations, No. 121 The World Bank, No. 140
Drug Policy	13. Is the Drug War Racist?	Families Against Mandatory Minimums, No. 44 National Institute on Drug Abuse, No. 76 War on Black People, No. 133
Economic Policy	25. The Business of Persuasion Thrives	Common Cause, No. 29 Ethics in the News, No. 42 National Voting Rights Institute, No. 82 STAT-USA/Internet, No. 114
	42. The Trade Weapon and Other Myths	A Catalog of New U. S. Unilateral Economic Sanctions for Foreign Policy Purposes, 1993–96, No. 17 China's Most Favored Nation Trade Status, No. 22 U. S. Backs Off on Sanctions, No. 122

	43. Dollar Diplomacy Returns	"Most Favored Nation Status for China Promotes
		    Freedom," No. 67
		North American Free Trade Agreement, No. 85
		Woodrow Wilson: Repudiation of "Dollar Diplomacy,"
		    No. 139

Elections and Campaigns	18. The Sleeping Giant Awakes	Latino National Political Survey, No. 62 Latino Voters Break the Trend, No. 63 National Association of Latino Elected Officials, No. 71 NES Guide to Public Opinion and Electoral Behavior, No. 84
	24. A Republic—If We Can Keep It	Campaign Finance Information Center, No. 15 Common Cause, No. 29 *Congressional Quarterly*: Campaign Finance, No. 31 National Voting Rights Institute, No. 82
	26. The Buying of the Bench	Campaign Finance Information Center, No. 15 Ethics in the News, No. 42 Voter's Guide to Judicial Elections, No. 131
Environmental Issues	16. Life in the 90s	Center for the Defense of Free Enterprise, No. 19 The Roadhog Info Trough, No. 102 The Sport Utility Vehicle Anti-Fan Club, No. 110 Ultimate Guide to Sports Utility Vehicles, No. 120
Federalism	7. Town-Building Is No Mickey Mouse Operation	Celebration: A Town Is Born, No. 18 Preservation, Mixed Use and Urban Vitality, No. 94

Topic Area	Treated in: Readings	Treated in: Web Sites
	9. The Disunited States	Center for the Study of Federalism, No. 21 U. S. State Constitutions and Web Sites, No. 124
	11. Power Grab	Contract with America, No. 34 National Conference of State Legislatures, No. 74 Reviewing the Revolution, No. 101 States News, No. 113 U. S. State Constitutions and Web Sites, No. 124
Foreign Policy	42. The Trade Weapon and Other Myths	A Catalog of New U. S. Unilateral Economic Sanctions for Foreign Policy Purposes, 1993–96, No. 17 China's Most Favored Nation Trade Status, No. 22 U. S. Backs Off Sanctions, No. 122
	43. Dollar Diplomacy Returns	"Most Favored Nation Status for China Promotes Freedom," No. 67 North American Free Trade Agreement, No. 85 Woodrow Wilson: Repudiation of "Dollar Diplomacy," No. 139
	44. Bits, Bytes, and Diplomacy	United Nations, No. 121 U. S. Department of State, No. 125 Foreign Affairs, No. 52
Gangs	17. Ganging Up on Civil Liberties	American Civil Liberties Union, No 3 Federal Gang Violence Act, No. 47 School Violence and the Legal Rights of Students, No. 106
Independent Counsel	32. Unchecked and Unbalanced	The Independent Counsel Law, No. 59 *Morrison v. Olson*, No. 66 The Starr Report, No. 111
Interest Groups and Political Parties	11. Power Grab	Contract with America, No. 34 Democratic Leadership Council, No. 36 Democratic National Committee. No. 37 Republican National Committee, No. 100 Reviewing the Revolution, No. 101
	24. A Republic— If We Can Keep It	Campaign Finance Information Center, No. 15 Common Cause, No. 29 *Congressional Quarterly*: Campaign Finance, No. 31 Ethics in the News, No. 42
	26. The Buying of the Bench	Ethics in the News, No. 42 Voters Guide to Judicial Elections, No. 131 National Center for State Courts, No. 73
Internet and Politics	5. Has Democracy a Future?	The Economist OnLine, No. 39 The Guardian of Liberalism: America, Cigars, and Arthur M. Schlesinger, Jr., No. 55 National Issues Convention, No. 77
	15. The Chador Hits Cyberspace	Internet Public Library/Ready Reference, No. 61 National Organization for Women, No. 78
	44. Bits, Bytes, and Diplomacy	U. S. Department of State, No. 125 United Nations, No. 121 The World Bank, No. 140
Judiciary	26. The Buying of the Bench	Ethics in the News, No. 42 National Center for State Courts, No. 73 Voter's Guide to Judicial Elections, No. 131
	33. Stroke of His Pen Subverts the Law	Federal Emergency Management Agency, No. 46 Search Executive Orders, No. 107 U. S. Constitution Online, No. 123

Topic Area	Treated in: Readings	Treated in: Web Sites
	39. Unrestrained: The Supreme Court	The Federalist Society, No. 51 Legal Information Institute, No. 64 Speech to the American Law Institute, No. 109 Supreme Court Justices of the United States, No. 115
	40. The Ten Commandments and the Constitution	Articles of Confederation, No. 12 The Federalist Papers, No. 50 The Federalist Society, No. 51 Religious Freedom Restoration Act, No. 99
	41. We the 50 Peoples	Center for the Study of Federalism, No. 21 Legal Information Institute, No. 64 National Center for State Courts, No. 73 State Constitutions, No. 112 U. S. State Constitutions and Web Sites, No. 124
Latinos and Politics	18. The Sleeping Giant Awakes	Latino National Political Survey, No. 62 Latino Voters Break the Trend, No. 63 National Association of Latino Elected Officials, No. 71
Legislating Abortion	29. The Senator's Dilemma	National Abortion and Reproductive Rights, No. 69 Family Research Council, No. 45 National Right to Life, No. 80
Media Criticism	21. Money Lust	Pew Center for Civic Journalism, No. 88 Rocky Mountain Media Watch, No. 103
	22. Network Failure	Fairness and Accuracy in Reporting, No. 43 Media Research Center, No. 65 Why Americans Hate the Media, No. 137
	23. Extra! The Press Is Liberal (So What?)	Fairness and Accuracy in Reporting, No. 43 Media Research Center, No. 65
Political Science	20. Monica Lewinsky's Contribution to Political Science	American Politics, No. 4 APSANet: The American Political Science Association Online, No. 10 Political Science Resources, No. 90 Political Science Virtual Library, No. 92 Roper Center for Public Opinion Research, No. 105
Pork Barrel Politics	27. Roll Out the Barrel	Citizens Against Government Waste: Pork Patrol, No. 25 Freshmen Learn to Love Pork Barrel, No. 53 The Pork Barrel Objection, No. 93
Presidency	32. Unchecked and Unbalanced	The Independent Counsel Law, No. 59 *Morrison v. Olson*, No. 66 The Starr Report, No. 111
	33. Stroke of His Pen Subverts the Law	Inaugural Addresses of the Presidents of the United States, No. 58 Presidents of the United States, No. 95 Search Executive Orders, No. 107 The White House, No. 136
Privacy	6. Is Nothing Private?	The American Civil Liberties Union, No. 3 Electronic Privacy Information Center, No. 40 The Privacy Forum, No. 96
	17. Ganging Up on Civil Liberties	American Civil Liberties Union, No. 3 Federal Gang Violence Act, No. 47 School Violence and the Legal Rights of Students, No. 106

Topic Area	Treated in: Readings	Treated in: Web Sites
Public Opinion	19. Democracy in Texas	Americans Talk Issues Foundation, No. 6 The Center for Deliberative Polling, No. 20 National Issues Convention, No. 77 National Voting Rights Institute, No. 82
	20. Monica Lewinsky's Contribution to Political Science	The Gallup Poll, No. 54 The Public Opinion Laboratory, No. 98 Roper Center for Public Opinion Research, No. 105
Social Welfare	12. Is Affirmative Action on the Way Out? Should It Be?	Affirmative Action Special Report, No. 1 Americans United for Affirmative Action, No. 7 Proposition 209, No. 97

Sports Stadiums	10. The Stadium Trap	Anti-Stadium, No. 8
		Are New Stadiums Worth the Cost?, No. 11
		Ballparks, No. 13
		Citizens for Leaders with Ethics and Accountability Now/
		  Stadiums, No. 26
		Top 10 Dumbest Reasons to Build a New Stadium,
		  No. 119

State and Local Government	8. Grassroots Graft	Citizens Against Government Waste, No. 24 Waste in Your State, No. 134
	9. The Disunited States	National Conference of State Legislatures, No. 74 National Governors Association, No. 75 State News, No. 113 U.S. State Constitutions and Web Sites, No. 124
	11. Power Grab	Contract with America, No. 34 National Conference of State Legislatures, No. 74 Reviewing the Revolution, No. 101 States News, No. 113 U.S. State Constitutions and Web Sites, No. 124
	26. The Buying of the Bench	Ethics in the News, No. 42 National Center for State Courts, No. 73 Voter's Guide to Judicial Elections, No. 131
	41. We the 50 Peoples	Center for the Study of Federalism, No. 21 Legal Information Institute, No. 64 National Center for State Courts, No. 73 State Constitutions, No. 112 U.S. State Constitutions and Web Sites, No. 124
Student Study/ Research Skills	1. Critical Reading Strategies	Effective Learning: Study Skills/Critical Thinking (see "A Note from the Publisher") Mission: Critical (see "A Note from the Publisher")
	2. Ten C's for Evaluating Internet Resources	The Complete Internet Researcher, No. 30

	3. Desperately Seeking Susan OR Suzie NOT Sushi	American Politics, No. 4
		Houghton Mifflin Documents Collection/American
		  Government, No. 56
		Political Science and Sociology Online Publications,
		  No. 91

Women's Rights	15. The Chador Hits Cyberspace	National Organization of Women, No. 78 Women in Politics, No. 138

INTRODUCTION

Critical Reading and Internet Research Skills

By sitting at a computer that has an Internet connection and a graphical browser for accessing the Web, we have at our fingertips a worldwide storehouse of information. We can search the Web to find information on just about anything. Need current statistics for a class assignment on political parties, voting patterns, or recently-passed laws . . . ? Find it on the Web. Want to test your knowledge of current events? Then go to any of a number of interactive Web sites where you can do so immediately. Curious about how your representative voted on an issue before Congress? Or are you interested in alternative health, school loans, and your favorite sports teams? Find it on the Web. No matter the topic, it's on the Web.

The readings in this **Introduction** will provide you with a solid overview of the Web, and they answer the most commonly asked questions about the Web, such as:

• What is the World Wide Web?

• How does it work?

• How do I avoid wasting time and maximize my online sessions?

• How do I evaluate online sources of information?

In addition, the first reading ("Critical Reading Strategies") offers specific techniques and study skills you can apply to any reading assignment. You will find that these techniques are especially useful for the kinds of selections reprinted here in *ReadingsPLUS*, and they are also useful for material you may download from the Internet.

Although there is a tremendous amount of information online, the quality is not uniformly good, and there is as much misinformation as there is useful and academically appropriate information. These readings can get you started in using the Web constructively for your courses.

Critical Reading Strategies

By Valerie Gray Hardcastle, Ph.D.

Here I present seven critical reading strategies that I have shamelessly stolen from someone else. These are strategies that you can learn readily and then apply not only to the reading selections in this class, but also to your other college reading. Although mastering these strategies will not make the critical reading process an easy one, it can make reading much more satisfying and productive and thus help you handle difficult material well and with confidence.

Fundamental to each of these strategies is annotating directly on the page: underlining key words, phrases, or sentences; writing comments or questions in the margins; bracketing important sections of the text; constructing ideas with lines or arrows; numbering related points in sequence; and making note of anything that strikes you as interesting, important, or questionable.

Most readers annotate in layers, adding further annotations on second and third readings. Annotations can be light or heavy, depending on the reader's purpose and the difficulty of the material.

PREVIEWING:

Learning about a text before really reading it.

Previewing enables readers to get a sense of what the text is about and how it is organized before reading it closely. This simple strategy includes seeing what you can learn from the headnotes or other introductory material, skimming to get an overview of the content and organization, and identifying the rhetorical situation.

CONTEXTUALIZING:

Placing a text in its historical, biographical, and cultural contexts.

When you read a text, you read it through the lens of your own experience. Your understanding of the words on the page and their significance is informed by what you have come to know and value from living in a particular time and place. But the texts you read were all written in the past, sometimes in a radically different time and place. To read critically, you need to contextualize, to recognize the differences between your contemporary values and attitudes and those represented in the text.

QUESTIONING TO UNDERSTAND AND REMEMBER:

Asking questions about the content.

As students, you are accustomed (I hope) to teachers asking you questions about your reading. These questions are designed to help you understand a reading and respond to it more fully, and often this technique works. When you need to understand and use new information though it is most beneficial if you write the questions, as you read the text for the first time. With this strategy, you can write questions any time, but in difficult academic readings, you will understand the material better and remember it longer if you write a question for every paragraph or brief section. Each question should focus on a main idea, not on illustrations or details, and each should be expressed in your own words, not just copied from parts of the paragraph.

REFLECTING ON CHALLENGES TO YOUR BELIEFS AND VALUES:

Examining your personal responses.

The reading that you do for this class might challenge your attitudes, your unconsciously held beliefs, or your positions on current issues. As you read a text for the first time, mark an X in the margin at each point where you felt a personal challenge to your attitudes, beliefs, or status. Make a brief note in the margin about what you feel or about what in the text created the challenge. Now look again at the places you marked in the text where you felt personally challenged. What patterns do you see?

OUTLINING AND SUMMARIZING:

Identifying the main ideas and restating them in your own words.

Outlining and summarizing are especially helpful strategies for understanding the content and structure of a reading selection. Whereas outlining reveals the basic structure of the text, summarizing synopsizes a selection's main argument in brief. Outlining may be part of the annotating process, or it may be done separately (as it is in this class). The key to both outlining and summarizing is being able to distinguish between the main ideas and the supporting ideas and examples. The main ideas form the backbone, the strand that holds the various parts and pieces of the text together. Outlining the main ideas helps you to discover this structure. When you make an outline, don't use the text's exact words.

Summarizing begins with outlining, but instead of merely listing the main ideas, a summary recomposes them to form a new text. Whereas outlining depends on a close analysis of each paragraph, summarizing also requires creative synthesis. Putting ideas together again—in your own words and in a condensed form—shows how reading critically can lead to deeper understanding of any text.

EVALUATING AN ARGUMENT:

Testing the logic of a text as well as its credibility and emotional impact.

All writers make assertions that they want you to accept as true. As a critical reader, you should not accept anything on face value but to recognize every assertion as an argument that must be carefully evaluated. An argument has two essential parts: a claim and support. The claim asserts a conclusion—an idea, an opinion, a judgment, or a point of view—that the writer wants you to accept. The support includes reasons (shared beliefs, assumptions, and values) and evidence (facts, examples, statistics, and authorities) that give readers the basis for accepting the conclusion. When you assess an argument, you are concerned with the process of reasoning as well as its truthfulness (these are not the same thing). At the most basic level, in order for an argument to be acceptable, the support must be appropriate to the claim and the statements must be consistent with one another.

COMPARING AND CONTRASTING RELATED READINGS:

Exploring likenesses and differences between texts to understand them better.

Many of the authors we read are concerned with the same issues or questions, but approach how to discuss them in different ways. Fitting a text into an ongoing dialectic helps increase understanding of why an author approached a particular issue or question in the way he or she did.

University of Wisconsin–Eau Claire
McIntyre Library

Ten C's for Evaluating Internet Resources

By Elizabeth B. Richmond

1. Content

What is the intent of the content? Are the title and author identified? Is the content "juried"? Is the content "popular" or "scholarly," satiric or serious? What is the date of the document or article? Is the "edition" current? Do you have the latest version? (Is this important?) How do you know?

2. Credibility

Is the author identifiable and reliable? Is the content credible? Authoritative? Should it be? What is the purpose of the information, that is, is it serious, satiric, humorous? Is the URL extension .edu, .com, .gov, or .org? What does this tell you about the "publisher"?

3. Critical Thinking

How can you apply critical thinking skills, including previous knowledge and experience, to evaluate Internet resources? Can you identify the author, publisher, edition, etc. as you would with a "traditionally" published resource? What criteria do you use to evaluate Internet resources?

4. Copyright

Even if the copyright notice does not appear prominently, someone wrote, or is responsible for, the creation of a document, graphic, sound, or image, and the material falls under the copyright conventions. "Fair use" applies to short, cited excerpts, usually as an example for commentary or research. Materials are in the "public domain" if this is explicitly stated. Internet users, as users of print media, must respect copyright.

5. Citation

Internet resources should be cited to identify sources used, both to give credit to the author and to provide the reader with avenues for further research. Standard style manuals (print and online) provide some examples of how to cite Internet documents, although standards have not yet been formally established.

6. Continuity

Will the Internet site be maintained and updated? Is it now and will it continue to be free? Can you rely on this source over time to provide up-to-date information? Some good .edu sites have moved to .com, with possible cost implications. Other sites offer partial use for free, and charge fees for continued or in-depth use.

7. Censorship

Is your discussion list "moderated"? What does this mean? Does your search engine or index look for all words or are some words excluded? Is this censorship? Does your institution, based on its mission, parent organization, or space limitations, apply some restrictions to Internet use? Consider censorship and privacy issues when using the Internet.

8. Connectivity

If more than one user will need to access a site, consider each users' access and "functionality." How do users connect to the Internet and what kind of connection does the assigned resource require? Does access to the resource require a graphical user interface? If it is a popular (busy) resource, will it be accessible in the time frame needed? Is it accessible by more than one Internet tool? Do users have access to the same Internet tools and applications? Are users familiar with the tools and applications? Is the site "viewable" by all Web browsers?

9. Comparability

Does the Internet resource have an identified comparable print or CD-ROM data set or source? Does the Internet site contain comparable and complete information? (For example, some newspapers have partial but not full text information on the Internet.) Do you need to compare data or statistics over time? Can you identify sources for comparable earlier or later data?

Comparability of data may or may not be important, depending on your project.

10. Context

What is the context for your research? Can you find "anything" on your topic, that is, commentary, opinion, narrative, statistics and your quest will be satisfied? Are you looking for current or historical information? Definitions? Research studies or articles? How does Internet information fit in the overall information context of your subject? Before you start searching, define the research context and research needs and decide what sources might be best to use to successfully fill information needs without data overload.

Editor: Elizabeth B. Richmond
Reference Department
McIntyre Library
University of Wisconsin–Eau Claire

Desperately Seeking Susan OR Suzie NOT Sushi

To Search the Web Successfully, Pick the Right Engine and Learn How to Use It

By Matt Lake

If the World Wide Web ever adopted a theme song, it could do worse than picking "I Still Haven't Found What I'm Looking For." Searching the Web is the most popular on-line activity—and often the most frustrating. In June, more than half of the top 10 most-visited domains were Web search sites, according to an Internet metering service, Media Metrix. But how many of the people visiting those sites found what they were looking for right away?

Not most, according to Karin Rex, whose Pennsylvania-based company Computer Ease conducts Internet search classes. "Most people type in words and get a bazillion hits," Ms. Rex said. "Some of the ones on the first page may pertain to what they're looking for, but most of them won't."

On the surface, it ought to be simple. You're looking for Lincoln's Gettysburg Address, you enter those three words, and assuming it's somewhere on the Internet (and that's a pretty safe assumption), the search site gives you a list of relevant Web pages. Right? Not so, Ms. Rex said. "You'll get sites about the Lincoln Continental and vacations in Gettysburg, and real-estate sites listing addresses," she said, "but often, nothing about Lincoln's Gettysburg Address."

Danny Sullivan, editor of the Search Engine Watch newsletter, agrees. His publication and Web site (www.searchenginewatch.com) monitor the world of Web searching, and despite improvements over the past two years, he said, he still sees problems.

"They've gotten better, faster and easier to use, but search engines have got a long way to go," Mr. Sullivan said. "They're poor for people who are doing really basic searches. Enter 'Disney' or 'travel' and it's a crapshoot whether they'll get the Disney site or any good travel sites."

One search site could provide 10 top results of pure gold, while another serves up either nothing or dross. Why is there a difference in results? Because there are three basic components of all search engines, and while there is often a lot of overlap, no two engines are exactly the same. One element is the index of Web sites or Web pages that your search roots through; each search site collects its information and updates its database differently. Each site's search function works differently, too, and the order in which the results are sorted is usually based on a proprietary algorithm that no company would be willing to share.

To make things harder, search sites generally do not do a good job of explaining how they work. Few people understand, for example, that Yahoo is fundamentally different from search sites like Hotbot, Alta Vista and Infoseek. Yahoo is not really a search engine but rather a Web directory, compiled by humans who classify Web sites under headings. The others are Web search engines, which use software agents called crawlers or spiders to index the contents of individual Web pages then follow links to other pages.

Web directories like Yahoo and Web search engines may look the same, but each type of site is good for finding different types of information.

The first step in creating more effective searches is picking the right search site for the job. "If people are doing a general search," Mr. Sullivan said, "they should start off at Yahoo or a Yahoo-like directory like Snap or Look Smart." A directory-style search provides two ways to research broad topics: dive through a

---

A Field Guide to Web Search Sites

Excite

www.excite.com

Good for searches on broad general topics, Excite adds interesting extras like a simultaneous search of the Web, news headlines, sports scores and company information—and groups the relevant results on a single page. Some reviewers have complained that the search results aren't always relevant.

Dogpile

www.dogpile.com

This metasearch site can go through 13 Web search engines, more than two dozen on-line news services or other types of sources, and sorts the results by the search engine that found them. While this is not the most useful presentation if you just want the facts, it's a good way to check which search engine works best for you.

Yahoo

www.yahoo.com

A human-compiled directory of Web sites, Yahoo doesn't help you search for the contents of individual Web pages. It's excellent for researching broad general topics, but tends to return too many results, many of them irrelevant.

Infoseek

www.infoseek.com

When searching for Web pages, news stories and Usenet postings, Infoseek produces very accurate and relevant results. But according to Search Engine Watch (www.searchenginewatch.com), it has a much smaller index of Web pages than many others.

Ask Jeeves

www.askjeeves.com

An excellent beginner's site that's also good for anyone's general queries, Ask Jeeves leads you through questions to help narrow your search, and also simultaneously searches six other search sites for relevant Web pages. Its ability to interpret natural language queries makes it easy to learn but also makes constructing precise queries difficult.

Hotbot

www.hotbot.com

This is the search site of Wired magazine, whose search engine Inktomi also powers Snap.com's and Yahoo's Web searches. It is an excellent tool for finding specific information. In addition to a thorough and up-to-date index, it provides an easy interface for constructing precise search queries—but this requires extra effort up front.

Lycos

www.lycos.com

Lycos provides a good selection of advanced search capabilities, like the ability to search for specific media types (JPEG files, Java scripts and so on). Its advanced search, Lycos Pro, provides even more options. But general Web searches can produce checkered results. Also, Lycos's index of Web pages is small.

Northern Light

www.nlsearch.com

In addition to its index of Web pages, Northern Light also searches through pay-per-view articles from periodicals and books not generally available on the Web. It sorts its results into topic headings, which can prove very useful.

Alta Vista

www.altavista.net

Another excellent tool for exhaustive and precise searches, Alta Vista makes it harder than Hotbot does for beginners to construct precise queries, but once you've mastered its search syntax, it's quick and easy to use. Its results, however, can include many duplicates.

Metacrawler

www.metacrawler.com

This is a metasearch site, simultaneously searching Yahoo, Excite, and five other search engines then aggregating the results. It's excellent for getting a quick hit of what's out there. But if you don't see what you want in the results, its limited search options make it tough to issue really precise queries.

Internet Sleuth

www.isleuth.com

Internet Sleuth is a 3,000-strong collection of specialized on-line databases, which can also simultaneously search up to six other search sites for Web pages, news and other types of information. It's excellent for highly specialized searches in any subjects in its detailed directory—but the metasearch results aren't sorted intuitively.

list of broad topics by clicking on the appropriate links or fill out a search box to find listings.

But directory searches are less effective when looking for specific information—things like the author of a book, the complete text of the Declaration of Independence or research on drug treatments for a medical condition. For this kind of information, search engines like Hotbot and Alta Vista are the way to go. Because they search an index of keywords drawn by spiders from millions of Web pages, the chances are greater that they will find obscure terms in obscure Web pages.

There's a third kind of search site, one that includes popular sites like Metacrawler, Ask Jeeves and Dogpile. These sites—also called metasearch tools—don't maintain any kind of index of their own but instead issue search requests to fistfuls of other Web search sites. When Yahoo, Hotbot, Alta Vista and the like return their results, the metasearch site collects them onto a single Web page for display.

BRAD HILL

Author, "World Wide Web Searching for Dummies" (IDG, 1997)
My Favorite Search Engine:
Yahoo

I'll go to different engines according to my needs, but I start with Yahoo. I consider it the most valuable site on the Web. Yahoo doesn't do any editorializing and hand-holding—the results you get from it are more of an overview. It can be overwhelming, but it's a good place to start.

Because no two search sites index exactly the same set of Web pages, metasearch tools give you a wider scope of results—but it's worth remembering that more does not necessarily equal better. What really counts is relevant results that are sorted in a relevant order. And that's the rub. Simply picking one of two or three types of sites to search from is no guarantee of good results. Brad Hill, the author of "World Wide Web Searching for Dummies" (IDG), says most search sites deliver too much information. "Search engines do a good job on indexing," he said. But because of that, they deliver more than you want.

So when you're faced with several hundred thousand results over dozens of pages, what should you do? "Don't go past the first page of results," Mr. Hill said. "If it doesn't have something of interest, you've probably entered the wrong search string."

Most people could get much more relevant results with a few simple tricks for constructing a search "string"—the words you enter in the search box. The most obvious is to type in several relevant words

---

PHILIPPE KAHN

President, Starfish Software
My Favorite Search Engine:
Excite and Yahoo

I usually use Excite or Yahoo when I have a good idea about the category: I think that Excite's relevance ranking is very good. I use Yahoo as much as Excite, though. It's really a tossup. When it comes to an extensive keyword search I tend to use Alta Vista or Hotbot.

---

instead of just one or two. In general, the fewer words you enter, the more general your results will be.

But not every search engine returns the most relevant results first—which leads to lots of pages about Lincoln Continentals instead of Lincoln's most famous speech. To give a search engine more instructions, it helps to master a site's instructions, which search techies call "operators."

"Search operators tell a search engine how to interpret your key words," Mr. Hill said. "Words like 'and' or 'not,' and quotation marks can really narrow down search results."

And it's narrowing the results—giving fewer, better pages—that really counts.

"The simplest techniques, like using quotes around a phrase, help the most people," Ms. Rex said. The result of slapping quotation marks around two or more words is remarkable. Type in "Gettysburg Address," with quotation marks, and you tell the search engine to look for a phrase instead of two separate words—knocking irrelevant vacation sites and real-estate listings out of your top 20 results. That trick works in many search sites, including Yahoo, Alta Vista, Hotbot, Excite and Infoseek.

Not all search sites use the same rules for making better searches. Most will let you exclude some terms from your results—which is great if you're trying to search for, say, the gross national product of Jordan and keep getting sports sites about Michael Jordan. Exclude the word Michael, and you'll trim a few hundred thousand irrelevant results right away.

DYLAN TWENEY

"Net Prophet" columnist for Infoworld, a management information journal
My Favorite Search Engine:
Hotbot

I used Alta Vista for a while, then it seemed to be returning too much stuff. Now I favor Hotbot. It's fast and its results seem more up to date. Also if you want to fine-tune your searches, it has some great search options.

Steps to Smart Searching

PICK YOUR SITE

No one site is good for every search. Search directories like Yahoo and Lycos's Top 5% are good for researching general topics. Search engines like Hotbot and Alta Vista are better for very specific information. Metasearch sites like Dogpile and Metacrawler cast the net a little wider on searches for specific information by using more than one search engine.

PICK YOUR WORDS

Most search engines do a poor job when seeking out a single word. Increase the number of words to increase the scope of your search. And pick the words well—many search engines ignore common words like 'the,' 'and' and 'Web.'

USE THE PHRASE THAT PAYS

Enter the two words Strawberry Fields in a search box, and you could get results as diverse as W. C. Fields and strawberry shortcake. Yahoo, Alta Vista, Hotbot and others recognize words in quotes —"Strawberry Fields"—as a phrase. Metacrawler and others provide phrase searching as an option.

TAKE ADVANTAGE OF THE OPERATORS

Most search sites use code words or symbols called operators to make searches more precise. The operators vary from site to site, but the common ones are AND, OR, NOT, quotation marks and the plus and minus signs (see the table below for details on how to use them).

USE BROWSER CLICK TRICKS

When checking out results, view them in a new browser window so you can quickly return to the results page without clicking the browser's Back button. In most browsers, you can open a link in a new browser window by holding down the Shift key while clicking on the link. And if a page fails to load the first time you click on a link, try clicking again.

CHECK YOUR SPELLING

Many Web sites are riddled with spelling errors, but for the ones that are worth finding, correct spelling helps. Ask Jeeves and Infoseek provide spelling help for the orthographically challenged. Also, vary the styling of terms, so that a search for CD-ROM, for example, will also turn up CDROM or CD ROM.

COVER ALL THE BASES

If you're looking for gardening tips, for example, you may need to account for several different words—garden, gardens, gardening, gardener and so on. Infoseek and Lycos handle plurals and word stems automatically. Alta Vista uses a different approach, the wildcard character. Enter garden* and you'll get results on all the different options. Search sites that don't recognize word stems or wildcards need you to think up variants by yourself and search for them all (e.g., garden OR gardening OR gardens).

ASK FOR DIRECTIONS

Not every search site works the same way, but all of them provide a help section and tips. A couple of minutes spent checking the help pages can pay dividends later.

DON'T STICK AROUND

If you don't find what you're looking for in the first couple of results screens, either go back and enter a different set of search terms or move on to another search site.

HOW OPERATORS WORK

" " (quotation marks) enclose words to search for a phrase "Strawberry Fields Forever"

AND connects two or more words, all of which must appear in the results: Strawberry AND Fields AND Forever

OR connects two or more search words, any of which may appear in the results: Strawberry Fields OR Strawberryfields

NOT excludes the word after it from the results: Strawberry Fields NOT W. C.

− (minus sign), like NOT, excludes the word that follows it: Strawberry Fields − W C

+ (plus sign) precedes a word that must appear: + Strawberry + Fields

Note that it's possible to string together several operators to construct a very precise query. To exclude certain cover versions of a certain song, for example, you could try: "Strawberry Fields" AND "The Beatles" NOT "Sandy Farina" NOT "Nashville Superpickers"

RON WHITE

"Net Kahuna" columnist for PC Computing and author of "How Computers Work" (Que, 1998).
My Favorite Search Engine:
Web Compass
(Quarterdeck, $49.95)

I don't use search engines so much as software on my PC that searches all the engines. Web Compass searches places I would never have thought of, like Brazil Online and Mr. Showbiz and places I've never heard of. It handles Boolean searches pretty well, and I get back a database I can search on my own PC. Another thing I've been experimenting with is Copernic 98. It's shareware that does the same thing, but it divides the searches into categories like news events, so you can concentrate your searches while spreading the scope.

But how you exclude words from a search depends on the search site. In the regular search forms at Yahoo, Excite and Alta Vista, for example, you put a minus sign before the word (−Michael). But in Hotbot, you click on the More Search Options button and select Must Not Contain in the Word Filter section.

It is hardly surprising that many people find Web searching confusing and inefficient. So how are you supposed to know which rules apply to which search site? Karin Rex includes a simple piece of advice in lesson one of her Internet search class.

"Read the instructions," she said. "The only way to learn the inner workings of each site is to read the help files or frequently asked questions document. Most people don't even realize there are help files, so they'll never be able to take advantage of advanced features."

Sage advice though this is, search sites tend to use jargon that's not easily understood by the uninitiated. A single mention of Boolean operators is enough to send many would-be searchers into a tailspin. (Named for a 19th-century British mathematician, George Boole, Boolean operators are words like AND, OR and NOT that many advanced search sites use to make searches

ROGER EBERT

Film critic and Yahoo Internet Life magazine's "Critical Eye" columnist
My Favorite Search Engine:
Metacrawler

Why start there? Because I can search them all at once, natch—Alta Vista, Infoseek, Excite, Yahoo—all with one query. Or I may go to Northern Light, which organizes the findings into folders and is therefore easier to use than engines with a long list of hits.

more precise.) But in truth, Boolean logic is not hard to learn—and in many cases, search sites label it with easy-to-understand phrasing like "search for ANY of these terms" or "search for these terms as a phrase."

There are options for sufferers of Boolean anxiety, though. One site with a novel approach is Ask Jeeves. When you enter a vague query, Ask Jeeves will throw back a series of questions. From the single-word query "travel," for example, it comes back with 10 possible interpretations of what you might be looking for, including "Where can I rent a cellular phone in a foreign country?" and "Where can I get tourist information about foreign countries?"

Another approach is to reduce the scope of your search. Searching the entire Web for a highly specialized piece of information isn't always the best way. For one thing many Web search engines index only Web pages in HTML format, and many Web pages are generated from databases that search engine spiders can't penetrate. To uncover information from these databases, you usually need to use the search engine provided at the database's Web site. There are literally thousands of these highly specialized Web search tools across the Web.

KARIN REX

Technology trainer and author of "Internet Search Techniques" (Ziff-Davis Education, 1998)
My Favorite Search Engine:
Alta Vista

Alta Vista is my favorite engine because I have studied its help files and I understand how to use some of its more advanced search techniques. Therefore I usually can find what I need. If I can't find what I am looking for, I then turn to a metasite search engine. Dogpile, for example, sends your query to 25 different Internet search tools.

So how can you find these specialized search tools? About 3,000 of them are listed at Internet Sleuth (**www.isleuth.com**) in Yahoo-style directories. But unlike Yahoo's directories, Internet Sleuth's include only searchable sites and include the search form to issue a query right away.

No matter what advice you get, however, you discover the best search techniques by experimenting. Danny Sullivan of Search Engine Watch uses all the major search sites frequently, and refuses to name his favorite site. His reason?

"Judging the results is subjective," Mr Sullivan said. "If your friend raves about a site and you don't like it, try another. Use whatever you find gives you the answers."

PART I

The Constitution and American Democracy

The United States Constitution endures. It is more than 200 years old, making it the oldest existing written constitution in the world. This fact is even more amazing when you consider that it has been changed only 27 times during that entire period. What accounts for the longevity of the Constitution?

Part of the genius of the Constitution is that it is a judicious mix of specific rules and abstract principles, which establishes a stable governmental structure while simultaneously permitting government to change in response to changing social conditions.

The Constitution establishes a governmental structure that is based on the idea that no one individual or institution should possess too much power. According to Founding Father James Madison in *Federalist No. 47*, "[t]he accumulation of all powers, legislative, executive, and judiciary, in the same hands . . . may justly be pronounced the very definition of tyranny." The framers of the Constitution built into the Constitution a system of separation of powers, in which governmental power is divided. It is divided among the three branches of government—Congress, the Presidency,

the Judiciary. It is further divided between the federal government and the state governments.

The Constitution is also filled with abstract principles that embody certain values that Americans hold but which are not capable of precise definition. For example, the Constitution affirms a commitment to "due process," "equal protection," and "freedom of speech." These phrases are difficult to define, and may change from time to time. For example, until 1954, racial segregation and the laws enforcing it were not thought to violate the portion of the Constitution that guarantees "equal protection of the laws." However, as segregation became less tolerated, the Supreme Court eventually declared that segregation does indeed violate that provision of the Constitution.

The Constitution is not without its flaws, but America has thrived under it. As you read the following selections, you should think about those aspects of the Constitution that work well and those that perhaps work less well. How much, if at all, should the Constitution be changed to reflect current society? What aspects would you change and why?

Please note: The following key documents in American history and politics can be found at Web sites listed in *WebLinks: A Directory of Web Sites* at the back of the book:

> **The Constitution of the United States**
> **The Articles of Confederation**
> **The Federalists Papers**

You will also find in WebLinks several Web sites containing State Constitutions and Supreme Court decisions.

A Reading for Critical Thinking

Unsound Constitution:

Oklahoma City and the Founding Fathers

By George P. Fletcher

When the police stopped Timothy McVeigh seventy-five miles from the freshly exploded Alfred P. Murrah Federal Building in Oklahoma City, he was wearing a T-shirt with an apparently incriminating message on the front: "Sic semper tyrannis." The message on the back was just as provocative: "The tree of liberty must be refreshed from time to time with the blood of patriots and tyrants." An illustration of "the tree of liberty" dripped blood.

At the trial in Denver, which concluded with a guilty verdict last week, prosecutors presented the content of McVeigh's shirt as evidence that he was a madman capable of killing scores of innocent people. Prosecutor Joseph Hartzler, who presented the case against McVeigh, implied as much in his opening statement to the jury. Referring to the language of the shirt and similar political slogans, Hartzler said, "These documents are virtually a manifesto declaring McVeigh's intention." The jury obviously agreed, finding McVeigh guilty on all charges against him, including eight counts of first degree murder.

Surely the verdict was reasonable. The case against McVeigh established fairly strongly that he was the Oklahoma City bomber. But the underlying assumption in the case—that McVeigh's beliefs define him as an extremist—is not quite right. After all, are the words that McVeigh carried on his chest really so radical? "Sic semper tyrannis" was popular among revolutionary leaders long before John Wilkes Booth gave it an infamous sting. Thomas Jefferson's metaphor of "the tree of liberty" is no more outrageous than Patrick Henry's "Give me liberty or give me death" or New Hampshire's license plate motto, "Live free or die."

More important, McVeigh's belief that the Constitution should be interpreted *exactly* as it was written is surprisingly conventional. Not only is it in line with the conceptions held by many of the nation's founders, but it lives on today in the works of an influential minority of legal scholars and advocates. Although we generally teach lawyers to read the Constitution as judges have read it over time, many contemporary judges—Antonin Scalia, William Rehnquist, Robert Bork—hold that we should read the Constitution precisely as it is written. If these "originalists" are right, then McVeigh had a reason to think the Brady Bill's restrictions on gun ownership were a direct assault on the Second Amendment's right to bear arms. Similarly, McVeigh was employing—if perhaps stretching—originalist logic when he concluded that the federal raid on Waco violated the Branch Davidians' First Amendment guarantee of religious freedom.

Faced with a government that he believed had systematically violated the Constitution's core rights, McVeigh also had at least some reason to believe it was appropriate to take up arms. As Alexander Hamilton wrote in Federalist 28: "[I]f the persons intrusted with supreme power become usurpers . . . The citizens must rush tumultuously to arms, without concert, without system, without resource. . . ." Of course, the concept of "arms" may not have included Ryder trucks wired to explode next to federal buildings, but the idea of armed resistance against "usurpers" is rooted in the original understanding of the Constitution.

Let me be clear: this is not at all to say that McVeigh had any legitimate reason to kill 168 people, nor is it to say that originalist legal scholars are

From *The New Republic* (June 23, 1997), pp. 14, 16–18. Reprinted by permission of *The New Republic*. Copyright © 1997, *The New Republic, Inc.*

responsible for McVeigh and his terrorist ilk. But McVeigh's notion of the Constitution, a notion that in his deranged mind led to terrorism, is far more influential than we commonly assume. And it is fundamentally wrong.

With the shots "heard round the world," Americans rebelled against an oppressive foreign authority. Then, after a generation as semi-independent states, they entered into a compact as "the People" in order, as the Preamble to the Constitution reads, to "secure the Blessings of Liberty to ourselves and our Posterity." The purpose of the 1789 Constitution was to charter a government of limited powers that could never become a tyrannical overlord. To guard against government's tendency toward self-aggrandizement, the framers not only expressly delimited the powers of Congress but tried in the Bill of Rights to carve out certain areas of freedom—speech, press, assembly, religion, arms—that would remain beyond the federal government's reach. They would remain vested in "the People," who preceded and superseded the Constitution they established.

Of all the myths that support Timothy McVeigh's antigovernment reading of the Constitution, the greatest is the idea that the People are sovereign and superior to the Constitution. In this argument, the People—represented if necessary by McVeigh and alleged accomplice Terry Nichols—are superior to constituted government authority. They are in a position to judge whether the government has exceeded its authority. Sitting as jurors, they can nullify laws democratically enacted and properly applied. As freemen they must be prepared, as Hamilton argued, "to rush tumultuously to arms" as soon as "the persons intrusted with supreme power become usurpers."

This is exactly what some on the radical right are starting to do. The illegal stockpiling of weapons helped prompt the federal siege at Waco, which outraged McVeigh so deeply. And the Fully Informed Jury Association (FIJA), a small nationwide movement, has begun a major campaign in many western states to inform those called for jury duty of their power and supposed right to nullify the law as instructed to them by the trial judge. To many, the distribution of leaflets near courthouses urging juries not to apply democratically enacted law looks very much like obstruction of justice, if not overt sedition against the government. But the devout believers of FIJA see themselves as doing no more than engaging in civic education. They are joined in this campaign to exploit the jury's power to say no by outspoken members of the black left, who argue, as does George Washington University law professor Paul Butler, that justice for blacks requires jury nullification in certain cases in

which African Americans are likely to be targeted. Right and left are able to cite on their behalf—accurately—academic writing that praises the jury's ultimate power to pass on the wisdom of laws it is supposed to apply.

If only eccentrics of the fringe believed in this exalted power of the People, we could dismiss them as mere and uninfluential anarchists. But these views are not foreign to the academy of constitutional law teachers, nor are they the exclusive province of the fringe. In *We the People*, an influential study of constitutional history, Yale professor Bruce Ackerman, a liberal, argues that the People retain the authority to legitimate illegal constitutional transformations, such as the adoption of the Constitution itself, which was illegal under the amendment provisions of the Articles of Confederation, and the transformation of Supreme Court jurisprudence after FDR's high-handed court-packing threat. The People can provide their imprimatur at the ballot box, as they did when they voted by a large majority for Roosevelt, or, implicitly, by adopting a practice of support and adherence to new laws. However they do it, the mythical People still function as the ultimate source of legitimacy. The power to say "yes" entails, of course, the power to say "no." And therefore it is but a short step from Ackerman's view to the right wing's faith in jury nullification as a legitimate response to unjust authority and the necessity of being armed to say "no" to the "usurpers."

Writing in the *Yale Law Journal* in 1991, Yale law professor Akhil Amar interpreted the First Amendment's "right of the people peaceably to assemble and to petition the Government for a redress of grievances" as "an express reservation of the collective right of We the People to assemble in a future convention and exercise our sovereign right to alter or abolish our government by a simple majority vote." The thought that a convention could abolish the federal government, including the Supreme Court, before the Court could rule on the convention's legality, goes to the heart of our constitutional confusion. We tolerate and encourage views about the constitutional power of the People that some receptive minds take to be an invitation to fight for the original republic.

Some might think that a clear distinction presents itself between fighting the British and taking up arms against a federal government that appears to be encroaching on our freedoms. As prosecutor Hartzler argued to the jury, "Our forefathers didn't fight British women and children. They fought other soldiers. They fought them face to face, hand to hand. They didn't plant bombs and run away wearing earplugs."

That is so, but, as McVeigh might well have seen it, the federal government had shown by its own example that the rules of engagement had changed. After all, women and children perished at Waco, too.

Still, there's a more fundamental problem with the originalist line of reasoning. The "original republic"—the one for which our "forefathers" fought "face to face, hand to hand"—exists only in the minds of academics and fundamentalist patriots. The republic created in 1789 is long gone. It died with the 600,000 Americans killed in the Civil War. That conflict decided once and forever that the People and the States do not have the power to govern their local lives apart from the nation as a whole. The People have no power either to secede as states or to abolish the national government.

The original republic died because it was grounded in a contradiction. It glorified the freedom of some and condoned the slavery of others. It valued persons "not free" at only three-fifths the Census value of those defined as free persons. It required free states to return runaway slaves to their owners. The flaw that spelled its demise was the failure of the framers to recognize the principle of human equality. Neither the word "equality" nor its practical equivalent appears in the document. (The "Privileges and Immunities" clause of Article IV could have become the near equivalent, but it became a dead letter instead.) Today, it would be unthinkable to adopt a constitution anyplace in the world without a commitment to equality. But in late eighteenth-century America, equality was less important than the fear that a federal government might infringe our liberties.

The new Constitution—the one that shapes and guides the national government and disturbs the new patriots to their core—begins to take hold in the Gettysburg Address, in which Lincoln skips over the original Constitution and reconstitutes it according to the principles of equality articulated in the Declaration of Independence. This short speech functions as the Preamble to a new charter that crystallizes after the war in the Thirteenth, Fourteenth and Fifteenth Amendments. The Gettysburg Address signals the beginning of a new Constitution. The language is so familiar that we do not realize the implicit transformation:

> Four score and seven years ago our fathers brought forth on this continent a new nation, conceived in liberty and dedicated to the proposition that all men are created equal . . . that we here highly resolve that these dead shall not have died in vain—that the nation, under God, shall have a new birth of freedom—and that government of the people, by the people, for the people, shall not perish from the earth.

Three changes signaled by Lincoln's words shake the foundation of our constitutional identity: the notion of organic nationhood—including the dead and the unborn—replaces the sovereignty of the (living) People. Equality, absent from the original document, comes front and center. And the United States evolves from an elitist republic into a democracy "of the people, by the people, for the people." The reconstituting of "We the People" as the American nation defines the spirit of the new Constitution. The new nation, mentioned four times in Lincoln's 272 indelible words, is shaped by its past as well as its future. The entire focus of the Gettysburg Address is whether the nation "can long endure," whether the "nation might live." A nation born in a historic struggle will not hold itself hostage to those who say they speak in the here and now in the name of the People. Lincoln's nation could not be dismembered.

In contrast, those who wrote the 1789 Constitution had little sense of an American nation originating in the past and inhabiting the future; they wrote and argued as though they thought primarily of their moment, their generation, as unique. Those living then, and by extension any cohort who loved freedom as they did, could simply decide to dismantle the United States—it was merely a creation of the present. It was Jefferson, after all, who famously wrote that no constitution should be valid past nineteen years.

The recognition that the People are one group, an American nation, makes possible the sustained campaign to convert the elitist Constitution of 1789 into an egalitarian constitution of popular suffrage—that is, a constitution that bases democratic rule on the majority of *all* the people. Beginning with the Fifteenth Amendment, securing the right to vote for emancipated slaves, the United States begins to take democracy seriously. Of the ensuing twelve amendments to the Constitution, five are devoted to increasing the franchise and the role of the citizenry in running the country.

Nationhood, equality and democracy—these are the ideas that forge a new Constitution. But Lincoln was a good lawyer, and lawyers always seek to camouflage conceptual transformations as the continuous outgrowth of language used in the past. That's why he invoked government "by the people" to capture the new principle of democratic rule. But the significance of the People had changed. They no longer exist as the guarantors of the Constitution, the bestowers of legitimacy. States and individuals can no longer set themselves apart from the nation. The people exist exclusively as voters, as office holders and as beneficiaries of legislation.

The relevant concept in the new Constitution, then, is not "We the People" but "We the citizens of the nation"—and this transformation is apparent in the

14

post-Civil War amendments. The Fourteenth Amendment, for example, gives us our first concept of national citizenship. "All persons born or naturalized in the United States, and subject to the jurisdiction thereof" are henceforth citizens. Prior to the Civil War, we allowed each state to define for itself who could become a citizen of the state and, on that basis, a citizen of the country. The new definition of who belongs to the polity marks a new beginning.

The Fourteenth Amendment further confirms the new sense of the United States as a national community with its clause prohibiting the states from "depriv[ing] any person of life, liberty, or property, without due process of law; [or denying] to any person within its jurisdiction the equal protection of the laws." These clauses account for the enormous expansion of judge-made constitutional law in the last fifty years, particularly in the field of criminal justice. Under these clauses of the new Constitution, virtually all the constitutional guarantees of the Bill of Rights apply, for the first time, to the states. Yet, as do all proper constitutions, the Fourteenth Amendment contains its own grant of legislative authority to Congress to implement its principles by appropriate legislation.

The Thirteenth Amendment also wreaks a radical transformation. On the surface, it merely abolishes slavery—expected in the wake of the war. But the Thirteenth Amendment also signals a new conception of constitutional power. The original Constitution limits only government power; the Thirteenth Amendment is the first direct intervention into the private affairs of citizens. The amendment invalidates a certain kind of private relationship—namely, involuntary servitude—and provides the legal hook for the first Civil Rights Acts, by recognizing that citizens — not just government—can deprive an individual of his or her constitutional rights. (This is the constitutional basis for the federal government's prosecuting and convicting Lemrick Nelson for violating the civil rights of Yankel Rosenbaum by fatally wounding him on a public thoroughfare.)

The most significant and, for funndamentalists, the most threatening aspect of the new Constitution is that it necessitates an activist federal government committed to preserving some semblance of equality—in other words, the government must intervene in the states and in private affairs to protect the disadvantaged. Early efforts in this direction—the income tax amendment, prohibition—represented significant moves to level the playing field and protect the weak. And, after the economic collapse of 1929, national government took its new role even more seriously with the New Deal. This is the point at which the conflict with the original Constitution becomes acute. Some constitutional fundamentalists, like McVeigh, explicitly reject the new Constitution in their propaganda. They maintain that the original Constitution—everything that comes before the Thirteenth Amendment—is the only legitimate one, and they believe their task as freemen is to protect the People against the "usurpers" who would have the federal government exceed its minimalist origins.

So if the extremists can grasp this distinction, why is it foreign to the rest of us? Quite simply, because we do not teach this historical rupture—not in our grade schools, not in our law schools. We are all good lawyers and therefore, like Lincoln, we pretend that the second Constitution is simply the natural continuation of the founding document. According to the official story, we corrected the racist mistakes of 1789 and got the Constitution on the right track. "We the People" are still in power. Our constitutional situation would be much clearer if we marked the discontinuity in our history by calling the first Constitution the "founding republic" and the second, say, the "egalitarian republic." This new terminology would acknowledge that our constitutional history is close to that of France, with its multiple constitutions, including some legal institutions such as the Declaration of the Rights of Man and the *Code civil* that date back as far as the late eighteenth century.

The sentencing of Timothy McVeigh and the ensuing trial of Terry Nichols will presumably play out without any serious attention to the defendants' constitutional beliefs. But there was more at stake in this trial than the terrorism of one or two men. The basic question is whether we as a legal and intellectual community will face up to the truth about the false view of the Constitution that we have nurtured for generations. We have propagated myths about the binding force of the 1789 Constitution that some people, unfortunately, take too zealously. We have planted the ideas that have grown crooked in the minds of some. On the basis of the evidence presented at the trial, the jury reached a well founded verdict on McVeigh's guilt. Yet we should be filled with horror that this heinous crime was committed with motives derived from the basic teachings of the republic.

George P. Fletcher is Cardozo Professor of Jurisprudence at the Columbia Law School. He is the author, most recently, of With Justice for Some: Victims' Rights in Criminal Trials *(Addison-Wesley).*

HAS DEMOCRACY A FUTURE?

By Arthur Schlesinger, Jr.

THROUGH A GLASS DARKLY

The twentieth century has no doubt been, as Isaiah Berlin has said, "the most terrible century in Western history." But this terrible century has—or appears to be having—a happy ending. As in melodramas of old, the maiden democracy, bound by villains to the railroad track, is rescued in the nick of time from the onrushing train. As the century draws to a close, both major villains have perished, fascism with a bang, communism with a whimper.

A season of triumphalism has followed. Two centuries ago Kant argued in his *Idea for a Universal History* that the republican form of government was destined to supersede all others. At last the prophecy seemed on the way to fulfillment. Savants hailed "the end of history." "For the first time in all history," President Clinton declared in his second inaugural address, "more people on this planet live under democracy than dictatorship." *The New York Times*, after careful checking, approved: 3.1 billion people live in democracies, 2.66 billion do not. According to end-of-history doctrine as expounded by its prophet, the minority can look forward to "the universalization of Western liberal democracy as the final form of human government."

For historians, this euphoria rang a bell of memory. Did not the same radiant hope accompany the transition from the nineteenth to the twentieth century? This most terrible hundred years in Western history started out in an atmosphere of optimism and high expectations. People of good will in 1900 believed in the inevitability of democracy, the invincibility of progress, the decency of human nature, and the coming reign of reason and peace. David Starr Jordan, the president of Stanford University, expressed the mood in his turn-of-the-century book *The Call of the Twentieth Century*. "The man of the Twentieth Century," Jordan predicted, "will be a hopeful man. He will love the world and the world will love him."

Looking back, we recall a century marked a good deal less by love than by hate, irrationality, and atrocity, one that for a long dark passage inspired the gravest forebodings about the very survival of the human race. Democracy, striding confidently into the 1900s, found itself almost at once on the defensive. The Great War, exposing the pretension that democracy would guarantee peace, shattered old structures of security and order and unleashed angry energies of revolution—revolution not for democracy but against it. Bolshevism in Russia, Fascism in Italy, Nazism in Germany, militarism in Japan all despised, denounced, and, wherever they could, destroyed individual rights and the processes of self-government.

In another decade the Great Depression came along to expose the pretension that democracy would guarantee prosperity. A third of the way into the century, democracy seemed a helpless thing, spiritless, paralyzed, doomed. Contempt for democracy spread among elites and masses alike: contempt for parliamentary dithering, for "talking-shops," for liberties of expression and opposition, for bourgeois civility and cowardice, for pragmatic muddling through.

In another decade the Second World War threatened to administer the coup de grace. Liberal society, its back to the wall, fought for its life. There was considerable defeatism in the West. The title of Anne Morrow Lindbergh's 1940 bestseller proclaimed

From *Foreign Affairs* (September/October 1997, Vol. 76, No. 5), pp. 2–12. Reprinted by permission of *Foreign Affairs*. Copyright © 1997 by the Council on Foreign Relations, Inc.

totalitarianism *The Wave of the Future*. It was, she wrote, a "new, and perhaps even ultimately good, conception of humanity trying to come to birth." Hitlerism and Stalinism were merely "scum on the wave of the future . . . The wave of the future is coming and there is no fighting it." By 1941 only about a dozen democracies were left on the planet.

The political, economic, and moral failures of democracy had handed the initiative to totalitarianism. Something like this could happen again. If liberal democracy fails in the 21st century, as it failed in the twentieth, to construct a humane, prosperous, and peaceful world, it will invite the rise of alternative creeds apt to be based, like fascism and communism, on flight from freedom and surrender to authority.

Democracy's failures handed the initiative to totalitarianism. It could happen again.

After all, democracy in its modern version—representative government, party competition, the secret ballot, all founded on guarantees of individual rights and freedoms—is at most 200 years old. A majority of the world's inhabitants may be living under democracy in 1997, but democratic hegemony is a mere flash in the long vistas of recorded history. One wonders how deeply democracy has sunk roots in previously nondemocratic countries in the years since the collapse of the totalitarian challenges. Now the democratic adventure must confront tremendous pent-up energies that threaten to blow it off course and even drive it onto the rocks.

THE LAW OF ACCELERATION

Much of this energy is pent up within democracy itself. The most fateful source in the United States is race. "The problem of the twentieth century," W.E.B. Du Bois observed in 1900, "is the problem of the color line." His prediction will come to full flower in the 21st century. Minorities seek full membership in the larger American society. Doors slammed in their faces drive them to protest. The revolt against racism has taken time to gather strength. White America belatedly awakens to the cruelties long practiced against nonwhite peoples, and the revolt intensifies. As Tocqueville explained long ago, "Patiently endured so long as it seemed beyond redress, a grievance comes to appear intolerable once the possibility of removing it crosses men's minds. For the mere fact that certain abuses have been remedied draws attention to others,

and they now appear more galling; people may suffer less, but their sensibility is exacerbated."

There are other pent-up energies. Modern democracy itself is the political offspring of technology and capitalism, the two most dynamic—that is to say, destabilizing—forces loose in the world today. Both are driven ever onward by self-generated momentum that strains the bonds of social control and of political sovereignty.

Technology created the clock, the printing press, the compass, the steam engine, the power loom, and the other innovations that laid the foundation for capitalism and that in time generated rationalism, individualism, and democracy. At first technological advance was unsystematic and intermittent. Soon it was institutionalized. "The greatest invention of the nineteenth century," said Alfred North Whitehead, "was the invention of the method of invention."

In the twentieth century, scientific and technological innovation increased at an exponential rate. Henry Adams, the most brilliant of American historians, meditated on the acceleration of history. "The world did not double or treble its movement between 1800 and 1900," Adams wrote in 1909, "but, measured by any standard . . . the tension and vibration and volume and so-called progression of society were fully a thousand times greater in 1900 than in 1800;—the force had doubled ten times over, and the speed, when measured by electrical standards as in telegraphy, approached infinity, and had annihilated both space and time." Nothing, Adams thought, could slow this process, for "the law of acceleration . . . cannot be supposed to relax its energy to suit the convenience of man."

The law of acceleration now hurtles us into a new age. The shift from a factory-based to a computer-based economy is more traumatic even than our great-grandparents shift from a farm-based to a factory-based economy. The Industrial Revolution extended over generations and allowed time for human and institutional adjustment. The Computer Revolution is far swifter, more concentrated, and more drastic in its impact.

HYPERINTERACTIVE STATE

The computerized world poses problems for democracy. Where the Industrial Revolution created more jobs than it destroyed, the Computer Revolution threatens to destroy more jobs than it creates. It also threatens to erect new and rigid class barriers, especially between the well-educated and the ill-educated. Economic inequality has already grown in the United States to the point where disparities are greater in egalitarian America than in the class-ridden societies of Europe. Felix Rohatyn, the investment banker and rescuer of a bankrupt New York City, speaks of the "huge transfers of wealth from lower-skilled middle-class workers to the owners of capital assets and to a new technological aristocracy." Those who skip or flunk the computer will fall into the *Blade Runner* proletariat, a snarling, embittered, violent underclass.

The computer will also affect the procedures of democratic politics. James Madison in *The Federalist Papers* distinguished between "pure democracy," by which he meant a system in which citizens assemble and administer the government in person, and a republic, by which he meant a system in which the majority expresses its will through "a scheme of representation." For most of American history, "pure democracy" was necessarily limited to town meetings in small villages. Now the interactivity introduced by the Computer Revolution makes "pure democracy" technically feasible on a national scale.

Brian Beedham in an article in the December 21, 1996, *Economist* applauds this development, claiming representative democracy is "a half-finished thing." Every citizen, Beedham argues, is entitled to an equal say in the conduct of public affairs. The rise of public opinion polls, focus groups, and referendums suggests popular demand for a finished democracy. With a nation of computers plugged into information and communication networks, "full democracy" is just around the corner. Full democracy, pure democracy, plebiscitary democracy, direct democracy, cyberdemocracy, the electronic town hall: under whatever name, is this a desirable prospect?

Perhaps not. Interactivity encourages instant responses, discourages second thoughts, and offers outlets for demagoguery, egomania, insult, and hate. Listen to talk radio! In too interactive a polity, a "common passion," as Madison thought, could sweep through a people and lead to emotional and ill-judged actions. Remembering the explosion of popular indignation when President Truman fired General Douglas MacArthur, one is grateful that the electronic town hall was not running the country in 1951. The Internet has done little thus far to foster the reasoned exchanges that in Madison's words "refine and enlarge the public views."

UNBRIDLED CAPITALISM

While the onrush of technology creates new substantive problems and promises to revise the political system through which we deal with them, the onrush of capitalism may have even more disruptive consequences. Let us understand the relationship between capitalism and democracy. Democracy is impossible without private ownership because private property—

resources beyond the arbitrary reach of the state—provides the only secure basis for political opposition and intellectual freedom. But the capitalist market is no guarantee of democracy, as Deng Xiaoping, Lee Kuan Yew, Pinochet, and Franco, not to mention Hitler and Mussolini, have amply demonstrated. Democracy requires capitalism, but capitalism does not require democracy, at least in the short run.

Capitalism has proved itself the supreme engine of innovation, production, and distribution. But its method, as it careens ahead, heedless of little beyond its own profits, is what Joseph Schumpeter called "creative destruction." In its economic theory, capitalism rests on the concept of equilibrium. In practice, its very virtues drive it toward disequilibrium. This is the dilemma of contemporary conservatism. The unfettered market conservatives worship undermines the values—stability, morality, family, community, work, discipline, delayed gratification—conservatives avow. The glitter of the marketplace, the greed, the short-termism, the exploitation of prurient appetites, the ease of fraud, the devil-take-the-hindmost ethos—all these are at war with purported conservative ideals. "Stationary capitalism," as Schumpeter said, "is a contradiction in terms."

Even premier capitalists are appalled by what runaway capitalism has wrought. If understanding of capitalism can be measured by success in making money out of it, no one understands contemporary capitalism better than the financier and philanthropist George Soros. "Although I have made a fortune in the financial markets," Soros writes, "I now fear that the untrammeled intensification of laissez-faire capitalism and the spread of market values into all areas of life is endangering our open and democratic society." The "uninhibited pursuit of self-interest," Soros continues, results in "intolerable inequities and instability."

The Computer Revolution offers wondrous new possibilities for creative destruction. One goal of capitalist creativity is the globalized economy. One—unplanned—candidate for capitalist destruction is the nation-state, the traditional site of democracy. The computer turns the untrammeled market into a global juggernaut crashing across frontiers, enfeebling national powers of taxation and regulation, undercutting national management of interest rates and exchange rates, widening disparities of wealth both within and between nations, dragging down labor standards, degrading the environment, denying nations the shaping of their own economic destiny, accountable to no one, creating a world economy without a world polity. Cyberspace is beyond national control. No authorities exist to provide international control. Where is democracy now?

THE ASIAN SHIFT

The end of the Eurocentric era raises further problems for democracy. Self-government, individual rights, equality before the law are European inventions. Now the age of the Pacific is upon us. The breakthrough of Japan in the century coming to an end heralds the breakthrough of China and India in the century ahead. The economic magnetism of Asia is already altering the contours of the global economy, and foreshadows historic shifts in the planetary balance of power.

I am not greatly concerned about the "clash of civilizations" that worries some thoughtful analysts. Civilizations are rarely unified. Countries within the same civilization are more likely to fight with each other than to join in monolithic assaults on other civilizations. But the impact of the rise of Asia on the future of democracy is worth consideration. The Asian tradition, we are told, values the group more than the individual, order more than argument, authority more than liberty, solidarity more than freedom. Some Asian leaders, notably Lee Kuan Yew of Singapore and Mahathir bin Mohamad of Malaysia, love to contrast Asian discipline and stability with the disorder and decadence they impute to the individualistic West. They denounce the attempt to hold Asian countries to Western democratic standards as the new form of Western imperialism.

Nevertheless, both India and Japan are functioning democracies. If the claim that human rights are universal is proof of Western arrogance, the restriction of those rights to Europe and the Americas brands non-Western peoples as lesser breeds incapable of appreciating personal liberty and self-government, and that is surely Western arrogance too. In fact, many Asians fight for human rights, and at the risk of their freedom and their lives. "Why do we assume," asks Christopher Patten, the last British governor of Hong Kong, "that Lee Kuan Yew is the embodiment of Asian values rather than Daw Aung San Suu Kyi," the courageous opposition leader under prolonged house arrest in Burma? A pre-Tiananmen Square wall poster in Beijing proclaimed: "We cannot tolerate that human rights and democracy are only slogans of the Western bourgeoisie and the Eastern proletariat only needs dictatorship." In the words of the Indian economist Amartya Sen, "The so-called Asian values that are invoked to justify authoritarianism are not especially Asian in any significant sense." Chris Patten concludes, "I think the Asian value debate is piffle. What are these Asian values? When you home in on what one or two Asian leaders mean by them, what they actually mean is that anyone who disagrees with me should shut up."

Still, the new salience of Asia on the world scene, the absence of historical predilections for democracy, and the self-interest of rulers who see democracy as a threat to their power suggest a period of Asian resistance to the spread of the democratic idea.

CULTURE LASHES BACK

That resistance will be reinforced by the defensive reaction around the planet to relentless globalization—a reaction that takes the form of withdrawal from modernity. The world today is torn in opposite directions. Globalization is in the saddle and rides mankind, but at the same time drives people to seek refuge from its powerful forces beyond their control and comprehension. They retreat into familiar, intelligible, protective units. They crave the politics of identity. The faster the world integrates, the more people will huddle in their religious or ethnic or tribal enclaves. Integration and disintegration feed on each other.

A militant expression of what Samuel Huntington calls cultural backlash is the upsurge of religious fundamentalism. Islamic fundamentalism seems especially hostile to freedom of expression, to women's rights, and, contrary to historical Islam, to other religions. Nor is the fundamentalist revival confined to the Third World. Many people living lives of quiet desperation in modern societies hunger for transcendent meaning and turn to inerrant faith for solace and support.

According to a 1995 Gallup poll, more than a third of American adults claim that God speaks to them directly. One hopes it is the God of love rather than the God of wrath on the other end of the line. Fundamentalism, carried too far, has ominous implications for democracy. Those who believe they are executing the will of the Almighty are notably harsh on nonbelievers. A fanatic, as the Irish-American wit Finley Peter Dunne's Mr. Dooley once observed, "does what he thinks th' Lord wud do if He only knew th' facts in th' case." Fanaticism is the mortal enemy of democracy.

Back to the question: Has democracy a future? Yes, Virginia, it does, but not the glorious future predicted in the triumphalist moment. Democracy has survived the twentieth century by the skin of its teeth. It will not enjoy a free ride through the century to come.

In America, democracy must run a gauntlet of challenges. The most crucial is still Du Bois' color line. Much depends on the availability of jobs, especially in the inner city. If employment remains high, political action will mitigate racial tensions, particularly when minorities understand that in the longer run ethnic gerrymandering will reduce, not increase, their influence. Tension will be mitigated even more by intermarriage.

Sex—and love—between people of different creeds and colors can probably be counted on to arrest the disuniting of America.

The national capacity to absorb and assimilate newcomers will remain powerful. The call of the mainstream will appeal far more than linguistic or ethnic ghettos, above all to the young. English will continue as the dominant language. Indeed, in essentials the national character will be recognizably much as it has been for a couple of centuries. People seeking clues to the American mystery will still read, and quote, Tocqueville.

Globalization rides mankind, but drives people to take refuge from its powerful forces.

Technology will rush on according to Adams' law of acceleration. But for all the temptations of interactivity and all the unpopularity of elected officials, I doubt that Americans will sanction the degradation of representative democracy into a system of plebiscites. Capitalism too will career on, through downs as well as ups, but laissez-faire ideology will probably wane as capitalists discover the range of troubles the unfettered market cannot solve, or makes worse. Unbridled capitalism, with low wages, long hours, and exploited workers, excites social resentment, revives class warfare, and infuses Marxism with new life. To move along constructive lines, capitalism must subordinate short-term plans and profits to such long-term social necessities as investment in education, research and development, environmental protection, the extension of health care, the rehabilitation of infrastructure, the redemption of the city. Capitalists are not likely to do this by themselves. Long-term perspectives demand public leadership and affirmative government.

In the world at large, can capitalism, once loose from national moorings, be held to social accountability? Will international institutions acquire the authority to impose, for example, a global SEC? This won't happen next week, but continuing abuse of power will build a constituency for reform. Wars will still disturb the tenor of life, but where in the past they generally arose from aggression across national frontiers, the wars of the 21st century will more likely be between ethnic, religious, ideological, or tribal factions within the same country. Such wars are harder to define and to control. Let us pray that no factional zealot gets hold of an atomic bomb. Nation-states will continue to decline as effective power units: too small for the big problems, as the sociologist Daniel Bell has said, and too big for the small problems. Despite this decline, nationalism will persist as the most potent of political emotions. Whether democracy, a Western creation, can be transplanted to parts of the world with different cultures and traditions is far from certain. Yet I would expect a gradual expansion of democratic institutions and ideals. It is hard to believe that the instinct for political and intellectual freedom is limited to a happy few around the North Atlantic littoral.

Democracy in the 21st century must manage the pressures of race, of technology, and of capitalism, and it must cope with the spiritual frustrations and yearnings generated in the vast anonymity of global society. The great strength of democracy is its capacity for self-correction. Intelligent diagnosis and guidance are essential. "Perhaps no form of government," said the historian and diplomat Lord Bryce, "needs great leaders so much as democracy." Yet even the greatest of democratic leaders lack the talent to cajole violent, retrograde, and intractable humankind into utopia. Still, with the failures of democracy in the twentieth century at the back of their minds, leaders in the century to come may do a better job than we have done of making the world safe for democracy.

Arthur Schlesinger, Jr., is a writer, historian, and former Special Assistant to President Kennedy. This article is based on the James Bryce Lecture on the American Commonwealth, to be delivered at the Institute of United States Studies of the University of London in September.

IS NOTHING PRIVATE?

A Reading for Critical Thinking

The right to protect our most intimate secrets is being chipped away.

By Jeffrey Rosen

In February, during a speech to the Democratic Business Council, in Miami, the White House aide Paul Begala told a joke. "Bill Clinton taught me that there are some good Republicans out there," he said, "which is not something I would have known just from reading their F.B.I. files." As the audience chuckled politely, Begala added, "You know, I mean that was just a joke, Your Honor."

Several days later, Begala received a notice ordering him to testify, and at first he thought that it was a joke, too. Issued by Larry Klayman, a conservative lawyer who has filed suit on behalf of the Reagan and Bush Administration employees whose F.B.I. files turned up in the Clinton White House, the notice demanded that Begala produce any records, notes, correspondence, or diaries that might cast light on the Clinton Administration's possible mishandling of the confidential information in those files. "I was living in Texas when Filegate broke," Begala told me. "I tried to explain over and over that I don't know anything about the use of the F.B.I. files."

Nevertheless, Klayman subjected the White House aide to a six-hour deposition. "He was going through the list of every person I ever had lunch with," Begala recalled. "He asked the most personal stuff." As Klayman combed through Begala's appointment calendar, Begala explained that he was scheduled to meet with a friend of his priest in Texas, whereupon Klayman exclaimed, "Name your priest; I will name my rabbi!" Begala said afterward, "If you had told me that in America I'd be sitting, under oath, arguing about the name of my priest—it was a surreal experience. And then he turned over the videotape of the deposition to Geraldo."

As we talked, in Begala's office, his twenty-three-year-old assistant, Stacy Parker, typed quietly at a desk next to his. Begala explained that he and Parker aren't allowed to discuss the Klayman suit, because, after she sifted through Begala's papers and E-mail in an attempt to respond to Klayman's demands, Klayman deposed her, too. In the course of her deposition, Parker told Klayman that she had been a White House intern at the same time as Monica Lewinsky, and that she had dined, on occasion, with Vernon Jordan. This prompted Klayman to ask if Jordan had offered Parker counsel about whether she should tell the truth in her deposition; he also asked if she had discussed her testimony with her boyfriend, whose name Klayman was eager to know. (Klayman has also subpoenaed other White House aides and journalists, including Jane Mayer, of The New Yorker. His theory is that the Administration has used confidential information in government files to smear adversaries, one of whom, Linda Tripp, was the subject of an article by Jane Mayer. Mayer has moved to quash the subpoena.)

It may seem ironic that a lawsuit filed to protect privacy could produce so many privacy violations of its own. But this has been the recurring dynamic of the Clinton scandals. It was The American Spectator's invasion of Paula Jones's privacy four years ago that set in motion the ever-expanding investigation that eventually led the special prosecutor Kenneth Starr to fish for Monica Lewinsky's sexual secrets by wiring her friend, interrogating her mother, and issuing subpoenas for her bookstore receipts. Similarly, when Dan Burton, the head of the House Committee on Government Reform and Oversight, was accused a few weeks ago of violating the privacy of former Associate Attorney General Webster Hubbell by releasing edited transcripts of his telephone calls from federal prison, Burton's response was to distribute *unedited* copies of the tapes to all those who asked for them. And so I recently found myself sitting at home and eavesdropping on Hubbell and his wife as Mrs. Hubbell discussed her plans for dinner. She remarked that the children wanted meat loaf. Hubbell gently reminded his wife that meat loaf wasn't his favorite food. "Have it before I get home," he said. "I just don't like meat loaf—O.K.?" His wife clucked indulgently, then sighed, "Poor Webby."

As Starr prepares to submit his X-rated report to Congress, one virtue of his seemingly endless inquisition has been to remind Americans how little our legal system cares about privacy today. The subpoenas issued by Starr and Klayman are perfectly legal under current law, but a hundred years ago many of them would have been suppressed as clear violations of the right to privacy. In the most famous essay on privacy ever written, which was published in the *Harvard Law Review* in 1890, Louis Brandeis, the future Supreme Court Justice, and Samuel Warren, his former law partner, announced confidently that "the common law secures to each individual the right of determining ordinarily, to what extent his thoughts, sentiments, and emotions shall be communicated to others." Yet over the past century this right has been eroded so gradually and imperceptibly that many people have scarcely noticed the transformation.

The legal principle that prevented prosecutors from scrutinizing diaries, letters, books, and private papers, Warren and Brandeis wrote, was the same principle that, in their view, should prevent gossip columnists from writing about the sex lives of private citizens. They called that principle the right to an "inviolate personality," and said that it was part of the more general "right to be let alone." In asserting a right to privacy that could constrain the press, the two lawyers were treading on adventurous ground, but it was a matter of general agreement in the eighteen-nineties that the Constitution prohibited prosecutors and other government officials from rummaging through private papers in search of sexual secrets or anything else. And to appreciate just how far that consensus has been eroded it's useful to compare the stories of two coltish legislators—John Wilkes, an eighteenth-century Englishman, and Bob Packwood, a twentieth-century American— who tried to conceal their private diaries from overreaching prosecutors, with very different results.

Wilkes is largely forgotten today, but his suit against King George's minions for breaking into his London house, in 1763, and seizing his private diaries so galvanized the American revolutionaries that the Sons of Liberty, in Boston—a group that included John Adams and John Hancock—insisted that "the fate of Wilkes and America must stand or fall together." Nearly thirty years later, when the framers of the Constitution drafted the Fourth Amendment, banning "unreasonable searches and seizures" of "persons, houses, papers, and effects," it was Wilkes's house and Wilkes's papers that they had in mind.

Wilkes had been elected to Parliament in 1757. Though Samuel Johnson considered him to be one of the ugliest men he had ever met, Wilkes boasted that it took him "only half an hour to talk away my face," and he was a highly successful womanizer. He belonged to a secret society known as the Hell-Fire Club, whose members held delirious orgies in a secret chapel adorned by an enormous sculpture of a phallus. But Wilkes got into trouble by founding a Whiggish scandal sheet called the *North Briton*, a kind of eighteenth-century Drudge Report, whose politics are a little hard to reconstruct today. Several issues were devoted to accusing Lord Bute, the Secretary of State, of having an affair with George III's mother.

The King, however, was especially offended by *North Briton* No. 45, which contained a violent attack on a speech of his praising an obscure German peace treaty. Lord Halifax, the Ken Starr figure, issued a general warrant authorizing the arrest of the printers, publishers, and authors of *North Briton* No. 45, without identifying them by name. Wilkes was arrested in his house and transported to the Tower; the King's minions then broke into his house, forced open the drawers of his writing desk, and seized his diaries and private papers. At his trial, Wilkes objected, "My house [has been] ransacked and plundered; my most private and secret concerns divulged. . . . Such inhuman principles of star-chamber tyranny will, I trust, by this court . . . be finally extirpated." The presiding judge, Lord Camden, sided with Wilkes, and ruled that unless private papers were protected from leering government officials "the secret cabinets and bureaus of every subject in this kingdom will be thrown open to the search and inspection of a messenger." In two subsequent cases, juries agreed, and they awarded Wilkes ruinous punitive damages of a thousand pounds and four thousand pounds. Giddy Americans commemorated the victory by naming towns and infants, from Wilkes-Barre, Pennsylvania, to John Wilkes Booth, in his honor.

Yet more than two centuries later, when Senator Bob Packwood, Republican from Oregon, tried to conceal his diaries from his fellow-legislators, he found that the legal protections for private papers had evaporated. He served as a senator for twenty-six years—from 1969 to 1995. More than two dozen former female employees and lobbyists accused him of making unwanted sexual advances during this time, but most of them described incidents that had happened before the Supreme Court decision, in 1986, that definitively recognized sexual harassment as a punishable offense. The exception was Packwood's former press secretary, who claimed that in 1990, after an evening of drinking with colleagues, he had tried to kiss her good night but had retreated after being rebuffed. Summoned before the Senate Ethics Committee, Packwood tried to argue that the advance wasn't unwanted, on the ground that a year after the incident, while drinking wine and listening to Frank Sinatra in his office, the press secretary had made so bold as to kiss him. On being asked to corroborate this claim, Packwood confessed that he had written about it in his diary.

The Ethics Committee then decided to subpoena all of Packwood's diaries written between 1989 and 1993. Packwood maintained that, rather than allow Congress to rummage freely through his most private thoughts, the committee should appoint an "independent examiner" to review the diaries and decide which passages were relevant to the charges of sexual misconduct. In an odd coincidence, the person whom Packwood suggested to conduct the review was Kenneth Starr, a former appellate judge. When the committee rejected this request, Packwood's lawyers contested the subpoenas, citing a famous case from 1886, Boyd v. United States. In the Boyd opinion, the Supreme Court had recited the story of John Wilkes and had then announced that subpoenaing a defendant's private business papers to be used as evidence against him was both an unreasonable search and a form of compelled self-incrimination. Nevertheless, in a remarkably breezy opinion, Judge Thomas Penfield Jackson, of the United States District Court in Washington, D.C., ordered Packwood to turn over the diaries, holding that the late-nineteenth-century right to privacy had been chipped away by subsequent Supreme Court decisions.

Those decisions were initially motivated by a single purpose: white-collar crime. In the years leading up to the Progressive era, it became clear that if people could refuse to turn over their corporate records in response to grand jury subpoenas it would be impossible to enforce antitrust laws or railroad laws, or any other government regulation. Well before the New Deal, the Court decided that the only way to investigate corporate crime would be to give prosecutors broad powers to subpoena witnesses and to obtain documents. But it was the purportedly liberal Warren and Burger Courts that inadvertently gutted the right to privacy, during the civil-rights era. In the nineteen-sixties, as part of an effort to constrain violent and racist Southern police, the Warren Court held that evidence obtained in unconstitutional searches had to be excluded from criminal trials. But the Justices soon realized that they had painted themselves into a corner: if every search, no matter how trivial, had to meet elaborate Constitution standards, including a judicial warrant and a Miranda warning, law enforcement would be impossible. The Court's hastily improvised solution was to pretend that all sorts of dramatic intrusions on privacy, such as planting bugs in people's clothing, rummaging through their trash, and spying on them with high-powered binoculars, weren't really searches or seizures anyway.

In a dubious series of related rulings, the Court also held that if you share information with someone else you relinquish all "reasonable expectation of privacy." In the 1971 case that made Linda Tripp's wiring possible, four Justices said that a government informer carrying a radio transmitter could secretly broadcast his conversation with a suspected drug dealer to an agent waiting in a nearby room, because all of us, when we confide in our friends, run the risk that they might betray us. And, in a series of cases that laid the groundwork for subpoenaing records of Monica Lewinsky's book purchases, the Burger Court decided, in the nineteen-seventies, that you have no expectation of privacy for information such as bank records and telephone logs which you voluntarily turn over to a third party. The implication of these rulings is chilling in an electronic age, when intimate personal data, ranging from medical records to E-mail, are stored outside the home. And the law has evolved in such a way that even your home is not secure. Until the Packwood affair, some courts were still trying to maintain the embattled distinction between corporate and personal papers. (In 1992, a Virginia court held a hearing about whether pocket diaries and beach-house records were business-related or personal.) But as a result of the Packwood decision citizens can no longer reasonably expect that their diaries will be considered any more private than their financial records.

In a recent hearing before Judge Norma Holloway Johnson, the deputy independent counsel Robert Bittman defended the decision to subpoena records of Monica Lewinsky's bookstore purchases by noting that federal prosecutors in the Unabomber and the Oklahoma City bombing cases had also examined the suspects' reading habits. "She has not been charged with anything," one of Lewinsky's lawyers countered, and therefore "she has the right to have her privacy protected." In the light of recent case law, however, he couldn't make the stronger legal argument that, even if Lewinsky were to be accused of perjury, there is a world of difference between committing mass murder and lying about sexual indiscretion, and any sane legal system that prohibits "unreasonable" searches and seizures should at least try to distinguish between the two crimes.

The lesson of John Wilkes, then, is that he may have been guilty of seditious libel but was lucky enough to live in an age when judges and juries didn't think that seditious libel was a serious enough offense to justify sifting through a man's private papers and divulging his sexual secrets. In the nineteenth century, judges understood that they could weigh privacy interests against the interests of prosecutors on a sliding scale, tipping in favor of one side or the other on the basis of the seriousness of the crime.

That balancing act looks very different, however, when we think about threats to privacy posed by the press, because of the strong First Amendment interests on the other side. The cruelest moment in the Bob Packwood drama wasn't the congressional subpoena; it was the gratuitously mean-spirited decision, by the Washington *Post*, to publish excerpts from Packwood's diaries. The excerpts had nothing to do with the sexual-harassment charges but instead held up for ridicule Packwood's private musings on his favorite recipe for baked apples, his preferred Washington supermarket, and his fondness for the music of Edward Grieg. "I just felt violated," Packwood told me when I visited Sunrise Research, the new lobbying firm he runs out of a basement office in Washington.

What's offensive about the exposure of Packwood's food preferences—or Webster Hubbell's—isn't that the information itself is secret or illicit. It is, instead, the breaching of boundaries: information that it might be appropriate to share with friends has been wrenched out of context and exposed to the world. In the same spirit, Brandeis and Warren talked about privacy in geographical or spatial terms. "The press is overstepping in every direction the obvious bounds of propriety and of decency," they wrote in their famous article. "To occupy the indolent, column upon column is filled with idle gossip, which can only be procured by intrusion upon the domestic circle."

The eighteen-nineties, of course, were a simpler time. What outraged Brandeis and Warren was a mild society item in the Boston *Saturday Evening Gazette*, which described a lavish breakfast party that Warren himself had put on for his daughter's wedding. Today, even truly humiliating facts can be printed, since the courts tend to dismiss suits by the embarrassed parties on the ground that personal disclosures are a matter of legitimate public concern. In 1937, for example, this magazine published a "Where Are They Now?" article by James Thurber, which included intimate details about a math prodigy who had graduated from Harvard at sixteen, then fizzled out, and was languishing as an eccentric recluse. The man sued and lost, on the ground that former child prodigies are inherently newsworthy. Then, in 1993, an African-American man named Luther Haynes sued Nicholas Lemann, the author of a book about the migration of blacks from the rural South to the North, entitled "The Promised Land," and the book's publisher, for describing his drinking, philandering, and neglect of his children. He lost, too. The social history of blacks in the inner city, Chief Judge Richard Posner held for the U. S. Court of Appeals in Chicago, is a subject of "transcendent public significance."

But it's not clear whether the same defense can be made for the recent epidemic of sexual memoirs, exemplified by Naomi Wolf's "Promiscuities," Elizabeth Wurtzel's "Prozac Nation," Kathryn Harrison's "The Kiss," and a stream of lesser-known effusions. Many of these books describe X-rated encounters that are mortifying for all concerned. I asked Judge Posner whether the unsuspecting former sex partners might be able to sue for invasion of privacy. "It's conceivable," he said, but he then noted the Catch-22 of privacy law: "If you were smart, you'd say, 'If I bring a lawsuit, that will make it additionally newsworthy.'"

It's a little unsettling to think that every time you go on a date you have to assume the risk that your prospective partner may be scribbling notes for a book proposal. Without a commitment to privacy, Charles Fried, who is now a Massachusetts Supreme Court Justice, has written, in one of the most thoughtful essays on the subject, "respect, love, friendship and trust" are "simply inconceivable." Friendship and love can't be achieved without intimacy, and intimacy depends on the selective parceling out of personal information, which we don't share with everyone else. A sexual memoir is the equivalent of a literary strip search, depriving the unsuspecting partner of the most basic attribute of self-definition, which is the ability to control the face we present to the world.

So, too, is a public "outing" of someone who prefers to keep his or her sexual orientation private. A few months ago, the conservative writer David Brock apologized to President Clinton for having published the article about Paula Jones in *The American Spectator* which provoked her lawsuit. In trying to explain Brock's change of heart, Jones's spokeswoman, Susan Carpenter-McMillan, suggested, on television, that Brock was having a love affair with Hillary Clinton's former press secretary, Neel Lattimore. "I was sitting in my office and looked up and there was Susan Carpenter-McMillan saying on TV that I was the love of David Brock's life and we had been living together," Lattimore told me. "It was completely ridiculous—we're just friends—but all of a sudden it ended up on 'Meet the Press.'"

Although Lattimore had never concealed his sexual orientation from friends and colleagues, he had chosen to keep his personal life private. Suddenly hearing it discussed on network TV "was an out-of-body experience," he says. "You want to breathe, but you can't think about how to bring air back in your lungs again. . . . It's like watching a storm destroy your house when you're not in it."

Lattimore considered suing for invasion of privacy, but then thought better of it. Courts have been generally unsympathetic to suits by public figures who have been outed, reasoning, with exquisite circularity, that the sexual orientation of celebrities is newsworthy because readers tend to be interested in it. In 1975, when an ex-marine named Oliver Sipple saved President Ford's life by striking the arm of his assailant, Sara Jane Moore, just before she fired her gun, the San Francisco *Chronicle* reported that Sipple was prominent in the gay community. Sipple sued for invasion of privacy, but a California court dismissed the suit, holding that the article had been prompted by "legitimate political considerations"; namely, the desire to combat the stereotype of gays as "timid, weak and unheroic."

The court's logic—asking how any man can object to being portrayed as manly—seems exactly backward: Sipple hadn't chosen to cast himself as a role model. But in suits over public disclosure of private facts, courts ask not only whether the information is newsworthy but also whether its publication "would be highly offensive to a reasonable person." And it's this part of the legal test which makes Brandeis's vision of the right to privacy hard to resurrect today. Who can say whether a reasonable person in San Francisco in 1975 would object to being portrayed as gay?

More generally, in an age that is beyond embarrassment, it's rarely clear what a "reasonable person" would find offensive. For every Duchess of York who objects to being captured, by telephoto lens, in a topless romp, there's a Jennifer Ringley, a twenty-one-year old exhibitionist in Washington, D.C., who has a camera trained on her bedroom twenty-four hours a day, transmitting images on the Internet at Jennicam.org. Who's the more reasonable person—Fergie or Jenni? And who gets to choose the group of reasonable people who would ultimately decide what's reasonable? "In everyday life, if you violate your friends' privacy you're not going to have many friends," says Robert Post, a professor of law at Berkeley's Boalt Hall, who has written provocative articles on privacy. "But in the social sphere there's a sense in which we love to see the norms violated, and gossip is one way of defining community."

Privacy, in fact, is a little like Al Gore: admired in the abstract but searching for a devoted constituency in a pinch. So when Gore, in a commencement speech at New York University on May 14th, declared that "privacy is a basic American value," his topic was less bland than it sounded: the dirty secret about the politics of privacy is that although polls show that a majority of people are for it, many of the best organized interest groups are strenuously against it. Corporations oppose any privacy protections that would restrict their ability to use personal information in marketing schemes. In the nineteen-nineties, some feminists have been arguing that the courts, by protecting privacy at home and at work, have created a zone of peril for women, where men are free to batter and harass them with impunity. This line of argument culminated in statutes such as Megan's law, which can be seen as invading the privacy of former sex offenders by informing new neighbors of their past crimes. At the other end of the spectrum, Focus on the Family, which lobbies for the Christian right, recently squelched a proposed right-to-privacy amendment to the Colorado constitution, on the ground that it might encourage abortion and gay rights and allow children to lock their bedroom doors without parental consent. State and federal law enforcement groups are also powerful foes of privacy reform. In fact, the only consistently pro-privacy group in national politics has been the Ruby Ridge wing of the libertarian right, which opposes federal authority in all its forms.

As a result, the politics of privacy tends to be largely reactive, fired by heartstring-tugging anecdotes that capture the public imagination. When journalists obtained copies of Robert Bork's video-rental records during his Supreme Court confirmation hearings, in 1987, for example, anxious legislators responded with the Video Privacy Protection Act. Princess Diana's death has encouraged Senator Dianne Feinstein and Senator Orrin Hatch to propose an anti-paparazzi bill, which would hold photographers liable for repeatedly threatening the safety of celebrities for commercial purposes. And Al Gore's endorsement of a medical-privacy-protection act, in his speech at N.Y.U., may have been prompted by recent articles describing the embarrassment of customers at Washington drugstores who received letters from pharmaceutical companies offering treatments for their most private ailments.

The most significant proposal in Gore's speech, however, dealt with the "electronic bill of rights." In an age when anyone who uses the World Wide Web leaves "a trail of personal data that can be used or abused by others," Gore declared, "You should have the right to choose whether your personal information is disclosed." He announced plans for a new Web site, sponsored by the Federal Trade Commission, which would help Internet users negotiate protocols about privacy before they decide to enter other sites, and so would increase their control over how much personal information they chose to reveal.

Although Gore's specific proposals are modest, his decision to embrace the issue of electronic privacy recognizes an important principle: that the shape of privacy in the future will be determined by technology, but our choices about how to construct this technology will ultimately be political. A few days after Gore's speech, Lawrence Lessig, who teaches at Harvard Law School, testified before a House committee on behalf of the anti-paparazzi bill, and lamented the crumbling "architectures of privacy." The last twenty years, he said, "have seen an explosion in technologies for invading people's privacy. Parabolic microphones that permit listening from a football field away . . . security cameras that watch as we move around a city. . . . E-mail becomes a permanently searchable record, for employers or universities."

In December, Judge Thomas Penfield Jackson, the same judge who had ordered Packwood to produce his diaries, chose Lessig to advise him in overseeing the antitrust dispute between the government and Microsoft. When Microsoft challenged Lessig's appointment as "special master," Netscape officials turned over to the Justice Department an E-mail letter that Lessig had written to a friend at Netscape in which he joked that he was selling his soul by installing Microsoft's Explorer. The Justice Department, in turn, gave Lessig's E-mail letter to Microsoft, thereby prompting calls for his resignation. Although Lessig refused to discuss his E-mail with me, the experience confirmed the central point of his congressional testimony: in a world in which most electronic footsteps are recorded and all records can be instantly retrieved, it's very easy for sentiments to be wrenched out of their original context by people who want to do you ill.

Lessig is appalled, he told the House Judiciary Committee, by Americans' passive response to what he called "the increasing Sovietization of our personal and private life." Just as the Soviets responded to constant surveillance by having private conversations in parks and making telephone calls from the subway, he said, Americans, too, have been "bovine," simply adjusting their behavior to the intrusions of technology—by avoiding the use of E-mail for private communications, for example, and paying with cash to evade direct marketers.

The fact is, Lessig argues, that new technologies have the ability to strengthen privacy, not just erode it. Electronic cash cards, like telephone cards, could enable people like Monica Lewinsky to order books over the Internet with complete anonymity, thus avoiding the risk not only of credit-card subpoenas but also of running into Linda Tripp in the bookstore. Digital encryption can insure that the content of documents is far more secure than it would be if it were locked in John Wilkes's desk. And Web sites can be configured to permit you to disclose selected details about yourself, such as your age, without revealing your actual identity. "The architecture of cyberspace is political, and we have to make a choice about it," Lessig told me. "We can embed one set of values or another, and these values either will be privacy-enhancing or will accelerate the destruction of privacy."

This assumes, of course, that we can reach some kind of social consensus about how much privacy it's reasonable to expect. The legal protections of privacy that have been allowed to atrophy over the past few decades presuppose that society can distinguish "reasonable" from "unreasonable" searches, and can agree about what kind of sexual exposure would offend a "reasonable" person. Now that judges and journalists are no longer confident about their ability to make these judgments, maybe it's too much to ask special prosecutors to make them for us. There is, in other words, a little Ken Starr in all of us, an inquisitorial imp eager to sift through diaries and listen to sex tapes, even as it purports to abhor them. But can we devour tabloid accounts of Princess Diana's cell-phone-intimacies and then deplore invasive questions about sex? "If we don't sanction people socially who violate privacy, we can't expect the law to do much of that work for us," Robert Post says. "The point is that we should actually care about privacy, and it's not clear that we do."

PART 2

Federalism
and
Federal-State Relations

The struggle for power between the states and the federal government may be the defining feature of American political history. America's first "constitution," the Articles of Confederation, failed because the federal government was far too weak to be effective. When the states ratified the Constitution, they agreed to give up some of their power to the federal government. Even so, conflicts soon arose as to how much power the states had given up, disagreements which culminated in the Civil War.

Since that time, the federal government has generally had the advantage. It has obtained more power through the efforts of presidents such as Franklin Roosevelt and Lyndon Johnson, and with the acquiescence of Congress and the Supreme Court. However, the tide has begun to turn. Presidents Nixon and Reagan argued that the federal government was too distant and had grown too large to be effective, and that power ought to be returned to the states. These arguments were increasingly well received by a nation that had grown distrustful of political institutions, and in 1994, Republicans took control of Congress on a platform that promised to return power to the statehouses.

For the time being, the conservatives have won. Even President Clinton, a Democrat, has declared, "the era of big government is over." The Supreme Court has begun issuing decisions restraining the power of the national government. However, the ultimate success of these efforts remains to be seen. Congress has returned control of some issues to the states, most notably in the area of welfare. But Congress has also increased the power of the federal government in some areas. As you read the following selections, you should think about what the federal government does well and where its limitations are most apparent. You should also consider whether state and local government are equipped to handle increased responsibilities.

TOWN-BUILDING IS NO MICKEY MOUSE OPERATION

In carefully planned Celebration, Fla.,
Disney has created a script it can only partly control.
A real community is messy, ever changing and inevitably political.

By Michael Pollan

The sun was barely up over the brand-new town of Celebration, Fla., and the Rotarians had gathered in the clubhouse at the golf course for their weekly breakfast meeting. I'd come fully expecting to meet a bunch of white guys in polo shirts who'd remind me of my father, and there were quite enough of them. And yet right there across the table sat several other Celebration Rotarians who, in age and outlook and appearance, reminded me a whole lot more of, well, me.

Only two years ago, the spot on which we were getting acquainted, these implausible Rotarians and I, was an impenetrable cypress swamp on the farthest edge of Walt Disney World. Now there is a handsome and lively town (population 1,500, eventually to reach 20,000) built by Disney, which has deployed its considerable capital and place-making skills to create, in the choral refrain of just about every company executive I met, "not just a housing development but a community." Viewed from that perspective, Celebration is nothing more than an elaborate contraption for the production of Rotarians—for transforming isolated and disaffected American suburbanites (not unlike myself) into civic-minded members of a community. By one measure the contraption seemed to be working: scarcely 18 months after the first family moved in, Celebration has become ground for a luxuriant growth of scout troops, religious groups and hobbyist clubs of every conceivable stripe. No doubt any housing development that markets itself as an old-fashioned town

would tend to attract more than its share of joiners. There is, too, the fact that Disney has been quietly working behind the scenes (for there is always a "backstage" at Disney) to seed and nourish all these groups.

But none of this explained the presence, across from me at breakfast, of someone like Todd Hill—an urbane landscape architect from Atlanta who doesn't fit anyone's stereotype of a Rotary member. Hill is, by his own lights, living proof that the "neotradtional" design of a subdivision can transform a young urban professional into what can best be described as a neo-Rotarian.

"Before I moved here I was not a big volunteer type," he told me over microbrewed beers on his porch one evening. "I worked all the time." Hill, who is 37, and his wife, Lisa, live on Mulberry Street in a Charleston side row, one of the six historical-house styles permitted in Celebration. They moved here from a condo in Atlanta, and their home has a two-career, no-kids spareness about it—lightly inhabited, with somewhat less in the way of furniture than high-end home audio and video equipment.

As a design professional, Hill had long been familiar with the ideas of neotraditionalism, the planning movement, also known as the New Urbanism, whose principles Disney has drawn upon in building Celebration; his experience living here has already convinced him that "it works"—that walkable streets, attractive public spaces and a close-by downtown can profoundly affect peoples' daily lives.

"It's a physical thing that becomes a spiritual thing," Hill said, by way of explaining his belated discovery of his Rotarian self. "About two months after we moved into Celebration, I was back in Atlanta on a job, and it hit me: for the first time in my life, I felt as though I was part of a community. That's when I decided I should join something. Me! When I first went to Rotary, I thought it was going to be, you know, Fred Flintstone in the bullhorn hat. I mean, what was all this 'fellowship' stuff? It's kind of hokey, and I'm not ordinarily that kind of person, but I see it as a community thing."

If it looks like a town and acts like a town, does that mean it is a town?

"Community" is a word we hear a lot these days, not only in the speeches of the President and in books by self-described "communitarian" thinkers in several different fields, but also in the focus groups and brochures of real-estate developers. (Community has emerged as one of the "features" most prized by new home buyers, according to the trade journal Builder.) Americans seem to sense, and regret, the fraying of our "civil society"— the informal network of clubs, volunteer groups and civic and religious organizations that traditionally knit a community together.

The town of Celebration represents the Disney Company's ambitious answer to the perceived lack of community in American life, but it is an answer that raises a couple of difficult questions. To what extent can redesigning the physical world we inhabit— the streets, public spaces and buildings—foster a greater sense of community? And what exactly does "a sense of" mean here?—for the word community hardly ever goes abroad in Celebration without that dubious prefix.

Disney occupies a special place in the American landscape and culture. Few companies are as skillful at making places, at shaping the physical environment to affect our behavior. Disney's theme parks deserve credit for helping to keep alive not only a large part of America's vernacular architecture but, on Main Street, the very experience of walkable streets and pleasing public spaces—this at precisely the time when Americans were abandoning real Main Streets for their cars and suburban cul-de-sacs.

But Disney's expertise is in building theme parks for paying guests, not towns for citizens. A real community is messy, ever changing and inevitably political—three adjectives that pretty much sum up everything the culture of Disney cannot abide. Very soon after the first homeowners moved into Celebration,

Disney got its first taste of the unpredictability of community life, and of the difference between consumers and citizens. A bruising controversy erupted over the curriculum at the Celebration public school, and Disney suddenly found itself in a most unfamiliar environment, one that has tested the company's vaunted skills at managing reality.

Disney's expertise at making places and synthesizing urban experience cannot be separated from its legendary obsession with control; it is, even more than most, a corporation that lives by scripts of its own scrupulous devising. At Celebration, however, Disney has set in motion a story whose script it can only partly control. It is this experiment that I recently traveled to Celebration to observe: just how does a corporation go about manufacturing a community? And what happens when it actually succeeds, and that community starts to act like one?

THE STREET

One Sunday afternoon, I took a long walk through the streets of Celebration, hoping to understand just what Robert A.M. Stern meant when he told me that "the street is the key to everything else we're trying to accomplish here." Stern is, along with Jaquelin Robertson, a fellow New York architect, Celebration's master planner; the two laid out the town's network of streets, its downtown commercial district, its parks and school and "wellness center." If a neotraditional town like Celebration represents a technology for the creation of community, the street, Stern was suggesting, is its most crucial component—its flywheel or microprocessor.

The streets of Celebration are loosely gridded, which means lots of stop signs, and narrow enough to force cars to crawl, so a pedestrian senses at once that he belongs here. The first thing I noticed as I headed up Longmeadow toward Hippodrome Park was just how much there is to look at. The houses are close enough to one another, and sufficiently varied in style, to unfold before the pedestrian in a pleasing rhythm. Even the grandest houses—and Longmeadow is a street of "Estate Homes"— are on tiny lots pulled up to the curb, and their faces engage the passerby with ceremonial front doors, nicely detailed windows and columns and sociable front porches.

Though I spotted no porch sitters on my walk, I spoke to several residents who swear by their porches, especially in the winter, when Orlando's temperatures and mosquitoes let up. Lise Juneman, a young mother of two, said her family "spends every Saturday morning out on the porch, having coffee, playing Barbies with the girls, catching up with the neighbors strolling by." A cliché, perhaps, but not an unappealing one.

Stern had spoken of the importance of making the street into an outdoor room—a public space in its own right, not just a connector—and the best of Celebration's streets have already achieved this quality. The orderly ranks of trees (Disney has planted thousands of handsome, mature specimens) present a unifying street wall, the dead faces of garages have been banished to backyards (where they are accessible by service alleys) and the house fronts have been carefully scaled so as not to overwhelm the space. I found it easy to strike up conversations on the street, and my notebook quickly filled with slightly astonished testimonials to the forgotten pleasures of small-town life: "I used to just wave at my neighbors from the car. Now we stop and gossip on the corner." "Everyone's so friendly here, it's like the first week of college."

It may be Disney's boldest innovation at Celebration to have established a rather novel form of democracy, one that is based on consumerist principles. For many of the people I met there the measure is not self-rule but corporate sensitivity to their needs.

If the typical suburb represents a kind of monoculture, street after street of architecturally and socioeconomically identical houses, Celebration has already achieved a striking degree of diversity. During my walk, I strolled down a street of million-dollar homes facing the golf course and then turned to find a lane of modest cottages that sell for a fifth as much; walking another block or two, I came to a broad crescent of town house apartments that rent for as little as $600 a month. This sort of diversity, while limited—there are no poor in Celebration, and the town is extremely white—is nevertheless rare today in the suburbs, where it is an article of the real-estate faith that people will live next door only to neighbors of the same class. In Celebration, houses of roughly the same price do face each other across a street, but the service alleys behind those houses deliberately mix high and low forcing the surgeon and the firefighter to mingle while taking out the trash or getting into their cars. Stern spoke of deliberately setting up such encounters as one of the many ways that "design can help to orchestrate community."

This is, of course, a very old utopian idea, with deep roots in the American landscape: that the proper arrangement of streets and houses can help usher in a specific sort of community. When, in the 1630's, the Puritans established a town on Massachusetts Bay, they specified exactly how far from the meeting house anyone could build—no more than a mile and a half—and laid out their village in concentric circles to enforce the social compact. In our own century, a long succession of middle-class utopias—Radburn, N.J.; Reston, Va.; Columbia, Md., Levittown, N.Y., and countless unheralded others—have been staked out, platted and built on blank stretches of land in the conviction that a considered arrangement of streets, houses, public spaces and, increasingly these days, walls and gates will help to realize a specific vision of the good society.

In the mid-60's, Walt Disney decided he had something to add to this tradition. He originally conceived Epcot (an acronym for the Experimental Prototype Community of Tomorrow) not as a theme park but as a high-tech model city of 20,000 residents. But it was not to be: shortly after his death in 1966, company executives, no doubt worried about profit margins and the likelihood that a city populated by real people might prove more difficult to manage than a theme park, decided to shelve Walt's utopia.

Today, Disney executives from Michael Eisner, the company's chairman, on down speak of Celebration as the fulfillment of Walt Disney's old dream to build a City on a Hill—a model held up to the world.

"Eisner was very clear from the beginning that he didn't want to do just another residential community," Bob Shinn said over dinner downtown at Max's Cafe. Shinn is senior vice president of Walt Disney Imagineering, giving him responsibility for the company's operations in Florida. "With Celebration, we're giving something back, trying to blaze a trail to improve American family life, education and health. This project allows us to fulfill Walt's idea for a town of tomorrow."

Of course, fulfilling the founder's vision was not the only motivation for building Celebration: if it is a City on a Hill, it is at the same time an element in a larger corporate strategy and very simply, a $2.5 billion real-estate deal, a creative way of packaging and selling Florida swampland. (Disney paid approximately $200 an acre for this land in the 60's; it is selling quarter-acre lots at Celebration for upward of $80,000.)

According to Tom Lewis, perhaps the Disney executive most closely involved with Celebration's early planning, the town had its more earthly origins on Wall Street, in the bloody battle for control of Disney in the early 80's. Part of what made the corporation such an attractive takeover target was the vast acreage of undeveloped real estate it owned in Orlando—the theme parks and hotels occupied only a small fraction of the company's 27,000-acre holdings. After Michael

Eisner took over the company in 1984, he ordered a study of the real estate that determined that some 10,000 acres of it, lying on the south side of Route 192, would never be needed by Walt Disney World. Developing that land in some way would render Disney that much less attractive to a raider.

Another consideration was the fact that Disney's relations with local governments in central Florida had grown somewhat strained. Walt Disney World occupies a state-chartered and virtually sovereign municipality called the Reedy Creek Improvement District, which contributes relatively little in the way of taxes to Osceola County, one of the two counties it straddles. By "de-annexing" the 10,000 acres and populating them with taxpayers, Disney could please local governments and smooth the approval process for future theme-park projects, like its new Animal Kingdom. (Had Celebration remained within Reedy Creek, it would also have given Disney's private municipality something it can't afford to have: independent voters.)

Of course, Disney could have accomplished these goals far more cheaply and easily by building a conventional housing development or resort community—and this is where the company's old utopian streak probably came into play. In a bit of local lore cherished by Celebration residents and executives alike, Eisner is said to have instructed his real-estate-development team that Celebration—the town's name was chosen from a focus-grouped list by Eisner and his wife—needs to make money for stockholders, but if its not going to be state of the art, Disney shouldn't bother.

The state of the art has changed considerably since Walt Disney's time. Disney's corporate vision of the future has undergone a revolution since 1966, from Epcot's sleek technological sublime (the city of tomorrow was to have people movers and a vast dome overhead) to neotraditionalism. Perhaps most closely identified with Seaside, the Florida resort community designed in the 80's by Andres Duany and Elizabeth Plater-Zyberk, neotraditional town planning has until now enjoyed rather more success nationally with the media than the marketplace. Many New Urbanists are counting on Disney's success at Celebration to sell developers and home buyers on the idea that the next American utopia should look like a neotraditional town.

They could be right. Some 5,000 home buyers entered a lottery for the privilege of purchasing the first 350 homes at Celebration, and sales since then have been brisk enough (Celebration is currently the fastest selling development in its price range in the Orlando area) to catch the attention of developers and planning officials from across the nation. Indeed, walking the streets of Celebration, bumping into visitors from all over the world doing much the same thing I was, I realized that Disney's town has already become what Disney's founder intended—a stop on the architectural tour or the American future.

It was hard not to come away from that tour impressed by the extraordinary care Disney has taken in every aspect of the town's physical design. And yet by the end of my walk the very designed-ness of Celebration had started to weigh on me. Eventually the streetscape began to feel a little too perfect, a little *too* considered. After a while my eye longed for something not quite so orchestrated.

From my research I knew that every last visual detail my eyes had taken in during my two-hour walk, from the precise ration of lawn to perennials in the front yards to the scrollwork on the Victorian porches to the exact relationship of column, capital and entablature on the facades of every Colonial Revival, had been stipulated—had in fact been spelled out in the gorgeous and obsessively detailed "Pattern Book" that governs every facet of architectural and even horticultural life at Celebration. I knew all that, yet now I felt it, too, and how it felt was packaged, less than real, somewhat more like a theme park than a town.

When I offered these impressions to Robert Stern, he said, wait for "the buildings to take on the patina of age, the landscaping to get luxurious" and for time to put its mark on a place that is still very, very, new. I noticed that he spoke of time leaving its mark, not people. In fact, not one can make the slightest change to his house's exterior without first obtaining written permission from the company; even the choice of trees and shrubs is subject to approval, and will remain so indefinitely. That doesn't leave much room for history.

> *When I visited Celebration last year, before any residents had moved in, there was enthusiastic off-the-record talk among the executives of rolling Disney towns out nationally. Not anymore: Celebration is an experiment that the company has decided it won't repeat.*

"Will Celebration always look so newly minted? That's a real question," Stern acknowledged. "They do have people power-washing the streets at night"—which is exactly what they do in the theme parks. But then the architect, who also happens to sit on Disney's board, remembered himself. "You know it's a really sad commentary," he said. "that for something to look 'real,' it has to be run-down." That is one sort of history, certainly, though not the one I had in mind.

DOWNTOWN

From the air, Celebration vaguely resembles a river delta, with the residential lanes flowing south and collecting at the head of Market Street, a commercial thoroughfare lined with stately palms that carry down to a pretty man-made lake. The whole neotraditional town idea is predicated on providing residents with a vibrant downtown area, a center of social gravity. Downtown Celebration is a sleepy little grid of streets lined with upscale shops and restaurants, a two-screen movie theater (designed by Cesar Pelli), a bank (by Robert Venturi), a neat toy of a post office (Michael Graves), and a visitors' center (really a sales office, designed by the late Charles Moore). Leaving aside these generally whimsical "signature" buildings, downtown resembles a miniature Santa Barbara—vaguely historical, lots of pastel stucco (actually a synthetic material called Dryvit), with most of the parking deftly hidden behind Main Street.

It is tempting to dismiss Celebration's downtown as a shopping mall without a roof, but that wouldn't be quite accurate: for one thing, there are no big national chains (most of the shops are appealing mom and pop operations); for another, there are rental apartments and a handful of offices above the shops. Andres Duany judges it "a spectacular achievement."

Many residents regard living within a five-minute walk of downtown as one of the best things about life at Celebration. "I am much less dependent on my car," Lise Juneman said; some, like Ramond Chiaramonte, have actually scaled back their fleets. Kids in particular enjoy a freedom in Celebration that is almost inconceivable today anywhere else. By the time children have reached the age of 10 or so, most parents are willing to let them wander freely, and after-school hours once filled with television are now taken up with Rollerblading to the parks and pool or expeditions downtown, where preteens go to check out the clothes at Village Mercantile or cadge samples of the coffee coolers at Barnie's.

For grown-ups, downtown offers a quasi-urban experience that can't be had elsewhere in the suburbs. Brian Haas and his wife, Dianne, are doctors who met while in medical school in Manhattan in the 80's. Career took the Haases to the Orlando area, but both miss the experience of walking to bars and jazz clubs in New York. They can get some of that here, Brian said.

We're a high-powered New York-Washington couple," he explained, as I joined him early one morning for breakfast before he walked his children, Julian and Zachary, to school. "Morning Edition" was on the radio, that week's New Yorker on the kitchen counter. Except for the cavernous space, the Haas home could easily pass for the apartment of an over-scheduled two-income Manhattan family.

"I'm an inveterate New Yorker," Brian said. "I could not at first imagine ever living in a Disney town—too Mickey Mouse, to use a cynical New Yorker's expression. But cynicism is often a mask for frustrated idealism. After visiting Celebration, I realized there were virtues to Disney's involvement. With all the publicity"—and here he gestured in my direction—"they can't afford to let Celebration fail."

After a while I began to see how someone as "high-powered" as Brian Haas, a busy surgeon who probably devotes very little time in a day to doubt, might learn to suspend disbelief about something like the urbanity of his adopted hometown. "It's the best of New York," Brian declared. And then, a moment later, "I love it because of the kids." Which is, of course, the classic pre-neotraditional rationale for moving to the suburbs.

So what is Celebration? A town or a suburb? A subdivision with a few streets of restaurants and shops, or a plausible alternative to the general sprawl of suburban cul-de-sacs spilling their cars onto commercial strips? From one perspective, Celebration allows people like Brian Haas, Todd Hill, Lise Juneman and their children to have a different life style than they would in a subdivision without a town center. Yet one has only to climb the tower at the visitors' center to see that the new town is really just one more in a series of residential pods hanging off the classic suburban strip—in this case, Route 192—by a single asphalt thread. Like all but a very few New Urbanist projects, Disney's town offers few real places to shop —there's no hardware store or pharmacy—and few serious employment opportunities; it also leaves the larger patterns of transportation undisturbed. Celebration might look like a railroad suburb, and its residents may walk downtown on the weekends, but on Monday morning most of them will have no choice but to climb back into their cars for the half-hour commute to Orlando.

Rosemary Cordingley laughed when I asked her whether she felt as though she lived in a town: "Oh, yes, a new town! We're pioneers! Please. I can't even get my hair cut downtown. Oh, it's very nice, you can walk to the movies with your friends—that part is great. But a town? It's not even close."

THE SCHOOL

Celebration School, a dignified campus of classrooms linked by covered walkways, is right in the middle of town. In brochures for Celebration, Disney resurrects

Walt Disney's dream of "a school of tomorrow" and depicts its K-12 public school "as a model for education into the next century." Florida schools are notoriously poor, and the promise of a "state-of-the-art school" in central Florida has proven to be the town's strongest selling point—the main reason home buyers are prepared to pay a 25 percent to 40 percent premium over comparable real estate to live in Celebration.

Given the expectations, it isn't surprising that the school should have emerged as the first real test of Disney's management and Celebration's community. Very soon after school opened in fall '96, a couple dozen parents began expressing dissatisfaction about the quality of the education their children were receiving. Many objected to the school's notably progressive curriculum: there are multi-age classrooms; reading is taught using the "whole language" method; tests are few, and there are "narrative assessments" instead of grades. ("This is a place," the principal said, "where nobody fails.")

Some of these approaches are quite controversial—the state of California, for example, is currently abandoning whole language in the face of plummeting reading scores, and while multi-age classrooms are catching on in places, combining six grades in one space is virtually unheard of. So why would Disney have opted for such a radical school, particularly in a neotraditional town? Possibly because a more conventional school would have been hard to distinguish from any other Osceola County public school.

At any rate, problems—or, as the company prefers to call them, "growing pains"—emerged right away. A group of some 30 parents began meeting to discuss their concerns and push for changes—hardly an unusual occurrence, but Celebration is an unusual place, and it all but suffered a nervous breakdown. Here was a faction of its young community flexing its muscles for the first time, and it gave everyone a chance to see how Disney would react. As parents trooped in to complain, executives listened patiently, even sympathetically, but finally disclaimed responsibility—this was, after all, a public school, and the company had its hands tied. All of which was true, but did little to assuage the anger of parents who had put so much faith in Disney.

For Roger Burton a successful small-business owner who had moved his family to Celebration from Chicago largely because of the school, the episode was disillusioning. "Sure it was a public school, but we figured if Disney was behind it, it would be as fabulous as everything else they do," he said. "I knew Celebration was going to be a very controlled situation, but controlled in a good way. But as soon as you run into a problem, you find there is no mechanism to

change things. The only person you can call is a corporate vice president, but he's not interested in the school, not really. He's interested in selling real estate."

Frustrated at the lack of response, Burton and a group of his neighbors began speaking out in the press. Celebration residents have discovered that they possess a powerful political tool few of the rest of us can lay claim to: merely by picking up the phone, they can put a local school squabble on the front page and the evening news. The press descended on the Celebration School story, and Disney realized it had a problem.

Soon after the first negative articles appeared, the great majority of Celebration residents suddenly rose up in full-throated support of the school, though just how spontaneously is open to question. One Disney executive told me that "the negative publicity galvanized the whole community in support of the school," but several residents see Disney's hand behind a lot of the galvanizing. Jackson Mumey, one of the parents most articulate in support of the school, was put on the Disney payroll as an "educational consultant"; he gave interviews to the press, educated benighted parents about the curriculum and helped organize something called the Dream Team—a parents organization that lent moral support to the teachers, who were thought to be demoralized by the controversy. A plane was hired to fly a "Great Job Bobbi" banner above downtown Celebration on Teacher Appreciation Day. (Bobbi Vogel, the principal, quit not long after, as did 6 of the 19 teachers.)

Brent Herrington, Celebration's "community services manager," emerged as one of the school's biggest cheerleaders. Herrington is paid by Disney to manage town affairs, but professes to represent "all the stakeholders." From his office in town hall, Herrington helped to organize a series of "pep rallies" and picnics for the teachers and helped raise funds to buy them small gifts—things like Celebration School jerseys.

All of this might seem harmless enough, yet there was a dark side to the frenzied show of support. At one point early in the controversy, Herrington used his monthly newsletter to solicit contributions for a "positive parents" fund, and school boosters soon took to calling themselves "the positive parents." Surely this was an insidious choice of words, for it immediately cast critics of the school as "negative parents." Dissent had been framed as destructive. The critics took to calling themselves "refuseniks."

Tensions quickly mounted, to the point where "the Hatfields and McCoys"—as Brian Haas described the warring factions—virtually stopped speaking to one another. "As soon as you say anything," Burton told me, "you become an outcast. If you don't like Celebration, you should leave, people would say. Keep quiet or get out." Rosemary Cordingley, another school critic, told of being harangued on the street by Margo Schwartz, single mother in her 40's who emerged as one of the most vociferous "positives." I can imagine it, for when Schwartz spotted me on Water Street interviewing a refusenik, she strode up to us and, jabbing her index finger at my notebook, informed me that "Beulah here was one of the negative ones who only wants to bash this place." (Schwartz and I had never met before.)

Cordingley refers to the positive parents as the "pixie-dust" brigade.

"Those of us who weren't quite so sprinkled with pixie dust were ostracized," Cordingley said. "And it was orchestrated by Disney. We were treated in a very ugly manner. There was a lot of talk about property values. Instead of facing up to the problems—and believe me, the majority agrees there are problems—they hold pep rallies! Disneymania is fine at the park, but not in a school." Cordingley pulled her children out of school, and now drives them 25 miles to a parochial school. All told, some 30 children—16 percent of the total—withdrew from Celebration School last year, and the defections have continued.

Joseph Palacios, who has been active in efforts to reform the school, lays much of the blame for the polarization of the community at the steps of town hall: "A real town manager isn't going to try to create division in his community, but Brent Herrington did exactly that. Brent treated everyone as either positive or negative, and if you were negative, he would literally turn his back on you on the street. Your phone calls to town hall wouldn't get returned." Palacios, the father of a second grader, was one of the few residents willing to criticize Herrington on the record, but three others reported similar treatment.

"Brent is supposed to represent all of us," Palacios said, "but it became clear during the school fight that he's representing Disney." Asked about this, Herrington told me, "This perception is mistaken." It would appear, however, that "community building" has been less of a priority than damage control. Large unscripted public meetings where residents might speak freely have been scrupulously avoided; in their place, Disney has held "focus groups" about the school.

Perhaps the most telling episode in the whole school drama came a year ago when a handful of families—including Roger Burton's—decided to pack up and leave Celebration. According to the contract that buyers sign, a homeowner may not profit from the sale of a house held less than one year unless he can prove hardship. Disney offered to exempt the disgruntled families from the rule but only on condition of signing an agreement promising never to reveal their reasons for leaving Celebration. "They were treating me like a Russian dissident," Rich Adams said. "You know, 'Sign here and you can go.'" Adams, who was one of the first to move to Celebration, became the first to move out. In the end, he signed nothing and Disney did nothing to stop him or the others. Herrington said that in retrospect the confidentiality agreement "probably wasn't the best choice."

TOWN HALL

Celebration's town hall is prominently situated at the head of Market Street, and to see it for the first time is to wonder if its architecture doesn't represent one of wily old Philip Johnson's more clever inside jokes. Johnson's design begins with the obligatory white columns, the same ones that have symbolized democratic values in American civic architecture since the time of Thomas Jefferson. Yet Johnson has taken this venerable convention and multiplied it ad absurdum, until the entrance to Celebration's town hall is all but lost in a shadowy forest of columns—52 of them in all. A straightforward symbol of republican self-government is thus transformed into a disconcerting image of obscurity. It couldn't be more fitting, for Celebration's town hall is privately owned—by Disney.

"Town hall offers residents one-stop shopping for services" is how Tom Lewis, the Disney executive, characterizes what happens in the building; "shopping" is not a bad metaphor either, because the whole panoply of municipal services—everything from garbage pick-up to street lighting, from the provision of recreational facilities and (a portion of) public safety to the enforcement of town rules—has been privatized at Celebration, as indeed they have been at hundreds of thousands of other master planned communities across America.

The responsibility for managing these private governments—for that is what they are—generally falls to a homeowners' association whose board is elected by the residents. Homeowners' associations are now the fastest-growing form of political organization in the country, forming a kind of alternative political universe in which one of every eight Americans now resides.

The Celebration homeowners' association has its offices in the town hall, and that is where I met the town manager, Brent Herrington, the man Tom Lewis had called "sort of the Mayor of Celebration." Herrington is a big, bluff 37-year-old Texan whose friendly demeanor was hard to reconcile with the image of Disney enforcer that several residents had painted. He is a product of the master-planned world: he grew up in Kingwood, a "highly amenitized" community in Houston, and has spent most of his working life as a professional manager of various master-planned developments.

When I mentioned to Herrington that I'd heard him described as Celebration's Mayor, he smiled and demurred. "I'm more like a small-town manager—I'm the go-to guy, but I don't see myself as a politician." Indeed, Herrington sees running a town like Celebration not as a matter of politics at all, but of "good communication and consensus building."

In Herrington's view, his actions during the school crisis fall squarely under that heading. When I suggested that some residents felt he had taken sides, and that the rhetoric of "positive parents" is perhaps not as post-political as it sounds, Herrington said, "There was no perception on my part or the developer's part that we were pursuing a controversial path or taking sides."

Surely the most ticklish part of Herrington's job is enforcing the myriad rules that typically govern life in a master-planned community. To anyone living outside the walls of such a community, these rules can sound outrageous, but inside residents generally view them favorably, as a way to keep property values high at a time when many suburbs have entered a period of decline. As one Celebration resident explained it, "The rules are there to make sure your neighbor's front yard doesn't turn into 'Sanford and Son.'" It should be said that this was the only racist remark I heard at Celebration.

All the rules governing life at Celebration would (in fact do) fill a book, but here are some of the more striking: All visible window coverings must be either white or off-white. A resident may hold only one garage sale in any 12-month period. A single political sign (measuring 18 by 24 inches) may be posted for 45 days prior to an election. Any activity that "detracts from the overall appearance of the properties" is prohibited—including the parking of residents' pickup trucks on the street.

"A violation is usually just an oversight," Herrington explained. "We try to solve problems as neighbors."

While I was walking around Celebration, I noticed some bright red curtains in the windows of a new Victorian on Longmeadow. Only then did I fully grasp the import of a cryptic little item I'd spotted in Herrington's monthly newsletter: "Please refrain from using colored or pattered material in the windows. This can look pretty 'icky' from the street!"

Icky?! So this is the voice of private government in the 90's? It all struck me as fairly creepy, Big Brother with a smiley face, but then I am probably not temperamentally suited to life in Celebration. As Kenneth Wong, president of Walt Disney Imagineering,

pointedly reminded me, "Everyone is here on a voluntary basis."

Master Planner Stern is vigorous in his defense of Celebration's rules: "In a freewheeling capitalist society, you need controls—you can't have community without them. It's right there in Tocqueville: in the absence of an aristocratic hierarchy, you need firm rules to maintain decorum. I'm convinced these controls are actually liberating to people. It makes them feel their investment is safe. Regimentation can release you."

The best defense of the regulatory regime at Celebration is that the people here have chosen to live under it and, if not now then eventually, those people can vote to change it. At least that's what I kept hearing from both the past and current "mayors" of Celebration. "In 8 or 10 years," Herrington assured me, "all power will revert to the homeowners." Lewis said the same thing.

But it turns out that matters are not quite that simple. Buried in the legal thickets of Celebration's "Covenants, Codes and Restrictions," the quasi-constitution that all home buyers are required to sign, can be found the underlying political script Disney wrote for the future of its town, and it reads very differently from the public script about community building and participation that company executives lay out for residents and reporters.

For while it is true that Celebration residents will eventually elect the directors of the homeowners' association, the covenants guarantee that that body will remain a creature of Disney's for as long as the company wishes—specifically, for as long as it owns a single acre of land within, or adjacent to, Celebration. The homeowners' association cannot change any rule or restriction in Celebration without prior notice to and the written approval of the Celebration Company," according to the covenants. Disney further retains the right to control every aspect of the physical character of Celebration as long as it wishes to. Thus, however vital the community that evolves in Celebration turns out to be, ultimate power over its affairs will remain backstage, with Disney.

"It is absolute top-down control," said Evan McKenzie, a lawyer and expert on homeowners' associations when I showed him the copy of the covenants I had obtained from a sales agent. "The homeowners are powerless against the association and the association is powerless against Disney. I can't imagine anything more undemocratic."

When I went back to Tom Lewis for clarification, he said that, as far as he understood, Celebration's covenants were "standard master-planned community boilerplate" and referred me to Wayne S. Hyatt, the Atlanta lawyer who was the principal author of them.

Hyatt specializes in master-planned governments; he is, in effect, the "framer" of Celebration's constitution, which he has described in speeches to professional groups as "progressive," part of a "shift from people and property management to building community."

Only after I cited specific articles of the covenants did Hyatt acknowledge that Disney would indeed retain a veto over the homeowners' association indefinitely and that this was unusual. "The residents can still make decisions, but the veto stays with the developer," he said. I asked him if he saw any contradiction between the goal of building community and the fact that Disney planned to keep that community's representative body on a short and permanent leash.

"Not at all," he replied. "This will result in more progressive governance: you can't change things arbitrarily to my detriment and I can't change things arbitrarily to your detriment. It's a system of checks and balances. This is not a dictatorial Disney. This is a participatory Disney."

For many residents, it is precisely Disney's participation that attracted them to Celebration in the first place. Most people I met expressed complete confidence in Disney's ability to run the town just as well as it runs its other enterprises. "Who's going to do a better job of it?" a prospective homeowner I met at the visitors' center asked me. "The homeowners? Come on!" Lise Juneman said: "Disney gives me a sense of security. They will insure a quality product, and keep property values up."

Somewhat sheepishly, I started asking everyone I met if they felt they were living in a democracy. To a great extent, the answers I got depended on where a resident stood on the school issue. Predictably, school critics did not feel they were living in a democracy; the far more numerous "positive parents" did. But what was striking was that the two groups held entirely different conceptions of what a democracy is. Critics like Rosemary Cordingley and Joseph Palacios described democracy in terms of power and voting, rights and self-rule, the traditional copybook maxims learned in elementary school.

The "positives" spoke with equal fervor of something more . . . well, neo. "It is definitely a democracy," Margo Schwartz said, "because we can go to town hall and express our feelings. It's a very responsive government."

Tom Lewis said, "Democracy is being listened to, so I'd say it's clearly a democracy." Charlie Rogers, a Rotarian who heads up the Sun Trust Bank branch in town, told me: "Everyone's input is welcome. Disney's doing an excellent job of staying in the background. Behind the scenes they're doing a lot, and while they have to control things, I think they really want to step back."

It may be Disney's boldest innovation at Celebration to have established a rather novel form of democracy, one that is based on consumerism, rather than republican, principles. For many of the people I met at Celebration, the measure of democracy is not self-rule but responsiveness—they're prepared to surrender power over their lives to a corporation as long as that corporation remains sensitive to their needs. This is the streamlined, focus-grouped responsiveness of the marketplace, rather than the much rougher responsiveness of elected government—which for many Americans was discredited a long time ago. Of course, the consumerism democracy holds only as long as the interests of the corporation and the consumer are one. So far, this has largely been the case, if only because all the community's "stakeholders" have dedicated themselves to the proposition of maintaining high property values—which is one way, I suppose, to define the public interest.

Todd Hill's answer to my question about democracy was slightly different than his neighbors' and, befitting his general post-modern slant on life, completely without illusion and undefensive. "This is no democracy, I know that. But, hey," he shrugged, "it's the 90's." Hill sees no necessary connection between community, which he cherishes, and self-rule, which is . . . old.

Maybe Hill is right. Maybe Disney has developed a new kind of community for the 90's, one that has been shorn of politics and transformed into a commodity—something people buy and consume rather than produce, an amenity rather than an achievement. Certainly Celebration is, as many residents noted, an "apolitical" place. Mention the word "politics" to people here, and they will talk about "divisiveness"; for in this view, politics is the enemy of community, rather than its natural expression.

I put this idea to Daniel Kemmis, who served until recently as the Mayor of Missoula, Mont. (population 88,520), and is the author of two books about community and place. "I don't believe you can create genuine community in the absence of self-government," he said. "Community finally depends on people taking responsibility for their own lives and the place where they live. That's a messy, troublesome—and also deeply satisfying—process.

"The interesting question here is, What will people do with the civic skills they're apt to acquire in this community? My guess is they will put them to political use—that there will be building pressure for the people to have more of a say."

Kemmis hasn't been to Celebration, but he may be onto something. For Disney seems to have set in motion two powerful forces that are bound sooner or later to collide. They have built a most impressive landscape of community—a place expressly designed to encourage neighbors to engage one another, to form associations and acquire the "civic virtues"—yet they have built it atop a subsoil of authoritarianism, which limits participation to only the most trivial matters of that community's business.

Why would Disney do two such contradictory things—undercut the very community it has worked so hard to create? Tocqueville suggested an answer 150 years ago when he pointed out that "civil associations . . . facilitate political association" by teaching people the "strength that they may acquire by uniting together."

It may be that the very same contraption that produces neo-Rotarians like Todd Hill will eventually produce political activists, too. If Disney truly believed in its benign, post-political vision of community—as an end in itself, as something that confines its energies to block parties and rotary meetings—it would never have bothered to make everyone in it sign such an onerous constitution. But Disney, who is nothing if not an astute observer of the American character, understands that sooner or later the people of Celebration will find their political voice, and when they do they're likely to make a mess of the company's carefully crafted script.

In a future history of the town of Celebration, the skirmish over the schools may well mark the beginning of that process. Certainly the episode has been a political education. "A real town has a voting process," Rosemay Cordingley said, "but this place is run by Disney. Could it ever change? There might have to be an uprising first." For now, people like Cordingley are keeping their heads down. "Last year was traumatic," she explained. There's talk among residents of an informal "moratorium on bad press." But politics could rear its head again at any time.

No doubt the school crisis has been an education for Disney, too. Brian Haas, who is generally supportive of the company, believes that "Disney has learned a lesson—that this isn't just selling someone on a theme park. You're playing with people's lives." That's one lesson. Another is that a community of citizens is a lot more difficult to control than a community of employees or tourists, especially when those citizens have access to the microphones of national publicity. Robert Stern mentioned that the company has been "amazed" by the amount of attention, good and bad, its City on a Hill has received, and is now "mindful of the fact its name will forever be linked with Celebration." To a degree Disney couldn't have foreseen, it has tied its good corporate name to the destiny of this town—and therefore to the deeds and words of people like Roger Burton, Rosemary Cordingley and Joseph Palacios. For a company like Disney to suddenly find itself in such an environment—volatile and, despite heroic efforts, ultimately unscriptable—must be disconcerting, to say the very least.

When I first visited Celebration early in 1996, before any people had moved in, there was enthusiastic off-the-record talk among executives of rolling Disney towns out nationally. Not anymore: Celebration is an experiment the company has decided it won't repeat.

Indeed, there are signs, subtle but unmistakable, that the company would like nothing better than to put a little distance between itself and its unruly new community. Early in the fall, a crew of workers climbed the fake water tower at the entrance to Celebration and took down a banner proclaiming "Disney's Town of Celebration." Now there are just the words "Town of Celebration." It got people talking, so in last month's newsletter, Brent Herrington wrote an item aimed at dispelling the rumor "that Disney may be 'pulling out of Celebration.'" There's nothing to it, Disney's sort-of Mayor wrote; the company has merely been "eager for the public to begin recognizing Celebration as a real, thriving community with its own unique identity."

Michael Pollan, a contributing writer to the Magazine, is the author of "A Place of My Own: The Education of an Amateur Builder."

Grassroots Graft:
Corruption in State Governments

By John Hood

Let me stipulate right up front that Washington is a fetid swamp of scandal. During the past two decades, whatever respect Americans might have had for their national political leaders has steadily sunk into the soft muck of Watergate, Abscam, Iran-Contra, Whitewater, Filegate, Chinagate, Fornigate, etc.

I'll make a bold statement, however. Government corruption is less rampant in Washington than in Albany, Sacramento, or (especially) Little Rock. It is striking that many of the Clintons' most egregious ethical lapses—involving state pension funds, kickbacks, shady land deals, illegal federal loans, and cattle futures—occurred while Bill was governor of Arkansas. Presidents and congressmen make headlines with giggling interns and intricate campaign finance irregularities. State politicians still do it the old-fashioned way: lobbyists with sacks of money, all-powerful committee chairmen who give themselves state contracts, business executives who pay cash for government appointments or regulatory nods.

State officials do this sort of thing a lot—mostly because they keep getting away with it. They typically face less scrutiny than national politicians do, and they have many opportunities to enrich or impoverish individual firms. By contrast, Congress does things that affect whole industries, making it simultaneously more powerful and less amenable to garden-variety graft.

While political observers can count on a couple of hands the federal legislators who've resigned in disgrace during the last decade—Dan Rostenkowski and Bob Packwood come to mind—recent scandals in state legislatures have embroiled dozens, if not hundreds, of lawmakers in tawdry investigations and costly prosecutions. In the last few years, newspapers have been rife with stories of corruption in states such as Arizona, South Carolina, Rhode Island, Kentucky, New York, New Jersey, New Mexico, and Massachusetts. And no one knows what the final body count will be in poor Arkansas, where the Whitewater investigation has turned into a broader scandal of bid rigging, insider deals, and thievery throughout state government.

Let me illustrate my point about state corruption with a few examples. Beginning in the late 1980s, the Kentucky state legislature underwent two major scandals, both involving regulatory oversight.

> *When it comes to corruption,*
> *state governments*
> *are second to none.*

In the first case, lawmakers enacted measures in 1988 and 1990 that hurt a small harness racing operation on the Ohio River. Its owner sought relief in the state capital, only to be told by a prominent lobbyist that it would probably cost around $100,000—in campaign cash to various lawmakers—to make his problems go away. The racetrack owner, to his credit, didn't pay up. Instead, he went to the FBI, which began an elaborate sting to catch lobbyists and lawmakers in the act of buying and selling votes for cash. The feds eventually netted 11 bribery convictions, including one involving the speaker of the state House.

The second Kentucky scandal involved health care regulation. Humana Inc., based in Louisville, got a special exemption from state licensing rules for some of its health care facilities. Later, an investigation found that a Humana vice president had paid $10,000 for the necessary legislative votes. Kentucky's penal system swelled again.

Rhode Island politicians were also buffeted by corruption charges in the early 1990s. The wide-ranging scandal involved a mayor taking kickbacks from city vendors, a former governor fined for steering state contracts to his political supporters, and judges tripped up on bribery and fraud charges. In perhaps the most colorful incident, state police put a North Providence clothing store under surveillance based on a suspicion that mobsters regularly met there. The suspicion proved correct but incomplete: One regular attendee at the meetings was the chief justice of the state Supreme Court, who later resigned.

This case may sound like a DeNiro movie treatment, but it's hardly unique. Many state scandals feature dramatic scenes. In "AzScam," the Grand Canyon State's brush with slime, a state representative in line to chair the House Judiciary Committee was caught on camera bringing a nylon gym bag to the office of a lobbyist and stuffing $55,000 into it. Another Arizona lawmaker was actually caught on tape saying, "I don't give a [expletive] about issues. . . . My favorite line is, 'What's in it for me?'" If that bit of dialogue were used in a screenplay, it would be ridiculed as unrealistically blunt.

I used to think my home state of North Carolina—where I run a think tank, the John Locke Foundation—was different. During the past two years, I've discovered how wrong I was. It all started the day after Christmas in 1996. Entering a crowded supermarket, I picked up a copy of a local black-owned newspaper to read in the checkout line. I was greeted with a glowing story about two local politicians, elected to the state Senate the previous month, who had given out $100,000 in "discretionary funds" to several nonprofits in minority neighborhoods. "That's my Merry Christmas present," said one of the senators-elect. "[We] are already having a positive effect."

The notion of passing out taxpayer money like Christmas candy was bad enough. But then I started to wonder how someone who had not yet taken office, much less served long enough to slip some pork into the state budget, could get his hands on "discretionary funds." After some digging, reporters for the Locke Foundation's *Carolina Journal* discovered that the money had come from a secret $21 million slush fund, known to only a few legislative leaders. The money had been "reappropriated" from surplus funds in a reserve account for the repair and renovation of state buildings. As is typical of such shenanigans, negotiators had inserted the reappropriation with four cryptic lines in the middle of the night during the previous year's state budget deliberations.

Legislative insiders and their political consultants doled out this money with abandon. Several grants were timed to help embattled incumbents cut ribbons a few weeks before an election. In other cases, the money appeared to be payback for favors done by rank-and-file lawmakers or wealthy contributors.

The grants were hard to justify on policy grounds. Wealthy Pinehurst, home to some of the world's ritziest and most famous golf resorts, got money for a new fire truck. Several senators and representatives steered money to local nonprofits which they served as board members. The Andrew Jackson Memorial and Museum, located along the South Carolina line near a "birthplace" most historians view as mythical, got a $200,000 check—twice its annual operating budget. The same state senator who obtained that grant (and who serves on the museum's board), gave government money to another non-profit (for which he is also a board member) in a revealing manner. According to a local newspaper, *The Enquirer-Journal*, he attached the check to a football and threw it across the room to the group's founder during a benefit roast. It seems that dispensing taxpayer money had become a game to him and many of his colleagues.

Some lawmakers used the money to entice private groups onto the public dole. In one case, Playspace, a nonprofit museum and entertainment facility for children in Raleigh, had been on the verge of establishing itself as a self-sufficient organization. After years of receiving state and local grants, Playspace had ended its grant requests, planning to rely on admissions and membership fees as well as private donations. But in December 1996, at the urging of Sen. Eric Reeves (D-Raleigh), Playspace accepted a $5,000 check from the state.

Legal action on some of the improprieties we uncovered is pending. But to our dismay, the slush fund scandal was only the beginning. The Locke Foundation began receiving a steady stream of anonymous tips about wasteful spending and political influence. In 1996, a former employee of the state's Division of Motor Vehicles named Algie Toomer received a controversial $100,000 settlement from the state for employment discrimination. As lawmakers convened hearings in 1997 to investigate the matter, we obtained an exclusive interview with Toomer and his attorneys. He told us about illegal campaign fund raising among rank-and-file DMV employees.

There seemed to be a climate of "pay to play" at the DMV, with workers not so subtly promised that the governor would be apprised of their financial support or lack thereof. On a single day in February 1995, Toomer and some 80 of his Department of Transportation colleagues made contributions to Gov.

Jim Hunt's 1996 campaign kitty. More than one-third of the employee donors received pay raises or promotions within a couple of months. According to a report by the watchdog group Democracy South, the contributions were often collected and "bundled" by politically appointed DOT supervisors, who used the cash to strengthen their connections to the governor's office.

By the time we published Toomer's allegations in the August 1997 *Carolina Journal*, the rest of the news media had begun their own scandal investigations. In September, *The* (Wilmington) *Star-News* reported evidence that the governor, his secretary of transportation, Garland Garrett, and his campaign finance director, Jim Bennett, had promised a seat on the North Carolina Board of Transportation, a powerful appointed panel, to a campaign contributor for $25,000. The allegation came to light because the donor, James Allen Cartrette, didn't get the appointment and started complaining about it.

Is selling a government post and then reneging on the deal, among other things, a case of mail and telephone fraud? Columbus County District Attorney Rex Gore looked into the matter and decided not to indict anyone, but he made it clear that he believed the charge. "I personally believe that Mr. Cartrette fully expected to get a DOT position," he said. "I personally believe that Mr. Garrett and Mr. Bennett did little to lead him to believe otherwise. I might get a conviction at the corner store, but I could not in the courtroom." A federal investigation is ongoing.

Another spate of news stories, in *The Charlotte Observer* and *The* (Raleigh) *News & Observer*, reported that several Board of Transportation members—and even, in at least one case, the governor himself—had pushed for highway projects to benefit themselves or political patrons. In August 1997 the Locke Foundation joined with three left-of-center policy groups in a joint request for a state performance audit of DOT and prosecution of wrongdoers. The resulting audit called for significant changes in DOT structure and operations.

The problems in North Carolina's transportation department—from excessive politics to insider dealings and mismanagement—led to the resignation of the secretary of transportation, the state highway administrator, and two board members. In February 1998, the FBI, the U.S. Department of Transportation, and the Postmaster General's Office (which handles mail fraud) announced a wide-ranging investigation of North Carolina's DOT.

Last year, the governor announced reforms aimed at reducing the number of patronage employees in the department and tightening procedures for hiring and promotion. State lawmakers are debating DOT reforms that include downsizing the board, tightening ethics guidelines, reorganizing and privatizing transportation divisions, and handing over highway revenues and authority to local governments.

You might think this long ordeal has validated rather than tarnished the processes through which North Carolina fights corruption. After all, the news media, with a little prodding, did leap into the fray. The legal system, creaking and groaning all the way, did begin investigations and forced some crooks from office. Hunt was forced to cede some power and go through the toughest political scandal of his career. Yet the governor's approval numbers are through the roof. North Carolina voters have either tuned out the scandal stories or concluded that "everyone does it, so why pick on Hunt?"

State corruption is far harder to combat than corruption in high-profile Washington or in local government, where decisions receive more local media coverage and where citizens can attend meetings and corral officeholders. States are the middle, "missing" layer of government. Press contingent's in state capitals have been shrinking for years. Many voters lack basic information about who governs their state and what they do.

It will take more than exposés and lawsuits to clean things up in state capitals. It will take basic changes in what state governments do and how they do it. Here are a few of the most important reforms:

• *Toughen civil service and contracting rules.* I was a reluctant convert to this idea. I used to think that rigid rules for hiring state employees and awarding contracts were unnecessary impediments to running government more like a business. Now I recognize the truth: Government can't and shouldn't be run like a business. It doesn't face the discipline of the profit motive. It relies on attitudes and behaviors fundamentally different from those confronting entrepreneurs. The alternative to civil service protections for employees is not a merit system but selling jobs to campaign donors. Exempting state agencies from bidding procedures means buying office supplies from an agency head's cousin.

• *Cut back regulation.* There are good economic and moral reasons for minimizing the encroachment of the state into private decisions. But one of the most persuasive arguments is that appointments to regulatory agencies and specific regulatory decisions are often bought by high-dollar donors. One glaring example is nursing home regulation, as the Kentucky case showed. In many states, operators who want to open new homes must obtain a "certificate of need" from state regulators. Coupled with state authority over nursing home reimbursements from Medicaid and other programs, this power makes the nursing home industry a reliable source of campaign cash. Other big campaign players in most states include the gaming industry, real estate developers, home builders, and health care lobbies such as optometrists and chiropractors—all of which worry about regulation.

> *Government will always be necessary to carry out essential functions such as law enforcement. Finding ways to carry out these functions without buying and selling influence is a critical challenge, one that advocates of limited government should make their own.*

• *Fight pork-barrel spending*. While discretionary funds tapped by lawmakers for pet projects in their districts make up a relatively small percentage of most state budgets, they consume a tremendous amount of time and result in a disproportionate amount of corruption. Consider state funding of the arts. While the Locke Foundation has long opposed such spending on principle, over the short term we have settled for reforming the process by which the money is distributed. Grants to local arts groups now must go through an open process of application, priority setting, merit consideration, and approval, which will reduce the amount of logrolling and waste.

As long as human nature remains what it is, there will be potential for official corruption. Government will always be necessary to carry out essential functions such as law enforcement. For the foreseeable future, education and some kind of social safety net are likely to remain government responsibilities as well. Finding ways to carry out these functions without buying and selling influence is a critical challenge, one that advocates of limited government should make their own.

Contributing Editor John Hood (locke@interpath.com) is president of the John Locke Foundation, a nonprofit think tank based in Raleigh.

A Reading for Critical Thinking

THE DISUNITED STATES

"Devolution"—shifting power from Washington to the fifty states—is no cure for what ails American government

By John D. Donahue

The wisdom of transferring governmental power away from Washington and toward the separate states enjoys something as close to consensus as American politics often sees. Devolution figured in the 1996 presidential election chiefly as a conventional piety, like family values or fiscal rectitude. Bob Dole brandished on the stump his pocket copy of the Tenth Amendment, affirming the principle of state primacy. Bill Clinton endorsed the "inexorable move to push more basic jobs of the public sector back to the state level," and the 1996 Democratic platform featured the taunt "Republicans talked about shifting power back to states and communities—Democrats are doing it."

Recent surveys conducted by the Gallup Organization, *The Wall Street Journal* and NBC News, *Business Week* and the Harris Group, and Hart and Teeter have discovered strong public support for state rather than federal leadership in education, crime control, welfare, job training, low-income housing, transportation, and farm policies. A bellwether poll conducted by Princeton Survey Research Associates in 1995 for *The Washington Post*, the Kaiser Family Foundation, and Harvard University found that by a margin of 61 to 24 percent, respondents trusted their state governments to "do a better job running things" than the federal government. Except for Jewish and black voters, every subgroup gave the edge to the states, including self-defined liberals, Democrats, and, by 72 to 21 percent, voters under thirty.

Enthusiasm for devolution, among elites and the electorate alike, has already reconfigured public authority. Welfare reform is only the most vivid recent instance of control over policy cascading to lower levels of government. Budget figures underscore Washington's eclipse. Federal spending is increasingly dominated by transfer programs, interest on the national debt, and the shrinking if still enormous defense budget. Within what most people think of as the government, states and cities occupy a huge and growing share of the terrain. State and local spending—the majority supported by state and local taxes, but some by federal grants—is over 13 percent of the gross domestic product: more than seven times the amount of federal domestic spending for other than transfers, debt service, and intergovernmental grants. If Congress and the Administration follow through on their budget-cutting plans, the federal government's domestic role will continue to shrivel. So the United States' public sector—already about a third smaller, as a share of the overall economy, than the average in other industrialized countries—will shrink further. Or the relative importance of the cities and states will soar. Or both.

∎ ∎ ∎

Some admittedly alluring logic supports the ascendency of the states. Supreme Court Justice Louis D. Brandeis popularized a resonant metaphor when he wrote that "a single courageous State may, if its citizens choose, serve as a laboratory; and try novel social and economic experiments without risk to the rest of the country." Varied state strategies test and winnow policy alternatives, providing the nation with information about what works and what doesn't. Beyond the laboratories-of-democracy scenario, in which diversity invites the discovery and diffusion of best practice, there can be value in diversity itself. Since priorities differ, the country may be better off if constituents can find arrayed within its borders alternative packages of services, regulatory regimes, and tax burdens from which to choose. A related line of reasoning stresses the virtues of competition. One engine of private-sector efficiency is the constant pressure that enterprises face to match the pace set by ambitious rivals. Extending that logic to government, states that are compelled to compete for citizens and investment *must* be more creative and more diligent in carrying out the tasks of governance than an unchallenged Leviathan in Washington.

A quite different argument for devolution as a core strategy for public-sector reform is commonest among those with direct experience in or around the federal government. It varies in its details, depending on one's specific exposure to the crippling debt and toxic politics that have come to dominate Washington. But in its essence it boils down to a kind of grim gratitude that since we have wrecked one level of government, the Founding Fathers had the foresight to provide a spare.

There is also a soothing a priori case for predicting that public-sector efficiency will increase as responsibilities flow to lower levels of government. Yet the states have, at best, a slightly milder case of the inefficiency that chronically plagues the federal public sector. And for at least some functions (public schools, license bureaus) claims of superior efficiency ring hollow indeed. Even where decentralization does promise significant economies, it is rare that economic or managerial logic will call for the reassignment of authority away from the central government but then stop at the states. State boundaries have been drawn by a capricious history, and only by accident does a state constitute the most logical economic unit for either making policy or delivering services.

Moreover, devolution is largely irrelevant to the debt service and middle-class entitlements that are straining citizens' tolerance for taxation. The ascendancy of the states, by the most optimistic assessment, will have only a minor impact on the cost of American government. This argument is not based on ideology or economic theory. It is a matter of arithmetic. In 1996 total public spending came to roughly $2.3 trillion. State and local activities, funded by state and local taxes, already accounted for about one third of this total. Another third consisted of check-writing programs, such as Social Security and Medicare. National defense (12 percent of the total), interest on the national debt (10 percent), and federal grants to state and local governments (another 10 percent) accounted for most of the remaining third of the public sector. All other federal domestic undertakings, taken together, claimed between four and five percent of total government spending.

Now, suppose that every last thing the federal government does, aside from running defense and foreign affairs and writing checks (to entitlement claimants, debt holders, and state and local governments), were transferred to the states—national parks and museums, air-traffic control, the FBI, the Border Patrol, the Centers for Disease Control, the National Weather Service, student loans, and all the rest. Suppose, then, that the states proved able to do everything that the federal government used to do, and do it a full 10 percent more efficiently. The cost of government would fall by less than half of one percent.

■ ■ ■

America is struggling to maintain itself as a middle-class society in a world grown inhospitable to that heritage, and our successors will judge this generation by whether we succeed or fail in the struggle. The reshaping of the industrial landscape, the maturation of the mid-century transportation and communications revolutions, and the emergence as economic rivals of huge populations long dismissed as backward are transforming the planet into an ever more integrated market. Like the industrial upheaval of the late 1800s, today's economic transformation is widening consumers' options, expanding opportunities for those who are able to seize them, conferring staggering wealth on a select few—and stranding those unable to adapt. Observers with the luxury of taking the long view, or those with no special stake in any single country, may find this moment in history to be richly promising. But it is by no means assured that America's magnificent achievement of broadly shared prosperity will survive.

Devolution will worsen the odds. Shared prosperity, in the maelstrom of economic change tearing away at the industrial underpinnings of middle-class culture, is an artifact of policy. Policies to shore up the middle class include work-based anti-poverty efforts that become both more important and more expensive as unskilled jobs evaporate, relentless investments in education and job training, measures to strengthen employees' leverage in the workplace, and a progressive tilt to the overall burden of taxation. The individual

The ascendancy of the states, by the most optimistic assessment, will barely affect the cost of government.

states—fearful of losing industry and richer residents to lower-tax rivals and anxious to minimize their burden of needy citizens—will find such policies nearly impossible to sustain.

As Washington sheds responsibilities, and interstate rivalry intensifies, it becomes unrealistic to contemplate anything but a small-government agenda. But even for principled conservatives, devolution is likely to prove less satisfying than expected. Since it has been justified as improving, not shrinking, government, the ascendancy of the states skirts the debate over the public sector's proper size and scope. Like the run-up in federal debt, devolution short-circuits deliberation over government's purpose by making activism impossible—for a time. America's federal system is sufficiently resilient that unless citizens are persuaded of small government's merits, the tilt toward the states that suppresses public-sector ambition will eventually (and after a hard-to-predict price has been paid) be reversed. By attempting to enthrone the states as the sole locus of legitimate government, conservatives muffle their own voices in the conversation over the country's future.

And by the standards of those who believe that what ails America is something other than big government, shifting authority to competing states, though it

Devolution risks truncating a vital conversation over the scale and purpose of America's public sector.

may solve minor problems, is likely to cause or perpetuate far graver ones. Federal officials, as a group, are certainly no wiser, more farsighted, or defter at implementation than their state counterparts. But America united remains much less subject to the flight of wealth and the influx of need than are its constituent states. Policies to shrink the underclass and solidify the middle class are thus far more sustainable at the federal level.

■ ■ ■

Five broad propositions suggest how we can readjust the federal-state balance to meet contemporary challenges. They will not be the last word on the proper structuring of America's federal system but are offered as a contribution, and perhaps a catalyst, to the next round of America's endless argument.

1. *Do devolve—where it makes sense.* Underscoring devolution's limits should not be misconstrued as belittling the benefits of moving duties as far down the governmental scale as possible. Many responsibilities do belong at the state level. Where states vary greatly in circumstances or goals, where external

impacts are minor or manageable, where the payoff from innovation exceeds the advantages of uniformity, or where competition can be expected to inspire efficiency gains instead of destructive stratagems, the central government should stand clear—both to honor our culture's durable preference for decentralized power and to forestall federal overload. The list of public functions in which Washington has little legitimate interest is long and important. But it is shorter today than it was a quarter of a century ago, and will be shorter still another quarter century hence.

2. *Restore federal primacy in anti-poverty policy.* The devolution of anti-poverty policy will eventually be seen as a mistake, if perhaps an inevitable one. By the mid-1990s the Gordian knot of the welfare status quo may have been beyond untangling. We will never know; the first Clinton Administration lost its nerve on welfare reform and forfeited the issue to Congress. But with the first serious recession (if not before), the new state-based welfare policy's built-in bias toward undue harshness will be revealed. As hard times swell the ranks of needy families while hobbling job-creation efforts, as welfare is forced to compete with every other budget item for shrinking state funds, and as taxpayers and officials ponder the prospect that anything but the sparest safety net will lure the poor from other states, anti-poverty programs will spiral toward the deepest degree of austerity that citizens' consciences will permit. Budgetary and political realities at the federal level will preclude reversing course anytime soon. Nor is there yet any blueprint for achieving the humane, work-oriented welfare policy that virtually everyone endorses in principle. We have embarked upon a period of state-dominated anti-poverty policy, and may as well make the best of it by harvesting every bit of evidence that state experimentation produces, to be analyzed and stockpiled for the eventual reconstruction of a national system. And we should hope that the country does not become permanently coarsened by what we will witness in the meantime.

3. *Recognize the states' limits as stewards of education.* Revenue crunches and the accumulation of competing burdens may lead states to fumble their long-standing responsibilities for education and training—just when productive skills are soaring in importance. At a minimum Washington should enlarge its role in financing higher education, from which the states are already retreating. The federal role in primary and secondary education will, and should, remain limited, but national performance standards ought to undergird state and local reform efforts. And we must be vigilant against the prospect that budgetary pressures and fractious politics will lead states

to retreat from the campaign of sustained, universal education investment that is the best hope for America's middle class. The odds that this retreat will occur remain difficult to gauge; the calamitous consequences should it do so are all too clear.

4. *Curb the competition for business.* Not least to lower the risk that budgetary pressures will force states to retreat from education investment, Washington should place limits on the competition for business that is increasingly warping state taxing and spending policies. Bidding wars for business have intensified in recent years. Beyond the high profile rivalries for major plants and sports teams, there is a systematic evolution of state policies to favor footloose enterprises. What states surrender to lure or retain jobs, moreover, yields no net national gains; incentives may affect the location of economic activity within America, but don't appreciably augment the total. Politicians and businesses won't like it, but citizens would be well served by the sturdiest curbs that can pass constitutional muster on state location subsidies and tax incentives.

5. *Fix the federal government.* A feeble federal government served Americans badly in the 1780s and will do far worse today. We must redouble efforts to make federal operations more efficient, innovative, and accountable. Serious federal reform may not be gentler than devolution to the public-sector status quo. Quite the contrary—it will often involve privatization, vouchers, and more traumatic "reinvention" than Washington has yet seen. But there is no inconsistency in pursuing common goals through means that make the most of the market. Beyond such procedural improvements, we must confront the politically difficult budgetary decisions needed to rebalance federal priorities and to forestall Washington's scheduled retreat into near irrelevance throughout much of the domestic sphere.

The embrace of devolution risks truncating a painful but vital national conversation over the scale and purpose of America's public sector. "Shrink government" is one answer to America's problems but not the only answer. Paradoxically, if we want to have a free choice about whether and how we will prepare all willing workers for rewarding roles in the global economy, about the terms on which our citizens engage global capital, and about how we should share the burdens of economic change—if we want to have a choice, we must choose together, as a nation. Fifty separate choices add up to no choice at all.

The Stadium Trap

By Charles Mahtesian

From the beginning of football training camp in July to the end of the season in January, Pittsburgh is swathed in the black and gold colors of the city's beloved Steelers. Former star running back Franco Harris smiles down benignly from billboards. On game days, the streets empty and commerce slows to a trickle. For the past 26 years, despite the region's status as one of the smallest markets in pro sports, the Steelers have sold out every single seat in Three Rivers Stadium.

Nevertheless, on the 4th of November last year, when it came time to cast an up-or-down, love 'em-or-lose 'em, 11-county referendum to save both the Steelers and the baseball Pirates by building new football and baseball stadiums financed partially with a sales tax increase, the home teams lost. Not by a whisker, either. They suffered a crushing, humbling defeat. In Pittsburgh's own Allegheny County, the vote was 58 percent to 42 percent. In the 10 surrounding counties, the margin was even wider—in one county, the measure went down by 4 to 1.

How could a place that loves its professional sports teams so much reject an effort to keep them so decisively? Easily, it turns out. Pittsburgh is just the latest city gripped by stadium backlash. It is a phenomenon that is becoming almost as commonplace as a millionaire owner extorting city officials for more concessions or a well-paid athlete running into trouble with the law. After an overexuberant run of sweetheart stadium deals and giveaways, a bitter resistance to public financing of stadiums—especially when it involves tax increases—and to sports owner demands is unmistakably taking shape.

On the same day that Pittsburgh went to the polls, Minneapolis sent a similar message by voting overwhelmingly to set a $10 million limit on any financial assistance the city might provide to build a new ballpark for the Minnesota Twins or for construction of any other pro sports facilities. In 1996, Milwaukee and Seattle voters flatly rejected the idea of stadium taxes to finance construction of new sports facilities. The same happened last year in Columbus, Ohio, and this past February in neighboring Dublin, Ohio, where residents rejected a professional soccer stadium, even though the owner planned to finance the facility himself and the city would have paid only for land acquisition, road improvements and utility extensions. When taxpayer-financed stadium projects do pass muster these days, as one did in Dallas this January, it is almost always by a razor-thin majority: That measure squeaked through by just 1,700 votes.

Legislative scrutiny of public subsidies is no less withering. In the 1998 session alone, scores of stadium-related bills clogged statehouses from Pennsylvania to Minnesota to Colorado, ranging from prohibitions on the use of public resources for sports facilities without a public vote to capping taxpayer liability for stadium costs to calling for Green Bay Packers-style community ownership of sports teams.

Given this level of roiling resentment, you might think the era of public subsidies is over. But the truth is, new stadiums that are entirely privately financed remain the exception. For all the mounting evidence of a backlash, there is little to indicate that cities are any less willing to make sizable public investments to attract or retain sports franchises. Few public officials

From *Governing* (May 1998), pp. 22–24, 26. Reprinted with permission from *Governing* Magazine. Copyright © 1998.

are willing to interpret a public vote against taxpayer financing of a stadium as a willingness on the part of those taxpayers to see the team leave town.

To some extent, that explains why construction has begun on new stadiums in Milwaukee and Seattle despite bitterly contested public votes not to fund them. Or how in Ohio, despite a recent poll indicating that seven out of 10 residents oppose public financing of stadiums, several controversial stadium proposals are still alive, in addition to ongoing projects in Cincinnati and Cleveland where ground has already been broken. Or how in Pittsburgh the Steelers and Pirates might just get their new stadiums after all: A new proposal for financing the facilities includes no tax hikes and would not need the approval of the voters who vented their wrath on the original plan.

> *The message from the voters is clear: They don't want to pay for new professional sports stadiums. But that doesn't mean they don't want them.*

Given the virtual futility of any effort to win passage of a public referendum to finance new stadiums, bypassing the voters is rapidly becoming the strategy of choice. Never was that clearer than during last year's negotiations to lure the New England Patriots to Rhode Island when, despite having advocated for referendums in the past when the state considered public debt, Governor Lincoln Almond opposed either a binding vote on stadium bonds or a non-binding referendum in a special election. In February, pro soccer team owner Lamar Hunt offered this assessment of the political landscape. "Wherever it ends up," he said after his Dublin, Ohio, stadium proposal was trounced at the polls, "we'll make sure it's not a referendum situation."

Of course, voter resistance to taxpayer financing of pro sports facilities is not a new phenomenon. What's new is the widespread intensity of that resistance. Bolstered by an increasing body of evidence indicating that the economic benefits of new stadiums are at best modest, opponents now have the statistical ammunition to fight back against the dizzying array of rosy economic impact studies churned out by pro-stadium forces. It's no longer so easy to dismiss stadium foes as anti-tax zealots or as the usual mob of cranks and naysayers who oppose any public works project. Nor is it easy to overlook the experiences in other cities where taxpayers appeared to have been either purposely hoodwinked or inadvertently misinformed about the real numbers behind recently approved stadium projects. In Cincinnati, for example,

projected costs for a new stadium are now running $200 million more than anticipated.

Elsewhere, the stadium story is even more troubling. An Oakland grand jury is investigating the $192 million deal that lured the Raiders back to the city. In St. Louis, the convention and visitors bureau brought suit against the National Football League, charging unsuccessfully that the league conspired against the city to jack up the price paid to attract the franchise. During the 1997 trial, the city's own attorney referred to the stadium package as "the worst sports deal in history." The NFL's defense argued, in effect, that St. Louis has only itself to blame for being taken to the cleaners. That's why the $300 million domed stadium is widely referred to locally not by its proper title, the Trans World Dome, but as the "Taxpayer Dome."

Of course, not all stadium deals are matters of public ridicule. But without exception, all must weather the same firestorm of hostility toward the state of professional sports in general and toward wealthy owners and players in particular. Minnesota's ongoing stadium soap opera, for example, is complicated by publicity surrounding the finances of billionaire Twins owner Carl Pohlad. Combined with the exquisitely poor timing of Timberwolves basketball player Kevin Garnett's recent rejection of a $103.5 million salary offer, it served to undermine and undercut the efforts of pro-stadium legislators in a way that opponents never could.

As a result, the legislature has been preoccupied by the issue for the past two years; a 1997 special session convened expressly to find a solution failed to settle the question. The Twins stadium issue is even sparking controversy in faraway North Carolina: Four fast-food chains in the locale where Pohlad is threatening to relocate, North Carolina's Triad region, recently renounced their support for a tax to help fund a new stadium; two of them denied that they had ever favored it. Irate customers, it seems, were browbeating local businesses.

"The structure of professional sports and franchise-shifting certainly creates public antipathy toward them," says Frank Lucchino, the controller of Pittsburgh's Allegheny County. "When you add anti-tax fever, millionaire owners and boorish second-string athletes demanding millions, you have a volatile combination."

No one around Pittsburgh doubted that last year. Indeed, long before voters stepped into the voting booths in November, some of the staunchest supporters of the plan known as the Regional Renaissance Initiative had recognized that it was headed toward ignominious defeat.

The initiative was the brainstorm of downtown interests and the corporate community. Proponents spent millions in an effort to convince voters in Pittsburgh and its surrounding counties that the plan would keep the teams in Pittsburgh while creating thousands of new jobs. One way of muting the expected opposition was to craft the proposal to include a project that nearly everyone could agree on—expansion of the convention center. Funds also would be directed to the downtown cultural district. Various capital projects were included as sweeteners for the surrounding counties.

The half-cent sales-tax hike was designed to raise close to $700 million over seven years. Steelers ownership offered $50 million, or 27 percent of the estimated $185 million cost of a football facility. The Pirates pledged $35 million for their ballpark, a fraction of the estimated cost of between $185 million and $200 million.

The other attempt at softening the opposition took the form of scare tactics. There was no other alternative, voters were told. If the vote failed, there was no backup plan. A rejection of the measure virtually guaranteed the Pirates' exit. The Steelers were likely to follow.

Whether or not people believed that the teams would actually leave is still a matter of speculation. Everyone agrees that, in any case, initiative backers made several major miscalculations, the most serious of which was underestimating the level of voter hostility to a tax hike, especially one that stood to benefit professional sports.

At the heart of the problem, even its supporters would later admit, was the perception that the initiative, known as Plan A, was old-school economic development. It harkened back to the dynamism of post World War II Pittsburgh, when huge public works projects were accomplished through the sheer will of a few political and corporate titans. The plan failed to take into account all the ways the city, the region and its business community had changed in the intervening years. No longer could a single politician speak for all of the officeholders. No one corporate leader could speak for the private sector. In an era when the communities surrounding Pittsburgh are more populous than the city, Plan A's advocates were handicapped by the widespread perception of who was driving it: downtown business interests. "No people who had political skills or grassroots knowledge had any involvement with that vote," says City Councilman Jim Ferlo, who opposed the plan. "The corporate elite created it."

As in most other cities, the local newspaper, a variety of prominent elected officials and the downtown business community lined up in support of passage. The opposition was composed of an under-funded assortment of anti-tax activists and others who railed against the proposed subsidies as nothing less than corporate welfare.

The huge campaign-spending disparities between the two sides highlighted the divide. Just as stadium boosters in Columbus, Ohio, outspent their foes by more than 250 to 1, Regional Renaissance Initiative backers outspent the opposition by at least 200 to 1. And just as in Columbus, it made no difference. Voters concluded that the very interests that most strongly supported the new stadiums were the ones that stood to gain the most from them. "If you really want to keep the team, why should the little old lady down in the Mon Valley pay for it?" asks Jake Haulk, research director of the Allegheny Institute for Public Policy, a conservative think tank that spearheaded the opposition. "The only people that agree on this are the downtown people."

In the wake of Plan A's defeat, one question remained unanswered: What exactly were the voters saying? No public funds for stadiums, or no new taxes? Ultimately, city and county officials took the vote to mean that residents still wanted the new stadiums—they just didn't want to shoulder the burden themselves through increased taxes. "The debate has been framed here that no public funds should be involved. But the reality around the country is different," says Mayor Tom Murphy. "My feeling is that when people say no public money, they mean no money used from day-to-day operations."

By March, a proposal known as Plan B surfaced. During the campaign, voters had been told that no such backup plan existed. In truth, though, discussions for Plan B had begun just as Plan A was going down the tubes.

Stripped to its essentials, the $803 million Plan B calls for nearly everyone to get something and nearly everyone to give up something. Revenues from an existing countywide sales tax, state and federal aid, ticket surcharges and private investment would provide the bulk of the funding. Popular resentment over sports greed would be addressed through a proposed tax on player salaries.

The plan, of course, makes several assumptions. Harrisburg would have to kick in $300 million in state capital funds. The legislature approved stadium funding for Pittsburgh in last year's capital budget, but that was before Plan A went down in flames. State officials also must weigh another consideration: If Pittsburgh gets its money, it won't be long before Philadelphia stadium advocates are knocking on the legislature's doors.

The private financing component also needs to be worked out. As it stands, the teams have not committed any more money to the projects than they did under Plan A. It is not escaping notice that some of the Plan B revenue streams identified as "private investment"—such as the player tax—can be considered private only under the most generous of definitions.

Still, the key is that Plan B does not raise taxes. Instead, it is a reallocation of existing tax revenues. And Plan B has one big advantage over Plan A, despite the fact that it actually costs more: If finalized and agreed to by all sides, it would not have to go before the voters who crushed Plan A.

That's not to say the teams would get a free ride. Allegheny County Commissioner Bob Cranmer, one of the Plan B architects, has insisted that both teams need to increase their share of private financing, but that the Steelers, in particular, should up their contribution because—unlike the Pirates—their survival is not predicated on having a brand new stadium. Any windfall profits created by the new stadiums, Cranmer and other officials also suggested, ought to be shared with the public. Another county commissioner demanded full disclosure of both teams' financial statements, showing exactly how they expected to benefit from the new facilities.

"If the Steelers ever left town." says Pittsburgh's Mulugetta Birru, "elected officials would be hung."

All of those new demands shared the same underlying message. "We just can't subsidize these teams with unreasonable amounts of public dollars. Some cities have realized that," says Cranmer. "We tell the teams that we are willing to cooperate. That's a different story than them telling us what they *want* and us trying to figure out how to deliver it. Now it's them telling us what they *need* and us stating that this is what we're willing to do."

That distinction is one that other places are beginning to make as well. Before Rhode Island Governor Lincoln Almond decided last fall that the roughly $140 million price tag for a new stadium required by the New England Patriots was simply too high to justify the expenditure, it was already obvious that state and local officials were refusing to operate from a position of weakness. During negotiations, for example, Providence Mayor Buddy Cianci insisted that the team make special payments for the police and sanitation services that would be necessary on game days.

If there is a new resolve, though, it is a tenuous one. The local pressure to subsidize stadiums remains enormous, whether it is driven by the hospitality industry and the private sector or by voters who don't want to pay for a team's stadium but nevertheless do not want to see their home teams leave town. "If the Steelers ever left town," explains Mulugetta Birru, executive director of Pittsburgh's Urban Redevelopment Authority, "elected officials would be hung."

Every public official who sits down at the negotiating table with the idea of limiting public investment also recognizes that almost from the moment they begin talks with franchise owners, they are being undermined by their counterparts in other cities. "We have two options," says Dan Onorato, a Pittsburgh city councilman and member of the Stadium Authority. "Either get involved and commit significant amounts of public money, or no public money and say goodbye to your teams. Because there are at least five cities that will do it if we don't."

Cleveland learned that the hard way in 1995. The civic trauma inflicted on the city by Maryland's theft of the beloved Browns football team was instructive, not merely because it revealed the lengths that one city and state would go to to lure a franchise—Maryland offered to build a brand new, rent-free $200 million stadium in downtown Baltimore, along with a slew of other lucrative incentives—but also because it served notice to thrift-minded cities that their bargaining power was severely limited.

The NFL awarded an expansion franchise to Cleveland in March, nearly three years after the Browns became the Baltimore Ravens, but by then other similarly situated cities, such as Pittsburgh, had made their own assessments about the impact of a departed franchise. "We're not so far from Cleveland that we don't understand what happened," says Allegheny County Commissioner Mike Dawida, another key player in stadium negotiations. "It's stunning to think this could have happened to them."

Nothing, as Dawida and many other local officials caught between the demands of team owners and the resistance of taxpayers can attest, stands to slam the brakes on a city's revitalization momentum as abruptly as the loss of a sports franchise. And few other events highlight the decline of struggling, older urban centers so starkly as the loss of a cherished professional sports team. According to that calculus, the economic impact of a team is nearly irrelevant. Ultimately then, for a city such as Pittsburgh, the value of not losing a team will far outweigh the price it pays to keep it. "There's a big difference between never having a team and losing one," says Onorato. "So you grudgingly do this and hold your nose."

A Reading for Critical Thinking

Power Grab

The "Devolution" Revolution promised by congressional Republicans four years ago has mostly fizzled. Instead of handing over authority to state and local governments, they're taking it away.

By Eliza Newlin Carney

For fours years in a row, the Indiana legislature has tackled the emotionally charged issue of drunk driving, haggling over whether to reduce the legal blood alcohol limit from 0.10 to 0.08 per cent. So far, opponents of the change have prevailed. But state officials may have debated the issue for the last time. That's because Congress may decide it for them.

Last month, the Senate voted to withhold transportation funding from states that fail to lower their blood alcohol limits to 0.08 per cent. House members have thus far resisted the lower limit, but sponsors vow to push for it in House-Senate negotiations. Even for the Indiana officials who support tough new drunk-driving rules, the Senate vote came as a shock.

"You wonder, then, why did the legislature bother to debate it four years in a row?" said Paul Helmke, the mayor of Fort Wayne, Ind., and president of the U. S. Conference of Mayors. "The problem is that when we decide these things at a national level, we're adopting a one-size-fits-all approach that might not make sense every place."

Helmke's argument should ring a bell with Republicans on Capitol Hill. Not too long ago, they were singing a very similar tune. Remember devolution? That was the Republicans' battle cry when they seized control of Congress four years ago. The GOP majority's "New Federalism"—handed down from President Reagan and from President Nixon before him—was supposed to banish bureaucracy and waste by devolving power back to the states.

Republicans would deliver "a smaller government financed by lower taxes that engages the American people with greater respect and greater freedom to conduct their own affairs," declared House Majority Leader Richard K. Armey, R-Texas, at the time of the GOP takeover.

That was the theory, at least. In practice, the devolution revolution has largely fizzled. Except for passing welfare reform in 1996 and a bill a year earlier that banned "unfunded" federal mandates on the states, congressional Republicans have given up little federal power. This year, in fact, they're poised to usurp state authority on several fronts, from juvenile crime to electric utility deregulation to property rights.

"It's very disappointing to hear a lot of high-flown talk about devolution and then not see the reality," said Lucy Allen, the major of Louisburg, N.C. She's one of dozens of mayors, state legislators and governors alarmed by Congress's growing penchant for preempting their power.

The "counterdevolution" trend, as local officials call it, has particularly stung GOP governors, who also swept to a majority in 1994. Two years ago, they stood shoulder to shoulder with Republicans in Congress to usher through welfare reform. Now, the alliance between Republican leaders and their counterparts outside the Beltway is crumbling.

"The [federal] mandate has given way to the preemption," said Gov. Mike Leavitt, R-Utah. "Both have the effect of stifling local government and state government. And I honestly believe that that is contrary to the wishes of the people."

If national Democrats once burdened the states with rigid social-welfare directives, governors complain, the Republicans now want to be the nation's zoning and tax commissioner. They're telling states what they *can't* do—restrict local development, for example, or tax the booming Internet industry.

To some degree, Republicans at the federal level just can't resist doing things their way. As James Madison observed, the natural tendency of government is "to throw all power into the legislative vortex." After all, said Washington lawyer and devolution expert Charles J. Cooper, "federalism is a principle of convenience."

Congressional Republicans, moreover, owe divided allegiances. Their cozy relationship with big business increasingly trumps their romance with devolution. Corporate interests would rather follow one set of federal rules, not multiple state and local guidelines—making them the natural enemies of federalism. And they've got the big campaign dollars that GOP leaders crave. Most of the bills in Congress that are causing an uproar in city halls today are pro-business measures.

Observed Carl Tubbesing, deputy executive director in Washington for the Denver-based National Conference of State Legislatures: "A proposal like telecommunications reform [or] like electricity deregulation, whether the sponsor intended it or not, attracts all sorts of campaign money."

MIXED MESSAGES

Federalism still has its cheerleaders, of course. The Republican-sponsored 1996 law replacing the social welfare bureaucracy with block grants to the states has been a huge success, said Richard P. Nathan, director of the Rockefeller Institute of Government at the State University of New York (Albany). "I've never seen a period of so much state and local innovation and activism."

And some GOP members of Congress are still fighting the good fight. Rep. Thomas J, Bliley Jr., R-Va., for one, has proposed letting states introduce amendments to the Constitution. Bliley's measure would significantly shift the constitutional balance of power toward the states, its proponents argue.

Sens. Fred D. Thompson, R-Tenn., and Carl Levin, D-Mich., are backing a regulatory reform bill that would make it easier for state and local officials to influence the federal rule-making process. Thompson called the bill "the next step" to toughen the 1995 unfunded mandates law, which, according to a recent General Accounting Office report, has had little effect on how agencies write their regulations.

Governors welcome Thompson's effort; plenty of Clinton Administration proposals have made their hackles rise. (One example is the Administration's plan to push organ-transplant centers to share donated organs nationally, rather than regionally.) But Thompson's bill would do nothing to rein in what many city officials see as the real source of their headaches: Congress. Even Thompson acknowledged that congressional Republicans' record on states' rights has been "a very mixed bag."

"It's much easier to devolve when somebody else is in power," said Thompson, a staunch states' rights advocate. "When you've got the ball, the temptation is to replace those bad, old regulations with your good, new regulations, instead of sending it back to the states."

This has been a banner year, in fact, for congressional proposals that rankle state and local officials. Among those moving through the House and Senate are:

- A juvenile crime bill that offers states millions in federal grant money, but only if they agree to prosecute serious youth offenders as adults. Other mandates involve increased record-keeping, more drug testing and minimum jail times for juveniles. The National District Attorneys Association opposes the bill, as do state law enforcement officials represented by the National Criminal Justice Association.

- A bill that would bar state and local governments from taxing any form of Internet commerce for the next three to six years. Many governors and municipal officials warn that the moratorium would cost them millions of dollars in sales tax revenues. Gov. Leavitt calls the Internet tax fight "the most important federalism issue that we've had in decades."

- Private-property rights legislation that would allow landowners to bypass state courts and go directly to federal court when they disagree with local zoning decisions. The bill is "an attack on the fundamental rights of local governments when it comes to zoning and local land use issues," said Reginald N. Todd, legislative affairs director of the National Association of Counties (NACo).

- A bill that would deregulate the electric utility industry, requiring states to restructure electricity services by the end of 2000. The bill has "tremendous potential tax consequences," said William D. Steinmeier, national chairman of the Jefferson City (MO)-based Electric Utility Shareholders Alliance. Many communities rely on property taxes from electric utilities for the bulk of their revenue, Steinmeier pointed out, but that money will be in jeopardy if utilities go out of business because of competition.

Not to mention the preemptive laws already on the books. In 1996, Congress made it a federal crime to possess a gun within 1,000 feet of a school—despite a 1995 Supreme Court ruling that struck down an earlier version of the law, on the grounds that federal meddling wasn't justified. "Now we've got the FBI going into the little red school houses on gun cases," said Thompson. "That's not the way the FBI is supposed to be used."

Local government officials are still smarting over the 1996 Telecommunications Act, which gave broadcasters and telephone companies wide latitude in deciding where to put up mammoth digital television and cellular phone towers, regardless of whether citizens agreed. Vermont Sens. Patrick J. Leahy, a Democrat, and James M. Jeffords, a Republican, have introduced a bill that would make it easier for citizens to have the final say over tower sitings. Leahy voted against the 1996 law, he said, "because it wiped out all local control."

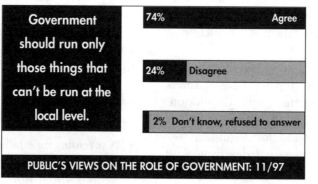

Government should run only those things that can't be run at the local level.

74% Agree

24% Disagree

2% Don't know, refused to answer

PUBLIC'S VIEWS ON THE ROLE OF GOVERNMENT: 11/97

Add to that Congress's first act this year: a bill to rename Washington National Airport after former President Reagan. State and local officials strenuously objected, citing cost and potential confusion to tourists. The irony of the name change, said Rep. Jim Moran, D-Va., whose district includes the airport, was that Reagan signed into law the bill that transferred control of the airport from the federal government to the Metropolitan Washington Airports Authority. Reagan "never would have wanted this, I'm sure," Moran said. "It's wholly contrary to his philosophy."

DAVID V. GOLIATH

State and local government groups, galvanized by what they say is an unprecedented federal power grab, are fighting back. Last month, the National League of Cities declared that "preserving municipal authority" is its highest federal priority for 1998.

"It's a tough time for local governments," said Brian J. O'Neill, a Philadelphia councilman and president of the league. "We're not being brought into the loop. We're not being asked: How would this affect you? Industry writes the bill, industry pressures the Congress and Congress produces the bill. It's a big change from what we've seen for the past couple of hundred years."

The league and other like-minded organizations—including the mayor's conference, the State Legislatures'

Conference, NACo and the National Governors' Association—are working together more closely than ever. They're also spending a lot more time in Washington these days.

Federal preemption "is going to be a principal focus of our organizations over the next several years," said NACo's Todd. "If you don't have authority to run your governments, then what else do you really have?"

But local officials are vastly outgunned when it comes to battles over land use, zoning and taxes. Take the pending Property Rights Implementation Act, known as the "takings" bill because it aims to enforce the constitutional ban on the government's taking of private property without just compensation.

The nation's developers, led by the National Association of Home Builders, have waged an aggressive lobbying campaign for the bill, which has passed the House and awaits Senate action. The Home Builders' political action committee gave $594,250 in campaign contributions last year alone. It also doled out $90,000 in "soft money" to the political parties. Developers argue that property owners who disagree with local zoning decisions now languish in state court for years without recourse and should be allowed to go straight to federal court.

Municipal officials, however, say that citizens know best whether a mega-mall belongs in a residential neighborhood, or an adult movie house near a school. Zoning disputes, in fact, go to the heart of what local governance is all about, municipal officials say. They argue that developers who win the power to sue in federal court may be ill-inclined to negotiate with local citizens.

"Faced with the prospect of a costly and time-consuming federal court lawsuit, local officials inevitably would feel pressure to approve land use proposals to avoid litigation, even if the proposed use might harm neighboring property owners and the community at large," warned the Justice Department in a February memo to Leahy, who opposes the bill.

City officials in Hudson, Ohio, know about costly lawsuits with developers. They've spent close to $400,000 since July 1996 on a legal battle with developers who object to a city growth-management ordinance, enacted in May of that year. The suit, spearheaded by the Home Builders Association of Greater Akron, eventually ended in Hudson's favor.

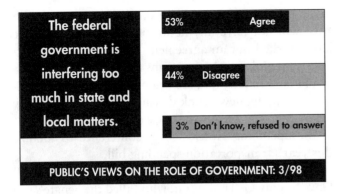

The federal government is interfering too much in state and local matters.	53% Agree
	44% Disagree
	3% Don't know, refused to answer

PUBLIC'S VIEWS ON THE ROLE OF GOVERNMENT: 3/98

But it cost the city time and money that would have been better spent on traffic, road and sewer improvements, said city manager James C. Smith.

The takings bill is unlikely to become law. Leahy, who says the measure "would have just totally trampled any local control," has threatened a filibuster, and the White House has promised a veto.

More likely to win approval this year is the Internet Tax Freedom Act, introduced by Rep. C. Christopher Cox, R-Calif., and Sen. Ron Wyden, D-Ore. The legislation pits state and local officials against an even more formidable foe than the nation's developers: the telecommunications industry.

Despite some key differences, both the Cox and Wyden bills aim to shield the Internet from burdensome new state and local taxes. They would place a moratorium on new Internet taxes until tax rules can be updated to fit the new technology. President Clinton, long a friend of Silicon Valley, has endorsed the legislation.

Though some governors—those from states with booming communication sectors—support the bill, most have reacted with panic. State and local governments depend on sales taxes and excise taxes for up to 50 per cent of their revenue. A tax-free Internet will attract more and more product sales, governors fear, gutting their tax base. Some see nothing less than the future of local government at stake.

"We're defining right now, I believe, the shape of government in the future," said Leavitt, who has helped spearhead the fight against the bill and warns that a general, national sales tax may be in the offing.

Who collects taxes is a key question that defines the state-federal relationship, foes of the moratorium agree. "It's always kind of a slippery slope," said Sen. Byron L. Dorgan, D-N.D., a bill opponent. "I worry that if we do something that dramatically reduces the state and local tax base, it's going to have long-term ramifications for how we construct tax revenue systems at both the state and federal level."

A complication for governors is that catalogue merchants—unless they have a physical presence in the states where they sell products—are not now subject to sales taxes. Governors are working with Cox on a compromise that would revamp catalogue and Internet sales-tax rules in one fell swoop. But the measure's future is uncertain, and Wyden is resistant.

Wyden's got plenty of powerful allies. The Internet tax bill is backed by a heavy-hitting coalition that includes America OnLine, International Business Machines Corp., MCI Communications Corp. and Microsoft Corp. Altogether, communications and electronics interests gave out a whopping $24 million in contributions to candidates and political parties in the 1996 election cycle, according to the Center for Responsive Politics, a Washington nonprofit group.

"I sometimes feel like we're a fifth-grade football team taking on NFL teams," said Frank H. Shafroth, director of policy and federal relations at the National League of Cities.

FREE MARKETS OR FEDERALISM?

Shafroth and other champions of state and local authority, however, acknowledge that larger economic forces—not just campaign contributions—are driving the anti-federalist movement.

A high-technology global economy demands uniform standards, and is not sensitive to state and local boundaries. And international trade treaties invariably preempt state environmental and health rules. "The American economy is changing very, very fast," Shafroth said. "And money and goods can now move around the world. It makes the concept of borders, whether it's between cities, between states or between countries, harder and harder to find."

Defending federalism, moreover, is tricky business. While the Constitution's 10th Amendment protects states' right to self-governance, the commerce clause gives the national government authority to wipe out state-imposed trade barriers. Many business-related policy issues, such as electricity deregulation, arguably relate to interstate commerce. The Constitution also protects property rights, as advocates of the takings bill like to point out.

"Republicans, in principle, certainly libertarian Republicans, don't stand any more for local tyranny than we do for federal tyranny," said Roger Pilon, director of the libertarian Cato Institute's Center for Constitutional Studies. "We're against tyranny, wherever it come from."

Still, Pilon deplores what he called congressional Republicans' "rank hypocrisy" in areas like the gun-free schools law. GOP leaders "are responding to the maelstrom of political pressures, without any constitutional compass to guide them through the thicket," Pilon complained.

Even when members of Congress see a constitutional reason to meddle in state affairs, some federalism experts argue, they should proceed with caution. "It's very hard to say that Congress doesn't have the raw power, and it's legitimate that that power be exercised" in areas such as interstate commerce, said Cooper, a partner with the Washington law firm of Cooper, Carvin & Rosenthal. "At the same time, a Congress genuinely devoted to respecting the rights of the states would exercise that power very carefully, and very grudgingly."

Mayors, state legislators and governors, in fact, may have more sway on Capitol Hill than they realize. They represent local constituents with the power to vote members of Congress in and out of office.

When 3,000 mayors and city officials descended on Washington for the National League of Cities' legislative conference last month, a delegation of them dropped in on Senate Majority Leader Trent Lott, R-Miss. Before the league members went home, Lott made them a public promise on the Internet tax bill: "We will not have any action in the Senate until we have worked out an agreement that you are comfortable with and you think is right for your people."

House leaders, too, are beginning to voice concerns about slapping new drunk-driving rules on states. They may beat back the Senate's lower blood alcohol limit in the upcoming House-Senate conference to finalize this year's transportation spending bill.

That should come as a relief to Wisconsin GOP Gov. Tommy G. Thompson, who called the Senate's use of transportation dollars to dictate state drunk-driving policy "a bad, bad precedent." Fortunately for Thompson, the fight over drunk-driving laws is one that, for once, places governors on the same side as an influential business lobby: the alcoholic beverage industry.

Increasingly, however, GOP members of Congress face a choice between satisfying their friends in big business and pleasing their friends in the statehouses. It may be impossible for them to consistently do both.

PART 3

Civil Rights and Civil Liberties

Few topics generate as much passion as civil rights and civil liberties. Abortion, affirmative action, gay rights, physician-assisted suicide, and the medical use of marijuana are just a few examples of controversial and divisive issues that have risen to the top of the American political agenda. Many people have even suggested that America is in the midst of a "cultural war" over these kinds of issues.

Why do these issues evoke such intense emotions? It is because these issues, more than others, tend to go to the very core of our belief systems. There appears to be little room for compromise on such issues. Other issues are more amenable to solutions that "split the difference." For example, if one person thinks that we should spend $10 billion on education, and another person thinks we should spend $20 billion on education, the two are likely to compromise on some figure in the middle, perhaps $15 billion. People find it much more difficult to compromise on issues that they see as moral or religious imperatives.

If you believe that human life begins at conception, it is virtually impossible to believe that abortion is anything other than murder, even if it occurs early in a pregnancy. Similarly, if you believe homosexuality is a choice and that it is unnatural and violates God's laws, then it is easy to see why homosexual behavior should be outlawed. On the other hand, if you believe that homosexuality is acceptable, then you probably find it difficult to understand why homosexual behavior should be criminalized.

Under the Constitution, church and state are separate. However, just because a law has some religious basis does not automatically mean that the law is invalid. For example, the Bible commands people not to kill. This does not mean that all laws against murder violate the separation of church and state—even most atheists probably agree that laws against murder are a good thing. Laws are usually based on some notion of morality. The important question is: under what conditions does the government have the right to impose one group's idea of morality on other groups? As you read the following selections, think about your own beliefs and how they influence your thoughts on these issues. Where do your own beliefs about morality come from? Are you open to compromise with people who believe differently than you?

A Reading
for
Critical
Thinking

Is Affirmative Action on the Way Out? Should it Be?

By Nathan Glazer

ffirmative Action has in part been a "hand up" to "people who have had a hard time," but its original design was so faulty that it soon became much more than that.

The categories placed under the special terms of affirmative action—the four minority groups of African-Americans, Hispanics, Asians, and American Indians ("Native Americans"), plus women—are so widely various in their histories, in the prejudice and indignities they have faced, in the obstacles they meet today, and in their claims to special treatment, that inevitably a great number of the policy's beneficiaries have not had a hard time, and have not needed a hand up. Two of these groups—Hispanics and Asians—are composed in large measure of immigrants and the children of immigrants who have come here since affirmative action began, and some are the beneficiaries of special programs for refugees. Have they needed the additional hand up? Asian immigrants in general so clearly did not need it that fifteen years ago colleges stopped recognizing their claim to beneficiary status and began discriminating *against* them—something that under the Civil Rights Act they were not allowed to do.

Did women need a hand up, beyond a general protection against discrimination? In some cases, perhaps. But in academia the preference for women, now abetted by the women's movement, has become excessive, and benefits a class that on the whole meets no discrimination.

Even the category for which affirmative action was originally instituted, African-Americans, includes many today from middle-class backgrounds who have not faced any noteworthy discrimination in academia for decades. Unfortunately, because affirmative action covers so many areas—jobs at all levels, contracts with federal and other government agencies, admission to colleges, universities, and professional schools—we do not know in detail just who has benefited and on what grounds. How many of the black students who have come under the aegis of affirmative action, for example, are from well-to-do homes in which they have received the standard array of middle-class assistance? Many? Few? Very few? We do not know.

We have a similar problem in weighing the general social costs and advantages of affirmative action.

A great black middle class has been created. But is it because of affirmative action? Stephan and Abigail Thernstrom, following on the research of Finis Welch and others, argue that the economic improvement in the black situation preceded affirmative action and would have continued without it. This seems reasonable to me. Although affirmative action has probably contributed something, one can hardly doubt that a good part of the movement by blacks into public jobs of all sorts would have occurred independently, as discrimination declined and as blacks became dominant, demographically and then politically, in so many cities.

On the cost side, has the level of public services declined as a result of the weakening of civil-service tests on which black applicants scored poorly and which were made less difficult because of the pressure of affirmative-action goals? The decline has perhaps been clearest in central-city teaching, where the number of black and Hispanic teachers and administrators has increased. Yet this change was inevitable as black and Hispanic students came to dominate central-city school systems, and as whites who might once have gone into teaching found more attractive employment opportunities elsewhere. It is hard to believe that the situation in New York and other big cities, where whites held almost all the administrative positions in school systems with a majority of black and Hispanic students, could have endured.

Perhaps the greatest cost has been exacted by the requirements for affirmative-action plans, with their elaborate record-keeping of recruitment, employment, and promotion, and the openings thus made possible for litigation. Affirmative action has undoubtedly burdened every employer, public and private. Some of the costs of this burden have been tallied, and they seem to me to exceed the benefit, however we calculate it.

Still another cost—the decline in the reputation of blacks for competence among nonblack citizens—cannot be easily quantified. But would this reputation have *improved* in the absence of affirmative action, and in the face of evidence that disproportionately fewer blacks were qualifying for jobs through traditional means? One cannot be sure.

This brings me to the question of "mending" or "ending" affirmative action. Certain forms seem to me necessary. We do need black members of police departments if we are to police black areas effectively; one recalls that there was a time when white firemen were harassed when they entered black residential areas. Similarly, we do need black teachers and administrators in our schools. Whatever the abstract force of the argument that the quality of the teacher is more important than his race or ethnicity, the degree of racial self-consciousness among African-Americans is so strong that, except under special circumstances, an educational system that does not take account of race and ethnicity will not succeed.

This position can be disputed by the experience of inner-city Catholic schools, which teach black children effectively even though, as I believe, their staffs include few blacks. But the Catholic schools, being both private and religious, do not face, and do not have to respond to, demands for black teachers and administrators. The public schools are another matter entirely. (In any case, wages are so poor in Catholic schools that they cannot compete with the public schools for staff.)

Brief as it has been, this discussion of just one area suggests how complicated it is to decide how and where to "mend" affirmative action. To me, the least satisfactory area is contracting. One does not create an entrepreneurial class by granting contracts to those who cannot otherwise compete; on the contrary one invites fraud and corruption. I would therefore be happy to see affirmative-action contracting fully eliminated. Nevertheless, the political realities are such that most cities and other public bodies now granting these preferences fight to maintain them, even in the face of Supreme Court proscriptions. It has become the current and accepted form of distributing political pork.

One of the most disputed areas of affirmative action, and also the most challenged, involves preferences in admission to selective colleges, universities, and professional schools. Thanks to widespread public belief in the legitimacy of granting admission according to academic qualifications, and the easily-obtainable facts of racial preference, we have seen such preference outlawed in the public higher-education systems of California (by action of the board of regents and by popular vote) and Texas (by action of a federal circuit court). Ironically, however, this form of affirmative action has on the whole been voluntarily adopted by the institutions involved, though of course not without pressure from militants, and also has its roots in at least one tradition of American higher education, which (unlike the European model) has never stressed the exclusive role of academic qualifications in admissions.

To my mind there is a good argument for maintaining this racial preference, or some part of it: because of its voluntarism, because of the diversity of the American system of higher education, and because the presence of blacks does change and on the whole benefit the education of all. But my principal reason is that our colleges, universities, and professional schools are the central gateways to positions of power, wealth, and influence, and applying strict meritocratic principles would lead to a catastrophic drop in the number of black students in these crucial institutions. That would deliver a terrible message to blacks, and would be bad for the country.

Is affirmative action on the way out? As we know, Congress has simply stayed away from the issue—it is too dangerous. It adopts occasional preferences itself (as in subcontracting for highway construction), with no extended discussion. The President will also do nothing. Indeed, even Presidents Reagan and Bush, both of whom opposed affirmative action, did nothing to weaken its central trunk—the executive order bringing the policy into being—which they could have modified or eliminated at the stroke of a pen. Why should anyone expect more from Clinton? Nothing has been mended yet.

If neither legislature nor executive will act, there remain the Supreme Court and the people. With regard to the Court, the most likely possibility is that, even if it has not yet done so, it will follow what seem to be the clear mandates of the Fourteenth Amendment and the Civil Rights Act to ban racial preference, as the circuit court did in the Texas case. I believe that would be going too far—something the Court has, however, often done. It is odd that conservatives, who have for so long criticized the Court for its sweeping judgments on abortion, school prayer, or flag burning, now see it as the means of eliminating affirmative action.

As for the people, they remain mixed in their views, as we see in, on the one hand, the California vote in favor of Proposition 209 and, on the other hand, the more recent defeat of a similar—though differently phrased—initiative in Houston. In other words, they oppose racial preferences, but may be persuaded to support some undefined form of affirmative action.

I would like colleges and universities, and employers and public contractors, to be freed to do what they feel impelled to do, on the basis of their ideology and their sentiments, as affected by political and market forces that shape them. That would be for the best, and much better than either a universal standard that says there must be preferences—we have lived under something like this for 25 years—or a universal standard that says there must not be preferences. With the free and voluntary action of autonomous institutions, I think we can move ahead, slowly, in dealing with our race problem.

Nathan Glazer, whose books include Affirmative Discrimination, The Limits of Social Policy, *and* We Are All Multiculturalists Now, *is professor emeritus of education and sociology at Harvard and co-editor of the* Public Interest.

A Reading for Critical Thinking

IS THE DRUG WAR RACIST?

The government's drug policy has scorched the inner cities and put a generation of young black men behind bars. Two leading African-American scholars reflect on the damage done.

By Samuel G. Freedman

America's war on drugs has ravished the inner cities it aspired to save. Without curbing drug traffic, the crusade has sent a generation of young black males into the criminal-justice system, which offers them not rehabilitation but firsthand instruction in violent crime. While blacks make up thirteen percent of the national population and thirteen percent of the country's monthly drug users, they account for thirty-five percent of arrests for drug possession, fifty-five percent of convictions and seventy-four percent of prison sentences, according to the Sentencing Project, a nonprofit that promotes criminal-justice reform. Between 1986 and 1991, the number of blacks held in state prisons on drug charges rose by 465 percent, the project also reported. That increase partly reflects the inequality of federal sentencing rules, under which a person convicted of possessing five grams of crack cocaine receives the same five-year mandatory minimum as someone caught selling 500 grams of powder cocaine.

Such evidence has turned Glenn C. Loury and Orlando Patterson into vociferous critics of the war. Two of America's leading public intellectuals, both men espouse cautious, unromantic liberalism on issues like affirmative action and are socially conservative about family values. Loury is an economist who won an American Book Award in 1996 for *One by One, From the Inside Out: Essays and Reviews on Race and Responsibility in America*. He also directs the Institute on Race and Social Division at Boston University and was one of thirty-four prominent scholars and law-enforcement officials who last September signed a set

of "principles for practical drug policies" that staked a middle ground between what it called "two positions stereotyped as 'drug warrior' and 'legalizer.'" Patterson is the John Cowles professor of Sociology at Harvard University and the winner of a 1991 National Book Award for *Freedom in the Making of Western Culture*. He decries the drug war in his current book, *The Ordeal of Integration*.

Both men speak as academics and as products of their divergent pasts. Loury, who is forty-nine, grew up in a black working-class neighborhood in Chicago. He later joined, then broke from, the neoconservative movement and now calls himself "a recovering reactionary." He is also a recovering freebase addict who went through a highly publicized arrest and finally got clean in a halfway house. Patterson, 57, was brought up in Jamaica, did graduate study in England and served in the Seventies as special advisor to the Democratic Socialist prime minister of Jamaica, Michael Manley.

Rolling Stone: If ten years ago you had said to people, "We're going to increase arrests and incarceration by several hundred percent over the next decade," the response probably would have been that there won't be any more drug problem. Arrests and incarcerations have gone up, as promised, but the drugs are still here. What makes it so difficult to reform our policy?

Loury: There's an anxiety among people about drugs. I mean, this is not just an inner-city issue. You've got it throughout rural and urban life; I hear about drugs in the Brookline [Massachusetts] schools, where my kids go. The War on Drugs is a way of doing something about it. It's a way that we're determined to fight back. It's easy to get that concern on the table. It's harder to get a concern about the consequences of a particular way of fighting drugs on the table.

What happens to the fellow who stands up and says, "Look at what's going on with the incarceration of racial minorities in the country. Look at the way in which we're criminalizing a whole class of young black men. There is a tremendous cost of this policy"? The person who stands up and says that isn't seen as credible. After all, he's advocating on behalf of these bad guys. They're the threat, right?

Rolling Stone: What is the cost when you criminalize a whole class of young men?

Patterson: Horrendous. You not only send these people to prison but you actually make them into criminals. The ones who go to prison end up as professional criminals committing major crimes later on —the costs of which are borne by the society in terms of property damage, murder and police costs.

It's often been pointed out, though, that many drug crimes are, in fact, victimless crimes. In a funny kind of way, that may well be what explains why people buy into this scorched-earth approach to controlling drugs. You don't have to account for people who are victimized as a result of making criminals of these people and sending them to prison.

> *You not only send these people to prison but you actually make them into criminals.*

Loury: You've got social policy being fueled by very significant resources on the ground. Peter Reuter, a criminologist who's a student of these matters, said that something like $30 billion is spent annually in the War on Drugs. So this is a massive mobilization; these are some significant resources. If we propose to spend $30 billion over five years on preschool education for kids, after-school programs, summer jobs or whatever, people would be up in arms in the Congress, saying, you know, "Midnight basketball doesn't work." Michael Tonry, in his book *Malign Neglect: Race, Crime and Punishment in America*, makes a very strong case that the anti-drug money substantially affects the behavior of police departments.

Rolling Stone: You mean that because the dollars are there, the public demands great numbers of arrests?

Loury: Yes, exactly. What's success? Success is locking people up. Success is cases, it's collars. And where does the police department find people? It's going to go to the point of least resistance, where there are transactions that are occurring on the street, where neighborhoods are poorly organized so that it's easy to infiltrate the rings that are selling the stuff.

I use this analogy: If we were having a war on prostitution and we decided we wanted to lock up as many prostitutes as possible, you're going to concentrate on people who are streetwalkers. You're going to go down by the docks, to the wrong side of the railroad tracks, the Combat Zone here in Boston. What you're going to find are poor women who are drug addicted, who are welfare dependent, who are going to be disproportionately minority. And you're going to lock them up.

Now we all know that sex for money is being transacted in this society at many different levels and in many different ways. But a policy designed to maximize the number of persons arrested for selling sex for money will predictably fill up the jails with women of a certain kind.

So the perspective from these communities well could be, "This is a war on us." I use that kind of rhetoric cautiously, because I don't mean to contribute to conspiracy theorizing.

Patterson: The difference between [the criminal penalties for] cocaine powder and crack cocaine is way out of proportion, and it doesn't matter what the original motivation is. One doesn't have to prove that this deplorable state of affairs originated in deliberate racist practices. In fact, I don't think it did. Because there's good evidence that members of the African-American community wanted a strong crackdown on crack and pushed for having extreme penalties.

Rolling Stone: Part of what went with that was the idea that crack was so addictive that you couldn't rehab from it. And once you believe that, you take the whole idea of treatment off the table and it becomes purely a debate over punishment.

Loury: The animus against crack that you find in the African-American community comes from the tremendous damage that crack addiction has done to so many people. The last thing you want to learn is that your son-in-law, your nephew, your cousin, is on the pipe. Because that's going to be trouble for a long time, and you know the downside is pretty far down.

Now, the anti-treatment people say treatment doesn't work, and it's true that on any given attempt treatment has a relatively low cure rate. You have to keep at it. But from my perspective, anybody who pulls themselves up out of the gutter and says, "I want to go and try to get my life together," there should be a place for them to go. And if it doesn't work this time, as long as there's a place there and they can go back—and they do go back—that should be paid for.

Rolling Stone: Would you talk to some extent from your own experience?

Loury: It's dangerous business to try to make social policy on the basis of one's biography. So I wouldn't, except to say that I have observed firsthand the difficulty of getting out from under the allure and the obsession with some of these substances.

Rolling Stone: How is it that criticizing the drug war has become perceived as tantamount to being soft on drugs?

Loury: You have to distinguish between the effect of a policy and the symbolic meaning of a policy, which I think is important politically. You know, we have sodomy laws on the books that are not enforced. My view is that they're bad laws in some demonstrable sense, but it might be very hard politically to get them off the books because an effort to take them off is understood to be endorsing a certain way of life.

Similarly, with drug policy, the discourse is shrouded with these symbolic meanings. If you have a lot of pot-smoking hippies running around denouncing all of the drug laws, then we know those are bad people. The fact that the image of drug users and dealers is that of a hooded-sweat-shirt-wearing, gun-toting sixteen-year-old hanging out in a doorway—the black, urban thug—gives you some indication of the demonization. Once these people become the face of this problem, those who say, "Let them out, don't hit them too hard" are people who don't take the problem seriously. That's the construction of symbolic meaning.

Patterson: There was a time when alcohol was also ethnically identified, and the Irish in America were criminalized as a result. As long as that association existed, no one could see alcoholism as an illness. It wasn't until people were able to persuade themselves that, in fact, alcoholism wasn't the problem of one single ethnic group that they were able to see it as an illness.

Loury: The degree of tolerance for alcohol use is relatively unique in American history. But the policy of Prohibition is universally recognized to have been a failure. It seems to me we need to recognize the same failure with drug policy.

Patterson: Having acknowledged all of this, the question is, "What do we do now?" And it seems to me that this is something that political will could be very effective in changing.

Rolling Stone: But virtually no politician is willing to stand up publicly and question the drug war. It's like the Cold War years and no one wants to normalize relations with China because they look soft on communism. This issue is waiting for its Nixon.

Patterson: This is a fundamental problem in the American political process, isn't it? There's nothing you can say about changing traditional attitudes toward law-breaking behavior because of the political fear that it will be used against you. I don't know how America got itself into this bind. But in the final analysis, it will only be a powerful leader who also is courageous enough to risk his popularity by saying, "This is ridiculous."

Loury: Look at what the Republicans tried to do in the last presidential election. When there was some statistic about marijuana use among high school students, there was a whole campaign about how Clinton had had some marijuana smokers in the White House so he's sending the wrong message. Which is ridiculous. These social trends are not driven by the symbols that are given off by somebody who sits in Washington, D.C. They're driven by the fundamentals on the ground in a nation of 270 million people.

Virtually no politician is willing to stand up publicly and question the drug war.

Patterson: I don't see why Clinton in his second term couldn't have selected a few issues that are ostensibly unpopular. This would have the political benefit for him of making him appear to be courageous. And given the fact that the African-American community constitutes such a major part of his base, he has a responsibility to take some unpopular stands on important issues. And drug policy is one I would certainly emphasize.

Loury: This is what Clinton's "national conversation on race" should partly be about. You don't have to frame it in terms of "You know the drug policy is racist." But you can say that the policy is creating distress and polarization and alienation among inner-city blacks. And that is a problem.

Patterson: What I find irritating is that in prison not only is there no rehabilitation but there's widespread use of drugs, which is quite incredible. At least we could get to drug users at that point. If you can't get at them in prison, you don't stand a chance in hell outside.

If Clinton and others decide to come down heavily on the need to do something about addiction in prison, that is politically easy to do. And it reinforces the heavy stick—the stick rather than the carrot approach.

Rolling Stone: To what degree might religious leaders have a role in turning the debate from punishment to treatment? Because you know religion is going to speak in a moral way about issues of substance abuse. At the same time, if you think about who houses Alcoholics Anonymous and Narcotics Anonymous groups, who runs rehab centers, it's the religious sector of society.

Loury: If you are looking for a Nixon today on this issue, that's one quarter where he or she might come from. Someone who is a Pat Robertson-type person or a Gary Bauer-type person who woke up one morning and said, "Oh, my God, I've looked at this. We're criminalizing a whole class of people. How big can the prison population be ? What manner of country

are we? Real resources go into that prison system, diverted from somewhere else. This is not the answer."

Patterson: I'm pessimistic about any such person coming on the scene any time soon. There is another way we can consider changing policy, and that is the enormous amount of money being spent on trying to stop the drugs from flowing in. I read some figure – it's preposterous. It's in the billions and billions of dollars. And it's gotten us nowhere.

We have not succeeded in preventing the drugs from coming in, and, therefore, we have to emphasize somehow trying to reduce the demand. Perhaps we should shift some of the billions of dollars we're now wasting on trying to prevent drugs coming in into rehabilitation. I'm not going to be spending any less, I'm not soft on drugs – I'm simply saying , as a practical matter, instead of spending $50 billion on Colombia or Bolivia, all of which is going just to sort of fill the pockets of these corrupt generals, spend it here.

Since we're in a prison-building mode, let's start getting a little creative and perhaps build some

Young, Vulnerable & Black

Black leaders are in a bind: it is on their turf that the drug war is being fought. For years black politicians and church leaders supported the War on Drugs because they saw the damage inflicted on their communities by drugs like crack. Even today, Atlanta's Democratic mayor, Bill Campbell, takes a tough line and tells Rolling Stone: "We must reject all proposals to legalize illicit drugs, because it is morally reprehensible to consider an action that would (a) erode our children's anti-drug attitudes of risk and social disapproval and (b) make harmful and addictive drugs far more accessible." Another black officeholder, Rep. J.C. Watts Jr., R-Okla., argues that drug use is a "widespread epidemic that is everyone's problem."

But the drug laws have had unforeseen and damaging consequences for African-Americans. The discrepancy in sentencing for crack-cocaine offenses (five years for possession of five grams of crack or sale of 500 grams of powder) is a notorious example. The U.S. Sentencing Commission, which was established by Congress, declared that Congress had made a mistake in enacting disparate sentences and recommended that crack penalties be reduced. President Clinton and Congress rejected the commission's recommendation. Many black politicians and leaders, however, have spoken out on the inequities of the drug war.

– Erika Fortgang

"In the absence of a real War on Drugs and an urban policy, we have a war on the young, vulnerable and black. Oddly, the rationale for the disparity is to protect blacks from crack. That is racial paternalism. What is at

stake is the essence of the 1954 Supreme Court decision – equal protection under the law."
– Rev. Jesse Jackson Sr., President, Rainbow/PUSH Coalition

"Our drug policy has become a tale of two cities or, more accurately, a tale of two classes – rich and poor."
– Rep. Donald Payne, D-N.J.

"It is not about being soft on crime. It is not about condoning drugs. It is about being able to look our children in the face and say: 'There is fairness in our system of justice. There is fairness in our laws.'"
– Rep. Melvin Watt, D-N.C.

"Cocaine and crack cannot be separated. The right thing to do would be to treat both of these lethal drugs under the same mode. The problem that we have in our society today is we misidentify drugs, we confuse the scene, and we have so many powerful burdens and powerful penalties that no one really understands it."
– Rep. James Traficant, D-Ohio

"Maintaining the sentencing disparity fuels the belief that our criminal-justice system is inherently unfair and racially unjust. Our judicial system must be fair if we ever expect it to earn the trust of our citizens. There is no such thing as a 'little justice.'" – Rep. Maxine Waters, D-Calif.

SOURCES: THE DRUG POLICY FOUNDATION: THE CONGRESSIONAL BLACK CAUCUS

kinds of prisons that are more rehabilitative centers rather than simply throwing these people among hardened criminals. One of the disturbing things that has come out in research in some ghetto areas is the fact that going to prison is not any longer seen as a big deterrent.

Rolling Stone: No, in fact it's become like a rite of passage.

Patterson: Right.

Rolling Stone: I remember reporting on South Africa and talking to people who'd been part of the resistance there and almost expected to go into prison for their political actions. There was a Zulu term for jail that translated to "the place of men."

Patterson: Then maybe we need to build a place of boys and relegate some first-time offenders and nonviolent offenders there. I would use some money on that instead of wasting it on military exercises in Bolivia.

Rolling Stone: Professor Loury, you've been a steadfast critic of liberal solutions to social problems. Does this sound like one that is both tough-minded and efficient?

Loury: We're not talking about washing our hands of drug abuse, becoming relativists and saying it doesn't matter. What's being said is, "Can we think sensibly about how we can enter into people's lives more constructively in order to try to produce something positive?" Now the idea of rehabilitation has a bad odor. People laugh at you when you talk about rehabilitation. Our prisons now don't rehabilitate; what they do is incapacitate.

I'd like to see much greater funding for treatment and a focus on the demand side of the drug market as well as the supply side. And a ratcheting down of the punitiveness of the mandatory-minimum sentencing. Those would be pillar of moderation.

Patterson: As a practical matter, it's simply politically not in the cards right now to have decriminalization. I personally would think that, in the long run, that may be the best approach. But in terms of what's possible, I do not see this ever taking place.

But there are alternatives. One we actually tried in an ad hoc sort of way in Jamaica. In the Seventies, we had a large number of young people being arrested for ganja—marijuana—and the jails were being filled up with people who perhaps aren't violent. What happened in response was not so much decriminalization but that the police were urged, essentially, to back off. And they did. The police themselves did not want to decriminalize, because they found the use of the ganja laws an effective strategy to get people for other things. So the laws are on the books and you can get arrested, but for the typical user the probability of being arrested is very low. Some version of that is one possibility for America.

Loury: Never mind the point that we have an enlightened self-interest in seeing that people come out of prison better than what they went in. Because we're not going to put them in a spaceship and ship them off to another planet. They're going to still be here, they're going to have children, they're going to have an impact. Because we're in this thing big time. I mean, 1.7 million under lock and key on any given day—and it's going up.

A Reading for Critical Thinking

WHO'S SORRY NOW?

White Americans wince when blacks call for **an apology for slavery.** It's time to get over our reluctance — because without an apology, blacks and whites will never get along.

By Naomi Wolf

We build memorials to what we want to remember, but a glance at our public monuments also shows just what we want to forget. Just off the Mall in Washington, D.C., there's a vast museum devoted to a holocaust that took place in Europe; near the Potomac, there's a beloved memorial to a slaughter that unfolded in Southeast Asia. But you'd have to look long and hard over the American landscape to find any prominent recognition of our own homegrown holocaust—of the 250 years during which up to one American in five was held, scourged, and bred as chattel.

America has a willful amnesia about its slave past. Daily life in Colonial Williamsburg has been painstakingly re-created for the sake of tourists. In the West, towns re-enact the days of the gold rush. But at the sites of the notorious slave markets—where thousands of African families were dispersed while sustaining the economies that supported white families—there is little or no commemoration. Ellis Island's makeover is a gleaming piece of historical preservation; but in Auburn, New York, the house of Harriet Tubman, which was a famous station on the Underground Railroad, now lies in disrepair, its preservation left to the amateur efforts of local citizens who raise funds to maintain it. The slave quarters at Mount Vernon carefully explain the production of horseshoes and tallow: Tools are displayed, but not whips or shackles. No multimedia archives bother to chronicle the histories of, and relationships between, the enslaved Americans who served the father of our country. Little attention is paid to the bitter irony that while George Washington allowed his slaves to wed, the state of Virginia refused to legally recognize those unions.

White America wants to forget. Two decades ago, the miniseries *Roots* was a major pop culture event because it gave names and faces to historical shadows, but its theme was palatable to whites only because it led, ultimately, to assimilation and redemption. In contrast, Steven Spielberg's recent *Amistad*—a straightforward and unsettling account of the subjection of Africans in the slave trade—sank like a stone.

Plenty of whites would say that memorializing our slave past is worse than unimportant, that it is destructive to the present. Controversy attended efforts to obtain congressional funding for a museum of slavery on the Mall. Southern struggles over the Confederate flag are routine and bitter. Whites' reactions to blacks' insistence on memorializing slavery are strong: "I didn't own any slaves. Why should I apologize?' as one recent caller to a talk-radio station characteristically argued. When Congressman Tony P. Hall, a white Democrat from Ohio, raised the subject of an apology for slavery as a "step toward healing," he was deluged with criticism. President Clinton typically waffled on this issue when, last August, he chose to leave the decision on whether to apologize for slavery up to his race advisory board. Eight months later, inching toward a more complete gesture, he sort of apologized for the slave trade—in Africa, to the descendants of Africans who were left behind by it; not in America to the descendants of those who were captured and bred in captivity. "The United States has not always done the right thing by Africa," he said with a truly farcical note of understatement. "Going back to the time before we were even a nation, European Americans received the fruits of the slave trade . . . and we were wrong in that."

Why does an apology matter? Why is memorializing our slave past important for the present? These things matter because without them, both sides remain stuck. The mass denial of slavery by the dominant culture creates what denial creates in any dysfunctional family: inflamed articulation of the denied truth by the injured party. The more one family member silences, the more the other symbolically over-emotes. When a black man was recently dragged to his death by three whites in Jasper, Texas, whites quoted in news coverage swore that the savage murder was an isolated event, as if they were unconscious of the history of lynching in towns just like theirs. In reaction to such denial, the African-Americans quoted were inclined toward conspiracy theories. "At this point," one woman reportedly said, "I'll believe anything."

How would proper memorials of slavery heal this stalemate? Memorials reflect the depth of our caring. As a Jew, I know rage wells within me toward contemporary Germans when I see a cheap tin marker over a subway entrance in the heart of Berlin commemorating a roundup of local Jews. The slightness of the marker undermines my trust in my German peers—even though the historic tragedy is now distant from us.

> One black woman said, with tears running down her cheeks, "I've been waiting all my life to hear a white man say that to me."

Apologies between groups matter for the same reason they matter between individuals in intimate relationships: They help keep the relationship healthy. The recent wave of international apologies speaks to the power of this fact. Why should we care whether Switzerland returns what are often insignificant amounts of money to Jews? Not because of the money but because of the lingering denial. Why did the pope's semiapology for the Catholic Church's collusion with Nazism reinforce Jewish distrust of Catholicism? Precisely because of its tone of self-exoneration. In contrast, France's unstinting apology for its collusion with the Vichy government and Australia's wholehearted Sorry Day, in which the entire continent expresses regret for separating Aboriginal children from their parents, will both go a long way toward genuine healing—the kind we in this country should note with envy.

Finally, particularly where children are concerned, apologies reflect the value as signed to a given relationship. Without an apology from whites for the centuries during which black children were bought and sold, black kids grow up wondering if the dominant culture will ever value them enough for their efforts within the system to really work. The fact is, conspiracies against black Americans have been real. Slavery itself was a conspiracy. So were the post-Reconstruction years, when whites banded together to cheat blacks out of fair prices for their cotton and white police forces conspired to frame black defendants. Without an apology that acknowledges this reality, black off-the-wall conspiracy theorizing will continue to assert itself. Hence, for example, the widespread beliefs that the CIA invented AIDS and that the LAPD framed O.J.

An apology in this case is not an expression of personal guilt. It is an expression of regret, of shared sorrow. Popular spiritualist Marianne Williamson, who is often mocked for saying things America isn't ready to hear, conducts an experiment with her audiences: She has white people stand and apologize to blacks in the audience for racism and the harm it has inflicted upon their families and children. I watched this once, squirming with discomfort; I was sure it would be offensive, a sham, superficial, insulting, phony—all the things we fear when the issue of an apology comes up. To my astonishment, after the apology the mood in the room changed in a way I have never before felt in America: There was an almost tangible lightening of tension for both the blacks and the whites. It was a mood in which one could actually move on. As one old black woman said, with tears running down her cheeks, "I've been waiting my whole life to hear a white man say that to me."

In a bad marriage, every little friction symbolizes the larger sense of being held in contempt or feeling betrayed. That's where we are now. In a good marriage, a fight, no matter how bad it gets, is just a fight. That's where an apology can take us. So in the interest of starting with what I can, I want to say, for the record, about this great harm: I am so sorry.

A Reading for Critical Thinking

The Chador Hits Cyberspace

PROTECTION OF FEMALE MODESTY ALWAYS LEADS TO INEQUALITY, EVEN ONLINE.

By Wendy Kaminer

In October 1997, the library board in Loudoun County, Virginia, voted to equip all library computers with software supposed to prohibit adults as well as children from viewing "pornography and obscene material" on the Internet. (Access to e-mail and chat rooms has been blocked as well.) This unusually repressive policy has been given a feminist spin: Titled "Policy on Internet Sexual Harassment," it is reportedly intended to protect women and children from encountering a "sexually hostile" environment.

Critics of feminist efforts to police pornography and purify workplace speech might be forgiven for saying, "I told you so." A preoccupation with self-esteem, assumptions about female fragility and mistrust of free speech have elasticized the concept of sexual harassment: Outside the courtroom, it can be stretched to cover virtually any situation in which a woman is allegedly offended or discomfited by a man. Or it can be invoked to critique apparently consensual sexual relationships in the workplace, including the White House. Feminists who failed to excoriate President Clinton for "harassing" Monica Lewinsky have been accused of hypocrisy: Assuming the allegations of a sexual relationship are true, we are also supposed to assume that she was incapable of consenting to it. Confusion about sex and sexual harassment, generated by some feminists, has brought us back to the fifties, when nice girls wouldn't even have sex with the President.

Feminist campaigns against pornography and questionable forms of harassment, like sexist speech, have always flirted with the double standard and its underlying notions of femininity. Its renaissance was predictable. Today, if few feminists will condone sexist denunciations of Lewinsky or endorse the Loudoun County library harassment policy, some share the blame for both. Anti-libertarian feminists have given new respectability to the old notion that adult women are apt to feel threatened and even traumatized by sexual banter, and the mere proximity of sexually explicit material, not to mention men who like it—and they have insisted that sexual equality depends on our willingness to make women feel safe, without second-guessing their sense of danger.

"This is a safe place," personal development experts coo at workshops and seminars where people are encouraged to "share." In this context, safety doesn't simply mean the absence of tangible physical or political danger. It implies psychic security, the promise of comfort and nurturance. Demands to make libraries, workplaces and other public spaces "safe" for presumptively fragile, frightened women focus similarly on psychic safety or comfort and reflect the influence of the therapeutic culture on public life. Loudoun County library officials are not claiming that Internet censorship is necessary to protect women from being raped in the library; attacking "pornography" and "sexual hostility" is apparently supposed to

From *The Nation*, Wendy Kaminer (March 9, 1998), pp. 21–22. Reprinted with permission from *The Nation* magazine. Copyright © 1998. www.thenation.com

insure that nothing in the library will make women feel vulnerable to rape. (They might as well censor the daily papers.)

When feeling safe becomes as paramount a public concern for women as being safe, the drive for equality is sacrificed to demands for protection. Civil liberties and civil rights suffer. In Massachusetts, the therapeutic feminist concern with establishing safe places for women has recently resulted in a new law allowing health clubs to maintain sexually discriminatory membership policies. Some women feel "uncomfortable" exercising in the presence of men, supporters of the law assert, noting that women are conditioned to be particularly self-conscious about their bodies and tend to be frightened by the presence of sweaty, partially clothed, physically aggressive men. All-female health clubs have been promoted as safe havens for women who feel alternately mocked by images of supermodels and tormented by the specter of sexual violence.

The trouble is that health clubs are places of public accommodation: Like movie theaters, restaurants and hotels, they are open to the general public and have no membership requirement other than the ability to pay a fee. In fact, the new Massachusetts law permitting female-only health clubs is an amendment to the state's public accommodations law. It is a direct attack on a basic principle of nondiscrimination embodied in the 1964 Civil Rights Act: Customer preference—like a desire not to associate with members of the opposite sex or particular racial, ethnic or religious groups—does not trump constitutional guarantees of equal access to public places.

Of course, the Massachusetts legislature would not have amended the public accommodations law to permit racially exclusory health clubs in deference to the sensibilities of white women who fear black men. The amendment permitting health clubs to exclude on the basis of sex, however, was quickly enacted, and while opposed by NOW, it generated relatively little public concern. Like the Supreme Court, the general public has never considered sex discrimination nearly as indefensible as race discrimination, because sex-based stereotypes are much more respectable than racial ones. Conventional wisdom holds that there are important cognitive, emotional and characterological differences between the sexes, and out of respect for difference, many people want to shield women from the indignities of interactions with men.

But you may sympathize with women who feel ill at ease in coed gyms or even in the presence of men viewing *Hustler* and still recognize that occasional discomfort is one minor cost of public life. Should we provide for all-female streets and beaches, and single-sex seating in movies, sports arenas and libraries? Should we permit men to re-establish exclusively male clubs and saloons where they can sweat and swear and watch football games "in private"? The rationale for single-sex health clubs and female friendly libraries—protection of female modesty—is the rationale for the chador. It always leads to inequality. In the end, there's no safety in separatism.

Wendy Kaminer is a public policy fellow at Radcliffe College and president of the National Coalition Against Censorship.

A Reading for Critical Thinking

LIFE IN THE 90'S:

Rights and Responsibilities in an Individualistic Culture

By Terry Golway

For some years now, we have heard from an assortment of critics the complaint that post-1960's America celebrates individual rights at the expense of individual responsibilities. We have, in the eyes of these observers, encouraged people to believe that they have a right to do pretty much whatever they want to do, whenever they want to do it, without regard for the consequences to society.

There's merit in the argument. After all, who can doubt that the rights revolution, as some have described it, has been extended well beyond what was envisioned in the first 10 amendments to the U.S. Constitution. Indeed, I have heard people state that they have a right to a vast array of entitlements James Madison never envisioned: the right to a pet-hair-free hotel room, the right to order a vegetarian meal at McDonald's and the right not to hear arguments, assertions and opinions with which they do not agree.

For the most part, this critique has come from conservatives, who fret, in many cases understandably, that our worship of individual freedom and our demand for more and more "rights" have come at great cost to society. According to a small army of public intellectuals and Op-Ed pundits, the emphasis on liberty over responsibility is at the heart of today's fractured society, the cause of such problems as teen pregnancy, deadbeat dads, drug addiction, personal bankruptcies and many others.

Believe it or not, this line of thought leads us directly to the raging debate over that highly important public policy issue: sport utility vehicles, those ubiquitous symbols of 1990's excess.

The Clinton Administration recently floated proposals to levy stiff taxes on the nation's ever-increasing fleet of trucks trying to pose as cars — and luxury cars at that. The Administration offered the opinion that since sport utility vehicles consume gasoline at pre-oil crisis rates, their existence is not in the interest of the general welfare, not to mention the fact that these monsters have created havoc on the highways. Television news magazines have delighted in filming staged crashes showing sport utility vehicles demolishing various goody-goody four cylinder sedans, and studies indicate that people in cars struck by S.U.V.'s are four times more likely to die than the folks in the S.U.V.

The White House's tentative notion to do something about the S.U.V. plague was hardly without precedent. Government has long held to the belief that it can and should tax behavior patterns that are not illegal but certainly not always helpful to society. That's why cigarette smokers need extensive lines of credit to support their habit, and why occasional tipplers like myself are forced to make involuntary contributions to the public treasury.

To judge by the howls of anguish from many conservative commentators, however, you'd have thought the White House had proposed something dangerously radical — a slight tax increase on annual incomes of more than $500 million, perhaps, or a bill that would require certain elements of corporate America to adhere to its professed love of competition. One commentator, who happens to be a member in good standing of the rights-responsibility crowd, harrumphed that the White House was trying to engage in liberal social engineering. By taxing sport utility vehicles, this commentator said, the Clinton Administration was trying to force Americans to settle for earnest little economy cars rather than exercise their right to buy whatever they want, regardless of cost, etc. He noted with pride that his spouse drove an S.U.V., and she shouldn't have to sacrifice her own safety because of some socialistic scheme to deprive the affluent of their toys.

Well, well; this *is* a dilemma.

Yes, we all have a right to buy a gas-guzzling, sedan-smashing sport utility vehicle. The question, though, is this: What about our responsibilities? Do we not owe society a little less self-indulgence? If we can purchase a car that will use fewer of the planet's resources and pose less of a danger to society's members in good standing, shouldn't we? Or does the right to own a sport utility vehicle transcend all the gooey talk about responsibilities?

Many commentators on the right, secure in their belief in free markets and intent on crippling any initiative from the White House, clearly have decided to rally around the dubious merits of the S.U.V. Every week, it seems, I read another conservative's complaint about the President's S.U.V. proposal.

About a quarter-century or so ago, certain left-wing types were tagged with the label "limousine liberals" when their private lives bumped up against their public positions. Now we have the spectacle of "S.U.V. conservatives," who believe that some of us should attend to our sober responsibilities while they burn up fossil fuels and endanger sedan drivers who can't afford the 30 to 50 grand or so that it costs for these status symbols on wheels.

There is, however, one pro-S.U.V. argument that resonates with me, although it's for all the wrong reasons. Another conservative commentator recently protested that S.U.V.'s are Detroit's most profitable vehicles and therefore shouldn't be subjected to any additional taxation. (It would cut into consumer demand, you see.)

Well, if Detroit has figured out a way of persuading the well-to-do that they simply must have an S.U.V. at a price approximately double what my parents paid for a house in 1967, and if that money is finding its way into the pockets of the United Auto Workers, I suppose there is something to be said about the S.U.V. fad after all.

But somehow I don't think that's what the pro-S.U.V. crowd has in mind.

A Reading for Critical Thinking

Ganging Up On Civil Liberties

By Nina Siegal

Sixteen-year-old Claudio Ceja of Anaheim, California, is an eleventh grader at Loara High School. From 8:00 A.M. until 2:35 P.M., he is in classes. From 4 P.M. to 6 P.M., he hands out fliers for a local business. From 6 P.M. to 9:30 P.M., he completes his homework before he goes to his second job at an Anaheim convention center.

But the Anaheim police don't see Ceja as a hard-working young student. In the past few years, they have stopped, detained, and photographed Ceja five times and put his photograph in the city's gang tracking computer database. Each time, Ceja told them he was not involved with a gang. But each time they ignored his claims, he says. Despite the police attention, Ceja has never been arrested or charged with any crime.

"They seem to be doing it for the fun of it," says Ceja. "They take my picture, and they put it in a gang file. But I'm not a gangster. I don't want to be identified as one."

Ceja says he recently contacted members of United Neighborhoods, an Anaheim-based group founded last year to help young people fight police abuse. Chairperson Jessica Castro told Ceja that he had a right to refuse to be photographed. So the next time he was stopped, says Ceja, "I told an officer that he couldn't take my picture because I was a minor. He said: 'Now you know your rights, huh?' and he took my picture anyway."

Ceja is one of thousands of young people across the nation who are being snared in a giant net cast by law-enforcement agencies to nab suspected gang members.

Two of the most popular gang-fighting strategies today—employed widely in California and under consideration in other states—are gang-tracking databases and civil gang injunctions. Although police and prosecutors herald both tactics as effective methods of gang control, opponents say the measures infringe on the basic civil liberties of young people and are biased against minorities.

Using the new practice of civil gang injunctions, prosecutors can prohibit alleged members of certain street gangs from criminal activities usually associated with gang-banging, such as vandalism, graffiti, and possessing weapons.

But the injunctions don't stop there. They include many activities that may not involve criminal activity at all. A San Jose injunction prohibits "standing, sitting, walking, driving, gathering, or appearing anywhere in public view" with any suspected gang member. Those named in the injunction are barred from carrying "glass bottles, rocks, bricks, chains, tire irons, screwdrivers, hammers, crowbars, bumper jacks, razor blades, razors, sling shots, marbles, [and] ball bearings." They are also enjoined from "approaching vehicles, engaging in conversation or otherwise communicating with the occupants of any vehicle," as well as "making, causing, or encouraging others to make loud noise of any kind."

The first civil gang injunction was issued in December 1987 against alleged members of the Playboy Gangster Crips of the Cadillac-Corning section of West Los Angeles. Now there are about a dozen in place in California cities, including San Jose, Los

Angeles, Oakland, Inglewood, Burbank, Pasadena, and Long Beach. Violators of the injunctions face fines or jail time.

Marty Vranicar, head of the gang unit for the Los Angeles city attorney's office, says injunctions imposed in West Los Angeles, Norwalk, and Pasadena have significantly decreased gang activity. "From our experience, it has had a tremendous suppressive effect on gangs," says Vranicar. "It provides breathing space for the neighborhoods to get out from under the constant intimidation caused by the gangs in the area."

But civil-liberties advocates are dismayed.

"When a person who has not been convicted of any gang-related activity or any criminal activity, for that person to be prohibited from being on a public sidewalk during daylight hours, runs against everything that our Constitution stands for," says Robin Toma, consultant and attorney at the Los Angeles County Human Relations Commission.

Vranicar disagrees. "The underlying legal theory is a simple one," he says, "and it has been supported by the California Supreme Court: Not every right of association is going to receive the same level of protection under the First Amendment."

New injunctions are now being considered throughout California. In July, a Los Angeles Superior Court judge imposed a ban on free association in a seventeen-block stretch of the Jefferson Park neighborhood in southwest Los Angeles, the hangout of the notorious Eighteenth Street Gang, according to the Associated Press. The most sweeping of its kind so far, this injunction would name and tag more than 500 people who live in a Latino neighborhood of just 28,000.

Ed Chen, staff attorney with the ACLU of Northern California, represented five teenagers in a suit against San Jose. An injunction filed in 1993 against thirty-eight suspected members of two Latino gangs in the Rocksprings neighborhood of San Jose included the names of several young people who had never been convicted of, or charged with, any crime.

"I was stopped by a policeman when I was walking down the street," Miguel Moreno, one of Chen's clients, testified to the court. "I was wearing a shirt and cap with RAIDERS on them, and the police officer told me that Raiders clothes were gang clothes. I was only wearing these clothes because I am a Raiders fan, and that is what I told the officer. The policeman took my picture without asking me, and said it was for his 'collection.' He asked me if I was in a gang, and I told him I was not."

Chen says prosecutors often use the civil gang injunction as a shortcut. It allows them to circumvent constitutional protections that require police departments to charge individuals with a crime, take them to court, and follow due-process procedures.

"Our first concern was the violation of people's due-process rights," says Chen. "Secondly, people were named solely because they were thought to be in a gang, not because they were doing anything that violated any laws. That's guilt by association, not guilt by individual conduct."

In January, however, the injunction was upheld by the California Supreme Court. The ACLU sought review from the U.S. Supreme Court, but in June the Court refused to hear the case.

Aside from the civil-liberties concerns, the injunctions may be ineffective. In 1993, the Los Angeles city attorney's office sought and obtained an injunction against hundreds of supposed members of the Latino Blythe Street Gang of San Fernando Valley. This May, the ACLU of Southern California published "False Premise/False Promise," the first comprehensive long-term study of the impact of injunctions. Examining crime data over the four-year period the injunction was in effect, the ACLU concluded that the tactic merely shifted criminal activity and drug trafficking to adjoining neighborhoods.

But San Jose city attorney Joan Gallo defends the effectiveness of the injunctions. "The neighborhoods where we have used this technique are neighborhoods where the residents were held hostage by gangs," Gallo says. "They could not leave their homes. They could not feel safe walking on the streets. The injunction immediately dispersed the gang, and the neighbors were able to reclaim their neighborhood. It's been a complete success. You can walk in those neighborhoods again today."

The making of gang databases began in the mid-1980's, but the pace has picked up. Police officers in Los Angeles, Garden Grove, Huntington Beach, Newport Beach, Orange, and other California cities now regularly harass, detain, and photograph youths who are only suspected of—not charged with—gang activity. Police then store that information in computer databases, so they now have files on citizens who have never committed a crime.

In March, California Governor Pete Wilson announced that he would invest $800,000 in state money to create a statewide gang-tracking program called CalGang.

"For less than $30, any law-enforcement agency in the state can purchase software that will put them on an Intranet [law-enforcement computer] network, where they can access a Master Name Gang Index and share information on the comings and goings of street gangs," Wilson told reporters.

CalGang now lists the names of almost a quarter of a million young people. The program culls the names from smaller lists compiled on roughly 600 computer terminals at 150 law-enforcement agencies throughout the state.

'It's hard to ignore the similarity to the blacklists created in the 1950s. Now people are being labeled gang members instead of communists. If it wasn't just happening to young people of color, I think it would be causing a lot of outcry.'

Johnny Carriro, a seventeen-year-old from the Boyle Heights neighborhood of Los Angeles, says the police stop him "almost every day" on his way home from work at the Jobs for a Future employment-training program. "They do that to us just because we look like gang members," says Carriro. "They stop us for no reason, sometimes they even point their guns at us, but we aren't doing anything. We're just walking home. They tell us to lie down, and if we don't lie down on the ground they start getting rough. Sometimes they put us in handcuffs, take us down to the station, and then they let us go." Carriro says he's never been charged with a crime, though the police fined him $135 one time for riding his bicycle on the sidewalk.

In July 1993, when Minh Tram was just fifteen, she and two friends, Quyen Pham and Annie Lee, all Vietnamese Americans, were waiting to use a pay phone outside a cafe in downtown Garden Grove. As Tram tells it, an unmarked car drove past them. The car's passenger, an Asian male, gave the girls the once-over. Tram thought he was trying to pick them up, but the car circled the block a second time, then stopped. Two men got out of the car and identified themselves as police officers.

"They detained us and said we looked like gang-bangers," says Tram, who is now eighteen and attending the University of California-Irvine. "We told them we were waiting for my brother to pick us up, and we said we were going to page him. They made some comment about how we were probably paging someone to get drugs. One officer sat us down and gave us a whole talk about how if you walk like a duck and talk like a duck . . . and then he said we were nothing more than street kids. This had never happened to us before, so we all started crying. Then they lined us up against a wall and took our pictures."

Although the police never charged the girls with a crime, they added their names to Garden Grove's gang database. Tram felt she and her friends had been unfairly targeted by the police because they were wearing baggy pants. All three girls were honor students. "We weren't affiliated with a gang," says Tram.

The young women contacted the ACLU of Southern California, which filed a class action lawsuit on their behalf. In 1995, the case was settled, and the women received $85,000 total. The Garden Grove Police Department agreed that officers would have to obtain voluntary consent in writing from detainees before taking their pictures. And they would no longer photograph people without "reasonable suspicion" that the individuals were engaged in criminal activity.

But officers routinely ignore those guidelines, says Tram. She regularly sees police harass young Asian students as part of Irvine's gang-tracking program, she says.

Daniel Tsang, an Irvine-based activist who co-founded Alliance Working for Asian Rights and Empowerment, says the Irvine police often treat Asian Americans who attend the University of California-Irvine as criminals. "Once you leave the campus, you feel that you're in a police state," says Tsang. "They'll follow any car that has been lowered, stop the drivers, get them out of the car, and take their photographs. It's a terrible intrusion."

John Crew, director of the Police Practices Project of the ACLU of Northern California, says the gang databases are now omnipresent in California. And he is afraid that the state's experience will be duplicated nationwide.

"It's hard to ignore the similarity to the blacklists created in the 1950s," he says. "Then, people were labeled based on who they associated with. People didn't know they were on the list. Once you got on the list you couldn't get off. Now the lists are on computers, and people are being labeled gang members instead of communists. If it wasn't just happening to young people of color, I think it would be causing a lot of outcry."

Each city that adopts California's database must follow the state's penal code before branding someone a gang member or affiliate, but the nine criteria the code uses are sweeping.

A person is a gang member or affiliate if that person "wears colors or clothing indicating affiliation." Another criterion legitimates guilt-by-association: A person is a gang member or affiliate if that person "is present in a photograph with other gang affiliates." The final criterion is a catch-all: "other documents indicate gang affiliation."

"The criteria are so varied that in one county I might not be considered a gang member while in another city I might be considered a gang member," says Castro of United Neighborhoods.

The policies have a disproportionate effect on people of color. While minorities make up less than 50 percent of Orange County's population, more than 90 percent of the names listed in the database are Latino, Asian, and African American, according to a July 14 article in the *Los Angeles Times*. While Latinos are only 27 percent of the county's population of 2.6 million, they are 73 percent of the gang database.

"There's a racially discriminatory aspect to all of these programs," says Chen of the ACLU. "In every case that we've seen, the targets are Latino or African American youth. They concentrate on young black, brown, and sometimes yellow men. It's rarely used against non-minorities."

Robert Hagler, who chairs the California Gang Node Advisory Committee for the CalGang program, denies the charge of racial discrimination.

"I try to assure that the people listed in the database are objectively verified gang members and that the gangs that they are members of have committed crimes," says Hagler. "If the chips fall in one particular neighborhood or another, then that's where they lie as far as racial makeup, but all neighborhoods are treated equally."

In 1985, the Los Angeles County Sheriff's Department developed its own computerized gang list, known as the Gang Reporting Evaluation and Tracking (GREAT) system. In 1992, a review of the GREAT database by the federal General Accounting Office found that the police had identified almost half—47 percent—of all black men in Los Angeles County between the ages of twenty-one and twenty-four as gang members. Upon completing a comprehensive review of GREAT during the same year, the Los Angeles County district attorney expressed concern about the inclusion of so many black men. "That number is so far out of line with other ethnic groups that a careful, professional examination is needed to determine whether police procedure may be systematically over-identifying black youths as gang members," he wrote.

Castro of United Neighborhoods says the databases in Orange County amount to a "mass racist labeling" of all Hispanic youth. "The attitude is 'gather them all up—they're all the same.'"

On May 29, the California Advisory Committee of the U.S. Commission on Civil Rights held a day-long community hearing in Costa Mesa about police harassment of minorities in communities with gang databases. During the hearing, law-enforcement officials in Orange County admitted that of the 20,000 individuals listed as gang members or affiliates in that area, almost half—9,000—had never been arrested or charged with any crime.

Young people are not the only ones who find that gang-tracking programs are infringing on their civil liberties.

In 1995, police stopped Yvonne Lugo, then a thirty-eight-year-old mother of six, while she was driving in her hometown of Santa Ana, California, on her way back from the supermarket. An officer questioned Lugo and her daughter, and then a gang-prevention team showed up and took her photograph for police files. Even though Lugo says she's never been in a gang in her life, the police added her name to Orange County's 20,000-person gang-affiliate database.

"I know I'm innocent," she says. "I didn't do anything, but now I am on file as a gang member, and I can't do any thing about it. Just thinking about it and talking about it gives me the creeps and makes me very upset. I don't know what they re going to do with my picture on file."

In Colorado, the police pass the information on to landlords and building managers, says Mark Silverstein, legal director of that state's ACLU chapter. This allows the police to issue "trespassing notices" to reputed gang members who enter their buildings.

As a result, Darrell Blair Horton of Aurora, Colorado, cannot visit his three year-old son. Aurora has a list of suspected gang members, and Horton is on it. The boy's mother, Chanda Glenn, a resident of federally subsidized housing in Aurora, received a threat of eviction for inviting her son's father to visit the child at her apartment. In June, she filed a law suit on behalf of her son to protect her constitutional right to family privacy and intimate association.

Like California, Colorado has a record of going after minorities. In 1993, *The New York Times* reported that two out of every three young black men in Denver were on that city's gang-suspect list.

The frenzy for cataloging names doesn't stop at the state level. In October 1995, the national Crime Information Center created a national gang database. According to the ACLU, the FBI is now encouraging law-enforcement agencies to contribute their own gang records to the national "Violent Gang and Terrorist Organization File."

Nina Siegal is a staff reporter with the San Francisco Bay Guardian.

PART 4

Public Opinion
and Political Participation

We live in a democracy. This suggests that our elected leaders should, to a large degree, do what the people want them to do. On the surface, this statement seems unobjectionable. But upon further reflection, it is fraught with practical problems.

First, how can elected leaders know what public opinion is? Public opinion polls are the most widely used method, but polls have their problems. Great care is taken to ensure the accuracy of polls, but any pollster will tell you that poll results can vary widely depending on the way that questions are worded. In addition, public opinion can change rapidly, casting some doubt on the strength of public opinion.

In addition, there is considerable debate regarding the extent to which our elected leaders should pay attention to public opinion. Polls may tell us what the public thinks, but they tell us little about the quality of public opinion.

There is a difference between having an opinion and having an *informed* opinion. Our elected leaders may have more knowledge about an issue than the public does. Should they ignore their own judgment?

In a sense, politicians can be criticized no matter what they do. If they ignore the polls, they may be accused of being arrogant or out of touch. If they follow polls too closely, they are accused of not having any principles. The latter charge has been frequently made against President Clinton.

Of course, citizens can make their views known in other ways: at the ballot box; through letters, phone calls, and e-mails; by participating in demonstrations and political associations; and by making donations to political campaigns. As you read the following selections, consider whether or not politicians can really know what the public thinks—and whether or not it should matter.

THE LATINO VOTE IS COMING TO AN ELECTION NEAR YOU—
AND NEITHER MAJOR PARTY IS READY FOR IT

The Sleeping Giant Awakes

By Dale Maharidge

Once again, California stands on the verge of a xenophobic tantrum. The outburst du jour: a special ballot initiative scheduled for June to ban bilingual education.

At first, the initiative sounds reasonable. The group pushing it, English for the Children, seeks to redress problems that transcend racial politics by banning public school instruction in a child's native language. Who doesn't want kids to speak English so they can succeed?

But like its predecessors on the state's list of measures affecting minority populations, the initiative, mostly aimed at Latinos (California's largest immigrant group), will likely morph into an electoral shriek.

In 1994, Proposition 187 sought to remove state services to undocumented immigrants; in 1996, Proposition 209 sought to end state-supported affirmative action. (Both passed, but Proposition 187 has been tied up in court challenges over its constitutionality.) In both of those precedent-setting campaigns, proponents, largely Republicans, exploited fear—plentiful in California, where whites will be a minority within a few years. Advertisements for Proposition 187 depicted an invading horde of illegal immigrants, the not-so-subtle message being, "Stop this takeover." Many Latinos saw this as a racial attack, and, two years later, nearly three-fourths voted for Bill Clinton.

Already, the Republican Party in California has endorsed this new initiative, upholding the GOP's record as the Democratic Party's best recruitment tool. Within two decades, Latinos will surpass African Americans as the country's largest minority. Latinos voted overwhelmingly for Democrats in the '96 elections in California and Texas, where close to half of the nation's 29 million Latinos live (9.1 million and 4.9 million, respectively).

It would seem the Democrats have a lock on the Latino vote. Take Art Torres, the chairman of California's Democratic Party, who crowed about his opponents' "image problem" at a debate last fall with state Republican Party chairman Michael Schroeder. "They've been great," Torres says of Republicans and their anti-minority message.

Such assuredness is a huge mistake. "Art can be as smug as he wants," says Schroeder, acknowledging that his party has an image problem. But Schroeder sees Republican potential in the Latino vote. Prior to the immigrant-bashing wave, Latinos voted in huge numbers for Ronald Reagan, and in 1990 California's Republican Gov. Pete Wilson got 45 percent of their vote. "[Torres] knows as well as I do that as long as everyone feels welcome, we will get a lot more Hispanics," Schroeder says.

One reason is social conservatism among some Latinos. Campus activism on race and identity issues exaggerates the perception that Latinos are liberal. But their conservative cultural background often influences their politics. In part due to Catholicism, in part to strong family institutions, issues such as abortion and "values" rhetoric play well with Latinos. ("So they didn't vote for [Bob] Dole," says Schroeder, conceding that in the past some Republican ads have been racist. "Even if they agree with him on the issues.")

From *Mother Jones* (January/February 1998), pp. 56–61. Reprinted with permission from *Mother Jones* Magazine. Copyright © 1998, Foundation for National Progress.

Another reason is the diversity of Latino cultures and, even more important, the difference in economic status among Latinos. From recent immigrants to generations-old, long-established families in the United States, Latinos are not a cohesive voting bloc, at least not like blacks, who, although often ignored by the Democrats, have stuck by them. Latinos, whose assimilation patterns have been compared to those of turn-of-the-century Italian immigrants, tend to vote more along class, not racial, lines, subjugating identity to economic concerns.

Nobody exemplifies the complexities of the Latino vote better than Rep. Loretta Sanchez (D-Calif.), who trumped six-term GOP incumbent Bob Dornan in the 1996 congressional race. The first generation Mexican American turned the Orange County, California,

A Portrait of the Latino Vote
Socially Conservative, Young—and Turning Out In Greater Numbers

According to estimates, Latinos will account for 44 percent of the growth of the nation's population from 1995 to 2025.

As of 1995, 35.7 percent of the California Latino population was under the age of 18.

In California, births minus deaths accounted for 85 percent of the change in the Latino population. Net immigration accounted for 15 percent.

In 1994, 64 percent of Latinos in the U. S. were of Mexican ancestry, 14 percent were Central/South American, 10 percent were Puerto Rican, 4 percent were Cuban, and 7 percent were of other ancestry.

In 1995, 74 percent of Latinos lived in California, Florida, Illinois, New York, and Texas. The top states for electoral votes are: CA (54), NY (33), TX (32), FL (25), PA (23), and IL (22).

According to a 1996 Tomas Rivera Policy Institute poll, 14 percent of Latino voters in the U. S considered themselves Republicans, 58 percent Democrats, 17 percent Independents, and 7 percent had no preference.

In 1992, 5.1 million Latinos were registered to vote. In 1996, 6.6 million Latinos were registered to vote.

Each month, approximately 18,000 Latino youths become eligible to vote.

In 1992, Bill Clinton received 61 percent of Latino votes. In 1996, he received more than 72 percent. 5 million Latinos voted in the 1996 presidential election, a 19 percent increase from 1992.

There are 18 Latinos in the 105th U. S. House of Representatives: 15 Democrats and three Republicans.

According to a Los Angeles Times poll, two months before election day, 52 percent of Latino voters favored Proposition 187 (California's ballot initiative denying social services to illegal immigrants). By election day, 77 percent opposed it.

After the Proposition 187 campaign, the Latino turnout in the 1994 California gubernatorial race increased 17 percentage points (to 57 percent) over the 1990 turnout rate.

63 percent of Latino voters polled in 1996 believed Gov. Pete Wilson's immigration proposals reflected racism toward Latinos. 16 percent of those polled voted for Democrats to punish the Republican Party.

Before the debate over Proposition 187, 60 percent of immigrants eligible for naturalization had not decided which political party to join. As of 1996, 80 percent of newly naturalized immigrants were registered as Democrats.

Average U.S. household income, 1993:
Whites $51,471
Latinos $31,124
Blacks $30,037

In 1994, 50 percent of Latino voters in Texas said their family's financial situation had improved in the past four years, 39 percent said their financial situation had remained the same, and 11 percent said it was worse.

67 percent of Latino voters surveyed in Texas opposed increasing benefits to mothers who continue to have children while dependent on welfare.

56 percent of Latino voters polled in California in 1996 cited "more jobs through economic reform" as their top political priority.

82 percent of Latino voters favored a Los Angeles Unified School District proposition to provide $2.4 billion for public school repairs and construction.

A 1996 poll found that more than 60 percent of Latino voters favored the death penalty, 80 percent felt long prison terms helped reduce crime, and 76 percent favored time limits on welfare.

– RESEARCH BY JEN WIECZOREK

seat Democratic and surprised the nation in the process. But until 1992, Sanchez herself was a Republican. She dropped the Anglo, married half of her name (Brixey) when she ran against Dornan. And while she's certainly no Dornan—she's pro-labor, for example, and labor largely supported her campaign—her priorities include small government and tax incentives for businesses.

For many years, the political cliche describing the Latino population was the "sleeping giant." If awakened, it would have a profound impact on America's political landscape. In many ways, Republicans and Democrats alike were happy that the giant slumbered. It made things easy.

Now, the Latino vote is a lot more up for grabs than people think. The number of Latino voters is growing—having increased by 19 percent nationally from 1992 to 1996. Some 5 million Latinos voted in the last presidential election, 1.3 million of them in California, where Latinos accounted for 10 percent of the total voting population. That number can and will hit 20 percent.

While Democrats and Republicans each believe they have some advantages in capturing that vote, both parties may be fooling themselves.

"Pendejos!" the woman said, deriding Latino politicians. Some in the room squirmed—it's akin to calling them "assholes" or "dick-heads." She was speaking at the opening assembly of the Latino Academy, a symposium held last year in San Antonio, Texas, by the Southwest Voter Registration Education Project, a major player in the record 1996 Latino voter turnout. This first-ever event, designed to develop Latino political awareness, featured sessions targeting activists, youths, and politicians; creating it had long been a dream of Southwest Voter, which has organized at the grass roots level for more than two decades.

The woman was essentially criticizing politicians for "turning white." About a third of the 93 attendees applauded. Many rolled their eyes. It was a moment that demonstrated the great division among Latinos—and it represented the focus of the entire week-long event. Concentrating on identity, and not strictly on hard political maneuvering, might seem odd at an event meant to advance Latino social and political power. But it's at the heart of the complexity of the Latino vote.

California's Proposition 187 was the turning point. At first, a majority of Latinos polled favored curbing the illegal immigration, no more sympathetic to undocumented workers than were blacks or whites. But when Proposition 187 grew into an attack on all Latinos, cultural identity kicked in. In 1994, even staunch Republican Latinos reluctantly switched sides. Democrats have admittedly had an easy sell ever since.

Gov. Pete Wilson's race-baiting tactics are so well known that rapper Tupac Shakur invoked his name in lyrics as a handy symbol of intolerance. Using Proposition 187 to help his re-election campaign in 1994 and Proposition 209 in his doomed presidential bid two years ago, Wilson has actively courted the white voter base: Even though they account for only half the California population, whites comprise three-fourths

Rep. Loretta Sanchez (D-Calif.) exemplifies the complexities of the Latino vote. She changed both her party and her name to trump ultra-conservative Bob Dornan in 1996.

of the state's electorate. Also problematic is Dornan. Ever since losing to Sanchez, he has been on a ceaseless bleat claiming illegals tipped the margin and, a year and a half later, is still seeking a rematch.

But Dornan will vanish, and this year term limits will keep Wilson from running again. What will the Democrats do then? Torres confidently says a new crop of race-baiting Republican poster children will take their place. "We'll have some others in the wings," he says. "Believe me."

Torres shouldn't be so sure. California, with its 54 electoral votes, is a Latino power base—time and again, a state in which precedents are set. But as the bilingual initiative heats up and candidates for the 1998 gubernatorial election begin to square off, it seems little is being done right.

Take Sen. Dianne Feinstein, who's a strong possibility for the governor's race. She's considered an odds-on favorite in the Democratic Party's white-black-liberal power axis. But she's equal to Wilson as an immigrant basher, scoring huge negatives in Republican polls (with more than 40 percent of Latino men opposing her, according to Schroeder). At press time, Feinstein hadn't announced her position on the bilingual measure, but she regularly uses "get tough on immigration" rhetoric and has supported Republican legislative proposals to crack down on immigration, including tightening border control measures.

Feinstein has written off Latinos, says Gloria Molina, a Los Angeles County supervisor, vice chair of the Democratic National Committee, and one of the nation's most prominent Latino politicians. "If she decides to run, she is going to have nothing but problems from our community, from a leader like me," Molina says.

Feinstein is so onerous that Molina says she could entertain the possibility of voting for Dan Lungren, the state attorney general running for the Republican nomination, as long as "Lungren would demonstrate leadership" on Latino issues. "I don't know who I'd pick," she says. "I know it would be a horrible thing . . . for me to encourage people to vote for a Republican. I hope that will never happen."

The scenario is not so far-fetched: Lungren was a reluctant supporter of Proposition 187, once telling the *Sacramento Bee*, "I don't fear immigration . . . [it] contributes to the greatness of this country." More recently, he has announced his intent to "court the Catholic vote" in his gubernatorial campaign (partially a euphemism for the largely Catholic Latino vote) and to emphasize education and family issues.

The national parties, of course, aren't on the streets in California trying to get out the vote; instead, they are wallowing in a corporate buckfest. The Democrats' Torres is openly contemptuous. "We try to stay away from them," he says of the Democratic National Committee. "They come into the state with their vacuum cleaners and take the money and run. They're doing their own thing—and we bless them," he adds sarcastically.

The Republicans aren't doing much better. At the California Republican State Convention early last year, the National Republican Hispanic Assembly sought a modest $500,000—first from the state party and then from the national party—to help organize and target Latino voters in California. At the end of the year, no support had come through, according to representatives of the NRHA's Sacramento chapter.

But there is a secret to connecting with Latino voters: old-fashioned, get-out-the-vote, door-to-door contact. A Southwest Voter study in Colorado demonstrated that rather than responding to slick TV ads and mailings, Latinos, more than any other group, respond to personal politics. In the study, voter turnout increased by 15 to 20 percent in neighborhoods where campaign workers visited each house. The party that canvasses will win much of the total vote.

Both California party chairmen agree this is key. Door knocking, says Torres, was what gave Loretta Sanchez her nearly 1,000-vote edge. His GOP counterpart, Schroeder, says, "You have to work it manually. Someone in the community has to stand up and say, 'I am a Republican.'" Schroeder is working hard to lay out the welcome mat for Latinos (despite his own position as Dornan's lawyer). Among his many efforts, he organized a statewide outreach appeal that drew 500 community leaders to a meeting last fall.

And California Republicans plan to attack Democrats in key districts. An NRHA project called Voto Dos Mil, or Vote 2000, which is intended to attract Latino voters to the GOP for the next presidential election, calls for concentrating in 16 areas where Democrats are considered vulnerable in the state.

Other high-profile Republicans are also in tune with the Latino vote. In Texas, Gov. George W. Bush has been outspoken against immigrant bashing. And there's New York Mayor Rudolph Giuliani, who has aggressively positioned himself as a champion of immigrant rights.

On the other coast, Richard Riordan, the mayor of Los Angeles, took 60 percent of the Latino vote when he ran for re-election in 1997. Riordan, a moderate who ranks high with voters on the issues of crime, business, and education, has stayed away from California's anti-immigrant fray. His election marked the first time that more Latinos than African Americans voted. Significantly, their vote split from the black vote, which went to Tom Hayden, the Democratic candidate.

"Giuliani and Riordan show all bets are off," says Antonio Gonzalez, president of the Southwest Voter Registration Education Project. "Right now you have an infusion into the Democratic Party, in places where

> *There is a secret to connecting with Latino voters: old-fashioned, door-to-door contact. Rather than responding to slick TV ads and mailings, Latinos, more than any other group, respond to personal politics.*

the immigration stuff is happening." But this, he warns, will change when the immigration debate dies down. "I see Latinos being split up."

Indeed, America's Latino immigrants may prove to be less like their turn-of-the-century Irish and Italian counterparts, who, at least for a generation, stayed with the Democratic Party. Rather, their party affiliation may more rapidly divide along class lines, and the question is whether Democrats and Republicans will wake up to this reality.

Dale Maharidge is the author of The Coming White Minority: California's Eruptions and the Nation's Future. *His last article for* Mother Jones, *"California Schemer," was a profile of Gov. Pete Wilson that appeared in the November/December 1995 issue.*

The *Economist*

Democracy in Texas:

The Frontier Spirit

Mirabeau Lamar, the second president of the Republic of Texas back in the 1830s, declared that "the cultivated mind is the guiding genius of democracy." James Fishkin, a professor of government at today's University of Texas, would like to prove that Lamar was right. Mr Fishkin proposes to introduce to American politics the idea of "deliberative polling". This is a process that would draw together a representative group of ordinary people, have them listen to all sides of an issue, and then cast their considered votes on behalf of their fellow citizens. He claims that the ancient Athenians used a similar system. Would it not be wonderful, Mr Fishkin muses, to resurrect the idea in a world where opinion polls are still merely a quick, come on, yes-or-no snapping up of instant reactions?

Instead of asking a random sample of people to decide instantaneously whether they think America should bomb Iraq, Mr Fishkin would invite his representatives to spend a weekend learning the basics of American foreign policy, of Iraqi politics and of military power. He would let them put their questions to experts, and debate the matter among themselves. Then he would ask them for their answer. That is responsible voting—the guiding genius, he argues, of democracy.

Deliberative polling has already been taken up by the more sober television stations. The Public Broadcasting System has commissioned such polls for presidential elections. It is in Texas, however, that deliberative polling is first dipping its toe into the waters of actual decision-making. The state's Public Utility Commission (PUC) has ruled that Texas's power companies must consult their customers about what the companies plan to do. To do this, the companies have turned to deliberative polling. "Initially I was skeptical," says Pat Wood, the chairman of the PUC, "but the results have been extraordinary."

How is it done? After selecting his representative sample, Mr. Fishkin provides them with a free weekend in a fancy hotel and a little money for expenses. They then go to school on the issues. Where electricity is concerned, you might thing this would be rather tedious. Yet the participants at a recent deliberative poll in Houston seemed genuinely enthralled to be given a voice. Their attention spans were prodigious; your correspondent nodded off several times, only to find on waking up that his companions were still bright-eyed and taking notes. The spirit of Frank Capra descended on one group when a verbose executive was asked to hush himself so that a teenage single mother could have her say.

Mirabeau Lamar would have liked the Houston proceedings. His "cultivation of minds" was done in small groups, so that everyone could be heard. The groups were led by trained chairmen who made sure that all sides of the question got addressed. "There are no wrong answers," everybody was told; this helped to keep the discussion surprisingly civil. Once they have learned the difference between gas and coal as sources of energy, the members of these little groups can put their questions to heavyweights like a utilities commissioner or the local power company's chief executive. "They have to feel that they are there to make a difference," says Mr Fishkin.

And they have. The Lone Star state is far more environmentally sensitive than most people had supposed. Texans want more renewable energy, from sources like wind and sun, and are willing to pay to get it.

Before its weekend, the Houston group did not want to reach into its pockets for renewable energy or for energy-efficiency schemes. After hearing all sides of the story, group members were prepared to add an average of $6.50 to their monthly bill for renewable energy and $3 for efficiency schemes. In Corpus Christi, the next city down the coast, 78% of those taking part in a similar exercise said they would be willing to pay a supplement for green energy. At the most recent deliberative poll, in Beaumont, near the Louisiana state line, support for renewables rose from 37% to 68% in the course of the proceedings.

It adds up to a vigorous prod in the ribs for the PUC. Mr Wood says he will try to give Texas's electricity customers the choice of buying green power. Already the interest in renewables has led to the construction of windmills in flat west Texas, paid for by supplementary charges.

Electricity is not the end of the the matter. Mr Fishkin wants to improve the "town hall" style of democracy President Clinton is so fond of. "For the first time in 2,400 years," he says, "a random sample of the population is being used to hear the voice of the people." The lobbyists are taking nervous note of all this. Already the coal lobby is said to be looking at ways of trying to discredit the results of deliberative polls. If they fail, the idea could spread into many other fields. And fail they may. Texans seem to enjoy being on the frontier of new ideas.

MONICA LEWINSKY'S CONTRIBUTION TO POLITICAL SCIENCE*

By John R. Zaller, University of California, Los Angeles

The bounce in President Clinton's job ratings that occurred in the initial 10 days of the Lewinsky imbroglio may offer as much insight into the dynamics of public opinion as any single event in recent memory. What it shows is not just the power of a booming economy to buttress presidential popularity. It shows, more generally, the importance of political substance, as against media hype, in American politics. Even when, as occurred in this case, public opinion is initially responsive to media reports of scandal, the public's concern with actual political achievement reasserts itself. This lesson, which was not nearly so clear before the Lewinsky matter as it is now, not only deepens our understanding of American politics. It also tends, as I argue in the second half of this article, to undermine the importance of one large branch of public opinion research, buttress the importance of another, and point toward some new research questions.

Whatever else may have transpired by the time this article gets into print, the Lewinsky poll bounce is something worth pondering. In a half-dozen commercial polls taken in the period just before the story broke, Clinton's job approval rating averaged about 60%. Ten days later, following intensive coverage of the story and Clinton's State of the Union address, presidential support was about 10 percentage points higher.[1] The fact that no analyst of public opinion could have credibly predicted this outcome makes the poll bounce especially important to examine. It is, in statistical parlance, a high leverage case.

I begin my analysis with an attempt to establish the parameters of the initial public response to the Lewinsky matter. Toward this end, the results of some three dozen commercial polls, gleaned from published sources, are summarized in Table 1. Although question wordings differ somewhat, all poll results refer to approval of Clinton's job performance as president. Also reported in Table 1 are the results of a content analysis of network TV news coverage during this period.

The content analysis, as shown in the top three rows of the table, gives average minutes of each network news program that were favorable or unfavorable to Clinton. Favorable references include Clinton's denials, attacks on Independent Prosecutor Ken Starr, statements of support for Clinton, and any other information (including non-scandal information) that might tend to enhance public support for the president. Unfavorable references include all statements indicating that the president had an affair with Lewinsky or tried to cover it up, attacks on Clinton or defense of Starr, and any other information that might tend to undermine public support for Clinton. I emphasize that, although journalists played a major role in creating the Lewinsky imbroglio, other actors, notably politicians, initiated some of the information that was reported. What the content analysis shows is that the frenzy began with two days of heavily negative coverage, but that coverage was relatively balanced after that (given that the matter continued to attract media attention at all). In fact, if the first two days are removed, the remaining period has about as many positive minutes as negative ones, including two days on which Clinton's coverage was decidedly positive.

I have divided the poll data into four partially overlapping periods. As the table indicates, the first two days of heavily negative scandal reportage had a considerable impact on public opinion. On the basis

From *PS: Political Science & Politics* (June 1998), pp. 182–189. Reprinted by permission from *PS: Political Science and Politics*. Copyright © 1998.

TABLE 1
Trends in Presidential Job Approval in the Initial Phase of the Lewinsky Matter

	Pre-event Baseline	Jan. 21 Story Breaks	22	23	24	25	26	27 Before Speech	27 After Speech	28	29	30	31	Feb. 1	Change
TV News Content															
Positive news minutes		0.7	2.0	4.2	2.5	2.4	2.9	4.9	—	4.6	1.9	4.0			
Negative news minutes		7.9	8.3	5.3	5.2	1.6	5.3	3.4	—	1.5	2.4	2.4			
Net news (positive minus negative)		−7.2	−6.3	−1.1	−2.8	+0.8	−2.5	+1.5		+3.1	−0.4	+1.6			
Phase I: Initial Frenzy (first two days)															
NBC News	62 (1/18/98)	61													−1
CBS News-*NYT*	58 (1/18)	55													−3
ABC News	62 (1/13)				57										−6
Time/CNN	59 (1/15)			52											−7
Newsweek	61 (1/18)			54											−7
Gallup	60 (1/18)				58										−2
ABC News-*Wash. Post*	59 (1/19)				51										−8
Phase II: Charge & Counter-charge (up to State of Union)															
NBC			61			61	63								+2
CBS News/*NYT*			55		56	56	57								+2
ABC News					57	59	60								+3
Gallup					58	60	59	67							+9
Phase III: State of Union address															
ABC News							60		60						0
NBC							63		68						+5
CBS News (respondents telephoned ahead to watch speech)									73						16?
Phase IV: Coverage of State of Union address															
Gallup								67		67			69		+2
CBS News							57			73			72		+15
ABC News							60				68	69			+9
Los Angeles Times					59							68			+9
Time/CNN				52							68				+16
Averages:	60	58	53	56	59	60	67	67	70	68	69	68	72		

Note: For sources of polls, see a PC Excel 5.0 file labeled "Lewpols" on my webpage, http://www.sscnet.ucla.edu/polisci/faculty/zaller/. Sizes and designs of polls vary.

of a half-dozen polls, Clinton's public support seems to have dropped about six or seven points.[2]

The scandal broke on a Wednesday, with the most heavily negative coverage on that day and Thursday. From Friday on, coverage was more balanced and public support for the president rose. By Monday, Clinton had regained everything lost in the first two days, and in Tuesday's Gallup poll, support for the President rose above pre-Lewinsky levels. There were two notable events in this period, both of which were amply reported on TV news. The first was Clinton's appearance on camera on Monday to make an emotional denial of a sexual relationship with Lewinsky; the other was Hillary Clinton's appearance on NBC's *Today Show* on Tuesday morning, where she charged the existence of a right-wing conspiracy against her husband.

If there is any particular spike in the data, it is the Tuesday Gallup poll, which was taken between six and nine in the evening and was therefore able to reflect news of Hillary Clinton's appearance on the *Today Show* that morning. Indeed, the poll was taken just as or just after many Americans were getting news of Mrs. Clinton's appearance; it may therefore, as other polls hint, have overstated its lasting importance on opinion. This poll showed a gain of eight percentage points from the day before, a difference that is statistically significant on a two-tailed test.[3]

Clinton's State of the Union address occurred on Tuesday evening, the end of the seventh day since the Lewinsky story broke. The speech attracted an unusually large audience, presumably because people wanted to see how the crisis-stricken President would perform. According to virtually all the pundits, he performed extremely well. "Good speech, too bad," as one commentator put it.[4]

Two national surveys were taken immediately after the speech. From baselines on the day before the speech—and therefore before Hillary Clinton's charge of right-wing conspiracy—one survey showed no change and the other showed a gain of five points, for an average gain of 2.5%.[5] There was also a CBS poll involving reinterviews with a panel of respondents who had been asked by telephone to watch the speech so that they could be polled afterward. This survey found that Clinton's post-speech job approval rating was 73%. No immediate prespeech base line for this poll is available, but if we take the best baseline we have—Clinton's 57% job approval in the CBS-New York Times poll from the day before the speech—then the combination of the speech and Mrs. Clinton's defense netted the president some 16 percentage points in support.

A little back-of-the-envelope arithmetic shows that these two sets of post-speech results—an average 2.5% gain in two polls and a 16 point gain among those asked to watch the speech—are not as far apart as they might seem. According to the Nielsen research firm, 53.1 million Americans saw the speech ("TV Ratings for Speech," 1998). This is a lot of people, but only about 25% of the adult population. If 16% of the 25% who watched the speech became more supportive of the president the overall increase in public support would be only 4.0 percentage points ($.16 \times .25 = .04$). If we assume that viewership of the speech was higher than 25% among those asked to watch it in preparation for a survey but still well under 100%, there is no real disagreement among the three polls on the size of the "speech plus Hillary" effect.

From the bottom panel of Table 1, it appears that public support for Clinton rose another three or so points after the State of the Union, perhaps in response to favorable news coverage of that event. But this gain, if real, is apparently small in relation to gains that had already occurred.

It is tempting to pursue more detailed analyses of particular events, but I have already pressed dangerously close to the limits of the data. Instead, I will step back and offer a somewhat less detailed and, I therefore hope, safer summary: In response to sharply negative media coverage of the Lewinsky matter, public support for the president fell. But support rebounded and then surpassed its initial level as the president, his wife, and their allies fought back.

One point seems especially clear and important: In the period in which Clinton's support fell about 7 percentage points, media coverage was sharply negative, but in the period in which he gained back those 7 points and added an additional 8 to 10 points of support, coverage was essentially balanced. Thus, while media coverage of the Lewinsky matter explains part of the opinion change that occurred, it cannot explain all of it. In particular, the notion that the public responded mechanically to media coverage cannot explain how Clinton ended up with higher job approval ratings than he began with. Additional explanation is needed.

An obvious possibility is to argue that the public makes a distinction between approving the way the president does his job and approving of the president as a person. There is, as it happens, some evidence for this view, but not a great deal. The president's personal favorability ratings fell more sharply than his job approval ratings and also recovered less well. In three NBC News polls, Clinton's favorability ratings were 57% before the Lewinsky matter broke, 40% after three days of scandal coverage, and 50% after the State of the Union. In what is apparently the only other set of surveys that made three such soundings of opinion, Time-CNN found that Clinton's favorability ratings went from 60% to 50% and then back to 60%.[6]

These data on favorability seem to me to do little to alleviate the mystery of Clinton's bounce in job approval ratings, since they show essentially the same trend. Even if we were examining the favorability data alone, we would still be hard-pressed to explain why Clinton, who looked nothing like a teflon president when he was pressing for gays in the military and health reform, stood up to the scandal coverage as well as he did. Nor could we explain why, amidst continued media attention to scandal, he actually recouped most of his initial loss.

Another argument might be that Clinton's specific defense against the allegations of sex and cover-up was simply very persuasive. But I find this hard to swallow—not because I disbelieve Clinton, but because he presented so little evidence to support his side and got so little support from witnesses that were in a position to give it. In particular, Clinton got no help from Lewinsky herself, who was semi-publicly negotiating a plea bargain with the independent prosecutor throughout this period. As I parse Clinton's defense, it has consisted of two flat assertions: "I didn't do it" and "my enemies are out to get me."

If the public believed this defense, it was because it wanted to. I suggest, therefore, that we consider the political context that presumably made the public want to believe Clinton's defense, namely, his record of achievement in office. Clinton made an excellent statement of this record in his State of the Union address. Although the address reached too few people and came too late to explain the bulk of Clinton's recovery in the polls, it is reasonable to suppose that the presidential record that the speech touted was well known to the majority of the public.

Clinton's speech was, first of all, a celebration of a list of "accomplishments" that would be any

TABLE 2
The Effect of Peace, Prosperity, and Moderation on Presidential Vote, 1948–1996

	B	S.E.	Two-sided p-value
War (52, 68=1, else=0)	−4.5	2.3	.04
Real Disposable Income[a] (range: 0% to 7.7%)	2.1	0.40	.001
Relative Extremism (see text)	−3 3	1.0	.005
Constant	43.6		
Adjusted r-square	.77		
N=	13		

Note: Dependent variable is percentage of the two-party vote for the incumbent party candidate.
[a] From Survey of Current Business, August, 1997, Table 4, p. 164–67.

president's dream: The economy was the strongest in 25 years, the federal budget was on the verge of balance for the first time in 20 years, crime was falling for the first time in living memory, and the country was at peace. In the main section of the speech, the president proposed a series of programs designed to appeal to the ideological center, as exemplified by a plan to use surplus funds to put Social Security on a sound footing, improve public education, and build more highways. Thus, what the president trumpeted in his speech—and what he would presumably continue by remaining in office—was a record of peace, prosperity, and moderation. Or, more succinctly, it was a record of "political substance." This record was so unassailable that, to much of what the president said in the State of the Union, the Republican leadership could only offer polite applause.

Can political substance, thus defined, move public opinion? Certainly it can. Thanks to a distinguished series of studies—including Key (1966), Kramer (1971), Mueller (1971), Fiorina (1981), and Rosenstone (1983) —political scientists have been aware of the importance of "bottom line" politics for sometime. Brody's (1991) work on presidential popularity, which stresses the effects of "outcomes" news coverage on approval, points in the same direction. In light of this, it seems entirely plausible to suggest that the poll bounce that Clinton got at the time of the Lewinsky matter was driven by the same thing that drives presidential election outcomes and presidential popularity in general—political substance. It was not admiration for Bill Clinton's character that first buttressed and then boosted his approval ratings. It was the public's reaction to the delivery of outcomes and policies that the public wants.

This argument is much more than a claim that "It's the economy, stupid." In fact, Clinton's economic performance has been only middling through most

of his presidency. Taking the average four-year growth in Real Disposable Income (RDI) for every president elected from 1948 on, Clinton's first term economy ranks tenth of 13. If presidential terms are rank-ordered by growth in the 12-month period prior to Election Day, Clinton's first term is still a mediocre tenth of 13 since World War II. Only recently has Clinton's economic performance become as strong as he described it in his State of the Union.

If Clinton's economy cannot by itself explain why he won by nine percentage points over Bob Dole in 1996, neither can it explain trends in his approval ratings. One big but easy-to-overlook factor is peace, which is a virtual prerequisite for popular support. Popular support for Presidents Truman and Johnson was so damaged by bloody wars that, despite reasonably good economies, they chose not to run for reelection.[7] Clinton's administration has not only avoided war, it has enjoyed a very notable success in Bosnia, for which the President was nominated for a Nobel Peace Prize.

The other big and also easy-to overlook plus for Clinton is his ideological moderation. This is a factor that scholars, with the exceptions of Rosenstone (1983) and Alesina, et al. (1993), have too often ignored. Let me first show anecdotally how moderation affected Clinton's support and then, insofar as possible, make a systematic case.

Since gays in the military and the debacle of health care reform, Clinton has hewed to centrist policies, including ones, like welfare reform (and NAFTA earlier on), that are hard for Democratic presidents to endorse. In his confrontation with the Republican Congress over balancing the budget, it was the president, rather than the Republicans, who held middle ground. And finally, after two decades of massive budget deficits, the president has, by means of an initially unpopular budget package in his first term, helped bring the centrist goal of a balanced budget within apparent grasp.

Consistent with the notion that moderation matters is this fragment of hard evidence: President Clinton's approval ratings were weaker at the midpoint of his first term, when the economy was stronger but he identified himself with noncentrist policies, than at the end of his first term, when the economy was weaker but he had remade himself as a policy moderate. Clinton's average job approval rating in Gallup polls taken in the sixth, seventh, and eighth quarters averaged 44.3% and the average percent change in RDI in these same quarters was 4.7%. In quarters fourteen through sixteen, these figures were 55.5% and 1.5%.

Systematic evidence that policy moderation affects presidential popularity is, as far as I know,

PART 4 – PUBLIC OPINION AND POLITICAL PARTICIPATION

non-existent. But as regards presidential elections, the evidence, though limited, is clear. The only published evidence comes from Rosenstone's *Forecasting Presidential Elections* (1983), which finds centrism to be a major determinant of cross-state and cross-time voting. In another cut at this problem, my research assistant rated each of the candidates in elections from 1948 to 1996 on a seven-point scale, running from liberal (+3) to conservative (−3). The ratings of each pair of candidates were then summed to produce a measure of relative distance from the center—i.e., a measure of relative extremism—such that higher scores indicated greater relative distance from the midpoint by the candidate of the incumbent party. For example, Lyndon Johnson was rated +2 in 1964 and Barry Goldwater as −3, so that Goldwater was one point further from the center than Johnson. Obviously, such ratings are subject to error and bias. But I note that they were developed in connection with another project (press bias in presidential primaries), and that they correlate highly with the ratings of Rosenstone with which they overlap. These ratings also correlate well with a new set of ideological location scores produced by Poole (forthcoming) for presidential candidates who earlier served in Congress.[8]

The results for a standard voting model are shown in Table 2. War is coded as "1" in 1952 and 1968 and "0" otherwise. Economic performance is measured as average percent change in RDI in the four quarters prior to the election; that is, in the 12th through 15th quarters of each term. As examination of the regression coefficients in Table 2 shows, ideological extremism rivals economic performance as a determinant of vote for the incumbent party. Being one point closer to the center on a seven-point ideology scale (as Johnson was in 1964) is worth about 3 percentage points of the vote; by way of comparison, each additional percent of growth in RDI is worth about 2.1 percentage points. Finally, war costs the incumbent party about 4.5 percentage points of the vote.[9]

From all this I conclude that peace, prosperity, and moderation very heavily influence the dynamics of presidential support, probably in matters of presidential popularity and certainly in general elections, for Clinton as well as for other presidents. What the Lewinsky bounce adds to this conclusion is confidence. Although evidence of the importance of political substance has been accumulating for some three decades, no one could have predicted that Clinton would survive the opening round of the Lewinsky affair nearly so well as he did. This is because it has never been quite so starkly clear just how relentlessly the majority of voters can stay focused on the bottom line. Nor, to my knowledge, has it ever been quite so clear that it is possible for public opinion and media opinion to go marching off in opposing directions.

To argue, as I am, that the public stays focused on a bottom line consisting of peace, prosperity, and moderation is not to say that the public is either wise or virtuous. For one thing, its sense of substance seems, in the aggregate, rather amoral—usually more like "what have you done for me lately" than "social justice." Nor is it clear that its decision criteria are very sophisticated. Suppose, for example, that the Watergate investigation of Richard Nixon had taken place in the context of Bill Clinton's booming economy rather than, as was the case, in the context of gasoline shortages and "stagflation" (the combination of high inflation and high unemployment). Would Nixon have been forced from office under these circumstances? Or, if Clinton were saddled with Nixon's economy, would Clinton be, at this point, on the verge of impeachment? These are, I believe, real questions, and the fact that they are does not speak well for the public's wisdom or virtue.

Perhaps future events will shed clearer light on these questions. From the vantage point of early April, when this essay is being finalized, I am keenly aware that issues relating to Lewinsky, Whitewater, and Paula Jones have by no means reached a conclusion. If clear evidence of sexual harassment, perjury, or obstruction of justice emerges, the public might still turn on Clinton. If so, one's judgment of public opinion would need to be more favorable: It waits for clear evidence before reaching a verdict, and it is, after all, concerned with higher values. My personal hunch, however, is that public support for Clinton will be more affected by future performance of the economy than by the clarity of the evidence concerning the charges against him.

I said in opening this article, the Lewinsky affair buttresses some work in political science and undermines the importance of other work. The tradition of studies on economic and retrospective voting, which maintains that the public responds to the substance of party performance, seems strengthened by the Lewinsky matter. On the other hand, the tradition of studies that focuses on the mass media, political psychology, and elite influence, including such diverse studies as Edelman's *Symbolic Uses of Politics* (1964) and my own *Nature and Origins of Mass Opinion* (1992), seems somewhat weaker. It is reasonable to contend that the ground has shifted beneath these two traditions in a way that scholars will need to accommodate. However poorly informed, psychologically driven, and "mass mediated" public opinion may be, it is capable of recognizing and focusing on its own conception of what matters. This is not a conclusion that comes naturally to the second tradition.

Let me amplify the nature of the aspersion I have just cast. A major development in American politics in the last 50 to 100 years has been the rise of what has been variously called *The Rhetorical Presidency* (Tulis 1987), the "political spectacle" (Edelman 1988) and, more simply, Media Politics. This form of politics stands in contrast to an older model of politics, Party Politics. The defining feature of what I prefer to call Media Politics is *the attempt to govern on the basis of words and images that diffuse through the mass media.* This communication—whether in the form of presidential speeches, press conferences, TV ads, media frenzies, spin, or ordinary news—creates a sort of virtual reality whose effects are arguably quite real and important. Typical of the attitude that prevails in this style of politics is Republican strategist Frank Luntz's assessment of the events I have just analyzed: "The problem with [the Lewinsky matter] is we are not going to learn the real impact for years. . . . It's going to leave an indelible mark on our psyche but I don't know what the mark will be . . ." (quoted in Connolly and Edsall 1998). Freely translated, what Luntz is saying is: "It may take us in the spin business a little time to figure out how to play this, but you can be sure we'll keep it alive until we come up with something that works for our side."

As a Republican strategist, Luntz has an obvious partisan interest in taking this view. But his occupational interest is equally great. He and his colleagues in both parties have an interest in "constructing" a public discourse in which events like the Lewinsky affair are important and in which political substance—in the sense of peace, prosperity, and moderation—is unimportant, except insofar as it is useful to emphasize it.

A sizeable part of political science has organized itself to study this new political style. My analysis of the Lewinsky affair, however, suggests that political science not go too far down this road, since old-fashioned political substance of the kind that party competition brings to the fore is not only thriving in the media age, but quite likely still dominant.

This is not to say that the new style of Media Politics is without importance. If only for the resources it consumes and the public attention it commands, Media Politics matters. More, perhaps, than we would like, Media Politics defines our political culture. But beyond that, the effects of Media Politics on political outcomes must be demonstrated on a case-by-case basis, because sometimes the effects are real and lasting and other times they are not.

One illuminating example of Media Politics that produced lasting effects is Gerald Ford's pardon of Richard Nixon in 1974. Coverage of the event was, of course, overwhelmingly negative. On the basis of the same coding categories as in Table 1, Ford got 11 minutes of negative coverage on the network news on the night following the pardon, as against two minutes of positive coverage. The next night, these figures were 10 and 2 minutes. Reporters were by no means the only source of the bad news. In the first two news days after the pardon, 12 Democratic members of Congress, including the House Speaker and Senate Majority Leader, were quoted on the network news attacking Ford, and within the first week the Democratic Congress passed a resolution condemning the pardon. Three Republican leaders also criticized Ford. In these circumstances, Ford's approval rating fell 17 percentage points in the first two days and about 30 points over the longer run.

The contrast with the Lewinsky case is striking. In the first two days of this case, only three Republican members of Congress, none from the leadership, were willing to be quoted on network TV news attacking Clinton—and not for want of opportunity. Reporters were scouring Capitol Hill for volunteers, but politicians (including Democratic politicians) were playing it safe. Thus, the media were forced to shoulder a much larger part of the Lewinsky story on their own. In these quite different circumstances, Clinton suffered limited short-term damage and made gains over the longer run.

It is a tempting conclusion that when the partisan opposition joins a media frenzy, the two together can move public opinion, but that the media alone cannot do it. But even if systematic research were to establish that this pattern is general, there would still be an obvious concern: Namely, that opposition politicians attack when they see an opportunity to score points and hold fire otherwise. By this account, Democratic politicians attacked Ford because they knew the attacks would play well, but Republican politicians refrained from attacking Clinton because they feared the attacks would backfire. If this argument is considered plausible, as I think it must be, it further underscores the central claim of this essay: That American politics tends to be driven more by political substance—in this case, public disapproval of the pardon of Nixon—than by the antics of Media Politics. It also points to a difficult future research problem: Sorting out whether partisan attacks and other media messages are the causes of public attitudes or their hidden (i.e., endogenous) effects. Surely, the answer is some of both.

Another media frenzy from the Ford administration is worth a brief look. When Ford stated in the second presidential debate that "there is no Soviet domination of Eastern Europe," the mass audience hardly noticed but reporters instantly saw the remark as a gaffe. Polls showed that, citizens polled immediately after the debate judged 44% to 33% that Ford had won. Once the media frenzy of this famous gaffe had run its course, however, the public's judgment was reversed: Several days after the debate, the public thought by a margin of 62–17% that Carter had won. More significantly, Ford also lost ground in straw poll surveys on how people intended to vote. But by about 10 days later, Ford's poll standing had recovered and the gaffe was left for political scientists to ponder (Chaffee and Sears 1979; Sabato 1993, 127–29).

According to a study by Daron Shaw (1995), this pattern is typical. Media frenzies over gaffes and alleged gaffes in presidential campaigns do affect public support for the candidates, but only briefly. The time it takes public opinion to bounce back may, as in the Ford example, disrupt a candidate's momentum and perhaps thereby affect the election, but the lasting direct effect of most media frenzies tends to be nil.

One way to think about this pattern is to assume that there is some "natural" level of support for candidates that is determined by political fundamentals such as the strength of the economy, the candidates' positions on issues, and other such matters. Media frenzies can briefly undermine a candidate's natural level support, but cannot permanently lower it. Thus, what happened to Clinton in the Lewinsky matter is similar to what happens to candidates who misstep in elections; he recovered from the initial attack. The fact that Clinton gained back more support than he lost is harder to explain in these terms, but I offer the following conjecture: In non-electoral periods, the public tunes out from politics, failing, *inter alia*, to keep its evaluation of presidential performance fully up-to-date. But when, as in the early days of the Lewinsky matter, Clinton's capacity to remain in office came into question, the public took stock and reached a conclusion that led to higher levels of overall support for the threatened leader.

These observations suggest a rough generalization about when media frenzies have lasting effects on opinion and when they don't: The closer media frenzies get to what I am calling political substance, the more likely the effects are to be lasting. The example of Ford's pardon of Nixon would seem to fit this pattern. To take one other example, it seems likely that sympathetic press coverage of attacks by racist southerners on peaceful civil rights protesters in the 1960s had an important effect on northern opinion and thereby congressional action. This was exactly what the Rev. Martin Luther King Jr. expected to happen, and it had lasting importance.

One lesson for political science from the Lewinsky poll bounce, then, is that more attention needs to be given to the general question of when Media Politics (in the sense of trying to mobilize public support through mass communication) matters and when it doesn't, and to do so in a manner that doesn't presuppose the answer. A current research project of Larry Bartels shows how this can be done: With a measure of the "real economy" from the Commerce Department and a measure of the "media economy" from content analysis of media coverage, he hopes to find out which has more influence on presidential approval. Among the auxiliary variables whose impact on presidential approval he will assess is the white-collar unemployment rate in Manhattan. The results will be interesting however they come out.

Another lesson for political science from the Lewinsky poll bounce is that the public is, within broad limits, functionally indifferent to presidential character. "Don't Ask, Don't Tell," as my colleague Art Stein summarizes the mass attitude. Given this, it seems appropriate to consider carefully whether research on the public's assessment of presidential character really helps us to understand the dynamics of American politics.

Contrary to this suggestion, it might be argued that private sexual misbehavior is different from public character, especially in light of changing sexual mores in this area, and that voters' assessments of public character will remain important. Perhaps. But if we view the character issue more broadly, it seems unlikely that voter concern about character has ever been very great. For example, Richard Nixon's peculiar shortcomings were deeply felt by a large number of voters from the moment he stepped onto the national stage in the 1940s. Further, the concerns about Nixon's public character were more serious than any that have been raised about Clinton's. Yet Nixon was elected to the presidency twice, once over Hubert Humphrey, a man whose sterling character has been almost universally acknowledged. Nixon's campaign against Humphrey was, of course, framed by urban riots and a stalemated war in Asia, and in these circumstances, Nixon chose to emphasize substance rather than character. "When you're in trouble," he told voters, "you don't turn to the men who got you in trouble to get you out of it. I say we can't be led in the '70s by the men who stumbled in the 60's."[10] Voters agreed with this emphasis, as they almost always do.

NOTES

*Thanks to Larry Bartels, Dick Brody, Mo Fiorina, Fred Greenstein, John Petrocik, and Daron Shaw for advice on early drafts of this paper.
1. Documentation of the sources of polls cited in this paper may be found in a PC Excel 5.0 file labeled "Lewpols" on

my web page (www.sscnet.ucla.edu/polisci/faculty/zaller). The polls used in determining the overall effect of the Lewinsky matter are: ABC News-*Washington Post*, January 19 and 31, job approval rates of 59% and 67%; ABC News, January 13 and 30, job approval of 62% and 69%; CBS News, January 18 and February 1, 58% and 72%, *Newsweek*, January 18 and 30, 61% and 70%, Time-CNN, January 15 and 31, 59% and 72%; *U.S. News and World Report*, January 11 and February 1, 58% and 66%. In cases in which polling occurred over several days, the date given is for the final day. Although wordings of the questions differ, all refer more or less directly to Clinton's job performance rather than to the Lewinsky matter *per se*.

2. Gallup conducted a poll on the afternoon of the first day of the episode, prior to the evening news. This poll showed Clinton's support rising to 62% from 60% two days earlier. However, I do not count this poll on the grounds that, although the story had broken at the time of the poll, few Americans could yet have learned about it.

3. The sizes of the two surveys were 864 and 672.

4. Peter Jennings, quoting an anonymous politician.

5. The baseline for the ABC poll was actually January 25–26, with a sample of 1023. The size of the ABC postspeech survey was 528. The NBC pre- and postspeech surveys both have reported sizes of 405.

6. For sources of these and other favorability polls, see the PC Excel file labeled "Lewpols" on my webpage (www.sscnet.ucla.edu/polisci/faculty/zaller).

7. President Bush showed that short, successful wars that cost few American lives do not harm popularity; but neither are they much help over the longer run.

8. Full details of the ideological coding are available upon request.

9. Though going beyond the direct evidence, this analysis suggests that Clinton's confrontation with Congress over the budget in early 1996, in which he reestablished his reputation as a defender of centrist policies, may have been as important to his November win as the economy.

10. Quoted in *Newsweek*, November 4, 1968, p. 28.

REFERENCES

Alesina, Alberto, John Londregan, and Howard Rosenthal. 1993. "A Model of the Political Economy of the United States."*American Political Science Review* 87(1): 12–33.

Brody, Richard. 1991. *Assessing the President: The Media, Elite Opinion, and Public Support*. Stanford: Stanford University Press.

Chaffee, Steven, and David Sears. 1979. "Uses and Effects of the 1976 Presidential Debates: An Overview of Empirical Studies."In *The Great Debates: Carter vs. Ford*, ed. Sidney Kraus. Bloomington: University of Indiana Press.

Connolly, Cecil, and Thomas B. Edsall. 1998. "Political Pros Looking for Explanations: Public Reaction Seems to Rewrite the Rules." *Washington Post*, February 9, A6.

Edelman, Murray. 1964. *Symbolic Uses of Politics*. Urbana: University of Illinois Press.

————. 1988. *Constructing the Political Spectacle*. Chicago: University of Chicago Press.

Fiorina, Morris. 1981. *Retrospective Voting in American National Elections*. New Haven: Yale University Press.

Key, V. O. Jr. 1966. *The Responsible Electorate: Rationality in Presidential Voting, 1936–60*. New York: Vintage.

Kramer, Gerald H. 1971. "Short-Term Fluctuations in U.S. Voting Behavior. 1896–1964." *American Political Science Review* 65(l):131–43.

Mueller, John. 1973. *War, Presidents, and Public Opinion*. New York: Wiley.

Poole, Keith. Forthcoming. "Recovering a Basic Space from a Set of Issue Scales." *American Journal of Political Science* 42(August).

Rosenstone, Steven. 1983. *Forecasting Presidential Elections*. New Haven: Yale University Press

Sabato, Larry. 1983. *Feeding Frenzy: How Attack Journalism has Transformed American Politics*. New York: Free Press.

Shaw, Daron. 1995. "Strong Persuasion? The Effect of Campaigns in U. S. Presidential Elections." Ph.D diss. UCLA

Tulis, Jeffrey. 1987. *The Rhetorical Presidency*. Princeton: Princeton University Press.

"TV Ratings from Speech." 1998. *Los Angeles Times*, January 29, A11.

Zaller, John. 1992. *Nature and Origins of Mass Opinion*. Cambridge: Cambridge University Press.

John R. Zaller is coauthor (with Herb McClosky) of American Ethos (1984) *and author of* Nature and Origins of Mass Opinion (1992). *He is completing a book called* Theory of Media Politics: How the Interests of Politicians, Journalists, and Citizens Shape the News *(University of Chicago Press). He received his Ph.D. from the University of California, Berkeley in 1984.*

PART 5

The Mass Media

Today it seems that the media are as unpopular as politicians. Media bashing has become a pastime for liberals and conservatives alike.

Conservatives accuse the media of having a liberal bias. They point to surveys that show a majority of reporters and news anchors identify themselves as Democrats. Conservatives argue that the media exaggerate mistakes made by conservative politicians and downplay mistakes made by liberal politicians. They argue that the media has a pro-environment, pro-civil liberties, anti-business bias that affects both the types of stories they chose to cover and the manner in which those stories are covered.

Liberals accuse the media of having a conservative bias. Liberals point out that the mass media are owned by big businesses. They contend that although most reporters may be liberal, the reporters' *bosses* are wealthy conservatives. As a result, reporters avoid investigating stories that might be harmful to the economic interests of the upper classes.

Both liberals and conservatives agree on another criticism: that the media has become more interested in generating profits than in covering serious news. This profit motive leads to news that is sensationalistic, with an excessive focus on sex and violence. As a result, important but less titillating stories go unreported. The media's fixation on the Monica Lewinsky scandal is cited as evidence of this trend. The media defends itself by arguing that it is just giving the public what it wants.

As you read the following selections, think about whether the media is biased, and if so, in which direction. Also, who is responsible for creating these problems—the media or the public?

MONEY LUST

How Pressure For Profit is Perverting Journalism

By Neil Hickey

Some random testimony from the far-flung precincts of journalism:

- "If a story needs a real investment of time and money, we don't do it anymore." The speaker is a forty-something reporter on a mid-sized Illinois daily. "In assignment meetings, we dream up 'talker' stories, stuff that will attract attention and get us talked about, tidbits for busy folks who clip items from the paper and stick them on the fridge." He adds ruefully: "Who the hell cares about corruption in city government, anyway, much less dying Bosnians?"

- A prominent network television newsman complains: "Instead of racing out of the newsroom with a camera crew when an important story breaks, we're more likely now to stay at our desks and work the phones, rewrite the wire copy, hire a local crew and a free-lance producer to get pictures at the scene, then dig out some file footage, maps, or still photos for the anchor to talk in front of, or maybe buy some coverage from a video news service like Reuters, AP, or World Television News. If we had our own correspondent and camera covering the story, we'd damned sure get something nobody else had, and be proud of it. But everything now is dollars and cents. When you're worried about how much it's going to cost, and you have to justify your decisions to your bosses, people are less willing to take risks. The journalism that gets on our air just isn't good enough, and it's a damned shame."

- A radio news director laments that his big-city station is cutting its news staff to the bone, virtually eliminating local news, and grabbing national news from a satellite delivered network feed. "That immediately shows a big gain in cash flow, so the owner can sell the station for a huge profit to one of the big chains, whose owners care nothing about public service to this community. One more journalistic voice is being killed off in the pursuit of profits. It's very sad."

- The editor of a profitable national magazine who's been ordered to reduce his budget 10 percent a year says: "OK, the first year I'll cut stuff I probably should have cut earlier anyway. Next year I'll have to reduce the number of editorial pages in every issue. In the third year, for damned sure, it's got to be people that will have to go: editors, writers, fact-checkers, art department staff. Then I'll hit a wall. Sooner or later I will have so cheapened the product that it will just go out of business. That's simple arithmetic."

A new era has dawned in American journalism. A *New York Times* editor describes its hallmark: "A massively increased sensitivity to all things financial." As competition grows ever more ferocious; as the audience continues to drift away from traditional news sources, both print and television; as the public's confidence in news organizations and news people continues to decline; as mainstream print and TV news outlets purvey more "life-style" stories, trivia, scandal, celebrity gossip, sensational crime, sex in high places, and tabloidism at the expense of serious news in a cynical effort to maximize readership and viewership; as editors collude ever more willingly with marketers,

The new hallmark: "Increased sensitivity to all things financial"

promotion "experts," and advertisers, thus ceding a portion of their sacred editorial trust; as editors shrink from tough coverage of major advertisers lest they jeopardize ad revenue; as news holes grow smaller in column inches to cosmeticize the bottom line; as news executives cut muscle and sinew from budgets to satisfy their corporate overseers' demands for higher profit margins each year; as top managers fail to reinvest profits in staff training, investigative reports, salaries, plant, and equipment — then the broadly-felt consequence of those factors and many others, collectively, is a diminished and deracinated journalism of a sort that hasn't been seen in this country until now and which, if it persists, will be a fatal erosion of the ancient bond between journalists and the public.

"It's the biggest story in American journalism," says Ray Cave, former managing editor of *Time*. Regrettably, it's also the least reported story in American journalism.

Sandra Mims Rowe, editor of *The Oregonian* of Portland and former president of the American Society of Newspaper Editors, told the ASNE convention in April that reporters "wonder whether their editors have sold out journalistic values for business ones. They long for the inspiration provided by leaders with abiding passion for the gritty world of journalism." She added that in some companies, "the talk has shifted to financial and marketing imperatives to such an extent that journalists have concluded their owners are blindly driven by Wall Street, and unconcerned about the quality of journalism."

In March, *Los Angeles Times* media reporter David Shaw wrote that while newspaper readership has been on the skids for more than thirty years and competition from cable TV news, the Internet, and magazines is on the rise, "stockholders and stock analysts have been demanding newspaper profit margins equal to — and in some cases greater than — those generated in earlier, less turbulent times."

Television's corporate chieftains, says Walter Cronkite, show little understanding of "the responsibilities of being news disseminators." They expect the news departments to generate the same sort of profits that entertainment programs do — an impossible task. The newspaper business isn't much different, he says. "Stockholders in publicly held newspaper chains

are expecting returns similar to those they'd get investing in industrial enterprises."

The "tabloidization" of TV news-magazines is strictly geared to ratings and profits. "A major tragedy of the moment," Cronkite maintains, is the use TV newsmagazines are making of the valuable prime time they occupy. "Instead of offering tough documentaries and background on the issues that so deeply affect all of us, they're turning those programs into television copies of *Photoplay* magazine." News executives know better, Cronkite says, and are "uncomfortable" with what they're doing. "But they are helpless when top management demands an increase in ratings to protect profits."

News chiefs themselves perceive that the press is perilously compromising quality in pursuit of gain. Nearly half the nation's editorial and business-side executives surveyed in a January *Editor & Publisher* poll think press coverage in general is shallow and inadequate, and fully two-thirds say newspapers concentrate more on personalities than important issues. J. Stewart Bryan III, C.E.O. of Media General, Inc., and publisher of the *Richmond Times-Dispatch*, told *E&P* that serious news is being sacrificed to profits as papers reduce news holes and produce softer stories. Said he: "I don't think we can put the bottom line ahead of our commitment to quality."

Journalistic values haven't completely disappeared, says Kurt Andersen, columnist for *The New Yorker* and former editor of *New York* magazine. "But they've been significantly subordinated to the general ascendancy of market factors, especially the maximizing of short-term profit." Magazine editors, he points out, "are much more explicitly responsible for business success than in the past. I'm not saying it's black and white; some of that has always been there. It was light gray, now it's dark gray."

Profit-hunger: "The biggest story in American journalism"

Even Brenda Starr, the comic strip reporter, has gotten into the act. She lamented: "Sometimes I think newspapers care more about profits than they do about people."

After scores of wide-ranging interviews conducted over several months with editors, reporters, publishers, media analysts, academics, and labor officials, CJR concludes that — more so than at any other moment in journalism's history — the news product that lands on newsstands, doorsteps, and television screens is indeed hurt by a heightened, unseemly lust at many companies for ever greater profits. In the service of that ambition, many editors are surrendering part of their birthright to marketers and advertising directors, and making news judgments based on criteria that would have been anathema only a few years ago.

But haven't media barons always wanted to prosper, like any other businessmen? Winston Churchill, an unrepentant Tory, once said: "It is a socialist idea that making profits is a vice; I consider the real vice is making losses." Journalism isn't philanthropy — no profits, no press. Some recent tendencies, however, alter the landscape:

- More Americans than ever are shareholders in public companies of all kinds and corporate executives, including those at media corporations, are sensitive to the vastly expanded interests of those investors.

- Top managers in media own ever larger piles of stock options — often a heftier source of income than their salaries — and thus have a direct, personal interest in their companies' profit picture. Higher profits mean a higher stock price and a bigger payoff when they cash in their holdings. Says a TV producer: "The more they can squeeze out of their people, the richer they'll be in the end."

- In an age of rampant consolidations and mergers, clamping down on operating costs and budgets — no matter the effect on news coverage — can fatten the bottom line and make a company a more attractive takeover target, with the consequent heavy windfall to major shareholders.

- Bonuses tied to profits tempt both editorial and business-side executives to trim costs, often to the detriment of news processing.

At the University of Iowa, three professors — John Soloski, Gil Cranberg, and Randy Bezanson — are embarked on an eighteen-month project (funded by philanthropist George Soros's Open Society Institute) studying how ownership structures of newspapers are affecting journalistic function; and examining journalists' complaints that their interests and readers' interests are being sacrificed for the interests of shareholders. "Publicly traded media companies are in a vicious circle they can't break out of," says Soloski, director of the university's journalism school. A huge percentage of their stock is owned by institutions — mutual funds, retirement funds, insurance companies — which care little about the quality of the journalism of the companies they invest in. "Those financial institutions are graded weekly, monthly, quarterly on their own performance. So they pass that pressure along — and it's a lot — to those media companies." They in turn pressure their editors and publishers to

raise their stock price by whatever means necessary. The land rush to go public in the 1980s and 1990s has had its residual effect: investors and analysts demand the kind of profits that often can be attained by mid-level papers, but are tougher for big-city dailies.

In 1990, when Geneva Overholser, editor of *The Des Moines Register*, was named Gannett's "editor of the year," she offered these thoughts in her acceptance speech:

> . . . As we sweat out the end of the ever-increasing quarterly earnings, as we necessarily attend to the needs and wishes of our shareholders and our advertisers, are we worrying enough about . . . our employees, our readers, and our communities?
>
> I'll answer that: no way. . . . We fret over declining readership and then cut our news holes. . . . We fret over a decline in service to our customers, and then pay reporters . . . wages that school districts would be ashamed of. . . . [O]ur communities are crying out for solutions, and newspapers can help — newspapers that are adequately staffed, with adequate news holes. But not newspapers where underpaid people work too hard, and ad stacks squeeze out editorial copy. . . .
>
> Too often by far, being an editor in America today feels like holding up an avalanche of pressure to do away with this piece of excellence, that piece of quality, so as to squeeze out just a little bit more money.

"Publicly traded media companies are in a vicious circle"

Other signs of the profit-pressure syndrome were apparent three years ago when a dramatic series of shut downs, layoffs, strikes, and the emotional departures of top editors afflicted the newspaper industry. The Times Mirror Company killed the Baltimore *Evening Sun* and *New York Newsday*. Knight Ridder Inc. slashed 300 full-time jobs at *The Miami Herald* and won major labor concessions in return for keeping the *Philadelphia Daily News* going.

Some of the biggest editors in the business have quit rather than make budget cuts that they felt would devastate editorial. As editor-in-chief of *Reader's Digest*, Ken Tomlinson grew weary of repeated demands to chop editorial costs up to 10 percent annually, year after year. In late 1995, management ordered a company-wide reduction of roughly 25 per cent, largely by inducing many edit people to retire. Tomlinson didn't want to be remembered as the editor who carried out this action. So he told C.E.O. Jim Schadt, "I've found a way for you to take a giant step toward your goal. Eliminate my salary." And so Tomlinson retired at 52. (He now raises racehorses in rural Virginia; Schadt's strategy failed to ease the *Digest's* continuing problems and he later resigned under pressure.)

That same year, James M. Naughton resigned as executive editor of *The Philadelphia Inquirer*. Among his reasons: "unrelenting pressures" on the newsroom. (And talk about pressure: half the respondents in an AP managing editors poll call their jobs "highly stressful." Their median workweek: fifty-two hours.) Last year, Maxwell King said upon resigning as the *Inquirer's* editor: "When I look at big newspaper companies across the board, the question that occurs to me is, 'Are they all too intent on taking profit now and not intent enough on investing in content for the future?'" The paper was under orders from Knight Ridder to ratchet up its profit margin from 8 percent in 1995 to 15 per cent last year.

The L.A. *Times's* David Shaw put the problem succinctly:

> Today, many newspaper owners insist on high quarterly dividends . . . thus depriving the papers of money that could be invested in improving quality; there is little question that the shift from individual and family ownership to public ownership has increased the demand for higher short-term profits. In order to make their stock attractive to investors, newspaper companies promise higher profits every year (if not every quarter). That sets up unrealistic expectations. . . . When revenues inevitably decline, even temporarily — because of recession, higher newsprint costs or other factors — most publicly held newspapers feel they must still increase profits. So they cut costs — and, ultimately, quality.

Money is one big reason that newsrooms at America's papers have an older and less satisfied workforce than ever before — more graying heads and reading glasses than fresh faces. Forty-four percent are 40 or over, says an ASNE survey. Between 1988 and 1996, the percentage of journalists 30 and under dipped from 29 percent to 20 percent. More journalists than ever are planning to quit the business before retirement age. The most oft-cited reason: money. (Average base pay at papers having 30,000–75,000 circulation: $23,000) But "working conditions" and "stress" are now a close second and third. The number of journalists rating their papers as "excellent" has dropped dramatically, and most think that newspapers will be "a less important part of American life" in ten years time. Over half of ASNE's sample said their newsroom budget had declined in the previous five years, and 71 percent called it inadequate.

Meanwhile, the revolutionary Telecommunications Act of 1996 set the stage for huge, disruptive changes in broadcasting. Its deregulatory effects and the resultant seismic shift to corporate gigantism has been at the public's expense, especially in the way the nation's information needs are met.

One example: the act removed all limitations on the number of radio stations any one company can own nationally and greatly increased the number a single entity can operate in any single city. That triggered an unprecedented wave of buyouts and consolidations in the radio industry (with 16,000 stations nationwide), which have left listeners with a less-than-nourishing news diet in many places. (CBS, the biggest owner of radio stations, has 155 in its stable.) At many stations, including CBS's flagship in New York, all-news WCBS-AM, anchorpersons and sports reporters routinely read commercials as part of their duties, an activity that seriously blurs the line between journalist and huckster. But it saves stations the cost of hiring an announcer to intone that advertising copy. And with fewer street reporters, writers, and editors than in past years, many stations are reduced to parroting news from the morning's papers.

Local radio and TV news in many cities have indeed suffered "crippling cutbacks as group owners trim staffs to enhance their bottom lines," says Louis C. Adler, former WCBS news chief, now a professor at Connecticut's Quinnipiac College. The agglomerating of radio stations in pursuit of economies of scale by rich corporations has left listeners in many communities with diminished service. In Connecticut, for example, three New Haven stations — WELI, WAVZ, and WKCI — now belong to Texas-based Clear Channels Communications. A second Texas company, SFX Broadcasting, is grabbing WPLR, WTNH-TV, and control of WYBC and WBNE-TV. In the 1970s, at least four locally owned radio stations in New Haven County had street reporters scouring the area for news. Now there's one, WQUN. Thus, says Adler, deregulation in broadcasting benefits "corporations whose allegiance is not to listeners or viewers but to stockholders who demand an ever-increasing return on their investment, a demand satisfied by cutting costs, reducing jobs, and generally sacrificing public service on the altar of greed."

At the major print newsmagazines, *Time* and *Newsweek*, the trend over ten years, 1987-1997, shows a distinct tilt toward more crowd-pleasing cover subjects and away from straight domestic and foreign news — in the effort to snare the interest of impulse buyers at the newsstand and thus boost revenue. (Reporting foreign news is expensive: a U. S. correspondent stationed in pricey posts such as Hong Kong, Paris, or Moscow can easily cost $500,000 a year in pay, perks, and expenses.)

In 1987, *Time* published eleven covers relating to foreign news — and only one in 1997. Its domestic hard-news covers dwindled from twelve to nine. Thus, the over-all total for straight news covers dipped from about 45 percent of the total ten years ago to only 20 percent last year. Studying the list of *Time's* 1997 cover choices, one sees stories on Ellen DeGeneres, Steven Spielberg, Generation X, the pop singer Jewel, Brad Pitt in a movie about Buddhism, Bill Cosby and the death of his son, plus "What's Cool this Summer," "Turning Fifty," (with a cover photo of Hillary Clinton), "How Mood Drugs Work . . . and Fail" and "The Most Fascinating People in America." *Newsweek* pitched in with 1997 covers on TV cartoon shows, JonBenet Ramsey, Bob Dylan, Deepak Chopra, plus "The Young Kennedys: A Dynasty in Decline," "Does It Matter What You Weigh? The Surprising New Facts About Fat," "The Scary Spread of Asthma and How to Protect Your Kids," "Behind the Mask: The Dark World of Andrew Cunanan . . . Versace's Life, Death and Legacy," "Buy? Sell? How to Invest Now," and a "Special Edition" on "Your Child From Birth to Three." Both *Time* and *Newsweek* ran covers on Princess Diana two weeks in a row, giving them the biggest newsstand sales in their histories.

"The balance has clearly shifted away from international news"

How come all this emphasis on soft news and life-style issues? There are at least two reasons, says Norman Pearlstine, editor-in-chief of Time Inc., the nation's most successful magazine publishing company.

First: The economy is thriving, "so there's probably less concern with what has traditionally been the hard news story."

Second: With the collapse of communism and the end of the cold war, "it's not surprising that the country has turned more inward. There's always been a balance between educating your reader and serving your reader, but we're not getting a lot of demand for international coverage these days in broad consumer publications." Addressing a readership the size of *Time's* (domestic circulation: 4 million) "you obviously balance telling them what you think they ought to read with giving them what they want to read, and that balance has clearly shifted away from international news in the last decade."

Pearlstine recalls that in 1995, his first year at Time Inc., among the magazine's five worst-selling covers were: two on Bosnia, two on Senator Bob Dole, and one on Social Security. (Among the best sellers: "How Did the Universe Begin?", "Is the Bible Fact or Fiction?", and "Mysteries of the Deep.")

For the recent May 18 issues of *Time* and *Newsweek*, two stories competed for the cover: India's detonation of a nuclear device, and the death of Frank Sinatra. Sinatra won both covers. Ten years ago, says Pearlstine, the decision probably would have gone the other way.

"The great threat today to intelligent coverage of foreign news," Seymour Topping, former managing editor of *The New York Times*, told CJR, "is not so much a lack of the public's interest as it is a concentration of ownership that is profit-driven and a lack of inclination to meet responsibilities, except that of the bottom line." In newspapers, foreign news has declined drastically as a percentage of the news hole. In the newsweeklies, *Hall's Magazine Editorial Reports* found that from 1985 to 1995, space devoted to international news slipped from 24 percent to 14 percent in *Time*, from 22 percent to 12 percent in *Newsweek*, and 20 percent to 14 percent in *U.S. News & World Report*. The evening TV news programs, according to the Shorenstein Center at Harvard, gave 45 percent of their time to foreign affairs in the 1970s and a mere 13.5 per cent in 1995. Result: the public is being drastically shortchanged in its capacity to learn what's going on in the world outside the U.S.'s borders.

Many news executives tiresomely argue that, in the late 1990s, all the research indicates that the public doesn't want to know about the rest of the world; that it's narcissisticly fixated on life at home in the U.S. — its economy, celebrities, scandals, fads, and folkways. Media companies aim to feed that appetite.

But, says Ray Cave: It's no good to say that people now are not interested in consequential news. "The general public has never been truly interested in it. But we delivered it, like it or not. By so doing, we piqued public interest in the very matters that must, to some degree, interest the citizens of a democracy."

In network television, the audience for evening news broadcasts continues to dwindle. Competition grows fiercer for larger slices of a smaller pizza, and the quality of those broadcasts has suffered as they, too, offer more life-style stories and soft news in search of bigger audiences. In 1980, 37.3 percent of tuned-in homes viewed the three network news programs every night; that slid to 24.3 percent in 1996–97.

The NBC *Nightly News with Tom Brokaw* has been the dominant newscast for almost two years. Staffers at CBS News and ABC News say that's because it has lowered its aim, too often substituting life style and soft features for hard news in a transparent tactic to increase audience, raise advertising rates, and meet the profit expectations of its powerful parent, GE, the nation's most successful conglomerate. NBC News denies the charge.

But the temptation is great in every news medium to sweeten the product for easier consumption. A survey by the Project for Excellence in Journalism of some 4,000 stories on the three network news programs, on newsmagazine covers, and on the front pages of major papers from 1977 to 1997 concludes that celebrity, scandal, gossip, and other "human interest" stories increased from 15 percent to an astonishing 43 percent of the total.

Indeed, an irreversible rot in the hulls of all three of the old-line networks (in entertainment as well as news) has TV executives scurrying for new ways to build viewership and counter the threat of cable, the Internet, pay-per view, and home satellite services. The ABC and CBS networks are operating in the red, and ratings-leader NBC's profit is melting from $500 million last year to about $100 million. "It's a time of total transition," CBS boss Leslie Moonves told *The New York Times* in May. "It's all ugly."

Newspapers: taking profit rather than investing in future

Ironically, all three networks are looking expectantly to their news divisions to help slow the decay. How? The major networks this fall will air TV news magazines six nights a week — up from two in 1983. Why? They're much cheaper than most entertainment shows to put on the air; the networks own them outright, unlike sitcoms and dramas, which they lease from outside producers; and those programs get respectable ratings. NBC's *Dateline* is expanding to five nights a week. ABC is fusing *20/20* and *PrimeTime Live* into a three-times-a week event. CBS hankers to make *60 Minutes* — its all-time most-successful series — a twice-weekly program.

Those unprecedented schedule shifts will bring more news-and-feature programming to network audiences than ever before, but there's a flaw in the strategy. The soup will be thinner than ever. Reporters, producers, editors, and crews will be stretched over more working hours a week. The pool of story ideas inevitably will become more polluted and noxious for series that already have gone down the low road in search of ratings: e.g., Diane Sawyer's interview with Michael Jackson and former wife Lisa Marie Presley; *Dateline NBC's* piece on *Baywatch* babe Pamela Anderson; *PrimeTime Live's* chat with sometime O.J. Simpson girlfriend Paula Barbieri. *60 Minutes's* executive producer Don Hewitt firmly opposes expanding his series to other nights, convinced that the program's quality can't possibly be maintained if diluted. But in CBS's no-holds-barred effort to squeeze more juice out of its prize property he'll almost surely be overruled.

Hewitt is fond of saying that *60 Minutes* ruined it for everybody in news, proving as it did that a news program could be a colossal money machine, and perking managers' hopes that comparable riches could be extracted from all news broadcasts. CNN, as well,

takes the rap for the broadcast networks' scorched-earth news budget cuts: Ted Turner established his all-news cable channel in a right-to-work state (Georgia), hired all nonunion journalists and staff, paid them far less than the going rates at ABC, CBS, and NBC, and built a hugely successful worldwide news organization. Corporate bosses at the broadcast networks mused: Why can't we be as lean, mean, and successful as CNN?" They've been trying.

Ever since Mel Karmazin took over as CBS president (and heir apparent to chairman Michael Jordan), drastic fiscal strategies have been bruited in the corridors of the erstwhile Tiffany network, none of them favorable for the news division. The most attention-grabbing: CBS Corp. would sell off its money-losing CBS Television Network — which, essentially, is merely a program supplier to local stations — while retaining its very profitable station division. It consists of eighteen valuable owned-and-operated outlets.

The fate of CBS News in such a deal is shrouded in uncertainty. Traditionally in the television industry, separating a network from its owned stations is a heretical, risky notion. But as Merrill Lynch analyst Jessica Reif Cohen points out, such ancient, entrenched theorems may be ready for the dustbin of history: "New CBS management is very aggressive," she writes, "toppling a variety of broadcast traditions in order to build shareholder value and willing to explore a large number of strategic options."

Indeed, Karmazin, who has no background in news, is the broadcast industry's model hero for cost-cutting schemes. When he arrived at CBS, *60 Minutes* humorist Andy Rooney told the Minneapolis *Star Tribune*: "Nothing good has happened around here for so long I can't imagine [Karmazin's accession] is going to be good. . . . The emphasis is so much more on money than content in every decision that's made that it's discouraging to be here."

"Crippling cutbacks" help owners trim the bottom line

Time was when the evening news programs assigned crews to cover (as one veteran puts it) "everything that moved" — every viable news story every day all over the world. The end began with the buyouts and downsizing of the mid-1980s. More and more coverage came from local stations and independent newsfilm services, and at far less expense. That shift allowed the networks to close many bureaus at home and abroad. Frequently sacrificed, though, was the incisive, polished authority that the best TV news correspondents had brought to the reporting of important news.

Even as TV news operations cut budgets and spread their staffs thinner and thinner to the detriment of news coverage, they continue to pay "star" performers princely sums in the conviction that those engaging faces and voices are their last bulwark against even further audience defection. Thus, Rather, Brokaw, Jennings, Sawyer, and Walters each receive compensation in the $7 million a year range for their putative appeal in attracting viewers — a talent that transcends the quality of the programs they inhabit. CNN's Larry King, host of cable's top-rated, celebrity-infested interview program, is also a $7 million-a-year property. "With everything that's included in the deal, I'll be in the same ballpark as the network guys," King said proudly when the contract was signed in May. Said CNN president Tom Johnson: "Larry's ratings were up sharply last year, and he's had a great first quarter. . . . "

That was good news for King, all right, but simultaneously CNN parent Time Warner cut almost a fourth of the staff — seventy jobs out of 300 — at its Headline News cable channel, thus saving about $2 million but leaving cable news viewers the poorer for it. A few weeks earlier, TV chairman Gerald Levin predicted the company would increase its cash flow by 16 to 18 percent annually for the next few years. The Time Inc. magazines, collectively, are expected to raise their profits by 15 percent a year.

Obsession with ratings is at an all-time high in television news. One former high-level news producer recalls: "When I first joined the network, you'd probably be fired if you talked about ratings in the newsroom. The newspapers didn't even publish ratings at that time. Nobody ever suggested we do a story because it would get ratings. If somebody from the entertainment side or the promotion department came to us and suggested we do a piece about a lesbian coming out in a prime-time sitcom, we would have yelled 'Forget about it!' It's unbelievable how much of that junk gets on the air."

The question (more relevant than ever) for journalists: Is news what the public is interested in or what's in the public interest? Says Reuven Frank, former president of NBC News: "This business of giving people what they want is a dope pusher's argument. News is something people don't know they're interested in until they hear about it. The job of a journalist is to take what's important and make it interesting."

Closing news bureaus at home and abroad has been one of the more conspicuous effects of cost-cutting ever since ABC, CBS, and NBC changed ownership in the mid-1980s. No broadcast network now has a full-fledged bureau (with correspondent, camera crews, and office staff) anywhere in Africa or Latin America; Europe is covered mostly from London, Moscow, and Tel Aviv. (CNN, on the other hand, maintains twenty-three bureaus outside the U.S.)

"Roving bands of free-lance camera men," says veteran TV news producer Av Westin, "shoot coverage at every crisis spot at home and abroad and sell it to networks and local stations." He calls them "the video equivalent of paparazzi." ABC News closed its San Francisco bureau in April, around the time the news division reportedly was figuring out how to comply with a ukase from parent Disney to cut between $25 million and $50 million from its $625 million budget.

Hour-long, single-subject documentaries on key issues virtually disappeared from broadcast networks years ago — illustrious series such as *CBS Reports*, *NBC White Paper*, and *ABC Close-Up*. Those programs had been the news divisions' crown jewels (But occasionally TV news surprises, with a spurt of its old energy. ABC News, for example, is embarked on the most ambitious documentary ever: *The Century*, a $20 million, twenty-seven-hour series to begin next March, a colossal survey of the last hundred years. And CNN in September will launch *Cold War*, a massively researched, twenty-four-segment history. But even series on so grand a scale are expected to pay their own way or even make a profit.)

In the newspaper industry, last year was a watershed for two big reasons: trafficking in papers was at an all-time high: and profits boomed, even as circulation continued to slide. It was dubbed The Year of the Deal: 162 dailies out of 1,509 changed hands, up 37 percent from the year before. Megadeals abounded: Knight Ridder bought *The Kansas City Star*, the *Fort Worth Star-Telegram*, and two other papers from Walt Disney Company for $1.65 billion; McClatchy Newspapers snared Cowles Media for $1.4 billion. Transactions for the year hit a record $6.23 billion. As of February 1, 81 percent of those 1,509 dailies were members of a chain or group. Gene Roberts, former managing editor of *The New York Times* and now a journalism professor at the University of Maryland, told a press group in California:

> News coverage is being shaped by corporate executives at headquarters far from the local scene. [The shaping] is seldom done by corporate directive or fiat. It rarely involves killing or slanting stories. Usually it is by the appointment of a pliable editor here, a corporate graphics conference there, that results in a more uniform look, a more cookie-cutter approach among the chain's newspapers, or the corporate research director's interpretation of reader surveys that see common denominator solutions to complex coverage problems. . . . As papers become increasingly shallow and niggardly, they lose their essentiality to their readers and their communities. And this is ultimately suicidal.

Alarmingly, only fifty-five American cities now have more than one paper. The sharp decline in the numbers of dailies competing vigorously against each other has damaged the quality and squeezed the amount of reporting in American papers. Studies show that in cities where competition is hot, the news holes tend to be larger and there are more reporters to fill them. "The absence of competition tends to affect the financial commitment of publishers to the news–editorial department," says a forthcoming survey by the Columbia Institute for Tele-Information.

What kind of returns do chains demand to justify high purchase prices? Steven S. Ross, a Columbia Journalism School associate professor, explains: "This is what is historically new. Today, if a paper underperforms, its stock price is threatened and it's vulnerable to takeover. A twenty-five percent return on gross revenues sounds pretty good to a paper's staff. But the new owner's board says, 'We paid $500 million for that company. How dare they earn only twenty five percent?'"

Complaints abound from editors of large chain papers that the investment they require to produce a superior paper is being drained away to meet owners' profit demands. That shows up in large ways and small: when Gannett took over *The Asbury Park Press* in New Jersey, it cut the staff from 225 to 180, and told the theater critic there was no money for him to cover Broadway plays.

A *"dope pusher's argument"*: Giving people what they want

A particularly instructive case history is that of *The Patriot-Ledger* of Quincy, Massachusetts. It's a 161-year-old daily that was sold in February to Newspaper Media LLC for about $95 million by the Low family, which had owned it for four generations. The paper actually was worth $70-$75 million, according to analysts. In need of larger operating margins to service their heavy debt, the new owners decreed that the editorial budget be slashed from $7 million to $5.5 million; 17 to 18 percent of the paper's costs had been devoted to news and editorial, but that was reduced to 10–12 percent. *The Patriot-Ledger* serves twenty-six communities near Boston, and had at least one full-time reporter in all of them — several in larger suburbs like Weymouth, Braintree, and Plymouth. Too expensive, said the paper's new publisher, James Plugh. Also: twelve vacancies existed in the newsroom at the time of the ownership change, but Newspaper Media declined to let them be filled. The paper's value to its readers has been grievously undermined as result of such economies.

Unwilling to function in that new environment, *The Patriot-Ledger's* editor of twenty years (and former president of ASNE) William Ketter, resigned on May 29. Speaking generically of the nation-wide profits-versus-quality controversy, Ketter says: "I'm concerned about the prices being paid for newspapers and the need for greater profit margins to meet those financial obligations. The squeezing of editorial budgets is a short-sighted way of dealing with that need. When you start diminishing and degrading the nature of newspapers' content, you run the risk of those papers being less valuable in the marketplace."

Says *The Oregonian's* Sandra Mims Rowe: "Newspapers don't invest nearly enough in their employees, especially in training and teaching. There are journalists in the streets of every town who cannot report, write, or edit with authority, cannot provide the rich, full, detailed, accurate story the reader wants."

Evidence mounts that the blurring of editorial-advertising distinctions — as the latest technique in profit-building — is compromising news judgments and decisions, resulting not so much in fawning pieces about major advertisers but rather in self-censorship, a reluctance by some editors to take the heat for doing stories critical of space-buyers.

Witness: the highly-publicized move by *Los Angeles Times* publisher Mark Willes to involve marketing/advertising executives in the paper's day-to-day editorial decisions, a tactic that continues to draw fire from journalists around the country. The big fear is that if journalists have to worry about advertising and profits, they may self-censor and shrink from producing tough coverage of stories inimical to advertisers' interests. But what Willes has done is being copied at many other papers in this new era of profit-worship.

In a self-justifying speech to ASNE in April, Willes pointed out that more than 200 papers have closed in the last twenty-five years; that overall newspaper circulation has declined 10 percent in the last dozen years (while the population has grown 12 percent); that newspapers now attract less than 22 percent of all advertising, down from 27 percent in 1980; that only 58 percent of adults read a daily newspaper, down from 81 percent in 1964; that barely a third of the population cites newspapers as their main source for national news; and that in a recent Gallup poll, Americans ranked the honesty and integrity of newspaper reporters behind police officers and TV reporters, and only slightly ahead of lawyers and building contractors. If those trends continue, Willes warned, "newspapers will be increasingly marginalized, less important and, therefore, less relevant." For such reasons, he argues, it behooves editors and business-side managers to work together, more closely than in the past, to help assure the good health of newspapers. Willes's diagnosis of newspapers' illness is impressive. But his ideas for the cure alarm many journalists.

The subject of compensation and incentive pay troubles the University of Iowa's Soloski. There are major implications when the bonuses of media executives depend solely on the economic — and not the journalistic — performance of their publications. With a direct interest in his paper's profits, can the editor truly exercise uncontaminated judgment in covering controversial subjects or advertisers that might take offense and defect? The answer is yes, of course, the honest editor can — but she or he must always be aware of the potential for conflict.

Many publishers are increasingly pressing for special sections of their papers as a magnet for advertisers and readers, even though the content of those (continuing or occasional) sections is often frivolous, and creating them places added stress on news staffs. *The Wall Street Journal* has its new Friday section called *Weekend Journal*, filled with entertainment and life-style advice and related advertising. In mid-May, *The New York Times* published a massive sixty-four-page special section on the charms of eastern Long Island, mostly the fashionable Hamptons, with articles on sailing, kayaking, land-development, dining, sport fishing, and (of course) the famous show biz and media folk who summer there — along with a tonnage of advertising from real estate agents, restaurants, clothing boutiques, liquor stores, nurseries, and country inns. (A study sponsored last year by ASNE and the Newspaper Association of America discovered that newspaper advertisements better meet readers' expectations than does the quality of news coverage.)

The questions: Are such sections an editor's vision of a value-added supplement that fills an important editorial need, or mainly a publisher's gambit for a quick-hit spike in revenue? And can those sections be executed without draining resources from the paper's main service?

Such one-time and continuing special sections are a greater strain on papers that don't have the legendary resources of *The Wall Street Journal* or *The New York Times*. But the criterion for success is usually the same: economic, not journalistic. At the *Los Angeles Times*, for example, where the editor of a daily section is yoked uncomfortably with a counterpart from the ad department, a section's survival chances depend heavily on its capacity to generate revenue, not on its journalistic excellence.

A comparable syndrome exists in the magazine industry: special issues, which exploit the value of a title in the effort to squeeze additional income from its brand-name identity. It's an old tactic that's employed with ever greater frequency these days to prettify the bottom line, even as editorial staffs have been pruned and there are often fewer people to take on the task. Can a magazine editor, who presumably occupies a full-time job, effectively oversee these special issues — on the passing of Frank Sinatra, Princess Diana, the Seinfeld sitcom — and still do his main job? "When the driving force is economic and not journalistic," says a senior editor of a national magazine, "the push is coming from the wrong direction. I would rather use that energy and that talent to improve my main product than to create a one-time offshoot. It's all very well to say I can do both, but I'm not sure anybody can, without weakening the core magazine."

The underlying debate continues. Profits. Return on investment. The public's right to know. Shareholder value. Journalistic responsibility. Are the terms incompatible? Not necessarily. Early in this century, the great labor leader Samuel Gompers said: "The worst crime against working people is a company which fails to operate at a profit."

"There are journalists on the street of every town who can't report, write, or edit"

But should news organizations reasonably expect the same profit levels as software companies, pharmaceutical firms, and computer makers? Or should stockholders and owners understand, when they wed their fortunes to those of working journalists, that news is a venture like no other? It's the only business protected by the Constitution of the United States, a status that brings obligations for both the shareholder and the journalist. "I wish investors and owners of media companies could be made to understand the incredible responsibility they've assumed," says Walter Cronkite, "and accept a reasonable return instead of the excessive profits that can be garnered elsewhere."

If that's too much to expect in this era of mega-media conglomerations, a surging economy, a galloping Wall Street, and chronic public dismay about the press, then the mission of journalism in America may be perilously debilitated. The big question: What doth it profit a media company to demand, unremittingly, steadily higher profit margins year after year and, in that very pursuit, lose its professional soul?

Neil Hickey is CJR's *editor at large. Additional reporting for this article was provided by David Cudaback, former editor of* Institutional Investor.

ALL THE NEWS THAT FITS

Network Failure

Are the major media frivolous or biased?
Some of each, find our reporters in the field.

By Brent H. Baker & Tim Graham

On May 15, the *New York Times* reported that Johnny Chung told investigators that part of the almost $100,000 he gave Democrats in the summer of 1996 came not just from Communist China but from the Peoples Liberation Army. It was a blockbuster story, confirming what had been the most sensational possibility when Asiagate first broke back in 1996. But none of the three network morning shows touched the story, devoting the majority of their air time to the death of Frank Sinatra.

That night, after three Sinatra stories and updates on Indonesia and Pakistan, ABC's Peter Jennings devoted a minute and a half to the story. On CBS, Dan Rather spent 27 seconds on it. On NBC, Tom Brokaw surrendered just 15 seconds. CNN's 8 P.M. newscast gave the story 2 minutes after 43 minutes of other news, including an estimate of the audience for the Seinfeld finale and a story about the recall of the new Volkswagen Beetle.

Two days later, the *Times* returned to the subject, detailing how President Clinton overrode the decision of Secretary of State Warren Christopher to limit permission to launch American-made satellites on Chinese rockets. Only ABC assigned a reporter to the story that night. CBS ignored it, although its newscast had time for a story on scientists' trying to determine whether Thomas Jefferson had offspring with slave Sally Hemings. NBC's basketball-shortened newscast covered the upcoming vote in Ireland on a peace plan and "Powerball fever."

Media critics once complained that the networks obsessively followed the lead of the *New York Times*.

Now, when it comes to the Clinton scandals, they don't even do that. The primary building blocks of TV news shows today are packages—"A Closer Look" on ABC, "In Depth" on NBC, "Eye on America" on CBS—devoted to themes such as the joys of Viagra, the fat content of French fries, or the latest gale of El Niño. These are great ratings grabbers—and they do not need to wait for the news of the day; indeed, they are often produced weeks in advance. Segments like these used to focus almost exclusively on serious policy issues concerning health and welfare, education, and the environment. Now they're more likely to report on male pattern baldness or the flaw in new diet drugs.

Network executives today seem completely comfortable making soft news a top priority. The ascent of 24-hour news outlets on television, radio, and the Internet makes the networks feel that public affairs have already been covered all day long; since a half-hour-long show can't compete with C-SPAN for the attention of political junkies, the reasoning goes, the networks may as well focus on the most attractive news for the greatest number. But 70 per cent of Americans tell pollsters they get most or all of their news from network television.

And C-SPAN can't always cover the big stories either. In 1997, when the Senate Governmental Affairs Committee convened to investigate fundraising abuses at the Democratic National Committee, Sen. Fred Thompson's hearings were not aired during the day on C-SPAN, because of its commitment to cover Congress. Most days, they were not covered live by CNN or MSNBC. Even the Public Broadcasting Service, originally created to counter the networks' commercialism, decided that Barney and Big Bird and Arthur the Aardvark were too important to be interrupted by Senate hearings.

With a longer list of affiliates than any of the other networks (and often with more than one station in a market), PBS insisted that its affiliates would not defer to someone else's notion of the public interest. Ellen Hume, head of PBS's "Democracy Project," explained: "A commitment to such open-ended coverage, including the House hearings which have not even started yet, was not a realistic option for PBS. PBS was in its infancy during Watergate, and, like MSNBC or the Fox cable channel today, it had little established programming to pre-empt. Today families rely on PBS's children's programming during the day, particularly when school is out during the summer."

If the Thompson hearings were not given live coverage, were they at least seriously reported on the network newscasts? No. Jennings and Brokaw and Rather all buried the hearings beneath lurid tabloid-style stories. The murder of Gianni Versace easily outranked the fundraising hearings on the evening newscasts, and the morning shows aired 7 segments on Versace for every 1 on the fundraising scandal. In the month after Princess Diana's death, the Diana-to-DNC ratio was 6 to 1 on the evening news, 10 to 1 in the morning.

> *Almost immediately, reporters began agonizing about how their coverage was hurting Clinton.*

Of course, there should be room in a half-hour-long show for both the ratings-grabber and the brainteaser. But the networks are terrified of viewers flipping to *Wheel of Fortune*. Indeed, the news shows now often start with a trivial item, and the more important political news arrives twenty minutes later —if it arrives at all. On July 16, 1997, the Thompson committee heard one of John Huang's bosses at the Commerce Department say Huang was "totally unqualified" for his post. But on ABC's *World News Tonight*, the lineup that evening was: three Versace stories, the NAACP convention, an FDA-approved implant for epilepsy, a bank robber who stuffed dollars in his pants and fled in his underwear when the dye on the bills ignited, and a fly-fishing program for breast-cancer victims.

In August, ABC's Cokie Roberts explained that the networks weren't covering the Thompson hearings much because of the low name recognition of the witnesses. The next month, when National Security Advisor Sandy Berger testified, ABC gave his testimony 18 seconds. That show had led with a poll showing that Brits want Prince William rather than Prince Charles to be their next king. Before getting to Berger, ABC gave its viewers another Diana-related story, studies on AIDS and osteoporosis, and sexual harassment in the Army.

Not only did Sen. Thompson and his committee colleagues go uncovered, they also went uninterviewed on the weekday morning shows. Those shows devoted only five interview segments to the hearings in July, and all five were with the networks' own pundits— NBC's Tim Russert and ABC's Cokie Roberts, George Stephanopoulos, and Bill Kristol. The use of in-house pundits is largely a business decision: it helps promote the networks' Sunday interview programs, it justifies multi-million-dollar contracts for the pundits, it sticks to people who are accustomed to speaking in soundbites, and, most importantly, it avoids giving air time to boring public officials who might focus on something other than who's up and who's down.

News Lite has worked to Bill Clinton's advantage, keeping most of his abuses of the public trust off the air—except in the case of Monica Lewinsky. With the ratings bonanza of the O. J. Simpson murder trial still warming television executives' hearts, the networks ran more stories on Monicagate in its first few days than they had run on all the other scandals combined over the previous five years—the FBI files (about 60 stories), Travelgate (many fewer than that), all the indictments of Cabinet members (next to none), the Asian fundraising scandal (see above). Was Monicagate definitive proof that there is no such thing as media bias? Ted Koppel suggested as much to Newt Gingrich on Nightline. But the course of that scandal has been instructive.

Almost immediately, reporters began agonizing about how their coverage was hurting Clinton. Just three days after the Lewinsky affair broke, ABC was focusing on the media's "overcoverage." CNN, with Clinton buddy Rick Kaplan at the helm, flayed the rest of the media—not for failing to cover the earlier stories but for covering this one—in a two-hour special. PBS's *NewsHour with Jim Lehrer* and the other network news shows followed suit. Then, having concluded that they themselves had gone too far, the media decided that Ken Starr had too.

Less than three weeks after the Lewinsky scandal broke, ABC's Michel McQueen concluded a piece: "The question now is whether Starr's tactics will prove more offensive to the courts and the public than any alleged wrongdoing by the President that Starr is investigating." A week later NBC's Tom Brokaw plugged an upcoming story: "Still ahead tonight: Investigating the President. A growing backlash against independent counsel Kenneth Starr. Is he out of bounds or just tone deaf? . . . Has Starr gone too far in his pursuit of Monica Lewinsky and the President?" The network trotted out polls asking: Has Starr gone too far? By contrast, of course, when Iran-Contra prosecutor Lawrence Walsh indicted Caspar Weinberger four days before the 1992 election, there was a barrage of media commentary pointing out how the indictment would hurt the Bush campaign, but the networks didn't even mention Walsh's name.

Even when it's a matter of policy debates rather than personalities, the same tired biases still apply. When the Senate considered a Republican proposal for tax-free education savings accounts, CBS's Dan Rather reported not on the proposal but only on the attack on it: "President Clinton today attacked a Republican proposal in Congress. This Republican proposal would let people set up education savings accounts that earn tax-free interest. The President said this GOP version benefits the rich and private schools at the expense of already decaying public schools."

CNN anchor Martin Savidge endorsed Democratic worries that "tax breaks for private tuition would benefit the wealthy at the expense of public education. And Democrats have numbers on their side. A Treasury Department report says 70 per cent of the benefits would go to just the top 20 per cent of income earners. Overall the education savings accounts would cost the government $1.6 billion in tax revenues."

Criticism of the media used to vary depending on whether the critic was on the Right or on the Left. Liberal critics would complain that the networks, in response to the market, were frivolous, while conservatives focused on their liberal bias. Frivolous or biased? Unfortunately, we don't have to choose.

Mr. Baker is Vice President for Research and publications at the Media Research Center in Alexandria, Virginia. Mr. Graham is the MRC's Director of Media Analysis.

A Reading for Critical Thinking

Extra! The Press Is Liberal (So What?)

By Richard M. Cohen

Classifying the politics of any group is dicey. Forty percent of all liberals are queer," the hard-hat social critic Joe announced to movie-goers a generation ago. Now it's the Republican leadership wielding the big bat. The press is leftist, they scream. From Dole to Gingrich to Reed. Tinkers to Evers to Chance. Reporters are liberals, liars and left-overs from another era. Three strikes, you're out.

How horrifying—except that maybe it's true. A Freedom Forum study released last year indicated that 22 percent of Washington journalists call themselves liberal while only 2 percent say they are conservative.

Some 89 percent of these reporters voted for Clinton over Bush in 1992 (apparently, that makes William Safire a liberal). Another study claimed that in 1972, 81 percent of Washington journalists went for McGovern over Nixon. If familiarity breeds contempt, four years of Bush and Nixon were probably quite enough for the crowd covering them. Those votes suggest a modicum of common sense more than a tendency to turn left.

Still, we journalists are so busy resisting the liberal label that it hasn't occurred to us that it's no crime. The countervailing bias of our bosses is generally conservative. Corporate news managers do not rock the boat, and they are in charge. News executives care more about holding on to customers and increasing profits than challenging the establishment. The status quo seems safe.

There is a perceived national swing to the right, so CBS News hires Laura Ingraham, a perfectly radiant righty, to play the role of political analyst. There is no sign of a liberal voice to provide even the appearance of balance. Who needs fairness when you're playing to conservative critics and the crowd?

Most reporters try to play it safe. We're not robots, though. We all have strong views and personal tilts. There is no such thing as pure objectivity as long as human beings cover the news. The only known human with no opinions about anything was Clarence Thomas at his confirmation hearings, using the old stealth strategy to win his seat on the Court. Journalists, many of them smart people, have opinions, but we don't all grow on the same tree.

Professionalism is the antidote for poison by bias. Professionalism is supposed to keep our own political visions out of our work. This is nothing less than a matter of integrity in our pursuit of a fair product.

What we don't want to admit in our newsrooms or to our mirrors in the morning, however, is that we invariably do end up left of center. Conservatives are crowing that the cup is half full. If that's true, we're stuck with the half-empty space that's left—our "yes, but" response. It's a bit elitist: We know best. And it may create a soft liberalism, more instinctive than ideological. If that humanizes stories and introduces an element of compassion, so be it.

"I would call it aesthetic liberalism," says David Brooks of the conservative *Weekly Standard*. "Reporters are so often out of the Ivy League. They have liberal social agendas, and they may also hold conservative economic ideas." Well, excuse me, but don't most Americans go for that combo platter?

If journalists are Starbucks liberals, as Brooks contends, Tom Rosenstiel believes newsrooms reflect a broader range of political beliefs than conservatives think. Rosenstiel has left *Newsweek* to run the Project for Excellence in Journalism for the Pew Charitable Trusts.

"Journalists, right now, are cultural liberals," Rosenstiel argues. "We came into this business covering the civil rights movement and Vietnam and Watergate. Those events shaped the way we view the world."

We baby boomers in the news business certainly did cut our teeth on huge stories that raised powerful emotions, though another generation of journalists is now also in place. It is the older journalists who have defined newsroom values, and for us, these events provided a fertile breeding ground for a low-key, back burner liberalism.

The press once seemed to have a conscience, thanks to history's painful social conflicts and questions of war and peace. The world has changed, however, and many of us may be in the time warp of old values. That may not be so bad.

I, for one, am tired of ideological labeling of reporters because it simply misses the point. With everything that is wrong with the press today, pointing fingers and assigning political identities and agendas to the media gets in the way of meaningful press criticism. The true crisis in journalism is that reporters and producers are in the entertainment business, responding to market pressures by replacing facts with emotions and, too frequently, seeking heat rather than light.

"They are adversarial," George Stephanopoulos told MSNBC, "in an obsession with conflict, controversy and scandal."

With television, the search for scandal is driven by ratings pressure. So is the fascination with the cult of celebrity, the personality fix, which is pushed by TV and in many papers. That's the *People* syndrome. It's an enticing diversion from the dialogue of democracy.

The real agenda most journalists serve is getting ahead in our careers, climbing that newsroom escalator. Reporters, like all of us, have houses and car and tuition payments to make. Nothing blunts a journalist's sword like a mortgage.

So we play the game. Every news organization has a culture, defined by its reward system. That's the unofficial rule book by which cub reporters are promoted to become cynical, seasoned tough guys. It's called giving the folks who sign the paychecks what they want, and it has nothing to do with coverage of politics and government. At networks and chain papers today, politics is out, anyway, because there is the perception that viewers and readers don't like politicians.

Reporters, like politicians, end up playing the high-stakes game of selling ourselves to the public. We follow the market now, and it can cause us to abandon our true mission. That should be of greater concern than whatever ideological dog tags some conservatives want to hang around our necks.

PART 6

Interest Groups and Political Parties

Political parties were once a major force in American political and social life. They provided jobs, social opportunities, and contributed to a sense of community. As a result, they commanded intense loyalty among their adherents. For many people, being a "Democrat" or a "Republican" was an important component of their identity.

Those days are gone. To be sure, there are still many people who are strongly dedicated to their political party. But the number of people who feel little or no loyalty to a political party has grown significantly. Each year, a higher percentage of Americans call themselves "independents." There is a significant longing in American society for a third political party, as seen in the presidential candidacies of Ross Perot and the rise of his Reform Party as a political force.

This concept is known as *dealignment* and it has had a number of effects on American politics. One of the consequences has been the increasing importance of interest groups. Rather than participating through political parties, (which are large and focus on many, varied issues) people have progressively turned to participation through interest groups (which are usually smaller and focus on a smaller number of issues of particular importance to their members).

But this development has been met with some concern. There is a good deal of criticism of "special interests." Special interests are accused of selfishly placing their own agendas ahead of the good of the nation as a whole, and by purchasing political influence through their campaign contributions. However, criticism of special interests is often self-serving and selective—people tend to criticize interest groups they oppose while conveniently ignoring the fact that some special interests work on their behalf. As you read the following selections, think about which political parties and interest groups work for causes that you believe in. Is their influence good or bad?

A Republic—
If We Can Keep It

*The present corrupt system of financing elections, a U.S. senator argues,
poses a serious threat to our democracy. The sad lesson
of the recent campaign-finance scandals is not only that the laws are vaporous
but also that politicians won't change their ways without public pressure*

By Joseph Lieberman

Of the many remarks uttered during the U. S. Senate investigation of the 1996 national elections—elections that saw the laws on campaign spending and contributions stretched to the point of absurdity—one of the most telling came in a brief comment by the former White House deputy chief of staff Harold Ickes. Challenged about his handling of a questionable transaction during the final week of the 1996 campaign, Ickes defended his conduct in part by pointing to the chaotic atmosphere all around him: "We were like Mad Hatters," he said.

This allusion to the fund-raising madness of the 1996 election cycle seems apt—too many good people were running around like Mad Hatters doing all kinds of bad things. There was a surreal quality to the whole scandal, with its bizarre cast of characters, the tortuous logic that many participants employed to rationalize their actions, and the sense as the investigation went on that the polity has fallen down a long, dark hole into a place that is far from the vision and values of those who founded our democracy.

In that strange place the law appears to be written in invisible ink. It is somehow possible for wealthy donors to give hundreds of thousands of dollars to political campaigns, even though the law is clearly intended to limit contributions to a tiny fraction of such sums. It is possible for labor unions and corporations to donate millions to political parties at the candidates' request, despite a decades-old prohibition on the involvement of unions and corporations in national elections. It is possible for tax-exempt groups to run millions of dollars' worth of television ads that clearly endorse or attack particular candidates, even though these groups are barred by law from engaging in such partisan activity. And it is possible for presidential nominees to continue putting the touch on contributors, even though they have pledged under the law not to raise any more money for their campaigns after receiving enormous lump sums ($62 million apiece for Bob Dole and Bill Clinton in 1996) in public funds.

The fundraising scandal of 1996 was a very real tragedy, with very real consequences for our democracy. People at the highest levels in both political parties did more than just strain credulity: they betrayed the public trust. In their breathless, unbounded rush to raise even more money for even more television advertising, they effectively hung a giant FOR SALE sign on our government and the whole of our political process. They also gave Americans, already beset by cynicism, good reason to doubt whether citizens have a true and equal voice in their own government. The dangers here must not be dismissed: corruption is a great killer of experiments in self-government. In 1787, as he left Independence Hall at the close of the Constitutional Convention, Benjamin Franklin was asked what kind

From *The Atlantic Monthly* (July 1998), pp. 14–17. Reprinted with permission from Joseph Lieberman. Copyright © 1998. Joseph Lieberman, Democratic Senator, Connecticut, serves on the Government's Affairs Committee, which last year (1997) investigated campaign abuses of the 1996 federal elections.

of government the country now had. He replied, "A republic, if you can keep it." Franklin was worried about a tendency toward monarchy. The threat today, imminent and real, is a state of affairs in which money itself is King.

One of the central problems exposed by the campaign-finance revelations has to do with the distinction we make between illegal conduct and improper conduct in public life, and the standards we use to judge such conduct. To this day some prominent elected officials contend that most of the scandals of 1996 involved violations of laws already on the books, and that therefore the appropriate response is simply tougher punishment and tougher enforcement. The reality is otherwise. Most of the sleazy behavior that characterized those elections was legal. The blatant skirting of limits on individual contributions; the subversion of restrictions on presidential candidates who receive public funds; the conversion of supposedly nonpartisan, tax-exempt groups into political agents; the fact that unions and corporations funneled millions of dollars into the two parties despite the law's absolute ban on their involvement in national campaigns—all these acts compromised the integrity of our elections and our government, and all plainly violate the spirit of our laws. Yet all of them also appear to be legal.

In effect, then, what the law permitted in 1996 was as outrageous as any crime that was committed. This point is enormously significant, not just in terms of gauging the import of this scandal but also for determining the steps we should take to repair our broken campaign finance system. It may be that enforcement of various kinds will curb some of the illegal activities that occurred during the 1996 elections. Yet we can make no similar statement about the wide range of corrosive activities that continue to be legal. In fact, just the opposite is true—it is certain that these behaviors will persist unless we make them illegal.

It is not only the political system that has been compromised and corrupted: so have the values and standards of those who operate within it. In politics as in many segments of our society today, from professional-sports leagues that wink at the shocking behavior of big stars to TV talk-show producers who achieve new lows in degradation and exploitation every day, the bottom line—raising money—has too often become the dominant line. Basic differences between right and wrong have become blurred. The moral standard for campaigns today is not what is unassailably proper but what is technically legal.

Plugging the most egregious loopholes to make the clearly improper clearly illegal will deter some future wrongdoing, which is sufficient reason to plug

them. But these changes won't be enough. The law serves as an expression of our values. It can stake out ethical boundaries, point us in the right direction, and punish actions that are wrong—but it cannot compel moral behavior. We cannot fully write into law what citizens have a right to expect from their representatives—that those who wish to write the rules for the nation will themselves respect the rules, rather than searching high and low for ways to evade legal requirements and eviscerate their intent; that those who have sworn to abide by the Constitution will honor the trust and responsibilities the Constitution places in their hands. rather than catering to the special interests depositing soft money in their pockets. For our democracy to function, we must rely on a common core of values beyond what the law requires, a system of moral checks and balances comparable to the ones built into the Constitution. But over the past several years the pressure to raise huge amounts of money has eroded those values among politicians—has "defined deviancy down"—and left them prey to their baser instincts.

The 1996 elections provided ample evidence of the threat that political money-scrounging poses to the legitimacy of our government. Although it has yet to be proved that any U.S. policy, foreign or domestic. was altered by any of the hustlers and opportunists who bought access to some of our top leaders, we cannot deny that the potential existed for this kind of purchase. Nor can we ignore the dangers inherent in the simple appearance of influence peddling. Consider some of the comments volunteered by the unsavory characters who sought to buy their way into our political system. Johnny Chung: "I see the White House is like a subway—you have to put in coins to open the gates." Roger Tamraz, explaining how money bought him political access that had been denied him through other channels: "If they kicked me from the door, I will come through the window."

Hearing these comments, the average American would have every reason to suspect the worst about the government and those who are running it, and to question just whose interests are being served. This may be the gravest consequence of the moral breakdown that our politics has suffered. Take away the Johnny Chungs and the Roger Tamrazes and the other shakedown artists, and we are still left with a system that bends over backward to indulge big donors and their special interests, a system that suggests to the public that power will be exercised chiefly in behalf of those who pay top dollar.

■ ■ ■

The breakdown in our political values is akin to a broader problem in our society—the sense that popular culture has disoriented our moral compass. In the intense competition for higher television ratings or more record sales, many good people working at great and honorable companies have debased themselves by conveying images of extreme violence, sexual promiscuity, and vulgarity into our children's minds. By extension they have debased us all. And they have defended their behavior by waving the First Amendment as if it were some kind of constitutional hall pass, whereby the right to speak freely justifies any and all behavior exercised under that right, no matter who is hurt.

What has happened within our culture is strikingly similar to what has happened within our polity. Both arenas are plagued by enormous competitive pressures, the powerful temptation of big money, and a reflexive reliance on the right of free speech to shield the unseemly and the corrosive. In Hollywood the thinking goes, If I can say it or portray it and people will pay, then I must indeed say it and portray it, because then I will succeed. In Washington the analogue is, If the law does not clearly prohibit me from doing it, then I must do it or I will lose.

Our experience in the so-called culture wars tells us that it is unrealistic to expect politicians to change their behavior and elevate their standards voluntarily. It is imperative to change the way our political process works—to suppress the temptation to stray from core values. And the only way to accomplish this is to reduce the unrelenting pressure to raise vast sums of money. The most promising step would be to close the soft-money loophole through which corporate and labor union money floods, making a mockery of the rules that bar those very entities from contributing to campaigns. A further step would be to prohibit presidential candidates who accept public money from raising any other money. Other steps might be to eliminate fake "issue ads" broadcast by political parties and independent groups and to encourage voluntary limits on campaign spending.

The mistrust and alienation that many Americans feel toward their government and their elected leaders are reflected over and over again in polls. A Gallup poll after the 1996 elections found that just 32 percent of the public trusts in government to "do what is right" most of the time. A survey done by Peter Hart and Robert Teeter for the Council for Excellence in Government found that when asked whether elected officials have honesty and integrity, nearly three quarters of the respondents said no.

One powerful indicator of the public's lack of confidence is its reaction to campaign-finance reform. When asked whether they believed that major changes in the laws could reduce the corrupting influence of big money in politics, nearly 60 percent of the respondents said that special interests will always find a way to maintain their power in Washington, no matter what laws we pass.

Such hopelessness is undoubtedly why the public has not been demanding campaign-finance reform. The first task for reformers in both parties is to raise the level of trust to the point where people believe that reform can make a difference, so that they will demand it from their representatives. Without that demand reform will not happen. The responsibility falls on us all, in and out of public life. We no longer have the luxury of waiting idly for others to take the lead.

The Business of Persuasion Thrives in Nation's Capital

By Jill Abramson

Washington, Sept. 28—"I haven't thought about Monica Lewinsky all day," mused Wright Andrews, a Washington lobbyist.

He was too busy. While the rest of Washington was obsessing over the President's sex scandal, Mr. Andrews and dozens of other business lobbyists were working on bankruptcy legislation that passed the Senate on Wednesday. Kenneth W. Starr's $40 million investigation may have dominated the headlines and caused misery for President Clinton, but $40 million was also spent on lobbying by the banking, credit card and retailing industries on a variety of bills, including bank legislation that would make it much tougher to declare personal bankruptcy.

This year has also, separately, been a banner year for K Street, the power corridor of law and lobbying firms that rims the White House in downtown Washington.

It started with extensive lobbying earlier in the year by the cigarette industry to crush a comprehensive tobacco bill, followed by efforts to influence major banking and bankruptcy legislation. With more lobbying yet to come on appropriations, trade and tax measures, Mr. Andrews and many lobbyists interviewed in recent months predicted that more would be spent on influencing the Federal Government this year than in 1997, when a record $1.2 billion was reportedly spent.

This rapid growth in spending has brought with it the rise of a new lobbying elite. At a time when the Democratic Administration and the Republican-led Congress are often at loggerheads and when Washington's agenda, dominated by scandal, seems inert, K Street's

portfolio has never been more robust. That portfolio includes multimillion-dollar lobbying campaigns on issues like product liability law, health care and computer privacy.

They are issues that do not necessarily receive a lot of media attention though they affect millions of people.

All last week, for example, while the klieg lights were shining on the House Judiciary Committee's debate about the Starr report, swarms of tax lobbyists were crisscrossing the hallways outside the House Ways and Means Committee, known as Gucci Gulch, in an effort to preserve an array of business tax breaks in the House's $80 billion tax-cut package.

The influence industry was already on a growth curve in the 1980's, but that growth has exploded in recent years with the advent of a divided Government.

A new cast of Republican Congressional committee and subcommittee chairmen as well as Washington's increasing impact on highly regulated industries like financial services, telecommunications and health care has meant that corporations and lobbying firms are reaching much deeper into the bureaucracy in order to wield influence.

When Kenneth J. Kies left his Congressional staff position last winter for a million-dollar job lobbying for PricewaterhouseCoopers, Congressional committee chairmen, senior Treasury Department and White House officials turned out for a lavish farewell in the House Ways and Means Committee room, a testament to his connectedness.

The eye-popping salary package commanded by Mr. Kies, a 46-year-old Republican tax lawyer who earned $132,000 as chief of staff of the Joint Committee on Taxation, was fresh evidence of a culture of money that in the 1990's has begun to transform Washington's image as a power city.

Another bureaucrat who was unknown outside Washington, Bruce Merlin Fried, a senior administrator for Medicare and Medicaid programs at the Department of Health and Human Services, was also courted like a superstar when he left the Government last January.

"I felt like I was representing Michael Jordan," said Susan Schneider, a legal headhunter who helped Mr. Fried choose among plum jobs at law and lobbying firms.

"The demand for knowledgeable people who can track what is going on on Capitol Hill and the Government and can figure out the pressure points that companies should be touching in Washington has greatly increased," said Richard Shapiro, executive director of the Congressional Management Foundation, a private organization that tries to educate Congress on running its business.

Almost anyone with significant political connections, including the spouses, family members and former aides of lawmakers, is highly marketable on K Street. Michelle Laxalt, for example, the daughter of Paul Laxalt, a former Republican Senator, is sought after as a lobbyist for her Senate connections.

Boutique firms that specialize in lobbying a single member or a single committee of Congress have also sprouted up and are flourishing. Ann M. Eppard, who for 22 years served as a top aide to Bud Shuster, the House Transportation Committee chairman, left her job in 1994 and hung out her shingle as a transportation lobbyist. Within months, she had lined up more than $1 million in retainers from an array of big transportation companies, including the FDX Corporation.

Some denizens of the capital say that K Street's explosion has fundamentally changed the city's atmosphere, with a new obsession with money eclipsing Washington's traditional obsession with power.

"New York was money, Los Angeles was glamour and Washington was always power," Victor Kamber, a lobbyist and a political consultant for 32 years whose firm billed $11 million last year. "Now this town is as much about money as power."

DOLLARS ON PARADE

A World Awash With Big Money

Washington has long been one of the nation's wealthiest metropolitan areas, with a large population of Government workers and white-collar professionals. But its elite, led by a stratum of highly paid lawyers and lobbyists, has never been as brazen in advertising its money or political connections.

At the Capital Grille, an expensive restaurant that opened near the Capitol in 1994, lobbyists flaunt their clients and their expensive tastes with brass name plaques on private wine lockers.

So many wealthy Washingtonians are buying second homes along Maryland's once quaint Eastern Shore that some areas are taking on the congested feel of New York's Hamptons on summer weekends. And a new glossy magazine, Capital Style, regularly profiles the lives of Washington's rich and famous.

Nothing seems to restrain this new culture. Not tighter revolving-door rules signed by President Clinton that lengthened the time that some lobbyists must refrain from lobbying their old agencies. Not a gift ban passed by the Congress to loosen the knot of friendship between lobbyists and lawmakers. Not even a major fund-raising scandal in which some of the city's premier lobbyists, including Haley Barbour, a former Republican Party chairman, and Peter S. Knight, a Democratic fund-raiser, were brought before Congressional oversight committees.

Some of the most expensive lobbying campaigns have sought to insure that nothing happens, like the $100 million effort to kill anti-tobacco legislation.

"A lot of the best lobbyists are like paid assassins," said Jennifer Shecter of the Center for Responsive Politics, a research group in Washington.

Lobbyists have always been part of the capital's political fabric, but have never before been so intimately interwoven into the government. Twenty years ago, for example, most Washington law firms did little or no lobbying. Now virtually all of them have bustling lobbying practices, and some have even hired non-lawyers to increase their political clout.

In his fight against impeachment, President Clinton has reached out to a network of Democratic lobbyists, lawyers and political consultants, including Thomas Hale Boggs Jr., Jody Powell, Joseph P. O'Neill and Anthony T. Podesta, who participate in a daily conference call with White House officials to plot strategy. This daily bull session is organized by Steve Ricchetti, who recently returned to the White House after leaving to become a lobbyist.

Both Vice President Al Gore and Speaker Newt Gingrich have tight coteries of lobbyists who regularly advise them on political matters.

Political analyst Kevin P. Phillips, author of "Arrogant Capital," worries that Washington has become what the Founding Fathers feared, a "capital so privileged and incestuous in its dealings, that average citizens believe it is no longer accessible to the general public."

Mr. Phillips added that there was nothing like Washington's "massive, permanent lobbying elite" in other foreign capitals.

Foreign countries, in fact, feel it is necessary to hire Washington lobbyists to have their voices heard. Tiny Azerbaijan is currently interviewing firms, even though the small republic has an embassy in Washington and limited resources. The reason? Its neighbors have Washington lobbyists.

At least 128 former members of Congress are now working as lobbyists. Although some found solace on K Street after they were defeated for re-election, others left office because they were offered giant salary increases to become lobbyists.

In 1993 and 1994, Ohio Republican Willis D. Gradison Jr. and Oklahoma Democrat Glenn English stepped down from their House seats in the middle of their terms for lucrative lobbying jobs.

Only 3 percent of the lawmakers who retired in the 1970's are currently on K Street; in the 1990's, at least 22 percent of those leaving have become lobbyists.

Even Robert Strauss, at 80 years old perhaps the most seasoned member of a generation of Democratic superlawyers, is amazed at how fast the revolving door spins. A former Democratic Party chairman and United States trade representative, Mr. Strauss said in a recent interview that lawyers now often went to work for the Government for a few years, not because they wanted a career in public service, but because "they know that enables them to move on out in a few years and become associated with a lobbying or law firm and their services are in tremendous demand."

To be sure, the long hours and lean salaries of Congressional aides have always led to turnover, but not this much, according to the Congressional Management Foundation. In 1987, for example, most administrative assistants in the House, the highest-ranking aides, had spent 5.5 years working in the Congress. In 1996, the average tenure had dropped to 4 years.

The length of tenure of senior Senate staffers has also dropped.

Second Careers on Capitol Hill

A review of the 1998 edition of "Washington Representatives," a directory of lobbyists, and of Congressional records, found 128 former members of Congress listed as lobbyists. This is less than 1 percent of the 17,000 lobbyists listed in the directory. Three percent of those who retired or who were defeated during the 70's are listed as lobbyists; 12 percent of those who left during the 80's as well as 22 percent of those who have left in the 90's are also listed. Overall, 12 percent of the Senators and Representatives who left Congress since 1970 are listed.

In a recent foundation survey, 58 percent of departing Congressional staffers cited a desire to earn more money as their reason for leaving; it was the second most frequent response given after a desire to pursue a different type of work.

THE MILLION-DOLLAR MAN

A Tax Analyst Joins the Fold

PricewaterhouseCoopers, the accounting firm that hired Mr. Kies to lobby on tax issues for its clients, may have already recouped its investment.

Last spring and summer, Mr. Kies led a lobbying blitz for some of the biggest names in corporate America, including the General Electric Company, to maintain a lucrative tax break. The provision, which Mr. Kies's old committee estimated would cost $1.8 billion in Federal revenue over 10 years, allowed United States corporations to reduce taxes on their overseas operations. Mr. Kies headed a team of 10 other PricewaterhouseCoopers analysts and lobbyists in a successful effort to maintain the status quo.

When the Treasury Department announced its intention to kill the provision, Mr. Kies swung into action, meeting many times with top Treasury officials, including Lawrence H. Summers, the Deputy Treasury Secretary. "We spent hours and hours with Donald C. Lubick, the Assistant Secretary for Tax Policy," Mr. Kies said in a recent interview. Mr. Kies dealt with both men at the Joint Tax Committee, which evaluates the tax implications of legislation.

Mr. Kies pushed hard with a central argument: that the provision was not really a loophole and would not result in a revenue loss from multinational companies shifting more of their operations overseas. Using Rube Goldberg-like diagrams that Mr. Kies likes to draw to illustrate complex tax issues, he carried the day. In June, the Treasury Department decided not to make the change, at least for the time being.

It also helped Mr. Kies that his old boss, the House Ways and Means Chairman Bill Archer, and other influential Republican tax writers, weighed in on his side. Federal lobbying laws prohibit Mr. Kies from lobbying Mr. Archer or his old committee for one year after his departure, but they are not much of an impediment. Former officials circumvent the law simply by designing the lobbying strategy and then letting their clients or colleagues do the direct lobbying until their one-year cooling-off period is over.

Coming from the Joint Tax Committee, Mr. Kies had free rein to lobby at Treasury, but on his team, which included lobbyists from other firms, was a former Treasury Department official.

In an interview, Mr. Kies said that the old fashioned stereotype of a back-slapping lobbyist trading on friendships was outmoded. Much of his time is spent crunching numbers and persuading Treasury officials and lawmakers that his analysis is on target. Of course, his political connections count, too, but Mr. Kies said of his old bosses, Mr. Archer and William V. Roth Jr., the Senate Finance Chairman, "Archer and Roth generally do what they believe is right."

"They don't do things because someone who's a buddy of theirs comes to see them," he said.

Ari Fleischer, an aide to Mr. Archer, had high praise for Mr. Kies.

"There are scores of top-notch lobbyists who have relationships but who don't have the great knowledge to go beyond a handshake," Mr. Fleischer said. "Ken Kies is an exception. He's a well-respected expert on tax law and he came to be one of the Hill's most admired strategists."

As the top aide at the Joint Tax Committee, Mr. Kies supervised a staff of more than 60. Almost every line of the sweeping tax bill passed last year was written by Mr. Kies. A year earlier, he helped break a three-year stalemate on how to make health coverage portable. Fortune Magazine named him "Mr. Tax" in a story on Washington's most powerful bureaucrats.

Without confirming or denying his salary, Mr. Kies stressed that he would have been making the same amount if he had stayed in the private sector instead of spending several years on a government salary. At Baker & Hostetler, the Cleveland-based law firm where he practiced tax law before 1994, he earned $500,000.

"The whole world was bidding for him and he's worth far

more than the great salary he is making," said former Congressman and Ways and Means Committee member Guy Vander Jagt, a Republican who worked with Mr. Kies when he was a Congressional staffer earlier in his career and who later practiced law with him at Baker & Hostetler. Mr. Vander Jagt tried to woo Mr.

MEMBERS OF THE HOUSE

Republicans

REPRESENTATIVE	STATE	SERVED	FIRM
John B. Anderson	Ill.	1961-81	Pres., World Federalist Assn.
Ed Bethune	Ark.	1979-85	Ed Bethune & Associates
Beau Boulter	Tex.	1985-89	
Donald G. Brotzman	Colo.	1963-65, 1967-75	Of counsel, Hopkins & Sutter
John H. Buchanan Jr.	Ala.	1965-81	Principal, Podesta Associates
Carroll A. Campbell Jr.	S.C.	1979-87	Pres. and C.E.O., American Council of Life Insurance
William Carney	N.Y.	1979-87	Pres., Bill Carney & Co.
Rod Chandler	Wash.	1983-93	Pres., Downey Chandler Inc.
Thomas J. Corcoran	Ill.	1977-85	Partner, O'Connor & Hannan
R. Lawrence Coughlin	Pa.	1969-93	Senior counsel, Eckert Seamans Cherin & Mellott
James K. Coyne	Pa.	1981-83	Pres., National Air Transportation Association
Robert W. Davis	Mich.	1979-93	Pres., Bob Davis & Associates
Edward J. Derwinski	Ill.	1959-83	Owner, Derwinski & Associates
William L. Dickinson	Ala.	1965-93	Senior partner, The Dickinson Group
Pete Du Pont	Del.	1971-77	Policy chairman, National Center for Policy Analysis
Jack Edwards	Ala.	1965-85	Associate, Ervin Technical Associates Inc.
Thomas B. Evans Jr.	Del.	1977-83	Pres., The Evans Group
Jack M. Fields Jr.	Tex.	1981-97	Pres. and C.E.O., Twenty-First Century Group
Paul Findley	Ill.	1961-83	Chairman, Council for the National Interest
Bill Frenzel	Minn.	1971-91	Pres., Ripon Society
Louis Frey Jr.	Fla.	1969-79	Pres., U.S. Assoc. of Former Members of Congress
Dan Frisa	N.Y.	1995-97	Partner, Federal Associates
Willis D. Gradison	Ohio	1975-93	Pres., Health Insurance Association of America
Fred Grandy	Iowa	1987-95	Pres. and C.E.O., Goodwill Industries International
Kent R. Hance	Tex.	1979-85	Partner, Hance, Scarborough, Woodward & Weisbart
Robert P. Hanrahan	Ill.	1973-75	Pres., R.P.H. & Associates
Frank Horton	N.Y.	1963-93	Of counsel, Venable, Baetjer, Howard & Civiletti
Hastings Keith	Mass.	1959-73	Co-chairman, National Committee on Public Employee Pension Systems
Greg Laughlin	Tex.	1989-97	Of counsel, Patton Boggs
Norman F. Lent	N.Y.	1971-93	Senior partner, Lent & Scrivner
Thomas G. Loeffler	Tex.	1979-87	Partner, Arter & Hadden
William D. Lowery	Calif.	1981-93	Partner, Copeland, Lowery & Jacquez
Jack H. McDonald	Mich.	1967-73	
Raymond J. McGrath	N.Y.	1981-93	Pres., Beer Institute
J. Alex McMillan	N.C.	1985-95	Consulting executive, The McMillan Group
Robert H. Michel	Ill.	1957-95	Sr. adviser, Corp. and Gov't Affairs, Hogan & Hartson
W. Henson Moore	La.	1975-87	Pres. and C.E.O., American Forest and Paper Assn.
Stanford E. Parris	Va.	1973-75, 1981-91	Of counsel, Dickstein Shapiro Morin & Oshinsky
John J. Rhodes 3d	Ariz.	1987-93	Hunton & Williams
Matthew J. Rinaldo	N.J.	1973-93	
Don Ritter	Pa.	1979-93	Chairman, National Enviornmental Policy Institute
Toby Roth	Wis.	1979-97	President, The Roth Group
James D. Santini	Nev.	1975-83	Santini, Chartered
Mark D. Siljander	Mich.	1981-87	Associate, Advantage Associates
Guy Vander Jagt	Mich.	1966-93	Of counsel, Baker & Hostetler
Robert S. Walker	Pa.	1977-97	Pres., The Wexler Group
Vin Weber	Minn.	1981-93	Partner, Clark, & Weinstock
Robert Whittaker	Kan.	1979-91	Senior legislative adviser, Fleshman-Hillard Inc.
George C. Wortley	N.Y.	1981-89	Exec. vice pres., Dierman, Wortley and Zola
Bill Zeliff	N.H.	1991-97	Associate, Advantage Associates
Roger H. Zion	Ind.	1967-75	Pres., Resources Development Inc.

Kies back to the firm, but failed because it could not compete with PricewaterhouseCoopers's seven-figure offer.

SHOW US THE MONEY

Fat Paychecks For Everyone

It has been nearly 15 years since Michael K. Deaver, a former Reagan White House aide turned lobbyist, sparked controversy when a Time Magazine cover story showed him flaunting his multimillion-dollar accounts and pictured him riding in a limousine. But earlier this year, Washingtonian Magazine, a glossy magazine that caters to the city's professional elite, had no trouble rounding up many of the city's 50 top lobbyists to pose for a group photo accompanying an article titled, "Show Me the Money!" Though he was not in the picture, Mr. Deaver is still a successful lobbyist at one of the city's premier public relations firms.

The nexus of lobbying and campaign fund-raising, which lawmakers and lobbyists used to make efforts to conceal, has also never been more graphically displayed. It is no coincidence that some of Washington's most successful lobbyists, such as Mr. Barbour and Daniel A. Dutko, a close adviser to Vice President Al Gore, are also leading fund-raisers for their respective parties.

Half of all political action committee contributions to Federal candidates and parties flow from Washington, with many donors listing K Street corridor zip codes. Two dozen lobbyists interviewed said they received hundreds of fund-raising solicitations from Congressmen and their parties last year, some shortly after a lobbying meeting with a particular lawmaker.

"You can almost count on getting some kind of fund-raising solicitation after you've been to the Hill," said one lobbyist who insisted he not be named. "The time in between has gotten shorter and shorter and it's gotten more and more brazen."

When Mr. Andrews, the business lobbyist, recently signed up a trade association of home equity lenders as a client, one of the first pieces of advice he gave the association was to establish a political action committee. "Under the current system, campaign giving and fund-raising are essential," he said. "When it isn't done, it's noticed."

Corporate interests that finance the largest portion of Washington's lobbying are fortifying their influence with record campaign contributions to Federal lawmakers. Even as the House moved to ban the large contributions to political parties that are known as soft money, the national parties scooped up $115 million in these big donations from business and other interests over the last 18 months. That is more than double the amount raised during a comparable period in the last non-Presidential election cycle. Microsoft Corporation, which opened a Washington government affairs office only three years ago but now has one of the largest fleets of lobbyists—more than a dozen people and firms—recently signed on through one of its executives as a member of the Republican Party's Team 100, its elite corps of $100,000 donors.

Labor unions, which are among the Democratic Party's biggest donors, also field large teams of lobbyists. Labor money and lobbyists played an important role late last year when the House defeated President Clinton's efforts to expand his trade authority.

In the past two years, serious scandals have erupted involving lobbyists and fund-raising, but few lobbyists have suffered serious consequences. James H. Lake, a prominent Republican lobbyist, was convicted of making illegal corporate campaign contributions as part of the Federal criminal investigation of Mike Espy, the former Agriculture Secretary. After Mr. Lake left the firm where he worked when the illicit contributions were made, he was offered a position as managing director of the Washington office of Burson-Marstellar, a public relations firm. Last January, Mr. Lake was fined $150,000, placed on probation and ordered to write a paper on Federal election laws. Mr. Lake's monograph was distributed to the 2,000 members of the American League of Lobbyists. In April, Ms. Eppard,

MEMBERS OF THE SENATE

Republicans

SENATOR	STATE	SERVED	FIRM
Mark Andrews	N.D.	1981-87	Chairman, Andrews Associates Inc. (also seerved in House, 1963-81)
Howard H. Baker Jr.	Tenn.	1967-85	Shareholder, Baker, Donelson, Bearman & Caldwell
John C. Danforth	Mo.	1976-95	Partner, Bryan Cave
David Durenberger	Minn.	1978-95	Vice pres., Public Policy Partners d.b.a. Durenberger/Foote
Paul Laxalt	Nev.	1974-87	Pres., The Paul Laxalt Group
James A. McClure	Idaho	1973-91	Principal, McClure, Gerard & Neuenschwander Inc. (House, 1967-73)
Bob Packwood	Ore.	1969-95	Sunrise Research Corp.
Larry Pressler	S.D.	1979-97	Pressler & Associates (House, 1975-79)
Warren B. Rudman	N.H.	1981-93	Partner, Paul, Weiss, Rifkin, Wharton & Garrison
Steven D. Symms	Idaho	1981-93	Pres., Symms, Lehn & Associates Inc.
Malcolm Wallop	Wyo.	1977-95	Chairman, Frontiers of Freedom Institute

the transportation lobbyist, was indicted by a Federal grand jury in Boston on charges of accepting improper payments from a lobbyist and a businessman while she was on the House Transportation Committee chairman's staff. She has denied wrongdoing and is still lobbying, having won provisions for her clients in the sweeping highway bill passed this summer.

A BIPARTISAN BAZAAR

Peddling on Both Sides of the Fence

"When I came to Washington, there was a small coterie of committee chairmen with iron-clad seniority and tremendous power," recalled Charls E. Walker, a former Treasury Department official during the Eisenhower administration who opened the capital's first non-lawyer lobbying shop in 1973, called Charls Walker Associates. "On a tax issue, if you had the agreement of the chairman of Ways and Means, you could go out and play golf" for the rest of the day.

These days, Mr. Walker said, "you can't rest easy unless you've worked all the members."

With new committee and subcommittee chairmen, and such a slender Republican majority, there are many more bases for lobbyists to cover. The demand for Democrats with ties to the Clinton-Gore administration and Republicans with connections to G.O.P. lawmakers has produced a veritable bazaar of political influence, with single companies and trade associations assembling all-star bipartisan lobbying teams. On the bankruptcy bill, for example, the American Financial Services Association showcased in its newsletter its "team of highly

MEMBERS OF THE HOUSE
Democrats

REPRESENTATIVE	STATE	SERVED	FIRM
Michael A. Andrews	Tex.	1983-95	Partner, Vinson & Elkins
Beryl F. Anthony Jr.	Ark.	1979-93	Partner and director, legislative and regulatory practice, Winston & Strawn
James Bacchus	Fla.	1991-95	Shareholder, Greenberg, Traurig, Hoffman, Lipoff, Rosen & Quentel
Michael D. Barnes	Md.	1979-87	Partner, Hogan & Hartson
James H. Bilbray	Nev.	1987-95	Partner, Alcalde & Fay
Lucien E. Blackwell	Pa.	1991-95	Whitten & Diamond
.James J. Blanchard	Mich.	1975-83	Member of firm, Verner, Liipfer, Bernhard, McPherson and Hand
Bill Brewster	Okla.	1991-97	Vice pres., R. Duffy Wall and Associates
Terry L. Bruce	Ill.	1985-93	Senior legislative advisor, Fleishman-Hillard Inc.
Jim Chapman	Tex.	1985-97	Partner, Arter & Hadden
Ronald D. Coleman	Tex.	1983-97	Senior vice pres., Advantage Associates
Thomas J. Downey	N.Y.	1975-93	Chairman, Downey Chandler Inc.
Dennis E. Eckart	Ohio	1981-93	Senior partner, Arter & Hadden
Glenn English	Okla.	1975-94	C.E.O., National Rural Electric Cooperative Association
Billy Lee Evans	Ga.	1977-83	Senior leagislative adviser, Fleishman-Hillard Inc.
Dave Evans	Ind.	1975-83	President, Dave Evans Associates
Dante B. Fascell	Fla.	1955-93	Holland & Knight
Don Fuqua	Fla.	1963-87	Pres., Aerospace Industries Association of America
Robert Garcia	N.Y.	1978-90	Washington rep., Robert Garcia and Associates
Sam M. Gibbons	Fla.	1963-97	Chairman, Gibbons & Company
Herbert E. Harris 2d	Va.	1978-81	Partner, Harris Ellsworth & Levin
Peter J. Hoagland	Neb.	1989-95	Partner, Arent Fox Kintner Plotkin & Kahn
Ed Jenkins	Ga.	1977-93	Vice pres., Winburn & Jenkins Inc.
Ray Kogovsek	Colo.	1979-85	Pres., Kogovsek & Associates
Michael J. Kopetski	Ore.	1991-95	Public affairs consultant, Downey Chandler Inc.
Peter H. Kostmayer	Pa.	1977-81 1983-93	Exec. director, Zero Population Growth Inc.
Peter N. Kyros	Me.	1967-75	Pres., Kyros & Cummins Associates
Larry LaRocco	Idaho	1991-95	Managing director, A.B.A. Securities Association, American Bankers Association
Marvin Leath	Tex.	1979-91	Partner, Marvin Leath Associates
Richard H. Lehman	Calif.	1983-95	Pres., Sacramento-Potomac Consulting Inc.
Meldon E. Levine	Calif.	1983-93	Partner, Gibson, Dunn & Crutcher
Elliott H. Levitas	Ga.	1975-85	Partner, Kilpatrick Stockton
M. Dawson Mathis	Ga.	1971-81	Dawson Mathis & Associates
Frank McCloskey	Ind.	1983-95	Partner, Barnes & Thornburg
Dave McCurdy	Okla.	1981-95	Chairman, The McCurdy Group
Lloyd Meeds	Wash.	1965-79	Of counsel, Preston Gates Ellis & Rouvelas Meeds
Daniel A. Mica	Fla.	1979-89	Pres., and C.E.O., Credit Union National Association
Anthony T. Moffett Jr.	Conn.	1975-83	Vice Pres., International Government Affairs, Monsanto
G. V. Montgomery	Miss.	1967-97	The Montgomery Group
Jim Moody	Wis.	1983-93	Pres. and C.E.O., Interaction
Bill Orton	Utah	1991-97	Jones, Waldo, Holbrook & McDonough
Paul G. Rogers	Fla.	1955-79	Partner, Hogan & Hartson
Fred B. Rooney	Pa.	1963-79	Senior consultant, Cassidy & Associates, Inc.
Charles Rose	N.C.	1973-97	Rose & Hefner Consulting
Marty A. Russo	Ill.	1975-93	Vice Chairman, Director and C.E.O., Cassidy & Associates
Patricia Schroeder	Colo.	1973-97	Pres., American Association of Publishers
Gerry E. Sikorski	Minn.	1983-93	Partner, Holland & Knight
Jim Slattery	Kan.	1983-95	Partner, Wiley, Rein & Fielding
Stephen J. Solarz	N.Y.	1975-93	Senior counselor, Apco Associates
James V. Stanton	Ohio	1971-77	Principal, Stanton & Associates
Al Swift	Wash.	1979-95	Partner, Colling, Swift & Hynes
James W. Syrnington	Mo.	1969-77	Partner, O'Connor & Hannan
Charles A. Vanik	Ohio	1955-81	Of counsel, Squire, Sanders & Dempsey
Charles Wilson	Tex.	1973-97	Principal, Hooper Hooper Owen & Gould
Leo C. Zeferetti	N.Y.	1975-83	Self-employed consultant; Legis. Dir. of A.F.L.-C.I.O. Building and Construction Trades Dept.

MEMBERS OF THE SENATE

Democrats

SENATOR	STATE	SERVED	FIRM
Birch Bayh	Ind.	1963-81	Partner, Oppenheimer Wolff Donnelly & Bayh
John C. Culver	Iowa	1975-81	Partner, Arent Fox Kintner Plotkin & Kahn (also served in House, 1965-75)
Dennis DeConcini	Ariz.	1977-95	Partner, Parry, Romani & DeConcini
Alan J. Dixon	Ill.	1981-93	Partner, Bryan Cave
Walter D. Huddleston	Ky.	1973-85	Consultant, Hecht, Spencer & Associates
J. Bennett Johnston	La.	1972-97	Johnston & Associates
Russell B. Long	La.	1948-87	Partner, Long Law Firm
Howard M. Metzenbaum	Ohio	1977-95	Chairman, Consumer Federation of America
George J. Mitchell	Me.	1980-95	Special counsel, Verner, Liipfert, Bernhard, McPherson and Hand
Donald W. Riegle Jr.	Mich.	1977-95	Deputy chairman, Shandwick International, Shandwick Public Affairs (House, 1967-76)
Joseph D. Tydings	Md.	1965-71	Partner, Dickstein Shapiro Morin & Oshinsky

experienced lobbyists and consultants," including two Republican firms, Barbour Griffith & Rogers and Timmons & Co., as well as Democratic bench strength from Verner, Liipfert, Bernard, McPherson and Hand, the law firm of former Treasury Secretary Lloyd Bentsen, and President Clinton's polling firm, Penn & Schoen Associates.

There have been many mergers of Democrats and Republicans in lobbying firms. In recent weeks there has been speculation that two respected House members, California Democrat Vic Fazio and New York Republican Bill Paxton, who are both retiring from the House this year, will join forces and open a new lobbying firm.

Parry, Romani & DeConcini, a firm that specializes in health and pharmaceutical lobbying, was long known for its connections to Orrin G. Hatch, the Republican Senate Judiciary Committee Chairman, and Dennis DeConcini, a former Democratic Senator from Arizona who joined the firm when he left the Senate in 1995.

Jack Valenti, president of the Motion Picture Association of America and a political veteran who was a top aide to President Lyndon Johnson, has been Hollywood's man in Washington for the last 32 years. He said he was nostalgic for the days when he employed a single lobbying firm, Akin, Gump, which is now one of seven firms that the film association keeps on retainer.

Mr. Valenti is himself a celebrated Washington insider who earns more than $1 million. Although he enjoys easy access to most lawmakers, he said he needed so many other lobbyists because the film association had an ever-broadening agenda of foreign and domestic issues before a host of committees and agencies, from the House Judiciary Committee to the

Office of the United States Trade Representative.

"I don't need any lobbyists for access or entree," Mr. Valenti said. "I need troops in the field."

Akin, Gump is still on Mr. Valenti's payroll, according to Congressional lobbying files. Another mainly Democratic firm, Verner, Liipfert, lobbies on Hollywood's trade and telecommunications issues. Still another Democrat in Mr. Valenti's lobbying arsenal is Mr. Podesta, whose brother, John, was once his lobbying partner and is now the President's top damage-control adviser on the Lewinsky imbroglio. Anthony Podesta lobbies on ratings issues for the television subsidiaries of the movie studios, according to the records. The film association has also hired Mr. DeConcini's firm and the firm of former Democratic Representative Marty Russo.

Mr. Valenti has also beefed up his Republican lobbying retinue, hiring Republicans like Mr. Vander Jagt, who said his services were in much greater demand after the Republicans won control of the House in 1994.

FIELD DRAWS MANY

The Experienced And the New Too

In an interview, Mr. Vander Jagt joked that his first years as a lobbyist after he retired in 1992 were so slow that, "I would have represented Al Capone or Fidel Castro." That all changed after the election in November 1994.

Mr. Vander Jagt can offer the motion picture industry and other clients a feel for what the Republican leadership is thinking because he continues to reap the perks of being a former Congressman, attending weekly meetings of several groups that are open only to current and former Republican lawmakers. "It's a lobbyist's dream to be sitting there with the committee chairmen and to find out what's going on," said Mr. Vander Jagt, who lobbies on tax and other issues. "You have all the benefits of your former life and none of the hardships," he adds.

Children, wives and even siblings of lawmakers have hung out lobbying shingles. There is Linda Hall Daschle, the wife of the Democratic Senate leader, and a former top official at Federal Aviation Administration who lobbies on aviation issues. Randy DeLay, the brother of House Whip Tom DeLay, also has transportation clients. (An ethics complaint against Representative DeLay that was sparked by his brother's lobbying activities was dismissed last year by the House Ethics Committee).

The son of former Louisiana Senator J. Bennett Johnston is one of the city's most successful lobbyists. Mr. Johnston, former chairman of the Senate energy committee, joined his son in the business after he retired in 1996, and so did one of the former Senator's top aides. Their client roster brims with energy interests and they also lobby for clients on trade issues involving China.

Former Senator Bob Packwood, a former chairman of the Senate Finance Committee, left office after the Ethics Committee decided he should be expelled because sexual misconduct and allegations that he had given legislative favors to a lobbyist. During the first half of this year, Mr. Packwood's firm, Sunrise Research Corporation, took in $440,000 lobbying on tax and trade issues for blue-chip clients such as Northwest Airlines and Marriott International.

But even the young and inexperienced are entering the field of lobbying. Lobbying has become an academic field, with American University offering a popular course on it.

Andrew Lacy, 23, for example, is an alumnus of a two-week intensive lobbying program at American. From his perch on K Street at Marlowe & Company, he enthusiastically sets up client meetings on Capitol Hill and attends fund-raisers for lawmakers.

"It's fun to meet a Senator or a Congressman and make your pitch," said Mr. Lacy, who is earning $25,000 as a beginner.

Mr. Lacy, who grew up on Maryland's Eastern Shore in a rural farm area where his father is in the agriculture business and his mother is a public school teacher, said he hopes to keep his lobbying job while he takes evening law classes.

James Thurber a professor who runs a lobbying institute at American, gets well-known lobbyists like Mr. Boggs to teach the trade to fledgling lobbyists like Mr. Lacy. Professor Thurber's students are required to develop a lobbying plan and to make their pitch to a panel of mock lawmakers. "We want them to feel the pressure of what it's like to be on a lobbying campaign," Professor Thurber said.

Mr. Lacy was persuasive in his lobbying assignment to discourage the mock lawmakers from restricting a computer practice known as "spamming," where businesses send unsolicited E-mail to consumers. He got an A and a job offer from one of the graders, lobbyist Howard Marlowe.

Mr. Marlowe's clients include property owners and localities trying to win financing for beach conservation, a cause that Mr. Lacy said he is comfortable embracing. He said some of his friends were working

for tobacco companies, something he said he understood but would not do. "They are making ends meet," Mr. Lacy said. "They are learning the system. They are getting a foot in the door of the business."

THE RIGHT CONNECTIONS

Gore or Gingrich: Gucci Gulch Ties

Thomas K. Downey, a New York Democrat, came to Washington in 1974 as the youngest of the Watergate Babies, the Young Turks who were elected to clean up Washington the year of President Nixon's resignation.

No longer a young reformer, Mr. Downey, who lost his seat in 1992, heads a lobbying firm, Downey & Chandler, that earned more than $2 million last year from clients like the Boeing Company, Microsoft and Time Warner Inc.

The former New York Congressman is also the most important member of Vice President Al Gore's kitchen cabinet of advisers. All of the members of this informal advisory group are expected to play pivotal roles in his Presidential campaign in 2000 and many are charter members of the K Street elite. The group includes top Democratic fund-raisers like Mr. Knight and Mr. Dutko and two former domestic policy advisers to Mr. Gore, Roy Neel and Greg Simon, who both lobby for telecommunications interests. Another member is Jack Quinn, the former White House counsel who was also Mr. Gore's chief of staff. Mr. Quinn was a lead lobbyist for a coalition of computer companies that pressed for a new administration policy, announced earlier this month by Mr. Gore, that loosened regulations on the export of sensitive software and hardware that shields information from public scrutiny.

In an interview, Mr. Downey said he kept his lobbying separate from his friendship with Mr. Gore, with whom he frequently socialized. (Mr. Gore tore a muscle while playing basketball with Mr. Downey in the House gym).

And far from feeling like he has sold out his old principles, Mr. Downey said, "I do more interesting things now than I did as a member of Congress." One thing that is different is how he lives. When he served in Congress, his family had a cramped Capitol Hill town house. They now live in a large home near the National Cathedral, a house with a hand-painted dining room mural, that, he joked, "looks like one of my fund-raisers should be living in it."

Mr. Gore's coziness with lobbyists is hardly unusual. The Federal Election Commission has been investigating whether the House majority whip John A. Boehner's weekly tête-à-têtes with business lobbyists involved unlawful coordination of their political activities, allegations that Mr. Boehner has denied.

Former Representative Vin Weber is among the most successful of a new crop of Republican lobbyists. Working as a tag team of political influence, Mr. Weber often pairs up with Mr. Downey for clients, including Microsoft. He works out of the gleaming offices of Clark & Wienstock, a Wall Street consulting firm that did not have a Washington outpost until Mr. Weber opened one in 1994, after he retired from Congress.

As one of Mr. Gingrich's best friends in the House, the Minnesota Republican was in immediate demand. "People were looking for G.O.P. consultants and lobbyists all over the place," Mr. Weber said in an interview. Mr. Weber now heads an eight-man office that reported lobbying revenues of $2.2 million in 1997.

Like Mr. Downey, Mr. Weber is still an inside player, jetting off earlier this year to join Mr. Gingrich at a Republican event in Palm Springs, Calif. And he, too, finds his new profession more rewarding in many ways. "With no disrespect to Congress," Mr. Weber said, "not everything you do as a Congressman is very exciting."

Mr. Weber and Mr. Downey also have the luxury of turning down clients. Both men refused to work for the tobacco industry and Mr. Weber said he would not be comfortable registering as an agent for a foreign client.

Another former Republican lawmaker in demand is Bob Dole, the Republican Presidential candidate in 1996. He is now "of counsel" at the Washington-based law firm of Verner, Liipfert, where he said he does not lobby but provides strategic advice to clients.

But his former political prominence still lands him national platforms, such as an appearance on David Letterman's talk show earlier this summer. There, between jokes, he took a moment to criticize President Clinton for his stance toward Taiwan. He did not disclose that his firm represents Taiwan, a relationship that required him to register as a foreign agent. Asked if he should have, Mr. Dole said that he had been a supporter of Taiwan for years before he joined Verner Liipfert.

Mr. Dole's firm, loaded with political superstars such as George J. Mitchell, the former Senate majority leader, and Ann W. Richards, the former Texas Governor, earned $19 million in lobbying fees last year, the most reported by any firm. Its partners also have contributed generously to Federal candidates and the political parties.

Senator John McCain, whose anti-tobacco and campaign finance overhaul bills were defeated amid a hailstorm of lobbying, said Washington would be dominated by moneyed interests as long as lobbyists remained at the hub of campaign fund-raising.

"The lobbyists give out the soft money," said the Arizona Republican, whose campaign finance bill would ban soft money contributions. "If you take away the soft money you do really reduce the influence of these people."

Consumer activist Ralph Nader, who has watched the growth of corporate influence in the capital for the last 30 years, agreed, but said Senator McCain did not go far enough. Mr. Nader advocates public funding of Federal elections as well as new mechanisms for building genuine citizens' lobbies.

"Trying to reform lobbying is like trying to stop a leak," he said. "You block the water here, and it just goes around the corner."

THE BUYING OF THE BENCH

By Sheila Kaplan and Zoë Davidson

The campaign fundraising scandal has drawn new attention to the way moneyed interests buy political favors in Washington. But far from the nation's capital, many of these same donors operate unchecked in a venue that may prove more disturbing than the Lincoln Bedroom: the state courts. In the thirty-nine states that elect judges at some level, the cost of judicial races is rising at least as fast as that of either Congressional races or presidential campaigns, as candidates for the bench pay for sophisticated ads, polls and consultants. A recent study by the California Commission on the Courts found that the cost of the average superior court race in the Los Angeles area more than doubled every year, increasing twenty-two-fold from 1976 to 1994. In Washington State, winners in 1980 spent between $30,000 and $50,000; by 1995 winners spent at least $150,000. In North Carolina, the American Judicature Society reported that the biggest spender for the Supreme Court in 1988 paid $90,330; by 1994 it was $241,709.

Fueling these campaigns is an influx of money from the tobacco industry, casinos, insurance companies, doctors and businesses. Upping the ante are defense lawyers and trial lawyers, along with unions and, recently, the religious right (in fact, John Dowless, executive director of the Christian Coalition of Florida, considers judicial elections "the next hot-button issue" for his group). It adds up to a system of justice in which judges are compromised by the time they take the bench—and those who are perceived as unsympathetic to whichever interest group has the most money that year often end up simply kicked out

of office. The Nation's analysis of campaign contributions in 1996 state Supreme Court races has found:

• In Texas, Chief Justice Thomas Phillips, first elected in 1988 on a campaign finance reform platform, raised $486,809 of his 1996 re-election funds from corporate defense lawyers; $213,016 from energy and natural-resource companies; and $159,498 from finance, insurance and real estate firms.

• In Ohio, Justice Evelyn Stratton raised $74,885 from finance, insurance and real estate firms; $134,900 from lawyers and lobbyists, most of whom represent big business before the court; and $16,476 from medical interests. The law firm that handled her campaign represents the tobacco industry in a case bound for her court. Stratton received the Ohio Chamber of Commerce's highest pro-business rating.

• In a notorious Alabama race, businesses determined to defeat incumbent Justice Kenneth Ingraham contributed more than $668,704 to opponent Harold See.

• In Nevada, Justice William Maupin received more than $80,000 from casinos and gambling interests, much of it while ruling favorably on a landmark casino case.

• In Pennsylvania, Justice Russell Nigro reaped more than $458,473, from lawyers, mostly the plaintiff's bar, in one of the few cases in 1996 in which they outspent the corporate contributors and defense lawyers.

• In West Virginia, Justice Elliot Maynard's largest contributors were coal companies and their employees, among them A.T. Massey Coal Company, Golden

Chance Coal Company and the lawyers who represent them.

"I can't think of a clearer conflict of interest than a judge taking cash from plaintiffs or defendants," says Charles Lewis, executive director of the Center for Public Integrity, which monitors government ethics. "That's about as direct a conflict of interest as we can have in our political system. The idea that a judge could take cash from them and issue an 'objective' ruling is complete hogwash."

Lewis's opinion is echoed by legal and civic organizations ranging from the American Bar Association (A.B.A.) to the American Judicature Society (A.J.S.) to the Fund for Modern Courts. But these groups can only make recommendations. Effecting change—setting spending caps for candidates, putting limits on donations, providing free advertising—is up to the states. Likewise, changes from election to merit selection (the A.J.S.-favored plan in which judges are appointed by a chief executive from a list named by a nonpartisan panel, and run for retention rather than re-election) can also only be accomplished through state action.

Further complicating the issue, many civil rights activists oppose merit selection, citing lack of diversity on the courts in states where it has been adopted and a reluctance to give up the ability to vote out bad judges in a timely manner. Yet in 1996, the National Voting Rights Institute filed suit in Los Angeles on behalf of a coalition of civil rights groups, challenging private financing of judicial elections there. The group says that under the current system, money determines the outcome of judicial races, effectively shutting out those without sufficient means.

"Our point is that thirty-nine states have a long tradition of holding some judicial elections, and if they're going to hold elections they should be free and fair, and not based on wealth," says John Bonifaz, executive director of the institute. "It's clear what's occurring in Los Angeles—the ones who can raise the most money or are personally wealthy become judges. For communities of color, their candidates are not able to get elected because of the disproportionate level of poverty."

The current system is troubling not only for people who worry about appearing before a judge who was underwritten by the opposing party or counsel but for anybody who has to live under the precedents being set by judges hand-picked by moneyed interests like oil companies and insurance firms.

"Donations, and the appearance by the donors in front of the judge, affect public trust and confidence in the judge's impartiality," says Kathleen Sampson, project director for the A.J.S. "Our concern is that

there not even be the appearance that a judge might favor a donor over another litigant in a case."

The A.J.S. and the A.B.A. have longstanding guidelines that call for judges to avoid compromising their courts by accepting all donations through a third party, thus shielding themselves from learning their patrons' identities. The A.B.A. acknowledges that this is untenable, but until recently has not addressed the issue. "I've heard many judicial candidates say publicly they won't look at the list of contributors," says James Mundy, former president of the Pennsylvania state bar and chairman of a state panel studying the issue. "Unfortunately, every time they say that, they admit they are breaching Pennsylvania election law. There's an affidavit accompanying each filing, where the candidate must attest under oath that he or she has personally reviewed every contribution and that each and every one of them is from the people listed, and all that."

Florida Circuit Court Judge Roberto Pineiro recalls that in his 1990 race, "I was told not to despair about raising the much-needed cash, as there would be many attorneys willing to give me money solely because they would be appearing before me in court. This I felt raised a moral dilemma. But I was told not to worry, as I would never actually ask attorneys for money, I would simply ask attorneys to ask other attorneys to give me money. This, I was told, would be ethically correct, even if utterly contrary to the legal principle that an agent's actions on behalf of a principal are deemed to be the actions of the principal."

'I can't think of a clearer conflict of interest than a judge taking cash from plaintiffs or defendant,' observes one ethics watchdog.

Like candidates for Congress, judicial candidates who try to avoid conflicts of interest by imposing their own limits on donations have a tough time raising enough money to campaign. In Pennsylvania last year, State Appeals Court Judge Kate Ford Elliott, who received the state bar's highest rating, restricted donations from lawyers to $100 a head in her Supreme Court race; there is no state limit. She lost in the primary by 2,000 votes after being outspent seven to one.

In such a system, it's easy to understand why lawyers often feel obliged to pay to play—even to campaigns of well-meaning judges during an election, or, like Kevin McCarthy, after it. Following McCarthy's campaign last year, his manager had an idea: Instead of throwing the traditional debt-burner party, the judge would sell sponsorships to his induction ceremony in the Green Room of the San Francisco War Memorial.

"I would be honored if you would serve as a sponsor of this event," he wrote to prospective donors, on letterhead that read, "Judge Kevin M. McCarthy, San Francisco Superior Court." "Your contribution," he continued, "will be used for election debt retirement. All sponsors will be listed on the invitation to the event, which will be mailed to members of the local bar, community leaders, and citizens in every neighborhood."

McCarthy sees nothing wrong with his pitch and calls it common practice in California. While he understands the potential conflicts caused by election of judges, McCarthy, who says he's the only openly gay judge on the bench, believes merit selection would prevent people like himself from holding office.

But the cost of maintaining the "diversity" yielded by that perspective is high. Consider recent events in Louisiana, where the state's oil and gas industry has been flexing its muscle in Supreme Court races for several years. The oil and gas industry is the source of most of the state's wealth, but also most of its pollution—and the basis for the Gulf Coast region's nickname as "Cancer Alley."

Among the toughest problems are the 2,500 abandoned oil wells that litter the landscape and leach toxic chemicals into nearby land and water. Lacking the resources to pursue the polluters, Louisiana Attorney General Richard Ieyoub offered private law firms a contingency fee on money awarded to the state through prosecution of those responsible for the orphaned wells. It's an arrangement often used by federal agencies and state attorneys general in tobacco cases and other complex litigation that strains government resources.

Louisiana businesses called the plan an environmental witch hunt and sued, sending the case on a two-year journey to the state Supreme Court. When it got there they were ready: Instead of just spending their money on lawyers, the business groups took a more modern tack and spent it on a judge.

An analysis by *The Nation* of campaign contributions to 1996 Louisiana Supreme Court candidate Chet Traylor shows that of $577,256 we could identify, more than $250,000 came from oil and gas industry executives, their lawyers and Louisiana for Business and Industry (LABI), which spearheaded Traylor's campaign against incumbent Joe Bleich. Individual LABI members gave more, among them Edward Diefenthal, whose family owns metal scrapyards and related businesses. They ponied up more than $70,000 and flew Traylor to fundraisers in his jet.

Traylor went on to win, and then cast his vote against the Attorney General, giving the industry

Dicey Justice

The casino industry doesn't like to gamble in court. In the past two years, the folks who run Nevada's roulette wheels and slot machines have poured more than $300,000 into the state's judicial races. To further pledge their support, the casinos, led by gambling mogul Steve Wynn, raised another $100,000 to defeat a proposal that would have imposed term limits on judges.

As the top moneymen behind the courts, the casinos can nearly always insure that their candidates win. It's a system that many Nevada lawyers say has skewed justice. And no cases better illustrate the point than those of the families of Ida Ray and Carol Pappas against the Fremont Street Experience.

Ray and Pappas, who have lived in Las Vegas for decades, owned property on an increasingly valuable downtown corner. In the late eighties, the city government joined forces with eight casinos to propose the Fremont Street Experience, a $63 million redevelopment project. Although the city had assured the property owners that their land was safe, in 1994 the city seized it under eminent domain and razed their buildings and those of two other landowners, Artemis Ham Jr. and former U.S. Senator Chic Hecht.

The Fremont Street partnership offered to reimburse Pappas $360,000 for 7,000 square feet of land, which she said did not compensate her for lost annual rent of more than $60,000 per year and was considerably less than the $6 million Wynn paid for a similar parcel nearby. Ray, Hecht and Ham were offered similar deals. Ham accepted; Hecht continued to fight the casinos.

Gaming interests heavily supported the two judges who heard the ensuing Ray and Pappas cases. Stephen Huffaker, the district court judge who first presided over the Pappas case, received full support from casino interests before and during his work on the case. In March 1995, Huffaker ruled against the Pappas claim of lack of due process in the eminent domain seizure. Huffaker also rejected the Pappas claim that the Fremont Street partnership had intentionally caused them to miss a crucial hearing by burying notice of a date change in an enormous stack of documents. After Huffaker disclosed that he owned 12,000 shares of stock in one of the casinos participating in the project, Pappas's lawyers asked him to step down from the case (they later learned that his son had been given a caddy job at Steve Wynn's golf course). He did, but by then his ruling for the city had enabled the partnership to construct a casino parking garage on Pappas's former land.

While the Pappases were in Huffaker's court, the Rays had a similar case before District Court Judge William Maupin. Like Huffaker, Maupin ruled consistently for the city-casino partnership. (Ida Ray died while an appeal was pending and her daughter settled.) At the time, casinos staked him more than $80,000 in his run for the Supreme Court. Huffaker was replaced by Judge Don Chairez, who ruled for the family and harshly criticized Huffaker and the Fremont Street Experience. Supported in the past by the casinos, Chairez will presumably be on his own in the next election.

S.K. and Z.D.

plaintiffs a four-to-three victory. He declined comment on the case, but LABI's political director, Virginia Sawyer, says, "If you had . . . Joe Bleich instead of Chet Traylor, you would have had a different decision." Noting a recent string of pro-business rulings, she adds, "In my view, any of those cases wouldn't have happened as they did."

That's a sore point for Ieyoub, who believes LABI's donations pose conflicts of interest for the judges. Among Traylor's donors, for example, are law firms that represent the tobacco industry, chemical companies, insurance firms, medical practices and other parties with cases pending before the high court.

"Everybody has a right to contribute to political races," Ieyoub says, "but when you threaten individuals with the fact that huge sums of money are going to be used against their candidacy if they don't toe the line, then that is almost extortionlike."

Sawyer is candid and unapologetic, the Roger Tamraz of judicial campaigns. Her goal is to raise and spend as much money as necessary to see pro-business, conservative judges ensconced in the courts. "We would prefer that judges not be elected, but as long as they are elected, we are going to be involved in the process," Sawyer says.

In the three elections since LABI has ventured into judicial races, the group has spent about $420,000 on campaigns, and had even wider impact by soliciting additional donations from members and pressing them to volunteer for phone banks and efforts to get out the business vote. It's been a wise investment. Not only has the Supreme Court increasingly ruled for business interests, it's even launched an investigation into the polluters' worst enemy: the Tulane Environmental Law Clinic. And LABI's success has made it a model for chambers of commerce elsewhere, which piggyback campaigns for business-friendly judges on tort reform drives that continue to play out around the country.

"I don't think there's any question that there's a greater awareness of the role the courts play," says Sherman Joyce, president of the American Tort Reform Association. "The conventional wisdom was you don't like the law, you go to the legislature and you get it changed. The dynamic has changed. You go to the legislature, you get the law changed, then you have to take the appropriate steps so that the law is not overturned by the courts."

One might expect a public backlash against such attempts to buy influence on the courts. But LABI and other state tort reform advocates throughout the country have mounted an effective public relations campaign that frames the debate not as lawyers versus lawyers or businesses versus citizens who might have

cases before the courts but as (like the tort reform fight) greedy trial lawyers versus helpless small businesses that want only to be good corporate citizens and survive. Yet while Sawyer says LABI represents small businesses, a look at contributors to its PAC war chest shows that these donations are buttressed by more generous sums from defense lawyers, oil and gas companies and tobacco giants like Philip Morris and R.J. Reynolds.

For the tobacco industry, LABI represents a backdoor channel to judicial candidates, who are wary of accepting direct donations. When Chet Traylor's opponent Joe Bleich revealed that the New York office of Philip Morris had contributed $5,000 to Traylor's campaign, he gave it back. But his finances didn't suffer: Lawyers retained by Philip Morris gave Traylor more than $15,000 on their own. And they gave $10,000 to LABI's PACs, as did R.J. Reynolds the same day. Philip Morris spokeswoman Darienne Dennis says the company has decided to stop making corporate contributions to judicial races, although she notes that individual lawyers and executives may continue to do so.

TEXAS: REFORMING THE REFORMER

When Thomas Phillips ran for the Texas Supreme Court back in 1988, he said that donations from lawyers and others with interests before the courts had undermined public confidence in the system. In his re-election bid in 1996, he took $1.4 million of it.

"I don't like the system," says Phillips, who serves on an A.B.A. panel charged with developing an alternative to it. "I've been a continual advocate of taking partisanship out of it and lessening the influence of money." But until a new system is adopted, Phillips invokes the same argument espoused by Bill Clinton and others who call themselves reformists while accepting huge sums of money: "I won't unilaterally disarm." He adds, "I think a judge's principal protection is to limit the size of contributions and seek to obtain as diverse a base of contributors as possible."

But Phillips hasn't really done so. Of the more than $1.2 million *The Nation* was able to identify, more than $1 million came from businesses, doctors and the lawyers who represent them. He received $185,278 from eight law firms that represent most of corporate America in Texas.

Phillips's colleague on the court, John Cornyn, also ran as a reformer. Cornyn's 1995–96 fundraising letters touted his role in helping "remove the taint of big money" from the court. He did this by taking $158,701 from eight of the top firms that represent businesses before the Texas courts, along with a healthy dose of oil, gas and insurance backing.

(Cornyn, now running for attorney general of Texas, declined requests for an interview.)

Phillips notes that he rules against donors regularly, and there is no reason to dispute him. But as more corporate money has poured into the courts, both Phillips and his colleagues have moved to the right. A recent study by Texas Citizen Action identified the "Terrible Ten," cases in which the Texas high court gave big business important wins that could endanger public welfare. Among them: a case in which the court made it tougher for injured consumers to find lawyers; another that erected a shield for hospitals that don't adequately screen physicians allowed to practice at their facilities. (Phillips was in the minority on that one; Cornyn ruled with the majority.) A third case permits cigarette manufacturers to escape some liability for the health effects of smoking, and a fourth allowed a property manager who failed to fix security problems at a shopping mall, and failed to report problems to a successor, to escape liability for a customer's death.

OHIO'S INDEPENDENT CITIZENS

The names of the political action committees sound innocuous: Citizens for an Independent Court and Citizens for Fair and Independent Justices. But the "citizens" referred to are the state's two biggest special-interest groups involved in judicial elections: a coalition of labor unions and trial lawyers (C.I.C.), and insurance companies and other business groups (C.F.I.J.).

The groups popped up in 1996 after Ohio adopted rules setting spending limits of $385,000 per candidate on judicial elections, just in time for the race between Democrat Marianna Brown Bettman and Republican Evelyn Stratton. The candidates raised substantial dollars on their own: Stratton's business-backed campaign raked in $457,078, while Bettman's trial-lawyer and labor-supported camp received $430,826. But the two committees made quite an impact, and, like independent expenditures in Congressional races, skirt the spirit of the law. Ohio newspapers reported that C.I.C. spent $290,000 for Bettman and Justice Andrew Douglas; C.F.I.J. spent $160,000 on Stratton, who won by a 51–49 margin. (The trouble with independent expenditures is that groups often try to remain secret about their membership and funding —making it impossible to determine if the groups then get favors in court. In Wisconsin, for example, the state is investigating the source of funding for a last-minute mailer sent to about 350,000 voters last year by the Wisconsin Coalition for Voter Participation. The G.O.P.-connected consultants who acknowledge writing the mailer, credited with helping elect

Supreme Court Justice Jon Wilcox, have so far declined to say who paid for it.)

A fundraising letter distributed by Robert Rabold, chairman of the Motorists Insurance Companies, to all Motorists agents in Ohio plumped heavily for Stratton by warning that the court incumbents "supported the interests of the trial lawyers and organized labor." Rabold himself gave $1,000 and insurance industry executives gave Stratton nearly $75,000, or 20 percent of her intake—more if you count the money from lawyers who represent insurance companies. The effort paid off. In the Ohio Chamber of Commerce's second annual "Business Evaluation of the Supreme Court of Ohio," issued in December, Stratton was rated 100 percent for her decisions regarding insurance cases.

The newest justice also received the chamber's highest overall rating, a 68 percent pro-business score, with 100 percent on insurance, medical malpractice and environmental cases. Charles McConville, director of the business group's project on political and candidate education, said he got the idea from similar reports issued in Michigan and Louisiana.

"The way I would characterize the Ohio Supreme Court in terms of its impact on business is right now it's more likely to do harm than good," McConville said. "This whole report figures into what we are doing. . . . We are trying to give a wake-up call to the business community as to why they might want to get involved in court elections." McConville said that although the Ohio chamber's PAC has not yet donated money directly to judicial races, it is likely to do so next time around.

One Ohio Supreme Court justice says her campaign contributors aren't seeking specific rulings but simply 'want a level playing field.'

Michael Thomas, a Middletown lawyer who works with the Ohio Academy of Trial Lawyers, was disturbed by the report's ratings of the justices. "We endorse justices, but we would never do it on how often they vote in our favor or against us. It's more overall judicial philosophy." But the trial lawyers do of course gear their contributions to those who vote with them. Justice Andrew Douglas, for example, who was re-elected in 1996 over a business-backed opponent, received much of his $441,348 from plaintiff's lawyers, with a sprinkling of corporate law firms looking to hedge their bets. Douglas also benefited from the independent expenditures of Citizens for an Independent Court.

Thomas sounds a lot like Stratton, who says her donors don't seek specific judicial favors but give out of support for her "philosophical approach." While Stratton readily acknowledges that her donors are often present in her court, she says recusal is unnecessary. "I don't think any of us on this bench really have recused ourselves because we got a contribution from one party," she says. "Everyone recognizes we exist in a system where you have to raise money. . . . I think I'm pretty well viewed as quite independent."

Stratton says the issue of conflict of interest is never raised in the high court. "Neither side wants to bring it up. If a plaintiff lawyer says you got a lot of money from this defense firm, the firm could write back and say, you got that from a trial lawyer. It cancels out." Stratton got less than 8 percent of her $134,900 lawyer intake from trial lawyers. She says her donors aren't seeking specific rulings but simply "want a level playing field."

Even if that were true, should they have to pay to get one? It's hard to find a judge or lawyer who thinks so. Reform efforts are now under way in North Carolina, Kentucky, Pennsylvania and other states, with proposals ranging from conversion to merit selection to maintaining elections but reducing the role of money by capping the amount judges can accept or by providing free advertising to candidates who accept spending limits. (Such efforts received a setback when the Ohio spending caps were overturned in federal court.) In addition, the A.B.A. hopes its forthcoming recommendations will prompt state bars to take up the issue.

Seth Anderson of the A.J.S. travels the country to push for change. "It's important that the politics be removed from the judiciary," Anderson says, "to insure that the third branch of government remains a check on the other two."

Washington journalist Sheila Kaplan is a former producer for MSNBC on the Internet, where she and Zoë Davidson conducted much of the research for this story. Kaplan is now co-producing a documentary for PBS's Frontline. Davidson is assistant director of the International Consortium of Investigative Journalists. This article is also posted on www.thenation.com and www.msnbc.com. Research assistance for this article was provided by the Investigative Fund of The Nation Institute.

PART 7

Congress

Congress has never been a beloved institution. Mark Twain got some of his biggest laughs by making fun of Congress. (Twain once said, "Suppose you were an idiot. And suppose you were a member of Congress. But I repeat myself.") Members of Congress are often perceived as being self-important, self-interested, and unethical.

But this only tells half the story. Scholars long ago identified a paradox regarding the way the American people view their national legislature. People seem to hate Congress, while at the same time they seem to love their own member of Congress. If Congress is such a terrible institution, why do its members usually easily win re-election year after year?

There are many reasons, but one of the most important is the fact that Congress as an institution is designed to help members of Congress be responsive to the needs of their constituents. The structure of Congress allows members to bring federal money (the "pork barrel") home to their districts and states. Members of Congress also do a lot of "case work." That is, they help individual constituents solve problems they are having with government. The result is a Congress that responds to the needs of 435 districts and 50 states, but which sometimes does so at the expense of the nation as a whole.

Congress also has an image as an institution in which partisan bickering takes precedence over finding common ground. But Congress is a reflection of the American people. We elect them, and if members of Congress find compromise difficult, that says something about the divide that separates citizens from each other. There are 270 million people in this nation, each with different ideas about what government should do, and Congress is assigned the task of reconciling these conflicting beliefs. As you read the following selections, keep in mind the many burdens that members of Congress are asked to bear.

A Reading for Critical Thinking

ROLL OUT THE BARREL:

The Case Against the Case Against Pork

By Jonathan Cohn

On most days, the lobby of the U. S. Chamber of Commerce's Washington, D. C., headquarters has a certain rarefied air. But on this Tuesday morning it is thick with the smell of greasy, grilled bacon. The aroma is appropriate, since the breakfast speaker is Republican Representative Bud Shuster of Pennsylvania, chairman of the House Transportation Committee and, his critics say, one of the most shameless promulgators of pork-barrel spending in all of Congress. The odor seems even more fitting given that the topic of Shuster's address is the Building Efficient Surface Transportation and Equity Act, [BESTEA] the six-year, $217 billion highway-spending package about to pass Congress—and, according to these same critics, the single biggest hunk of pork Washington has seen in a decade.

The critics, of course, are absolutely right. The House version of BESTEA, which hit the floor this week, contains at least $18 billion in so-called "demonstration" and "high-priority" projects. Those are the congressional euphemisms for pork—public works programs of dubious merit, specific to one congressional district, designed to curry favor with its voters. And Shuster's record for bringing home the bacon is indeed legendary. BESTEA's predecessor, which passed in 1991, included $287 million for 13 projects in Shuster's central Pennsylvania district. Today, visitors can see these and other shrines to his legislative clout by driving along the newly built Interstate 99, a shimmering stretch of asphalt the state has officially christened the Bud Shuster Highway.

None of this much bothers the suits at the Chamber of Commerce, who savor every line of Shuster's pitch as if it were just so much more fat-soaked sausage from the buffet table. Money for roads—whether in Shuster's district or anybody else's—means more ways to transport goods and more work for construction companies. But, outside the friendly confines of groups like this, a relentless chorus of high-minded watchdog groups and puritanical public officials complains that pork-barrel spending wastes government money. These critics also protest the way pork becomes law in the first place, as last-minute amendments designed to bypass the hearings and debate bills normally require.

To be sure, these arguments are not exactly novel. The very term "pork barrel" is a pre-Civil War term, derived from what was then a readily understandable (but, to modern ears, rather objectionable) analogy between congressmen gobbling up appropriations and slaves grabbing at salt pork distributed from giant barrels. "By the 1870s," William Safire writes in his *Political Dictionary*, "congressmen were regularly referring to 'pork,' and the word became part of the U. S. political lexicon." Criticizing pork, meanwhile, is just as venerable a tradition. Virtually every president from Abraham Lincoln to Ronald Reagan has promised to eliminate pork from the federal budget, and so have most congressmen, much to the satisfaction of muckraking journalists and similarly high-minded voters.

But rarely have the politicians actually meant it, and even more rarely have they succeeded. Until now. Thanks to an endless parade of media exposes on government waste, and a prevailing political consensus in favor of balanced budgets, pork critics have been gaining momentum. In 1994, anti-pork fervor nearly killed President Clinton's crime bill, in 1995, the same sentiment lay behind enactment of the line-item veto,

From *The New Republic* (April 20, 1998), pp. 19–23. Reprinted by permission of *The New Republic*. Copyright © 1998, *The New Republic, Inc.*

something budget-balancers had sought in vain for more than a decade. A few years ago, a handful of anti-pork legislators took to calling themselves "pork-busters." Thanks to their vigilance, says the nonprofit group Citizens Against Government Waste [CAGW], the amount of pork in the budget declined by about nine percent in 1998.

The influence of pork-busters reached a new peak in 1997, when they helped defeat a preliminary attempt at BESTEA. They probably won't be able to duplicate the feat this year—Shuster has nearly 400 votes behind his new pork-laden bill, which House Budget Chairman John Kasich has called an "abomination." But pork-busters won a major public relations victory last week when four House Republicans turned on Shuster and accused him of trying to buy them off with pet projects. "I told them my vote was not for sale," said Steve Largent of Oklahoma. "Shuster bought just about everyone," David Hobson of Ohio told *The Washington Post*. Three weeks ago, Republican Senator John McCain of Arizona, Capitol Hill's most determined pork-buster, won passage of an amendment that could cut at least some of the bill's pork. President Clinton has since joined the chorus, saying he too deplores the parochial waste Shuster and his cronies added to the measure.

In the popular telling, episodes like these represent epic struggles of good versus evil—of principled fiscal discipline versus craven political self-interest—with the nation's economic health and public faith in government at stake. But this narrative, related time and again by purveyors of elite wisdom and then repeated mindlessly by everyday citizens, has it exactly backward. The pork-busters are more anti-government than anti-waste. As for pork-barrel spending, it's good for American citizens and American democracy as well. Instead of criticizing it, we should be celebrating it, in all of its gluttonous glory.

Nearly a week has passed since Shuster made his appearance before the Chamber of Commerce, and now it is the pork-busters' turn to be making headlines. In what has become an annual rite of the budget process, Citizens Against Government Waste [CAGW] staging a press conference near Capitol Hill to release its compilation of pork in the 1997 federal budget—a 40-page, pink-covered booklet it calls the "Pig Book." (Actually, the pocket-sized, 40-page version is just a summary of the unabridged "Pig Book," which weighs in at a hefty 170 pages, in single-sided, legal-sized computer printouts.)

CAGW has been fighting this fight for more than a decade, and its steady stream of propaganda, reports, and testimony is in no small part responsible for pork-busting's Beltway resonance. Republican Representative Christopher Cox calls CAGW "the premier waste-fighting organization in America"; the 1995–1996 Congress sought CAGW testimony 20 times. The interest in today's press conference—attended by more than 60 reporters and a dozen television crews—is testimony to the group's high esteem among the Washington press corps, although it doesn't hurt that CAGW has also provided the TV crews with a good photo opportunity.

Like many press conferences in this city, this one features several members of Congress, including Mc-Cain and Democratic Senator Russell Feingold. Unlike many press conferences in this city, this one also features a man dressed in a bright pink pig's suit, rubber pig masks free for the media to take, plus a live, charcoal-gray potbellied pig named Porky. For the duration of the event, Porky does little except scarf down some vegetable shreds. But the beast's mere presence gets a few laughs, which is more than can be said for the puns that CAGW's president, Tom Schatz, makes as he rattles off the recipients of this year's "Oinker Awards."

Senator Daniel Inouye of Hawaii secured $127,000 in funding for research on edible seaweed; for this and other appropriations, Schatz says, Inouye (who is of Japanese ancestry) wins "The Sushi Slush Fund Award." Senator Ted Stevens of Alaska sponsored $100,000 for a project called Ship Creek, so he gets "The Up Ship's Creek Award." (Stevens is a double winner: for his other pork, totaling some $477 million since 1991, CAGW also presents him with "The Half Baked Alaska Award.") The Pentagon budget included $3 million for an observatory in South America: "It's supposed to peer back millions of years in time," Schatz says, his deadpan poker face now giving way to a smarmy, half-cocked smile. "Maybe they're looking for a balanced budget." This dubious-sounding project Schatz dubs "The Black Hole Award." And on. And on.

You might think cornball humor like this would earn CAGW the disdain of the famously cynical Washington press corps. But, when Schatz is done, and the question-and-answer period begins, the reporters display barely any skepticism. Instead, that evening, and during the following days, they will heap gobs of attention on the group. They don't flatter or endorse the organization per se, but the coverage shares a common assumption that the group's findings are evidence of political malfeasance. CNN, for example, will use the "Pig Book"'s release as a peg for stories bemoaning the persistence of pork in the federal budget. A story out of Knight Ridder's Washington bureau, which will run in nearly a dozen of the chain's newspapers, basically recapitulates the report. And all this comes on the heels of a front-page *Wall Street Journal* feature—sparked by a similar report from the

Tax Foundation—highlighting the profligate pork barreling of the Senate majority leader, Trent Lott of Mississippi. Its headline: "Mississippi's senators continue a tradition: getting federal money."

This is typical. Normally jaded Washingtonians, journalists especially, tend to view pork-busters not as ideologues but as politically disinterested watchdogs. Television producers, in particular, regularly summon CAGW experts to validate stories for such waste-focused segments as NBC's "The Fleecing of America" and ABC's "Your Money, Your Choice." While this image has a basis in reality—CAGW truly goes after pork-barreling Republicans with the same fervor it pursues Democrats—it is also a product of the organization's concerted attempt to wrap itself in the flag of nonpartisanship. "No matter how you slice it, pork is always on the menu in the halls of Congress," Schatz said at the press conference. "Some members of Congress simply couldn't resist the lure of easy money and putting partisan political interests over the best interest of taxpayers."

But it's not as if the pork-busters have no partisan or ideological agenda of their own. Some, like the, Cato Institute, are explicit about their anti-government predisposition. CAGW is a little more cagey, but it remains true to the spirit of its past chairman, perennial right-wing Republican candidate Alan Keyes, as well as its cofounder, J. Peter Grace, who headed President Reagan's 1984 commission on government waste and whose antipathy to government in general was widely known. "The government is the worst bunch of stupid jerks you've ever run into in your life," he said once at a CAGW fund-raising dinner. "These people just want to spend money, money, money all the time."

That is, of course, a forgivable overstatement of a plausible argument. But it is also an overtly ideological one, and it calls into question the group's reliability when it comes to making delicate distinctions about what is truly wasteful. After all, CAGW is not just against pork, but against much of what the mainstream conservative movement considers bad or overly intrusive public policy—which encompasses an awful lot. In 1995, CAGW was not bashful about embracing the Contract With America, whose expansive definition of waste included many regulatory programs Americans deem quite worthwhile. "Taxpayers . . . demonstrated in two consecutive elections of a Republican Congress that the Washington establishment at its peril ignores the taxpayers' voice," the group's annual report boasts. "CAGW stood shoulder to shoulder with the reformers and enjoyed a sense of accomplishment at this burst of energy from revitalized taxpayers." CAGW's contributor list, not surprisingly, reads like a who's who of conservative interests, from

Philip Morris Companies Inc. to the Columbia/HCA Healthcare Foundation Inc.

To be sure, CAGW is not the only Beltway organization whose partisan allegiances belie its nonprofit, nonpartisan status. At least a dozen other groups on both the left and the right do the exact same thing. Anyway, the fact that an argument may be ideologically motivated hardly means it's wrong.

But that doesn't mean it's right, either. Listen closely the next time some smug good-government type starts criticizing pork: it's an awful lot of fuss over what is in fact, a very small amount of money. In the "Pig Book," for example, CAGW claims last year's budget included pork worth about $13.2 billion—or, as a pork-buster would say, "$13.2 billion!" Yes, you could feed quite a few hungry people with that much money, or you could give a bigger tax cut. But it's less than one percent of the federal budget.

And it's not even clear that all of the $13.2 billion of waste is really, well, waste. A good chunk of CAGW's $13.2 billion in pork comes from a few dozen big-ticket items, costing tens of millions of dollars each scattered through various appropriations measures, particularly the Pentagon's. Among the programs: research of a space-based laser ($90 million), transportation improvements in Utah ($14 million), and military construction in Montana ($32 million).

But it's hardly self-evident that these all constitute waste, as the pork-busters suggest. At least some national security experts believe the space-based laser is a necessary defense against rogue nations that might get their hands on nuclear missiles. A lot of that Utah money is to help Salt Lake City prepare for Olympic traffic. And, if you've ever been to Montana, you know that there are a lot of military bases scattered across that vast state—which means a lot of soldiers who need buildings in which to live, eat, and work. In other words, all of these serve some credible purpose.

The wastefulness of the smaller items is similarly open to interpretation. Remember Senator Inouye's "Sushi Slush Fund Award"—the $127,000 for research on edible seaweed in Hawaii? It turns out that aquaculture is an emerging industry in Hawaii and that edible seaweed—known locally as "limu," "ogo," or "sea sprouts"—is "rich in complex carbohydrates and protein and low in calories," according to the *Honolulu Advertiser*. "It's a good source of vitamin A, calcium, and potassium, too."

Yes, the federal government is paying $3 million for a telescope in South America. But it has to, because the telescope is part of a U. S. effort to explore the southern hemisphere sky—which, of course, is only visible from the southern hemisphere. Although the telescope will be located in Chile, it will be operated remotely from the University of North Carolina at

Chapel Hill. "When completed, the telescope will hold tremendous promise for scientists and the federal government," the university chancellor said when Republican Senator Lauch Faircloth of North Carolina announced the appropriation. "We at the university also have high hopes for what the project will mean for the North Carolina economy as well as for students of all ages—on this campus, across our state, and beyond."

And Senator Stevens's "Up Ship's Creek Award"? The Ship Creek water project was part of a bill authorizing studies of environmental cleanup across the country. Some $100,000 went to the U. S. Army Corps of Engineers to assess the impact of development on Ship Creek, which is Anchorage's primary source of freshwater. Ironically, according to the Corps of Engineers, the study is exploring not only what kind of environmental precautions are necessary, but whether the federal government really has to pay for them, and whether local private entities might be convinced to foot part of the bill. In other words, one objective of the Ship Creek appropriation was to reduce government waste.

You could argue, as pork-busters do, that, while projects like these may serve some positive function in society—perhaps even deserving of government money—they should not be on the federal dime. Let the Hawaiians pay for their own calcium-rich dinners! Let Alaskans foot the bill for their own water study! But there's a respectable argument that sometimes parochial needs are in fact a legitimate federal interest, particularly when it involves things like pollution and commerce that cross state lines.

Certainly, that's the way a lot of people outside of Washington understand it. Last month, while the national media was busy flogging unthrifty lawmakers, several local newspapers rose to their defense. "We elect people to Congress not only to see to the nation's defense and keep the currency sound but also to bring home some pork," editorialized *The Fort Worth StarTelegram.* "Pork can mean local jobs, local beautification, local pride, etc." *The Dayton Daily News* defended one project, a museum on the history of flight, that appeared on CAGW's hit list: "It is at the heart of a community effort that has been painstakingly nurtured for years by all manner of Daytonians. It combines the legitimate national purpose of recognizing the history of flight with the top-priority local purpose of getting Dayton recognized as a center of the history of flight." Other papers were more critical: they wanted to know why their congressmen hadn't brought home more bacon. "Alaskans aren't going to sit still for being No. 2 for long," *Anchorage Daily News* columnist Mike Doogan wrote in a spirited defense of pork. "We need the money. And we have our pride."

This is not to say that all or even most of what gets called pork is defensible on its own terms. (Did Bedford County, Pennsylvania, which happens to be smack in the middle of Shuster's rural district, really need a new airport when there were two others nearby?) Nor is it to say that the local interest in getting federal money should always trump the national interest in balancing the budget and distributing the federal largesse fairly. (Couldn't the state of Pennsylvania have paid for the Bedford County airport instead?) Nor is it even to say that local interests defending pork aren't being incredibly hypocritical—no one thinks an appropriation is pork when it's his.

No, the point is simply that you can't call something waste just because it makes a clever pun. "From what we can tell," says John Raffetto, communications director for the Senate Transportation Committee, "CAGW does no research to determine what purpose the project serves other than to flip through the pages of the bill and find projects that sound funny. If it sounds funny, that's pork. I have not heard from any member's office that has told me they've received a call from CAGW to ask what purpose that project has served."

Pork-busters concede they lack the time or resources to investigate items thoroughly. "Some may be worthy of consideration," says CAGW media director Jim Campi. "Our concern is that, if the projects went through the process the way they were supposed to, there would be a better opportunity to judge them on their merits."

This is the same argument that most animates McCain, Feingold, and other pork-busting lawmakers. But what constitutes a fair appropriations process? CAGW would have everyone believe that a project is pork if it is "not requested by the president" or if it "greatly exceeds the president's budget request or the previous year's funding." Huh? The whole point of the appropriations process is to give Congress a chance to make independent judgments about spending priorities. Particularly when Republicans control one branch of government and Democrats the other—as is the case today— differences will exist. The Republican Congress used to routinely declare the president's budget "dead on arrival." Did this mean the entire congressional budget was pork?

Two other criteria for defining pork are equally shaky. Invoking the familiar pork-busting wisdom, CAGW says a program is pork if it was "not specifically authorized"—meaning it wasn't in the original budget which contains general spending limits, but rather added on as part of the subsequent appropriations process, in which money is specifically allocated to each item. But the rationale for a separate budget and appropriations process is to allow Congress (and,

READING 27 – ROLL OUT THE BARREL: THE CASE AGAINST THE CASE AGAINST PORK   127 for that matter, the president) an opportunity to change their minds about smaller items, as long as they stay within the broad guidelines of the budget agreement. CAGW also damns any projects "requested by only one chamber of Congress." But, just as Congress can disagree with the president over a project's merit, so the House can disagree with the Senate—that's the reason the architects of the Constitution created two houses in the first place. (Also, keep in mind that one reason the Senate doesn't propose as much pork is that senators—wary of getting stung in the national press for lacking frugality—will often wait to see how much pork the House passes. That way, they end up with the best of both worlds: they can quietly tell supporters that they backed the measure without ever incurring the wrath of pork-busting watchdogs.)

Make no mistake, though: Many pork-barrellers are trying to evade the scrutiny bills get when they move through the normal appropriations process. They stick in small bits of pork after hearings end because they know that nobody is going to vote against a multibillion-dollar bill just because it has a few million dollars of pork tucked in. And they can do so safe in the knowledge that, because there's very little in the way of a paper trail, they will not suffer any public consequences—unless, of course, a watchdog group or enthusiastic reporter manages to find out.

Pork-busters call this strategy sleazy, and it is. But remember, the whole point of our Constitution is to harness mankind's corrupt tendencies and channel them in constructive directions. In an oft-quoted passage of *The Federalist Number 51*, James Madison wrote, "if men were angels, no government would be necessary," and "the private interest of every individual may be a sentinel over the public rights." The Founders believed that sometimes local interests should trump national interests because they recognized it was a way to keep federal power in check. It's true this process lends itself to a skewed distribution of benefits, with disproportionate shares going to powerful lawmakers. But, again, pork is such a small portion of the budget that "equalizing" its distribution would mean only modest funding changes here and there.

Which brings us to the final defense of pork, one Madison would certainly endorse. Even if every single pork-barrel project really were a complete waste of federal money, pork still represents a very cheap way to keep our sputtering legislative process from grinding to a halt. In effect, pork is like putting oil in your car engine: it lubricates the parts and keeps friction to a minimum. This is particularly true when you are talking about controversial measures. "Buying off potential coalition members with spending programs they favor is exactly what the Founders not only ex-

pected, but practiced," political scientist James Q. Wilson has argued. He has also written: "If you agree with Madison, you believe in pork."

Think of the NAFTA battle in 1993. Contentious to the bitter end, the fate of the agreement ultimately fell on the shoulders of a handful of congressmen, all of whom privately supported it but feared the political backlash if they voted for it. Clinton gave each of them a little pork—for example, a development bank in border states that ostensibly would provide start-up money for entrepreneurs who had lost jobs because of NAFTA. The bank was just another way to pump some federal money into these districts, but that was the whole point. Thanks to that money, NAFTA became politically viable; these lawmakers could tell their constituents, plausibly and truthfully, that there was something in it for their districts.

To take a more current example, just look at BESTEA. U.S. transportation infrastructure is famously inadequate; the Department of Transportation says unsafe roads cause 30 percent of all traffic fatalities. But, when fiscal conservatives questioned the pork in the original BESTEA last year, the measure failed, forcing Congress to pass an emergency extension. This year, a more permanent, six-year version will likely pass, largely because the appearance of a budget surplus has tipped the scales just enough so that the pork seems tolerable. As John W. Ellwood and Eric M. Patashnik wrote in *The Public Interest* several years ago (in what was the best defense of pork in recent memory): "Favoring legislators with small gifts for their districts in order to achieve great things for the nation is an act not of sin but of statesmanship."

Last week, of course, BESTEA's high pork content had fiscal conservatives downright apoplectic. "Frankly, this bill really is a hog," Kasich said. "It is way over the top." But, without the pork, there might be no highway bill at all. As one highway lobbyist told *National Journal* last year, "The projects are the glue that's going to hold the damn thing together." A former transportation official said: "I've always taken the point of view that every business has some overhead. If that's what it costs to get a significant or a good highway bill, it's worth the price." Kasich would surely be aghast at such logic, but someday he and other fiscal conservatives might find it useful for their own purposes. Remember, they are the ones who say that balancing the budget will likely be impossible without severe and politically risky reforms of entitlements like Medicare. When the time comes to make those tough choices—and they need to pry a few extra votes from the opposition — you can bet they will gladly trade a little pork for their greater cause. They might feel guilty about it, but they shouldn't. Pork is good. Pork is virtuous. Pork is the American way.

75 Stars

A Reading for Critical Thinking

How to restore democracy in the U.S. Senate (and end the tyranny of Wyoming)

By Michael Lind

Here's a quiz question for you: What American institution has used its power to thwart desegregation, campaign finance reform, health care reform, New Deal programs, gun control, and midnight basketball—and gave Adolf Hitler time to conquer most of Europe without American opposition? The answer: the United States Senate. Because of our Senate—the least representative legislative body in the democratic world except for the British House of Lords—an ever shrinking minority of voters has the power to obstruct policies favored by an overwhelming majority of the American people. The Senate is the worst branch of government, and it's going to get even nastier in the century ahead.

If democracy means anything, it means one person, one vote—a principle flouted by the Senate's very design, which is based on an antiquated constitutional provision that provides equal suffrage in the Senate for government units (states) rather than suffrage based on the size of a constituency. As a result, a dwindling minority of Americans elects a majority of senators.

California has 66 times as many people as Wyoming—and yet on any given vote Wyoming's two senators can neutralize California's two senators. Texas, with more than 19 million people, has only two senators—as many as Montana, which has less than 1 million citizens. New York, the third most populous state in the union, can be outvoted by tiny Rhode Island (the *true* Empire State).

This malapportionment favors inhabitants of Rocky Mountain and New England states at the expense of Americans who live in densely populated megastates—not only Sun Belt states such as California,

Texas, and Florida, but also states in the Northeast and Midwest such as New York, Illinois, and Pennsylvania. True, the big states have more members in the House. But this misses the point: Why should Idahoans be represented in the House and the Senate, while Californians, Texans, and New Yorkers are effectively represented in the House alone? It's not an even trade. The majority of Americans get nothing in return for forgoing their right to democratic representation in one-half of their national legislature.

From the 18th century to the present, the ratio of large- to small-state populations has grown from 19–to–1 to 66–to–1. Today, half of the Senate can be elected by 15 percent of the American people—and the problem is only getting worse. Almost all of the population growth in the United States in the foreseeable future will be concentrated in a few populous states (chiefly California). By the middle of the next century, as few as 5 percent of the population, or even 1 percent, may have majority power in the Senate.

Even now, only 10 percent of the U.S. population elects 40 percent of the Senate. By filibustering, senators representing little more than one-tenth of the nation can block reforms supported by the House, the president—and their fellow senators, who represent the other 90 percent of the population. This is not democracy It is minority rule. For example:

- The Republican Party held the Senate from 1980–86 only because of Senate malapportionment. During that period, Republican senators as a group received fewer votes nationwide than Democratic senatorial candidates. If the Senate had been elected on the basis of population, President Ronald

From *Mother Jones* (January/February 1998), pp. 44–49. Reprinted with permission from *Mother Jones* magazine. Copyright © 1998, Foundation for National Progress

Reagan would have faced a Democratic Senate throughout his eight years in office.

- In 1991, the Senate voted 52–48 to appoint Clarence Thomas to the Supreme Court. The senators opposing Thomas (including those from California, New York, New Jersey, Ohio, and Texas) represented a majority of the American people—but found themselves in the minority in the Senate.

- In order to pass his budget package in 1993, President Clinton had to cave in to demands by senators from Montana, Arkansas, and Louisiana to lower the gasoline tax.

- Likewise, Clinton's 1993 domestic stimulus program, which was targeted at metropolitan areas in megastates like California, was killed by conservative Republican and Democratic senators from underpopulated states such as Oklahoma.

While the Senate exaggerates the power of anti-urban, anti-government conservatives in domestic policy, when it comes to foreign affairs, the Senate has always been the command post of isolationism. As late as 1940, a bipartisan team of isolationists in the Senate blocked the efforts of President Franklin Delano Roosevelt and the House to revise the country's misguided neutrality laws and rescue Britain from defeat at the hands of the Nazis. Thanks to the unrepresentative Senate, Hitler came close to winning World War II.

The only Americans whose views are consistently magnified by Senate malapportionment are white, rural, right-wing isolationists. If you are nonwhite or of mixed race, if you live in a major metropolitan area, if you are liberal or centrist, if you support an internationalist foreign policy, or even if you are a

Half of the Senate can be elected by 15 percent of the American people.

conservative who lives in a populous state, you should look on the Senate with loathing and apprehension.

Because of its role in screening executive and judicial appointees, the Senate also has a disproportionate influence on all three branches. To make matters worse, the senators staggered six-year terms—intended to insulate the enlightened statesmen of the upper house—have merely ensured that the Senate would be out of touch with the times, as well as out of touch with the American majority.

ORIGINAL CONTEMPT

Most of the founding fathers hated the Senate, which they created to satisfy small states, like Rhode Island, that demanded equal representation in the new federal government. In "The Federalist No. 22," Alexander Hamilton, criticizing the Senate by implication, identified equal representation of the states in the national government as one of the worst defects of the Articles of Confederation. Allotting representatives on the basis of statehood rather than population, he wrote, "contradicts the fundamental maxim of republican government, which requires that the sense of the majority should prevail." Hamilton predicted that "two-thirds of the people of America could not long be persuaded, upon the credit of artificial distinction and syllogistic subtleties," to be governed by a third of the population. "The larger States," he concluded,

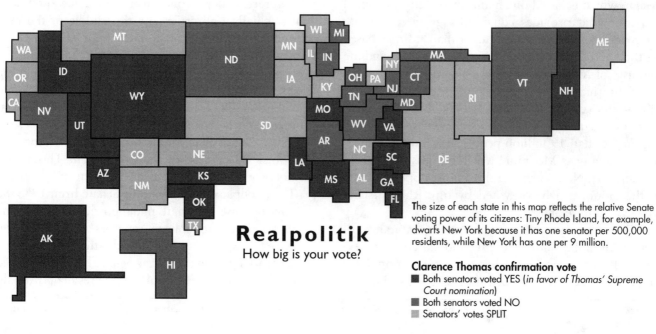

Realpolitik
How big is your vote?

The size of each state in this map reflects the relative Senate voting power of its citizens: Tiny Rhode Island, for example, dwarfs New York because it has one senator per 500,000 residents, while New York has one per 9 million.

Clarence Thomas confirmation vote
- ■ Both senators voted YES (*in favor of Thomas' Supreme Court nomination*)
- ■ Both senators voted NO
- ▨ Senators' votes SPLIT

"would after a while revolt from the idea of receiving the law from the smaller." If Hamilton returned today, he'd be amazed to learn that the citizens of large states have not yet revolted against the excessive power of the statelets in America's upper house.

In the early 1960s, the Supreme Court struck down malapportioned state legislatures as unconstitutional, arguing that they violated the principle of one person, one vote. In 1963, the Supreme Court declared in *Gray v. Sanders* that "the conception of political equality from the Declaration of Independence to Lincoln's Gettysburg Address to the 15th, 17th, and 19th Amendments can mean only one thing—one person, one vote." There you have it: The federal judiciary determined that the structural principle underlying state senates at that time—and the U.S. Senate today—was unjust and unconstitutional.

For much of American history, white Protestant rural constituencies were deliberately overrepresented in state legislatures in order to dilute the political influence of urban dwellers, who were more likely to be European immigrants. In the 21st century, the built-in corruption of our Senate may cause a constitutional and racial crisis. Just as European immigrants in the cities were stymied by rural Anglo-Protestant "rotten boroughs" in state legislatures in the 19th century, so the coming Hispanic, black, and Asian majorities in the megastates will have their votes diluted by the over representation of the white microstates in the Senate. As the Chicago lawyer and writer Tom Geoghegan has pointed out, the House will soon look like multiracial metropolitan America; the Senate will continue to look like white rural America.

The Senate has always functioned as the last bastion of white supremacy. The balance of slave states and free states in the Senate permitted the South to preserve slavery and weaken the federal government for a generation after its population had been surpassed by that of the North. In this century, Southern senators filibustered anti-lynching legislation, and later blocked civil rights reform. The gridlock they caused was one reason the federal courts eventually seized the initiative on desegregation. If the emergent multiracial majority in the United States perceives the Senate as the tool of selfish white obstructionists, pressure will grow on the judiciary or the president to take control and push through reforms that the majority needs and approves—at the cost of further weakening our constitutional order.

DIVIDE AND RULE

Can anything be done about the Senate and its weighted vote for white reactionaries? A distinguished New York senator once grumbled to me over dinner,

"You should write an article saying we should combine all those Western states into one." Alas, we can forget about creating a single populous "state of Deseret" by forcibly consolidating all those states with right-angle corners. The microstate delegations to the Constitutional Convention of 1787 managed to booby-trap the Constitution to protect themselves. Article V states that the American people cannot amend the Constitution to get rid of equal suffrage for the states: "No State, without its Consent, shall be deprived of its equal suffrage in the Senate." And Article IV, Section 3, provides that no state can "be formed by the Junction of two or more States, or parts of States, without the consent of the Legislatures of the States concerned as well as of the Congress." Not one, but two poison pill provisions.

Yet there is a way to address the problem of Senate malapportionment, one that doesn't require us to abandon the Constitution or to alter the two-senators-per-state rule. Let's go back and read Article IV, Section 3, in its entirety:

> New States may be admitted by the Congress into this Union; but no new State shall be formed or erected within the Jurisdiction of any other State; nor any State be formed by the Junction of two or more States, or Parts of States, without the Consent of the Legislatures of the States concerned as well as of the Congress.

Why not form new states within the jurisdictions of the existing megastates? Why not divide in order to rule? This is not as crazy as it sounds. Commentator Walter Russell Mead has suggested that no American should have to live in a state with more than 4 or 5 million citizens. If the 4-million-population rule were applied to the large states, California might be subdivided into eight new states; Texas, five; New York and Florida, four; Pennsylvania, Illinois, and Ohio, three; and Michigan and New Jersey, two.

Eight Californias? Five Texases? Four New Yorks? Why not?

With 25 new states in the union, the Senate would be far more representative of the American people. The citizens of the nine largest states, who today send a mere 18 senators to Washington, would soon have a total of 68 senators to defend their interests against senators from microstates like Vermont and Wyoming. The overall Senate representation of the voters in present-day California, Texas, and New York alone would jump from 6 to 34. The House functions with 435 representatives; a Senate with 150 members would be quite manageable.

This scheme would be perfectly constitutional under Article IV—as long as the small states as well as the populous states consented. Obviously the megastates would have to strike a deal with the microstates, so that they did not then subdivide into still tinier units (nanostates?). Under this proposal, states like Wyoming would still have roughly four times greater representation in the Senate than California's eight new states of 4 or 5 million citizens apiece—and would have reason to be grateful that California didn't divide into 32 new states.

How could the microstate politicians be persuaded to go along with the dilution of their unjust authority in the Senate? Perhaps the megastate majority in both parties would give the microstate senators no choice. The moment the Senate's malapportionment becomes a popular political issue, both parties are likely to sacrifice the wishes of their Rocky Mountain and New England minorities in order not to offend the megastate voters who will decide which party controls the House and the presidency.

LOSE A STATE, GAIN A CAUCUS

In 1997, British conservatives paid the price for ignoring an equally vexing problem of constitutional reform. The Conservative Party was decimated when voters in Scotland and Wales flocked to the Labor Liberal Democrat alliance that promised local legislatures for the two regions. In this country, the direct election of U.S. senators was proposed in minor-party platforms as early as 1876; it became part of the

Democratic Party platform in 1900; and it was not achieved until the 17th Amendment passed in 1913. This proves that, even in the United States, once a national majority is aroused, the Senate can be reformed—eventually (for 20 years, the Senate did not even let the amendment come to a vote, even though the House had approved it five times).

Selling subdivision to residents of Florida, New York, California, and other populous states should be much easier. (I am referring to legal and consensual division, of course, not to militiamen declaring that a ranch is a republic.) The states of the American union do not correspond to real geographic, social, or economic groups—and never have. Most of the state boundaries were drawn by surveyors, with little or no regard to the actual contours of the landscape. The map of the American states is like a section of wire mesh pressed down atop an abstract expressionist painting. The high mobility among Americans, coupled with the present high level of foreign immigration, renders state patriotism tenuous. Indeed, the voluntary division of some states would delight many of their inhabitants. In the 1960s there was a proposal to make New York City a state. In 1992, voters in a majority of California counties voted in favor of splitting California in two. Citizens of adjacent counties in Kansas, Colorado, Oklahoma, Nebraska, and Texas recently sought to form a new state, West Kansas. In

SPLITSVILLE, U.S.A

The newest states in the union

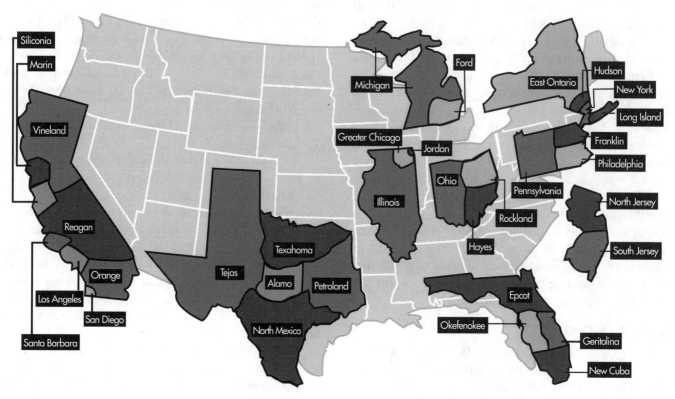

Texas, it would be sad to see the Lone Star flag lowered for the final time. But though the state song calls Texas an "empire wide and glorious," Texas is not an arbitrary political unit, but a distinctive cultural region, like New England or the Pacific Northwest. Lose a state, gain a caucus.

EIGHT Californias? Five Texases? Four New Yorks? WHY NOT?

Conservatives and populists who today denounce the centralized rule of the statehouses in Sacramento or Albany or Austin should be delighted with the idea of two dozen smaller states, whose legislatures would be more responsive to their smaller, more manageable constituencies. Liberals, too, should be pleased—voting power would shift away from almost exclusively white hinterland electorates toward urban, Hispanic, black, and immigrant voters. Libertarians could celebrate the choice of lifestyles offered by the states of Orange and Marin. And neo-Progressives who want to eliminate redundant levels of government might at last get their wish—at least in unitary city-states like those based on New York City, Los Angeles, and Philadelphia. Provision might be made for any state, once its population reaches 8 or 10 million, to split into two new states of 4 or 5 million citizens. Depending on the growth of the U.S. population and its density, the number of stars on the American flag might rise from 50 to 75 to 100.

Short of scrapping the Constitution altogether, the voluntary division of the big states into new, smaller states is the only way that the citizens of megastates can end their semicolonial subjugation to an electoral minority in the microstates. It may also be the only way to avoid a race war between the two houses of the U.S. Congress in the 21st century, when the real "white house" will be the Senate. If the majority cannot rule by constitutional means because of the Senate, then it will rule by extraconstitutional measures, through an imperial presidency or an imperial judiciary. We can use the Constitution to reform the Senate—or trash the Constitution to get around the Senate. The choice is ours.

Michael Lind is the author of The Next American Nation. *This article is first in a four-part series on democratic political reform. Forthcoming articles will look at new alternatives to our campaign finance and electoral systems.*

For further discussion, see the MoJo Wire (www.motherjones.com/mag/modest_proposals).

The Senator's Dilemma

For Rick Santorum, the partial-birth-abortion issue unexpectantly got personal.

By Joe Klein

On the evening of September 26, 1996, Karen Santorum was home with her three young children watching C-SPAN as her husband, Rick, who is a United States senator from Pennsylvania, debated an issue that has emerged as one of the most volatile social questions of the decade: the effort to outlaw partial-birth abortion, an extremely rare but highly controversial procedure that is used to end mid-to-late-term pregnancies. Since 1995, Congress has twice voted overwhelmingly to ban the operation, which doctors call intact dilation and extraction (or intact D&X), and President Clinton has twice vetoed the bill. During that time, the partial-birth question has led to a dramatic and unexpected reframing of the debate over legalized abortion—a debate that seemed destined to wane in intensity after the Supreme Court made it clear, in its 1992 Planned Parenthood v. Casey decision, that it had no intention of overturning the fundamental right to abortion established nineteen years earlier, in Roe v. Wade.

The Court, though, had left open a small area of contention: states could pass laws to regulate abortion—they could impose waiting periods, or demand mandatory counselling—as long as these laws didn't place an "undue burden" on the women seeking the operation. This seemed to promise a marginalized, technical debate—until, in the mid-nineties, antiabortion activists discovered, and seized upon, the existence of the partial-birth procedure. Though D&X is used infrequently, it is one of several ways—none of them pleasant—to end mid-to-late-term pregnancies: the fetus is maneuvered into a breech position and partly delivered; then, according to the American Medical Association, the doctor performs a "partial evacuation of the intracranial contents" while the fetal head remains inside the womb, in order "to effect vaginal delivery of a dead but otherwise intact fetus." In other words, in order to make the delivery possible the skull is punctured and its contents are suctioned out.

The decision made by abortion opponents to concentrate their lobbying efforts on the prohibition of one specific, rare, and morally questionable procedure was an unusual tactical choice—incrementalism, instead of total war—but it was quite appropriate to the Clinton era of sophisticated, small-bore message marketing. "It's been a clever strategy on their part," Joanne Blum, a legislative expert who serves as a vice-president of the National Abortion Rights Action League, said. "They haven't been interested in making the compromises necessary to get an actual piece of legislation passed. They want to undermine Roe v. Wade."

The strategy has paid off. Pro-choice activists have clearly been placed on the defensive. Indeed, there is some evidence, according to recent polls, that the partial-birth question has caused the public to grow more cautious in its support of abortion in general. Even politicians who favored abortion rights in the past have decided to oppose this form of it. "It is too close to infanticide," Senator Daniel Patrick Moynihan, a usually reliable pro-choice voter, has said.

In the fall of 1996, after the President vetoed the first partial-birth-abortion ban passed by Congress, Rick Santorum became—somewhat to his own surprise—the leader of the anti-partial-birth forces in the Senate. It was a role that placed him at the center of what soon became a very emotional, and personal, maelstrom. On the evening of September 26th, as a vote to override the President's veto approached, the floor debate became particularly intense. In one of the exchanges, as Karen Santorum watched at home, Senator Carol Moseley Braun, of Illinois, stared at Rick Santorum and said, "No member of the Senate can face the trauma that is represented by the issue of late-term abortion. . . . The men of this Senate cannot be pregnant, and I daresay for the women of the Senate pregnancy is a hypothetical matter of nostalgia."

At that point, Karen Santorum began to cry. She was eighteen weeks pregnant at the time, and the possibility of a late-term crisis was not "hypothetical" in her case. In three previous pregnancies, she had felt life by nineteen weeks, but this baby hadn't yet quickened. She had once been a neonatal-intensive-care nurse, and some of the heartbreaking things she'd seen flashed through her mind. "I was so angry at Moseley-Braun," she later recalled. "What if there was something wrong with my baby? How horrible that would be."

The moment passed. The vote to override the President's veto fell just short of the two-thirds majority needed. Karen forgot her twinge of fear: she had never had a problem with her other pregnancies; she had already heard this baby's heartbeat; and she was optimistic by nature. But the Santorums would soon endure an experience that few politicians have to face: they would be forced to test their ideological beliefs against the imprecise information and split-second decisions of a real-life crisis. A week later, when Karen and Rick went to a Washington-area radiologist for a routine five-month sonogram, Karen knew there was trouble as soon as she saw the image of her womb on the screen.

A dark ring was visible around the fetus. Their baby was suffering from a minuscule but almost invariably fatal problem. A tiny posterior urethral valve wasn't working properly, the baby's bladder wasn't emptying, and so there was no amniotic fluid (which is composed primarily of fetal urine). Without fluid, fetal movement and, eventually, growth in the womb become more difficult, and the development of the kidneys and the lungs is seriously impaired.

Santorum called Scott Adzick, whom he had met a few months earlier during an official visit to the Children's Hospital of Philadelphia. Adzick is a pediatric surgeon who is known for his ability to perform prenatal operations in which birth defects can be repaired and life-threatening tumors removed. "I called him from the hallway at the clinic," the Senator recalled.

Adzick offered some hope: there was a procedure that might work if the kidneys were still functioning. A plastic shunt could be inserted into the baby's bladder and used to channel the fetal urine into the womb; the post-urethral valve itself could easily be repaired after the baby was born.

The Santorums drove to Philadelphia the next morning. The first test results were not encouraging: the baby's kidneys didn't seem to be functioning properly. "The medical team took us into a consultation room, and a doctor gave us the options," Santorum recalled. "He said, 'I know this one is probably not for you, but you can terminate the pregnancy.' The other two options were to let the baby die or to try a bladder tap, testing the urine in the bladder to see if there was any kidney function at all. He said it looked pretty grim, but there was always a chance."

Doctors tried two bladder taps. The procedure was similar to amniocentesis but far more delicate: a long needle was inserted through Karen's abdomen into the baby's bladder, and urine was extracted. The doctors said they would phone with the results of the tests, and the Santorums drove to their home in Northern Virginia. On the way, they decided to name the baby Gabriel Michael—after the two archangels—and they prayed for his health. That evening, they attended Mass at St. Catherine's Church, in Great Falls, Virginia. "And the most amazing thing happened," Karen said. "The baby kicked for the first time. We later learned that the second tap had left a little hole in the bladder, which was allowing some urine to seep into the womb, and that gave Gabriel the room to kick."

The Senator said, "I was sitting in church and thinking that it was just a week after the vote to override the President's veto on partial birth, which was the first time I'd ever really taken an active role in this issue. I mean, it was like, What's God doing here?"

Rick Santorum is the youngest member of the Senate. He is thirty-nine years old, and has the look of a very mischievous altar boy. In 1994, after spending four years in the House of Representatives as an enthusiastic supporter of Newt Gingrich's Republican revolution, he was elected to the Senate, narrowly defeating the Democratic incumbent, Harris Wofford. Santorum was not a popular member of the Senate; his colleagues thought him callow and intemperate. "He was like a new golden-retriever puppy," his friend Senator Dan Coats, of Indiana, says. "There was incredible passion and energy, which some in the Senate saw as inappropriate." (A less politic assessment comes from a Senate Republican staff member: "I was once in a meeting where Santorum was just ranting about welfare reform. I thought he was a jerk, but I think he's learned a lot since then.")

Santorum was quite conservative, but more of a low-tax libertarian than a traditional-values sort. He had always tried to stay away from the abortion issue—which was difficult, given his wife's family. Karen's father, Kenneth L. Garver, was a pediatric geneticist, who was vehemently antiabortion. (The Garvers had twelve children, eight of whom were associated with the medical profession, including two doctors, two dentists, and three nurses.) "I hadn't really thought much about the issue," Santorum said during one of several conversations I had with him and Karen. "My first job was serving as an aide to a pro-choice member of the Pennsylvania State Senate, and I guess I thought of myself as being pro-choice, too. But when I decided to run for Congress Karen's father asked me what position I was going to take on abortion, and my reaction was 'Can't I just kind of skate by on this thing?' But he made me listen to his arguments. We had several long discussions about it, and I wrestled with it. I tried out several positions, like 'I'm personally against, but the law says abortion is legal.' None of them felt right, except to just say I was pro-life, and let it go at that."

When Karen became pregnant for the first time, in 1990, Santorum accompanied her to the five-week sonogram and saw the baby's heart beating; at twelve weeks, he saw the baby—his daughter Elizabeth—sucking her thumb, and he began to feel more strongly that he'd come to the right conclusion on the issue. Still, he avoided floor debates on abortion. "I didn't get involved, because it was politically risky to be an activist, on either side," he told me. "My feeling was, the public would respect your position, pro-choice or pro-life, as long as you didn't make much noise about it. That's the way most people up here feel."

Then, one day in the spring of 1996, he was sitting in his office watching C-SPAN as Senator Bob Smith, of New Hampshire, described partial-birth abortion—a procedure that Santorum hadn't previously known about—and Senator Barbara Boxer, of California, "ripped into Bob," Santorum recalled. "It just outraged me. I can understand how you could be pro-choice, but to vehemently defend something so ghoulish and horrible as partial birth was incomprehensible. I ran over to the Senate and made my first floor speech ever on abortion, supporting Bob Smith."

Some of Santorum's political advisers were horrified. "You don't want to be known as the partial-birth-abortion senator," he was told. The issue seemed more clear-cut than many other questions relating to abortion, but it was still extremely emotional and was studded with complications and exceptions. Furthermore, Santorum's own position on abortion was not absolute—he made exceptions in cases of rape and

incest, and also when the life of the mother was at stake. When I asked him if the exceptions he had made for rape and incest would hold into the middle trimester of a pregnancy, he said, "Oh, jeez, I don't know. . . . I've always said you had to deal with it within a few weeks. . . . By nineteen weeks, I'd have to say no."

Many of the most vexing questions were unanswerable. Twenty-five years ago this month, Roe v. Wade gave states the right to outlaw abortion after the point of "viability"—that is, the moment the baby could survive independently outside the womb—and forty states and the District of Columbia had restricted post-viability abortions. (In mid-December, the New Jersey Senate voted to override Governor Christine Todd Whitman's veto of a ban on the intact dilation-and-extraction procedure.) But, with advances in medical technology, viability comes much earlier now than it did twenty-five years ago. "It's probably sooner today than it was yesterday—the technology is changing that fast," I was told by John C. Nelson, a trustee of the American Medical Association from Salt Lake City, who helped formulate the organization's position on late-term abortions. Viability had been approximately thirty-two weeks when Roe v. Wade was decided, in 1973. "Now it's down to twenty-five weeks in some cases," Nelson said. "I've seen nine- or ten-ounce babies born who survive and do quite well."

A generation of young parents like the Santorums had seen the undeniable evidence of human life far earlier than the point of viability—in sonograms performed at five, twelve, and twenty weeks. According to Linda DiVall, a Republican pollster, the public's position on abortion has become more nuanced in recent years: a clear majority supports first-trimester abortion, but a clear majority also believes that there should be restrictions—especially on mid-to-late-term procedures. "This is where the squishy, middle-of-the-road pro-choicers peel off—especially Catholic boomer women," DiVall said. "They've seen the sonograms. They don't think abortions should be allowed so late. They think it's murder."

In the summer of 1996, when Bob Smith, who was facing a tough reelection campaign, said that he could no longer carry the burden of being the lead senator in the partial-birth-abortion fight, Santorum agreed to take it on. There were several striking moments in the debate that fall—Karen's recollection of Carol Moseley-Braun's remarks was among them—but perhaps the most memorable event occurred during Santorum's concluding remarks. "It was one of the most moving things I've ever seen happen on the floor," Dan Coats recalled. "Rick was saying, 'It's not just some cells, it's not just some tissue—it's a baby!'

And at that moment, up in the gallery, a baby began to wail, and the sound seemed to fill every cubic inch of the Senate."

A week later, the Santorums personal crisis began. After the initial bad news, there was a brief moment of hope: the second round of tests showed that the baby's kidneys were performing just well enough to make an operation possible. Rick and Karen returned to Philadelphia and, in a remarkable bit of outpatient microsurgery, a shunt was successfully inserted into Gabriel's bladder. The doctors had two caveats, though. There was a possibility that the shunt would fall out and the operation would have to be performed again. There was also a slight chance—one in two hundred—of infection: if Karen began to experience cramps or a fever in the next forty-eight hours, she should call a doctor immediately.

That was on Tuesday, October 8th. The next day, the Santorums went to Pittsburgh for Karen's parents' fiftieth wedding anniversary. "Wednesday night was a bad one," Karen said. "I didn't feel right. I didn't sleep well. And Thursday morning I wasn't feeling well at all. I took my temperature and was running a slight fever—one hundred degrees. I took it again, and it was up to one hundred point five. I felt cramping, too, but I was in denial—I didn't want to believe the operation had caused an infection. It was a one-in-two-hundred chance, they'd said. I decided to try another thermometer. My fever was up to one hundred and one."

There was no alternative now but to call the doctors in Philadelphia. They recommended that she head immediately for the labor-and-delivery unit at Magee Women's Hospital, in Pittsburgh. Karen's temperature was still rising; the cramps had become contractions. "They came in to do a sonogram, and it was the worst thing that could have happened," Karen said. "The baby was perfectly normal; I could see him kicking and moving around. The shunt was working perfectly. He finally had the perfect little environment—and it was just awful, because I was in labor and I knew that if he was born then he wouldn't survive."

Karen became adamant: she wanted the doctors to find a way to stop the labor. Her fever was still rising—it peaked at a hundred and five. She was shivering, even though she had been covered with several blankets; she was becoming delirious. The doctors said that Karen was probably suffering from an intrauterine infection and that there was the possibility of septic shock if they made any effort to stop the labor. "They said that if the infection wasn't treated there was a real chance it would kill Karen," the Senator recalled. "But Karen was really insistent. She kept saying 'No, no.'"

"In a situation like that, you are completely lost in the storm," Karen said. "Now I can see that I was caught up in the grief and the anguish. But I had three other children at home. It was wrong to even think about risking my life."

The Santorums, and especially the Senator, have difficulty talking about what they would have done if Karen hadn't gone into labor—if her life had been threatened. "There are cases where, for the life of the mother, you have to end a pregnancy early," Santorum said, steering away from the particular. "But that does not necessarily mean having an abortion. You can induce labor, using a drug like pitocin. After twenty weeks, the doctors say, abortion is twice as risky as childbirth. If there's a real emergency, you can do a cesarean section. But in no case is it necessary to kill the baby and then deliver it."

Santorum's view is supported—although not completely—by John Nelson, of the American Medical Association. He told me that in the "vast majority" of such cases induced labor is the safest and most humane course to take. But the "vast majority" does not include all cases. Abortion-rights activists argue that sometimes induced labor takes days, and that there may be occasions when an abortion, perhaps even the intact D&X procedure, is preferable in order to ease the suffering—if not to save the life—of the mother.

The Santorums had brushed very close to the heart of the late-term-abortion question, but they had been spared some of the toughest decisions. Gabriel had had a maddeningly tiny birth defect, but some mothers discover multiple, cataclysmic problems in their twenty-week sonograms. And some have had to face the horrifying prospect of carrying to term a baby who will not survive, or, at best, will be severely debilitated. Pro-choice lobbying groups had brought forth women who had decided, with genuine regret, to terminate their pregnancies using this controversial operation. The President surrounded himself with five such women when he chose to veto the partial-birth-abortion ban that April. "The Santorums had every right to make the choices they did," Kate Michelman, president of the National Abortion Rights Action League, says. "What we believe is that every mother in those circumstances should have the right to make her own choice, even if it is different from the one that the Santorums made."

There does, however, seem to be a growing uneasiness about late-term abortion as an elective procedure, a sense that perhaps it is time to impose stricter standards on most late-second-trimester operations. But what about the exceptional cases? Does a mother have the right to destroy an imperfect child? Who would find it easy to tell a woman that she has to carry a baby with severe, perhaps fatal, defects to term? Faced with this extremely difficult question, the Santorums are unflinching. It was a question that Rick had spent many hours discussing with Karen's father, who felt strongly—and had written a paper for the *American Journal of Human Genetics* arguing—that such decisions were a form of eugenics, an effort to tinker with the species which could lead to a virulent perfectionism, a Darwinian forced march in which the less than perfect would be brutally weeded out. "It's what the Nazis were about," Karen told me. A life, she believed—and Rick had come to believe—was a life, and no one, not even a mother, had the right to decide whether a child, however severely compromised, should live or die.

At twenty weeks, a human fetus usually weighs less than half a pound; its eyes are sealed shut; its head is disproportionately large. But it has all its fingers and toes, and its genitals, and it looks just like a baby. For Rick and Karen Santorum, the birth of Gabriel Michael confirmed their beliefs about partial-birth abortion; the idea that the state might condone violence against this tiny but undeniably human creature seemed impossibly barbaric. For Karen Santorum, the delivery was an incredibly painful experience. "I'll never forget those contractions," she said. "They were far worse than my other pregnancies. I think it was probably because I knew that I was going to go through this process, I was going to give birth and I would not hear the baby cry."

Shortly after midnight on Friday, October 11, 1996—just a week after the Santorums were told about their child's fatal defect—the baby was born, and he did not cry. He lived for two hours. His father baptized him with a few drops of water that had been blessed by a priest. Both parents held the child in their arms, and took pictures of him. When he died, Karen found that she couldn't part with him. "They wanted to take him to the morgue," she said. "I remembered taking babies to the morgue as a nurse, and I just didn't want him there with all these other dead babies. So we kept him with us all night and buried him the next day."

The Santorums had one other difficult decision to make. They decided that their other children should get to see and hold the tiny infant. "We were afraid they might have horrible thoughts about what he looked like," the Senator said. "We wanted them to see that he was a beautiful tiny little baby. Now my daughter Elizabeth will show people pictures of Gabriel and tell them, 'This is my baby brother. He's an angel.'"

The partial-birth-abortion congressional debate in 1997 was, if anything, uglier and more contentious than the debate of the previous year, although the apparent drift of public sentiment and of several important pro-choice politicians—and a clearer understanding of some of the facts—appeared to bolster the abortion opponents' case. In February, an abortion-rights lobbyist named Ron Fitzsimmons admitted that he had lied about the number of intact dilation and extractions that had been performed each year: he had cited four hundred and fifty, but those had been performed in the final trimester; many thousands—the exact number is unknown—were performed in the second trimester. Investigations by the Washington *Post* and the Bergen County (New Jersey) *Record* concluded that most of these mid-term abortions were elective, and had little to do with the physical health of the mother. In May of 1997, after several years of avoiding the issue, the American Medical Association said, in an extremely rare public-policy statement, that intact D&X was never "the only appropriate procedure"—although the group insisted that the decision as to whether it was "absolutely necessary" should be left to the presiding physician.

In response to these developments, the Senate Minority Leader, Tom Daschle, a Catholic, who was horrified by the partial-birth procedure, introduced a compromise proposal, a federal law that would have banned all post-viability abortions, with a carefully written exception made in cases of "grievous injury" to the health of the mother. But Santorum refused to negotiate, on two grounds: first, the Daschle bill would not have covered intact D&Xs performed in the second trimester; also, he didn't think the "grievous injury" language was tight enough. "It could mean anything," Santorum told me, overstating the case a bit. "It's unenforceable. It would perpetuate the system we have now—abortion on demand until birth—because no court is going to convict a doctor who says that he was making a decision based on the health of the mother. It's never happened, and it never will."

Eventually, Daschle chose to vote with Santorum against partial-birth abortions. The measure received sixty-four votes in the Senate, three short of the number needed to override a veto. "On balance, we were voting to eliminate what I consider to be a very grotesque procedure," Daschle told me. "And, from a strategy point of view, I thought this would accelerate the decision-making process by the courts."

Some abortion-rights activists were anxious to get the partial-birth issue off the table before further damage could be done to their cause. Linda DiVall, the Republican pollster, said that the percentage of people who described themselves as "pro-choice" as opposed to "pro-life" had declined from 53–35 (pro-choice over pro-life) to 45–45 in little more than a year, a shift that she attributed to the partial-birth controversy. "Our polls don't show that," said Kate Michelman, of the National Abortion Rights Action League. "I'm not in the business of public relations," she added. "Sometimes we have to take positions that enable reporters to label me and us as extreme . . . but this debate is a political strategy designed to overturn Roe v. Wade, to weaken the constitutional protections for a woman's right to an abortion, to put women at risk, and to put doctors under political supervision. I've never defended this particular procedure. I just believe that this is not an arena for political interference."

As for Rick Santorum, the death of his son and his growing involvement in the abortion controversy had caused him to grow both softer and harder. Friends and staff members said he'd become more sober, and more devout. "He's mellowed," said Karen, who also has become more deeply religious. But Santorum's feelings about abortion now seem every bit as vehement as Kate Michelman's. His bill allowed doctors to take any measures necessary to save the life of the mother. But his insistence that there could be no other health exceptions made even his allies at the American Medical Association a bit uneasy. John Nelson said, "You can't get the ink dry on a protocol"—a prescribed method for handling a medical situation—"before you find yourself in the operating room faced with a circumstance you haven't thought of." The American Medical Association helped to modify the specific language of Santorum's bill and reluctantly supported it as the least objectionable alternative; the American College of Obstetricians and Gynecologists opposed it. Nelson also said, "We just can't have a situation where a patient isn't allowed to receive the care she needs because of some law. The way the Santorum wording came out, we believed, you could prevent a doctor from going to jail for performing a partial-birth abortion, but we certainly didn't lobby very hard in favor of it."

Bill Clinton vetoed the partial birth-abortion ban for the second time on October 10, 1997—which Karen Santorum noted, was a day away from the first anniversary of Gabriel's death. Another attempt to override the veto will be made soon after Congress reconvenes in February.

A Reading for Critical Thinking

Congress and the Constitution

Each report of a committee on a bill or joint resolution of a public character shall include a statement citing the specific powers granted to the Congress in the Constitution to enact the law proposed by the bill or joint resolution.

—From the Rules of the House of Representatives

By Gary Benoit

If most members of Congress were to stand by their oath to "support and defend the Constitution of the United States against all enemies foreign and domestic" and to "bear true faith and allegiance to the same," big government would disappear. It could not be otherwise, since all of the powers granted to the federal government by the Constitution are enumerated, and those enumerated powers do not allow for either the Welfare State or the Warfare State. Yet most congressmen do not grasp this fundamental principle, imagining instead an ambiguous and expansive grant of power never intended by the Founding Fathers. Apparently, most don't even use the Constitution as a guide for the performance of their congressional duties, for if they did they would surely know the true scope of their powers—as well as those of the other branches of government.

This lack of interest in the Constitution was vividly displayed early last year when a group of "experts" appealed to the House International Relations Committee to support the U. S. Agency for International Development's Population Assistance Program. As recounted by a congressional aide who was present, Congressman Ron Paul's (R-TX) press secretary asked for the section of the Constitution that authorized this foreign assistance program, at which point "the room went dead—one, two, three, four, five seconds. Then one of the 'experts,' dazed and confused, asked, 'The . . . Con. . .sti. . .tu. . .tion?' More silence. Another 'expert' cautiously came to her rescue. 'Just to make a stab at this, the Constitution authorizes the

federal government to raise money to deal with foreign affairs.' Another 'expert' quoted some U. S. Code that 'authorized' their legal plunder. Then, they pounced, 'What office are you from?' The man replied, 'Congressman Ron Paul from the 14th District of Texas.' Then he thanked them and sat down. His question had been answered by their initial silence."

Most congressmen on the House International Relations Committee are no better informed on constitutional matters than the "experts"—or they would presumably not support international welfare without the proper constitutional authorization—an authorization which, of course, does not exist.

The House rule cited at the beginning of this article (Rule XI, Clause 2[1], Subparagraph [4]) was adopted at the start of the current 105th Congress as a means of reintroducing the Constitution to lawmakers and their staffs. Because the House committees are now required to cite the specific constitutional powers justifying the legislation they submit to the full House, they supposedly must read the Constitution and satisfy themselves that the powers are really contained therein. Also, any congressman is now able to refer to the committee's constitutional authorization prior to voting on a particular bill and to decide whether or not he agrees that the bill is constitutional. That is not a lot to ask, of course, of lawmakers who have taken an oath to uphold the Constitution.

Presuming that lawmakers would apply this constitutional litmus test in an honest way, the Rules Committee analysis of this requirement stated that "it is expected that committees will not rely only on the so-called 'elastic' or 'necessary and proper' clause and that they will not cite the preamble to the Constitution as a specific power granted to the Congress by the Constitution." This "expectation" notwithstanding, since the adoption of the rule in January 1997, committees have on a number of occasions cited only the "necessary and proper"—clause as the constitutional basis for legislation. They have similarly stretched the meanings of the "general welfare" and "interstate commerce" clauses, enabling them to justify virtually any social-welfare or regulatory program imaginable. And they have at times vaguely referenced Article I, Section 8 of the Constitution, the principal section enumerating congressional powers, without bothering to cite any particular power. In short, they have interpreted the Constitution not as a binding document authorizing specific powers, but as a blank check.

Of course, if lawmakers can legislate any law they want, then we have a democracy instead of a republic and there is no need for a written constitution limiting the powers of government. Moreover, if lawmakers can interpret the Constitution based on whatever liberal theory is in vogue at the moment, then the Constitution is an evolving document that holds no meaning as a fixed set of fundamental laws.

But lawmakers who subscribe to any such radical reconstruction are wrong, as can be readily demonstrated by referring to the Founders' own writings, such as *The Federalist Papers*. As James Madison, father of the Constitution, explained in *The Federalist*, No. 45, "The powers delegated by the proposed Constitution to the federal government are few and defined" and "will be exercised principally on external objects, as war, peace, negotiation, and foreign commerce." Its jurisdiction, he explained in *The Federalist*, No. 14, "is limited to certain enumerated objects, which concern all the members of the republic, but which are not to be attained by the separate provisions of any." All other powers are retained by the states or the people, a principle that was well understood at the time and was later reaffirmed in the Tenth Amendment.

Because federal powers are "few and defined," Congress does not have *carte blanche*. "No legislative act . . . contrary to the Constitution can be valid," Alexander Hamilton noted in *The Federalist*, No. 78. "To deny this would be to affirm that the deputy is greater than his principal; that the servant is above his master; that the representatives of the people are superior to the people themselves; that men acting by virtue of powers may do not only what their powers do not authorize, but what they forbid."

In *The Federalist*, No. 83, Hamilton added that since congressional powers are enumerated, "This specification of particulars evidently excludes all pretension to a general legislative authority, because an affirmative grant of special powers would be absurd as well as useless if a general authority was intended."

Let us now consider specific clauses which House committees have cited in their constitutional authorization statements in order to justify their supposed "general legislative authority."

Article I, Section 8, Clause 1 of the Constitution, also known as the "general welfare" clause, states: "The Congress shall have power to lay and collect taxes, duties, imposts and excises, to pay the debts and provide for the common defence and general welfare of the United States." House committees have cited this clause to justify legislation relating to vocational education, literacy programs, job training, charter schools, student loans, housing programs, welfare reform, foreign aid, crime control, child support, etc. Their rationale is that Congress has an open-ended power to pass whatever legislation it deems appropriate to provide for the general welfare, including the transfer of funds from taxpayers to private individuals and organizations.

But this broad interpretation makes no sense whatsoever, since the general statement in Clause 1 is immediately followed by a list of specific powers that Congress can exercise to provide for the general welfare. Condemning this broad interpretation in *The Federalist*, No. 41, Madison asked: "For what purpose could the enumeration of particular powers be inserted, if these and all others were meant to be included in the preceding general power? Nothing is more natural nor common than first to use a general phrase, and then to explain and qualify it by a recital of particulars. But the idea of an enumeration of particulars which neither explain nor qualify the general meaning, and can have no other effect than to confound and mislead, is an absurdity. . . ."

Addressing this subject during congressional debate on February 7, 1792, Madison warned that "if Congress can employ money indefinitely to the general welfare, and are the sole and supreme judges of the general welfare, they may take the care of religion into their own hands; they may appoint teachers in every state, county, and parish, and pay them out of their public treasury; they may take into their own hands the education of children establishing in like manner schools throughout the Union; they may assume the provision for the poor; they may undertake the regulation of all roads other than post-roads; in short, everything, from the highest object of state legislation down to the most minute object of police, would be thrown under the power of Congress. . . ."

In a letter on January 21st of the same year, Madison warned: "If Congress can do whatever in their discretion can be done by money, and will promote the General Welfare, the Government is no longer a limited one, possessing enumerated powers, but an indefinite one, subject to particular exceptions."

Of course, the Founders' intent with regard to the general welfare clause has been ignored and distorted, causing Madison's dire warnings to come true. But the modern-day interpretation was not yet in vogue in December 1831, when Madison wrote: "Beginning with the great question growing out of the terms 'common defence and general welfare,' my early opinion expressed in *The Federalist*, limiting the phrase to the specified powers, has been adhered to on every occasion which has called for a test of it."

Madison's understanding of the general welfare clause was echoed by many other Founding Fathers, including Thomas Jefferson, who in 1817 stated that Congress does not possess "unlimited powers to provide for the general welfare, but were restrained to those specifically enumerated. . . ."

The phrase "general welfare" is often misunderstood by present-day Americans because of the development of the Welfare State. But at the time the Constitution was written, the phrase did not refer to giving taxpayer money to the poor, but to the general welfare of the nation. On May 3, 1854, President

The Enumerated Powers of Congress

The very first sentence of the first Article of the Constitution states, "All legislative powers herein granted shall be vested in a Congress of the United States" — making that body the most powerful of the three branches of government. Neither the Presidency nor the Judiciary can make laws — except by usurpations tolerated by Congress. Congress could, for example, prohibit the federal judiciary from issuing usurping rulings in such cases as the infamous *Roe v. Wade* (abortion) decision simply by exercising its enumerated power to limit the jurisdiction of the federal courts (see Article III, Section 2). Also, Congress could employ its impeachment power in order to tame a corrupt and imperial President.

In the June 1997 issue of *The John Birch Society Bulletin*, constitutional analyst Don Fotheringham created an invaluable reference by listing all of the enumerated powers and duties of Congress. That list, which should be at the fingertips of every congressman, follows.

- Levy taxes.
- Borrow money on the credit of the United States.
- Spend.
- Pay the federal debts.
- Conduct tribunals inferior to the Supreme Court.
- Declare war.
- Raise armies, a navy, and provide for the common defense.
- Introduce constitutional amendments and choose the mode of ratification.
- Call a convention on the application of two-thirds of the states.
- Regulate interstate and foreign commerce.
- Coin money.
- Regulate (standardize) the value of currency.
- Regulate patents and copyrights.
- Establish federal courts lower than the Supreme Court.

- Limit the appellate jurisdiction of the federal courts, including the Supreme Court.
- Standardize weights and measures.
- Establish uniform times for elections.
- Control the postal system.
- Establish laws governing citizenship.
- Make its own rules and discipline its own members.
- Provide for the punishment of counterfeiting, piracy, treason, and other federal crimes.
- Exercise exclusive jurisdiction over the District of Columbia.
- Establish bankruptcy laws.
- Override presidential vetoes.
- Oversee all federal property and possessions.
- Fill a vacancy in the Presidency in cases of death or inability.
- Receive electoral votes for the Presidency.
- Keep and publish a journal of its proceedings.
- Conduct a census every ten years.
- Approve treaties, Cabinet-level appointments, and appointments to the Supreme Court (Senate only).
- Impeach (House only) and try (Senate only) federal officers.
- Initiate all bills for raising revenue (House only).

These are the powers of Congress: there are no non-enumerated powers. Leaving nothing to inference, the Constitution even specifies that Congress may pass the laws "necessary and proper" for executing its specified powers. Congressmen have simply to study and apply the Constitution in order to restore sound government. That most fail to do so is not the fault of the Founders, but of the people who elect the congressmen and send them to Washington.

— G.B.

Franklin Pierce vetoed a bill that (in his words) concerned "the constitutionality and propriety of the Federal Government assuming to enter into a novel and vast field of legislation, namely, that of providing for the care and support of all those . . . who by any form of calamity become fit objects of public philanthropy." Continued Pierce: "I cannot find any authority in the Constitution for making the Federal Government the great almoner of public charity throughout the United States. To do so would, in my judgment, be contrary to the letter and spirit of the Constitution and subversive of the whole theory upon which the Union of these States is founded."

On February 16, 1887, President Grover Cleveland vetoed a bill to appropriate money to provide seeds to drought-stricken counties of Texas because "I can find no warrant for such an appropriation in the Constitution, and I do not believe that the power and duty of the General Government ought to be extended to the relief of individual suffering which is in no manner properly related to the public service or benefit."

Even Franklin D. Roosevelt, father of the modern Welfare State, acknowledged while still governor of New York that the federal government did not have constitutional authority to provide social welfare. "As a matter of fact and law," he said in a March 2, 1930 address, "the governing rights of the states are all of those which have not been surrendered to the national government by the Constitution or its amendments." After noting that Prohibition was constitutional due to the 18th Amendment, he said that "this is not the case in the matter of a great number of other vital problems of government, such as the conduct of public utilities, of banks, of insurance, of business, of agriculture, of education, of social welfare, and of a dozen other important features. In these Washington must not be encouraged to interfere." No one can properly accuse FDR of installing statist policies out of ignorance of constitutional principles!

The House Appropriations Committee routinely cites Article I, Section 9, Clause 7 as the constitutional authorization for its mammoth and often unconstitutional spending bills, including appropriations for foreign aid, agricultural programs (including food stamps), and the Departments of Labor, Health and Human Services, and Education. Clause 7 states: "No money shall be drawn from the Treasury but in consequence of appropriations made by law. . . ." Of course! But the intent behind this requirement, as well as the power to "lay and collect taxes" to provide for "the general welfare," was that the money could be used only for constitutional purposes.

A report on the 1799–1800 Virginia Resolutions drafted by Madison explains: "[S]ubjoined to this authority [is] an enumeration of the cases to which their [Congress'] powers shall extend. Money cannot be applied to the general welfare, otherwise than by an application of it to some particular measure, conducive to the general welfare. Whenever, therefore, money has been raised by the general authority, and is to be applied to a particular measure, a question arises whether the particular measure be within the enumerated authorities vested in Congress. If it be, the money requisite for it may be applied to it. If it be not, no such application can be made. This fair and obvious interpretation coincides with and is enforced by the clause in the Constitution which declares that 'no money shall be drawn from the treasury but in consequence of appropriations made by law.'"

Few if any congressmen on the House Appropriations Committee apply any such standard to the legislation they draft. At the beginning of the 105th Congress, one congressman who would have applied this standard was denied a promised seat on the committee when he made known, in response to a question from the leadership, that he would not vote for any foreign aid appropriations.

Article I, Section 8, Clause 18, also known as the "necessary and proper" clause, authorizes Congress to "make all laws which shall be necessary and proper for carrying into execution the foregoing powers, and all other powers vested by this Constitution in the Government of the United States, or in any department or officer thereof." In spite of the Rules Committee's "expectation" that this clause would not be used as the sole basis for satisfying the constitutional authorization rule, House committees have nonetheless used it as their sole basis for funding unconstitutional agricultural research programs, dairy support payments, and small business programs.

Coming as it does after a list of specific congressional powers, this clause was obviously intended not as an undefined grant of "sweeping" powers, but as a simple declaration that Congress can make such laws as are "necessary and proper for carrying into execution" its enumerated powers. "Without the substance of this power," Madison wrote in *The Federalist*, No. 44, "the whole Constitution would be a dead letter." Yet this so-called "elastic clause" has been stretched to include virtually anything Congress deems "necessary and proper."

During Virginia's deliberations on whether or not to ratify the Constitution, George Nicholas correctly observed that "this clause only enables them [Congress] to carry into execution the powers given to them, but gives them no additional power." And during North Carolina's deliberations, Archibald Maclaine concluded, "This clause specifies that they [Congress] shall make laws to carry into execution *all the powers vested* by this Constitution; consequently, they can make no laws to execute any other power. This clause gives no new power, but declares that those already given are to be executed by proper laws."

This narrow definition made perfect sense since, as Maclaine also reasoned, "If they can assume powers not enumerated, there was no occasion for enumerating any powers." A report on the Virginia Resolutions drafted by Madison stated that this clause "is not a grant of new powers to Congress, but merely a declaration, for the removal of all uncertainty, that the means of carrying into execution those [powers] otherwise granted are included in the grant."

But what "means" should be employed? On February 15, 1791, Thomas Jefferson argued that "the Constitution allows only the means which are 'necessary,' not those which are merely 'convenient,' for effecting the enumerated powers. If such a latitude of construction be allowed to this phrase as to give any non-enumerated power, it will go to every one, for there is not one which ingenuity may not torture into a convenience in some instance or other, to some one of so long a list of enumerated powers. It would swallow up all the delegated powers, and reduce the whole to one power, as before observed ["that of instituting a Congress with power to do whatever would be for the good of the United States"]."

Article I, Section 8, Clause 3, also known as the interstate commerce clause, states that Congress has the power to "regulate commerce with foreign nations, and among the several States, and with the Indian tribes." Over the years the federal government's "interstate commerce" power has been expanded to include everything from the regulation of wetlands (deemed to be part of the navigable waters of the United States), to whom a restaurant must serve, to what or how much a farmer can grow, to wage and price controls. During the 105th Congress, House committees have cited this clause to justify legislation relating to underground storage tanks, homeowner's insurance protection, the U. S. Export-Import Bank, the Securities and Exchange Commission, energy policy, wildlife refuges, motor vehicle consumer protection, and labor standards.

The original intent, however, was not to manage the American economy, but to prevent the states, which were then operating almost as separate countries in a loose confederation, from inhibiting the interstate flow of goods through tariffs or other barriers. James Madison reaffirmed this intent when he wrote in a letter dated February 13, 1829 that "it is very certain that [the commerce clause] grew out of the abuse of the power by the importing States in taxing the

non-importing, and was intended as a negative and preventive provision against injustice among the States themselves, rather than as a power to be used for the positive purposes of the General Government. . . ."

Thomas Jefferson echoed the same sentiment on February 15, 1791 when he wrote that this clause "does not extend to the internal regulation of the commerce of a State (that is to say, of the commerce between citizen and citizen) . . . but to its external commerce only, that is to say, its commerce with another State, or with foreign nations, or with the Indian tribes."

But Franklin D. Roosevelt expressed a radically different view when he argued in a May 31, 1935 press conference that the commerce clause was written "in the horse-and-buggy age" and that "since that time . . . we have developed an entirely different philosophy." "We are interdependent, we are tied in together," he claimed. "And the hope has been that we could, through a period of years, interpret the interstate commerce clause of the Constitution in the light of these new things that have come to the country. It has been our hope that under the interstate commerce clause we could recognize by legislation and by judicial decision that a harmful practice in one section of the country could be prevented on the theory that it was doing harm to another section of the country. That was why the Congress for a good many years, and most lawyers, have had the thought that in drafting legislation we could depend on an interpretation that would enlarge the constitutional meaning of interstate commerce to include not only those matters of direct interstate commerce, but also those matters which indirectly affect interstate commerce." That is, change the meaning of the clause to fit the changing times—and don't worry about the intent of the Founders.

In his statement, Roosevelt was responding to a Supreme Court decision that defined the commerce clause narrowly enough to interfere with his statist schemes, including the regulation of farm products. "Are we going to take the hands of the federal government completely off any effort to adjust the growing of national crops," he complained, "and go right straight back to the old principle that every farmer is a lord of his own farm and can do anything he wants, raise anything, any old time, in any quantity, and sell any time he wants?" Certainly no such freedoms could be tolerated in the brave new world, which is why Roosevelt dealt with the justified judicial response by audaciously attempting to pack the Supreme Court.

Since that time the Supreme Court has interpreted the commerce clause much more broadly. Yet in its

1995 *Lopez* decision, the Court served notice that there are limits to this broad interpretation. In that landmark case the Court found unconstitutional a federal law that relied on the interstate commerce clause for prohibiting firearms in school zones. Justice Clarence Thomas, who joined the majority, correctly noted that "our case law has drifted far from the original understanding of the Commerce Clause" and has, in fact, "swallowed Art. I, Section 8."

Although the *Lopez* decision should have served as a shot across the bow, it is hard to detect any lessons learned on the part of interventionist congressmen who continue to pilot our ship of state through unconstitutional waters.

So far as this writer could determine, the House committees, abiding the expectation of the Rules Committee, have at least resisted the temptation to cite the Preamble in their constitutional authorization statements. Nor should they have cited the Preamble, since it was intended to be a statement of the ends to be achieved through the exercise of powers enumerated in the main body of the document. The Preamble states: "We the people of the United States, in order to form a more perfect union, establish justice, insure domestic tranquillity, provide for the common defence, promote the general welfare, and secure the blessings of liberty to ourselves and our posterity, do ordain and establish this Constitution for the United States of America."

"Had the states been despoiled of their sovereignty by the generality of the preamble," declared Virginia's General Assembly on January 23, 1799, "and had the Federal Government been endowed with whatever they should judge to be instrumental towards the union, justice, tranquility, common defence, general welfare, and the preservation of liberty, nothing could have been more frivolous than an enumeration of powers."

As we have already seen, of course, the same observation could be made with regard to liberal interpretations of the "general welfare," "necessary and proper," and "interstate commerce" clauses.

Jefferson observed in 1803 that "our peculiar security is in the possession of a written Constitution. Let us not make it a blank paper by construction." Most congressmen, with the willing participation of like-minded presidents and Supreme Court justices, have treated the Constitution as a blank piece of paper. And the people have not only allowed this radical reconstruction to occur, but have often encouraged it because of their own lack of understanding. But because the Constitution still exists and still constitutes the sole body of powers possessed by the federal government, all of the non-enumerated powers now exercised by the federal government fall in the category of usurpations that can be ended as soon as the understanding is created.

The understanding that is necessary includes a recognition that ours is a government of laws and not of men, a republic and not a democracy. Enough Americans must be brought to an understanding that Congress, acting in the name of the people for some greater good, cannot execute any non-enumerated powers, no matter how popular or tempting—unless the power in question is first granted to the Congress through the amendment process.

Of course, this does not mean that other levels of government cannot—or, for that matter, should not—execute any powers not embodied in the U.S. Constitution. Only the federal government cannot do so; the state governments can exercise powers authorized by their own state constitutions, and county and local governments can perform other functions allowed by law. But this concept of federalism, along with the concept of enumerated powers, has been largely forgotten, allowing a dangerous concentration of powers on the federal level that threatens not only the rights of the states, but the freedom of the individual.

The House rule requiring a constitutional authorization statement in committee reports could be a useful tool for building understanding among both lawmakers and constituents. What constitutional power is cited as authorization for a particular piece of legislation? Does the cited power truly authorize the legislation, or is the citation an embarrassing attempt to provide a fig leaf of cover for naked usurpation? Lawmakers should have no problem providing the claimed constitutional power(s) authorizing any bill or joint resolution when challenged, and informed constituents should not only ask such challenging questions, but inform others as to how the Constitution is being circumvented through misinterpretation.

As understanding grows, more Americans will recognize that the problem is not the Constitution or the government it created, but lack of adherence to the Constitution. And as they hear from a growing number of informed constituents, more busy congressmen will surely find the time to learn about the document they have sworn to uphold.

A Reading for Critical Thinking

CAPITOL FLIGHT:

Why congressmen are never in Washington

By Jennifer Bradley

The Congressional Directory says that Mark Sanford is a congressman, representing the citizens of the First District of South Carolina. But Sanford prefers to think of himself in slightly different terms: he is a citizen-congressman. "My belief is that the Founding Fathers wanted us to come up here, make a difference and go home," he says. "Given where I'm coming from, I have a belief that you want to stay immersed in what folks at home are thinking." Sanford, one of the Republican freshmen of 1994, has yet to rent an apartment in Washington. He sleeps on a futon in his office, then dashes home every week to Charleston, leaving late on Thursday or early on Friday. He says that the mere act of being home—out of Washington and in the company of his constituents—makes him a better congressman: "There is a fair amount of value found in having to go get a thing of milk on Friday evening because there wasn't any, and running into somebody," somebody who will give him an on-the-spot job evaluation.

Sanford is a courtly man, more self-effacing than many of his colleagues. His belief in the citizen-Congress is genuine. And it is widely shared. In 1994, Republicans overthrew the Democratic majority on Capitol Hill by running as anti-Congress outsiders. Their election has changed the culture of the Hill. The term limits amendment to the Constitution, destined to be brought to the floor every year the GOP stays in power, is only one manifestation of this change. Gone are the days when congressmen boasted of their seniority and their hard-won knowledge of the ways of the Capitol. Nowadays, to hear the members talk, every one is a Cincinnatus, who painfully

and regretfully leaves his real work at home to do his patriotic duty in wretched Washington.

At the root of the citizen-Congress myth is the notion that government is not a full-time job, that legislating is not so difficult a task that it requires constant attention. As Sanford once said of governing, "It's not like we're dealing with brain surgery." To the more extreme devotees of this populist agenda, time spent in Washington is not merely unnecessary but dangerous. The District is Babylon; the Beltway, the road to perdition. Washington corrupts and deforms, and the more time spent in the capital, the worse the damage.

This notion has its electoral charm. But it is a bad way to think about representative government; and it is creating a new kind of do-nothing Congress. Every week, on Thursday evening or Friday morning, more than half the members of the House abandon Washington, and its pernicious climate of government professionalism, and head home. They spend four cleansing, clarifying days with "real Americans" in their districts and return, reluctantly, to Washington as late as Monday night or Tuesday morning. To facilitate this, the House schedule is arranged so that little or no official business transpires on Mondays or Fridays. Most of their constituents may not know it, but these members have shoehorned the work of governing into three harried, tense, twelve-hour days. And that's during the regular session. Members also have district work periods, when they're home for a week or more at a time. The House rarely goes more than six weeks without a recess.

The truncated schedule was not invented in 1994, but in the 1960s, and not by Republicans, but by

Democrats who wanted to encourage more responsive (and electorally secure) members. In the years since, what started out as a compromise between governing and representing has become a commandment of congressional faith.

The result is a Congress that doesn't function properly because it simply isn't there often enough. Lawmaking may not be brain surgery, but it's not a no-brainer, either. It requires not merely representatives but legislators—people who spend enough time on the Hill to learn the substance and form of lawmaking. "We're the ones who write the budget each year for $1.7 trillion," says Anthony Beilenson, a California Democrat who retired in January after twenty years in the House. "In the past we had a much larger proportion of members than we do now who physically and mentally spent a decent proportion of their time doing legislative work, and that means mainly going to committee hearings. . . ." Now, he laments, there are "not 100 members out of 435 who are serious legislators." Budget cutting, he says, especially "needs a lot of members who, because they've spent a lot of time [here], understand where money can be wisely spent and other programs and areas where spending of money is not as useful. . . . You can't figure it out if you're flying back home. . . ."

Even Republican David Dreier, who goes home almost every weekend because, as he says, "I prefer living in California to living in Washington, D.C.," speaks of the importance of "maintaining the deliberative nature of this institution." Constituent views "should not be the sole determinant," he says. "I'm not merely echoing whatever I hear. . . . It's clearly part of the mix, [but] not the sole determinant." True. The other determinant is supposed to be what Dreier thinks is right. And what is right is supposed to be arrived at through deliberation—through conversation with other members. This process depends on familiarity, trust and respect—qualities that accrue through conversations in the elevator, chance meetings in the cafeteria and just being around each other. In the new citizen-Congress, this is disappearing. Many long-serving members link the partisan sniping that has characterized the last Congress to the ignorance that so many members have of one another. So tenuous are some of the personal bonds in the House that members spent the weekend of March 7 at a civility retreat in Hershey, Pennsylvania, just trying to get to know one another well enough to stop shouting at each other. "Part of our problem today," said Florida Republican Tilly Fowler at a news conference about the retreat, "is most of us go home every weekend, and we don't get a chance to know each other."

Spending time at the office doesn't just breed courtesy, it helps to produce good laws. Modern government is complicated. Members of Congress are called on to vote for national highway programs, for the repeal of the Glass-Steagall Act (which is—well, that's the point: they have to know what it is) and a hundred other bills. These are not issues to which constituents have all the answers. Mark Sanford thinks that members should "make [laws] simple enough so that the common man understands them." This sounds nice, but it means nothing, or worse than nothing: it means half-baked, poll-driven, faux-populist laws.

There is, finally, the problem of intellectual fraud. The rush to get back to "real Americans" betrays a serious confusion between living with people and living like them. Despite their good intentions, Sanford and his commuter colleagues don't live like most of their constituents. Their local addresses are conceits, because they don't really live anywhere. And this, arguably, makes them less in touch with the needs of "real people" than if they simply moved to Washington and brought their families with them. The new citizen-congressmen, sleeping on their futons and in their group homes on Capitol Hill, are divorcing themselves from the way most of their constituents live. "With no family in town, that lends itself to the 'Well, why not have late night sessions?' attitude, and all of the fraying nerves that come with that," says Colorado Democrat David Skaggs. "It means that most members do not have the normal experience of going home and having dinner with a spouse and kids that reminds us of a greater reality. It's impossible to quantify, but I know that just the general mind-set and demeanor of members would be different if they were going home at night to their families. It seems to me that's a much more normal and normalizing [life] than the pretense [of] leaving family out in the home district."

The anti-professionalists love to quote America's founders to bolster their distrust of government and feed their strangely flattering self-hatred. But George Washington said this in his farewell address: "You have in a common cause fought and triumphed together. The independence and liberty you possess are the work of joint counsels and joint efforts, of common dangers, sufferings and successes." The commonality of which Washington spoke, the space in which the people's representatives meet and debate and fight and legislate, is not an abstract or metaphorical place. It is a real, particular place, and it's called Washington, D.C.

Jennifer Bradley is a staff writer for Roll Call.

PART 8

The Presidency

It was more difficult to locate readings for this section than for any other section of this book. The intention was to find selections relating to the office of the presidency, rather than the man who holds that office. But, not surprisingly, virtually everything currently written about the presidency has focused on Bill Clinton's actions in the Monica Lewinsky scandal. Because the presidency is occupied by one individual, the fate of the office is inexorably tied to the fate of the man (and some day, the woman) who occupies it.

Whether or not Bill Clinton's presidency will ultimately be considered a success is unknown. There is no doubt that Clinton has achieved numerous political victories for his agenda. During his administration, the federal budget was balanced for the first time in twenty-five years and welfare was reformed. Clinton raised the minimum wage, passed the Brady Gun Control Bill, and achieved a number of other legislative victories. But Clinton's failures, both personal and political, are also notable.

During his administration, Democrats lost control of both houses of Congress for the first time in more than 40 years. Many of his major legislative priorities, including reform of the health care system and achieving greater regulation of tobacco, died in Congress. Several of his successes were initiated more so by Congress than by Clinton. And, of course, Clinton's personal failings are so well-known as to not be worth repeating here.

Our national ambivalence about Clinton parallels our ambivalence toward the office of the presidency. Often, we tend to want contradictory things from our presidents. For example, we want the president to be an exceptional person, more intelligent and moral than we are. However, we also want the president to be a "common man," someone who is in touch with our values and desires. As you read the following selections, you should attempt to come to some conclusion as to what qualities you believe are important in a president, and how the success of presidential administrations should be judged. Should the president serve as a role model for the nation, or should he just get his job done?

UNCHECKED AND UNBALANCED

WHY THE INDEPENDENT COUNSEL ACT MUST GO

By Cass R. Sunstein

A Reading for Critical Thinking

"The institutional design of the Independent Counsel is designed to heighten, not to check, all of the institutional hazards of the dedicated prosecutor; the danger of too narrow a focus, of the loss of perspective, of preoccupation with the pursuit of one alleged suspect to the exclusion of other interests." Thus wrote Supreme Court Justice Antonin Scalia nearly a decade ago, echoing the warning of three attorneys general, two of them staunch Republicans. In his dissenting vote to hold the Independent Counsel Act unconstitutional, Scalia objected that the supposedly independent counsel is a novel and dangerous means of law enforcement: a prosecutor who is effectively accountable to no one and entirely focused on a single person.

Kenneth Starr was appointed to investigate possible illegality in connection with the Whitewater affair in Arkansas. Nearly four years and $30 million later, Starr authorized and obtained tape recordings of private conversations with Monica Lewinsky, the former White House aide. As of this writing he has also threatened criminal charges against Lewinsky, issued subpoenas to a large number of people who may have talked to Lewinsky about her sex life, forced Lewinsky's own mother through two days of testimony before a grand jury, and sought testimony from members of the Secret Service and from Lewinsky's original lawyer. Whatever may be the outcome of this investigation—whatever its fate or that of President Clinton—it cannot be doubted that Starr's behavior extends far beyond the usual practice of the criminal prosecutor. Prosecutors do not ordinarily authorize

tape recordings designed to capture private accounts of alleged illicit sexual relations, and they rarely threaten to bring perjury charges as a result of affidavits in civil cases, especially when the affidavits involve such relations.

This article is not primarily about Starr's investigation. What is remarkable is that Starr's conduct has been paralleled by a large number of less publicized but drawn-out, expensive, and sometimes obsessive investigations by other independent prosecutors. The peculiar behavior is best understood as a product of the bizarre incentives created by the Independent Counsel Act, one of the most ill-conceived pieces of legislation in the last quarter century.

This is hardly a partisan issue. As Scalia foresaw and Republicans have long argued, the underlying problem is that the act eliminates the key safeguards built into the role of the prosecutor. Ordinary prosecutors have a large set of actual or potential targets of investigation. They also have limited budgets. They know that criminality of some sort or another is widespread and that not everyone suspected of a crime should be indicted. The safeguards that come from the combination of a limited budget and a wide focus are crucial contributors to human liberty under law—as crucial, perhaps, as any provision of the Bill of Rights. They discourage prosecutors from becoming single-mindedly preoccupied with one target of investigation and therefore tempted to abuse the powers of their office.

The Independent Counsel Act creates dangerous incentives not only for the independent counsel, but

From *The American Prospect* (May/June 1998), pp. 20–27. Reprinted with permission from *The American Prospect* Copyright © 1998. *The American Prospect*, P.O. Box 383080, Cambridge, MA 02138. And by permission of the author, Cass R. Sunstein, Professor of Law at the University of Chicago Law School.

for members of Congress and the press as well. Investigations under the act deflect attention from serious public issues and focus the attention of Congress, the press, and citizens alike on scandals that are sometimes imaginary and that, even if real, may not deserve the prominence that the possible or actual appointment of an independent prosecutor gives them. Sensational anecdotes, eye-catching accusations, and the dehumanization of political opponents have come to occupy so large a portion of our public life in America that they now obstruct the main business of democracy: attending to our problems and how they might be solved. The principal effect of the Independent Counsel Act is to fortify the worst tendencies in contemporary democracy. The act does a great deal of harm and little good. It is scheduled to expire in 1999 and it should not be re-enacted; better yet, it should be repealed as soon as possible.

THE COUNSEL'S DESIGN

One reason for the durability of the American Constitution is that the Framers had an acute understanding of the relationship of institutions to incentives. They sought to create a structure for the national government that would permit representatives to act in a reasoned fashion, above the fray of factions and misplaced passions. The institutional safeguards of the original Constitution, including both national representation and checks and balances, were designed to implement this deliberative ideal. The real problem with the independent prosecutor is not the individuals who occupy the office, but the unchecked discretionary power and unbalanced incentives of the institution itself.

The original goal of the Independent Counsel Act was simple, laudable, and entirely appealing: to ensure that the decision whether to prosecute high-level government officials would not be made by high-level government officials. In the aftermath of the Watergate scandal, which was a genuine constitutional crisis, the act seemed indispensable as a way of promoting public trust in government. The idea that no person should be the judge in his or her own cause is deeply rooted in American constitutional traditions; it seems only natural to think that those investigating high-level criminality should be insulated from control of the highest executive officers. In this way, the Independent Counsel Act might be seen as continuous with the Founders' effort to design institutions so as to respond to the incentive effects of different governmental arrangements.

The Constitution, of course, specifically provides for impeachment as the remedy for official misconduct at the highest level. But in the Watergate era, it seemed sensible to reply that impeachment is extremely difficult and unnecessarily strong medicine for many offenses and that it should be used very rarely. The act appeared far more precisely targeted. It would create an assurance that a disinterested person would investigate and if necessary prosecute high-level officials. But as sometimes happens, legislation driven by particular events may have created problems more serious than those that it was meant to prevent.

What sort of structure has emerged? Every year, of course, many complaints are made by people asserting that a high-level official has violated some law and that an independent counsel should be appointed. The Independent Counsel Act specifies a rigid procedure for handling these complaints. The attorney general must follow three steps. First, she must conduct a "preliminary investigation" whenever she receives "information sufficient to constitute grounds to investigate whether any" covered person may have violated the federal criminal law. Covered persons include the president and vice president, heads of the cabinet departments, assistant attorneys general, the director of the CIA, the deputy director of the CIA, the commissioner of the IRS and the chairs and treasurers of the principal national campaign committees seeking the election or re-election of the president. To consider whether a preliminary determination is warranted, the attorney general is allowed to consider only two factors: the specificity of the information received and the credibility of the source of information. She has 30 days to make the key decision.

> *The real problem with the independent prosecutor is not the individuals who occupy the office, but the unchecked discretionary power and unbalanced incentives of the institution itself.*

If she decides that a preliminary investigation is warranted the attorney general must decide within 90 days whether "there are reasonable grounds to believe that further investigation is warranted." During the preliminary investigation phase—and this is a crucial provision—the attorney general is not authorized to convene grand juries, plea bargain, grant immunity, or issue subpoenas. And she cannot decide against further investigation because the defendant lacked the necessary state of mind, "unless there is clear and convincing evidence" of that fact.

If the attorney general concludes that there are "reasonable grounds" for further investigation, she must apply to the court for the appointment of an independent counsel; this step is mandatory. The independent counsel, once appointed, has "full power and independent authority to exercise all investigative and prosecutorial functions and powers of the Department of Justice, the attorney general, and any other officer or employee of the Department of Justice." Among the expressly enumerated authorities are the power to apply for grant of immunity for any witness, to obtain tax returns, and to bring indictments. The independent counsel is also authorized to hire any employees he considers necessary. The attorney general may remove the independent counsel "only for good cause, physical disability, mental incapacity, or any other condition that substantially impairs the performance" of his duties.

This structure is remarkably rigid. How can the appointment of an independent counsel be stopped if it is undesirable? There are several methods. The first is via a preliminary determination that the charges are insufficiently credible and specific. But credibility may be hard to deny if, as is often the case, the allegation has been reported in the press and members of Congress think that there is reason for concern.

The second possible step is to conclude that there are no reasonable grounds for further investigation. Attorney General Janet Reno's decision not to seek appointment of an independent counsel for certain campaign-related activities by President Clinton and Vice President Gore attests to how controversial such decisions are likely to be. Judgments of law can stop the investigation at this stage. But under the act, any such judgment must be reached without convening grand juries, granting immunity, or issuing subpoenas, and without considering, in the normal fashion, the issue of intent. Often, of course, a prosecutor will drop a case at an early stage, after issuing subpoenas, considering the defendant's state of mind, or simply deciding, after an "all things considered" judgment, that this is not the kind of case that calls for a formal criminal investigation, even if there was a technical violation of law.

Such decisions not to investigate seriously or prosecute are a major safeguard of liberty under law. Not every technical violation of law should be subject to criminal prosecution, or even criminal investigation. If the law books were taken entirely seriously and every American were fully investigated with an unlimited budget for crimes committed within the last two decades, we could probably manage to put a high percentage of Americans behind bars and bring the economy to a grinding halt. High-level public officials are

particularly good targets for investigation, if only because of the complex network of statutes that regulate their behavior. Criminal prosecutors have limited budgets and exercise common sense in deciding to which cases they should allocate their limited resources. This is an important protection against liberty-threatening intrusions on people whose human frailties produce criminality that should hardly be celebrated but that ought not to result in an actual jail sentence, or even in the realistic fear of a jail sentence.

Consider a few of the examples of investigations under the act. President Carter's chief of staff Hamilton Jordan, was alleged to have used cocaine, and an independent counsel was appointed to investigate the allegation. The resulting investigation took several years and eventually cleared Jordan. President Reagan's assistant attorney general, Theodore Olson, was alleged to have lied before Congress in the context of a hotly disputed set of issues involving the behavior of Anne Gorsuch, the administrator of the Environmental Protection Agency. An independent counsel was appointed to investigate whether Olson should be indicted and sent to jail. Ultimately, Olson was "cleared." But is it reasonable for an assistant attorney general to have to fend off a criminal indictment because of the possibility that he has acted as an excessively zealous advocate in discussing constitutional issues relating to executive privilege? It is conceivable, though highly debatable, that Vice President Gore violated an old statute, the Pendleton Act, by making fundraising phone calls from the White House. But no reasonable criminal prosecutor would bring an indictment in such a case unless he were attempting to grandstand or to make a name for himself. It is not worth belaboring the point that in cases like this, calls for an independent counsel have nothing to do with a realistic claim that people should face criminal charges.

These suggestions raise an important question of law and fact: To what extent is the independent counsel within the technical control of the Department of Justice? As a matter of law, the question is not easy to answer. The counsel can be dismissed for "good cause," as the Supreme Court emphasized in *Morrison v. Olson*. It would be reasonable to think that the attorney general has considerable authority to discharge an independent counsel and perhaps also to control the counsel's performance. But however the legal issues might be resolved, the practical reality is that any attorney general will inevitably give a great deal of autonomy to the independent counsel. An attorney general who discharged a counsel, or attempted to control a counsel's operation, would face enormous political pressure, and any attorney general will know this. Thus while the law leaves room for dispute, the independent counsel is in practice an independent agent with an unlimited budget.

SMALL BENEFITS, LARGE COSTS

The Independent Counsel Act has probably served as a deterrent to crime by letting high-level officials know of the serious consequences of any illegal conduct. Moreover, some of the allegations pursued under the act are not trivial, and in some cases the use of an independent counsel has succeeded in bringing about convictions that might otherwise not have been obtained.

But these points hardly show that the act has made things better on balance. Many investigations have been a waste of taxpayer resources, in the process tarnishing the reputations of public officials and other possible defendants, not to mention imposing enormous legal costs on them. It is not clear that the 20 total convictions and 24 total guilty pleas offset these costs. But the most important harm to the nation is indirect and arises from the incentives created by the act for prosecutors, politicians, the media, and citizens themselves.

The independent counsel. By narrowing the prosecutor's focus to a single target of investigation and providing unlimited funds, the act eliminates the key safeguards built into the ordinary role of the prosecutor and creates an incentive for zealotry. After years in which your job is to investigate a single person or incident, all perspective is likely to be lost. An independent counsel who uncovers nothing will look as if he has wasted his time, not to mention millions of tax dollars. An announcement that no crime was committed, or that no crime can be proved, looks like a confession of failure. In contrast, an independent counsel who is able to bring a prosecution, or force the resignation of a top official, perhaps the president himself, may not just validate his work but perhaps even go down in history as another Archibald Cox, a true hero of democratic ideals. The act encourages independent prosecutors to do what, in a free society, no good prosecutor does: to take all imaginable steps to indict a single individual.

The contrast between the Framers' understanding of institutions and incentives and the office of the independent counsel could not be sharper. The system of checks and balances was designed to ensure deliberation, reflection, and accountability. Some of the most valuable developments in institutional reform—including the oversight role of the Office of Management and Budget with respect to both the budget and regulation—have also attempted to link incentives to institutions. The Independent Counsel Act, however, creates incentives for intense pursuit of a single target of investigation that dominates all other concerns.

Politicians. Consider how the incentives of politicians are affected by the act. It is hard to imagine any presidential administration in which there will not be at least a colorable claim of official illegality by someone covered by the act—a proposition supported by the fact that every administration has been subject to at least one independent counsel since the act's passage. Among political opponents of any administration, a number are likely to find it in their political interest to call for an independent counsel to investigate some real, possible, or even wholly imagined wrongdoing.

Any call for criminal investigation has the appearance of neutrality and statesmanship. How can a mere investigation do any real harm? From the standpoint of political self-interest, such a call will usually have the happy effect of attracting the attention of the press and the public. And if eventually some politician is likely to call for an independent counsel, might there not be special advantage in being among the first to do so? Once one or two politicians have called for an investigation, those who do not favor an independent counsel in the particular case, especially if they belong to the opposing party, may seem timid or unduly allied to the interests of the current administration.

An announcement by an independent counsel that no crime was committed, or that no crime can be proved, looks like a confession of failure.

Thus members of an opposition party may well find themselves in the position of publicly favoring—and by significant numbers—no less than a sustained criminal investigation and a possible jail sentence for their political opponents. Political disagreements turn into criminal charges. What is especially important is that everyone knows this before any scandal begins, and this knowledge will make the unfortunate scenario all the more likely.

In this light it should not be at all surprising that the act is used in a partisan manner. The problem is that it enlists the criminal justice system in partisan maneuvering. Criminal charges are easy to make and hard to rebut. The process is easy to start and hard to stop. And the stain on an official's name is easy to make and difficult to wash out.

Media. Newspapers and broadcasters already have strong economic incentives to focus on scandals, and the growing competition in the media in recent years has increased the preoccupation with scandals as a way of building circulation and ratings. It is far easier to attract readers and viewers by playing up a call for an independent counsel to investigate a high-level official than by running an exploration of, say, the effects of minimum-wage legislation. Thus there is a vicious circle, in which politicians and reporters follow their self-interest to the detriment of public discussion. Even before the recent events involving Monica Lewinsky, the preoccupation with independent counsel investigations had been growing. Front-page stories in the *New York Times* and *Washington Post* referring to such investigations have grown over time. There were just three such stories in the final years of the Carter administration; then 50 in the first four Reagan years; 225 in Reagan's second term; 63 under Bush; 220 during Clinton's first four years; and already 120 in Clinton's second term up to November 6, 1997. (Computer-equipped readers are invited to do their own search between November 6, 1997, and the present; needless to say, the number increases just about daily.)

Editorial writers also find it easy to assume a statesman-like posture favoring appointment of an independent counsel on the grounds that otherwise there can be no assurance that justice will be done. This is, for example, the typical stance of the *New York Times* editorial page, which is often focused, with all imaginable seriousness, on the legitimate concerns raised by new allegations and the need for "the air to be cleared." (The utter predictability of these editorials, admittedly, can make them appear a bit hilarious to longtime readers.) No one loses from a call for an independent counsel. Thus a kind of cycle is likely to build, in which political and media incentives fortify the interest in scandal-mongering.

Prospective public servants. In light of the experience of recent years, one prediction is pretty safe: so long as the law remains on the books, every future presidency will be faced with independent counsel investigations. It would be astonishing if "specific and credible" charges could not, over the course of four years, be made against at least a few members of any administration. Indeed, it would be astonishing if specific and credible charges could not be made against most Americans, based on their conduct over any four-year period, let alone their entire lives! But thankfully, most ordinary Americans will not face a prosecutor dedicated to investigating them alone, for prosecutors don't have the time and must pay attention only to the most serious crimes. For public service, the consequences of this asymmetry can be devastating. Prospective public officials know that by accepting a high-level appointment, they run the risk that someone, someday, will make a credible charge against them, that an independent counsel will be

appointed with no time or budgetary limit on the investigation, and that they will have to defend themselves against allegations that could put them in jail. Nor is an investigation by itself harmless; even without an indictment, defending yourself can cost millions of dollars, and thus even the innocent (and their families) face financial and other hardships. Why accept the job?

THE EFFECTS ON AMERICAN DEMOCRACY

No doubt, in many particular cases, those who approve of the current law or call for investigations by independent prosecutors have in mind the best interests of the country. But the general impact of such investigations—undertaken often for relatively trivial cases—is grave harm to American democracy as a whole. Scandals and sensationalism crowd out discussion of other issues. Instead of focusing on problems that deeply affect us, the nation becomes preoccupied with often impossibly technical questions about the violation of a statute that has marginal relevance to the national interest.

The result of all this is a disaster for the public: a belief that all politicians are crooks participating in cover-ups, a deflection of attention from substantive issues, a situation in which anyone contemplating public office faces a serious risk of being investigated. The Independent Counsel Act is not the prime source of public cynicism, but it contributes to distrust of government grounded not on an assessment of what policies do, but instead on a perception of pervasive corruption. This distrust can easily be exploited by conspiracy-mongers and political free-lancers such as Ross Perot, who may themselves be subject to character assassination but nonetheless draw ordinary officials into a skeptical cloud.

WHAT TO DO

How should we handle high-level criminality? If not the Independent Counsel Act, then what? For most of the nation's history—in fact, for more than 180 years—corruption in high places was addressed without any special procedures. Special procedures can hardly be indispensable if the nation managed well for nearly two centuries without them. The vigilance of opposing parties and the press are formidable obstacles to official wrongdoing and corruption. Before the Independent Counsel Act, political checks worked reasonably well. Scandals were occasionally handled by the appointment of an investigator in the Justice Department known to be relatively impartial and free from partisan control.

Usually invoked as a counterexample, the Watergate scandal is actually a case in point. Archibald Cox was made independent by Department of Justice rules, as was Leon Jaworski. After Robert Bork fired Cox, Jaworski was appointed and did his job well, and President Nixon had to resign. The system worked. And there was no independent counsel act. The lesson of the Watergate scandal is that political safeguards and ordinary procedures are perfectly sufficient.

In a highly politicized, two-party system filled with incentives to ferret out corruption, the possibilities of disgrace and impeachment are likely to do most of what needs to be done. If the choice is between the continued use of the Independent Counsel Act and its repeal, the better course is repeal. Scaling back the act—limiting the number of people covered or the power of the counsel—would be a bit better than the status quo but would leave untouched the basic problems of the office. The best approach would be to allow the act to die a peaceful death in 1999 or to repeal it even sooner.

> *The Independent Counsel Act was supposed to increase trust in government; instead, it has done exactly the opposite.*

If a sensible intermediate step is to be ventured, one possibility would be to create a highly professionalized institution, with a degree of independence, one of whose functions is to explore high-level illegality. This might be an office within the Department of Justice, perhaps modeled on the FBI and entrusted with several sensitive jobs, including that of investigating reports of illegality involving the president, the vice president, and the attorney general. People in such an office would have a history to draw on and a basis for reasonable comparisons. They would also have a menu of cases, and as career officials—not one-shot special appointees—they would have no special tendency toward zealotry. With a broader focus of work, they would have no reason to become obsessed with a single prosecution or think they would be judged a public disgrace for failing to secure an indictment. This proposal is hardly exotic. Among the analogs are not only the FBI but other Justice Department offices dealing with ethical issues and Freedom of Information requests.

The principal problem with the Independent Counsel Act is that by creating the wrong incentives, it makes our institutions work less well. It was supposed to increase trust in government; instead, it has diminished trust in government. It deflects public and congressional attention from substantive issues and turns disputes about policy into allegations of criminality. The Independent Counsel Act is thus a kind of parody of the achievement of the Framers, who merged an understanding of incentives and an understanding of institutional design.

The concern about favoritism in the criminal prosecution of high-level wrongdoing is legitimate, and in many countries it is a fundamental problem. It is not, however, one of the most serious issues facing American government. Our serious problems involve the effects of policies on people's actual lives. Official wrongdoing can and should be handled through means that are less destructive of public life. Whatever happens with Kenneth Starr's investigation of President Clinton, the Independent Counsel Act is itself a disastrous failure. On the merits there is little serious question. The only serious question is whether the Congress is prepared to do something about it.

—March 5, 1998

Stroke of His Pen Subverts the Law

A Reading for Critical Thinking

Summary: The Founders would be shocked to learn presidents now make law by executive order. But for Bill Clinton and many of his predecessors, it has been a potent political tool.

By Keith Russell

Trust no one. Especially not the Federal Emergency Management Agency. That's the immutable lesson FBI Special Agents Mulder and Scully, those extraterrestrial-chasing detectives played by David Duchovny (Mulder) and Gillian Anderson (Scully) learn in the blockbuster motion picture, The X-Files. In the film (based on the hit television series of the same name) Martin Landau, playing a conspiracy spinner whose tales of black helicopters and alien motherships ring true, tells Agent Mulder of a desperate plan concocted by federal villains: The secret transfer of dictatorial government power to the Federal Emergency Management Agency, or FEMA.

The mechanism that would allow bureaucrats to trample on the Constitution? A presidential executive order. "Think of it, Mulder!" Landau exclaims in the film. "A secret government, run by FEMA, with supreme powers!"

For most of us, it is purest fancy, straining credibility even by suggesting a president would use an executive order to seize total power. Even Mulder, a man paid to believe in conspiracies, has his doubts. "They call me the paranoid one," he quips when being told of the FEMA plot.

And yet, like all good science fiction, the threat of a presidential executive order abrogating constitutional authority is based on more than fantasy. Indeed, the truth about the use of executive orders by presidents to accumulate and exercise unauthorized power would seem a real-life nightmare to the Founding Fathers, say constitutional scholars and concerned members of Congress.

"We have virtually created a form of dictatorship," warns Idaho Republican Rep. Helen Chenoweth. "We must take back control of our government."

Chenoweth, who came into Congress as part of the GOP's 1994 conservative revolution, speaks from experience. For nearly two years she has fought the Clinton administration over the president's controversial American Heritage Rivers Initiative program, announced in his 1997 State of the Union address, under which local communities near designated "American heritage" rivers are made eligible for money and other development assistance from federal agencies. Though Chenoweth opposed the program on its merits, fearing it was an attempt to undermine private property rights in favor of expanded federal land management, it was how Clinton did it that steamed the gentlelady from Idaho.

Clinton did not go to the people's Congress for an enabling act but established the program dictatorially through executive order. In short, the president created a controversial new federal program, appropriating federal tax dollars that Congress likely would never have approved.

"It's purpose was a federal land grab, or a federal takeover of power that rightfully belonged to the states," Chenoweth tells Insight. "And they didn't do it through statutory authority. Instead, they created a new animal called an 'initiative.' I am so amazed."

To stop funding for the heritage rivers initiative, Chenoweth introduced a bill, cosponsored by 52 other representatives, recently voted out of the House Resources Committee. Along with Republican Reps.

Don Young of Alaska, Richard Pombo of California and Bob Schaeffer of Colorado, she also has filed a federal lawsuit to kill the initiative.

But Chenoweth and her allies are not the only ones amazed by the willingness of Clinton to act dictatorially without benefit of constitutional color through presidential executive orders. In November 1996, for instance, legislators in Utah were flabbergasted when they heard President Clinton had issued an executive order seizing 1.7 million acres of land in the Beehive state as a national monument—without so much as consulting Congress or the state. "The manner in which the White House hid this decision from the people of Utah displays an alarming disregard for the Constitution," Utah Republican Rep. James Hansen says of the affair.

More recently, executive orders have been used to add controversial language inserting "sexual orientation" into affirmative-action provisions affecting federal hiring practices, and even have been used to change the rules concerning how federal agencies decide when and whether to intervene when issues of federalism arise. Adam Thierer, a fellow in economic policy at the Heritage Foundation, called the effort "a grotesque distortion of the Framers' language establishing the original federalist system." And it was all done without a single vote by Congress.

Even more curious is that the mechanism used to override the balance of powers carefully worked out by the Framers never was intended to be there. Forrest McDonald, a professor of history at the University of Alabama and author of *The American Presidency: An Intellectual History*, explains that executive orders were created about 100 years after the Constitution was written. They were first authorized by Congress as part of a civil-service bill in the go-go 1880s. Since then, executive orders gradually have evolved into a powerful executive tool, and the judiciary has tolerated the expansion of presidential authority. "The courts have held that if the order falls within a president's constitutional duty or is authorized by Congress then it has the force of law," McDonald explains.

Executive orders can be innocuous declarations, such as when Clinton declared a national day in honor of the youth drug-awareness program, D.A.R.E., earlier this year. Defenders of the Constitution's separation of powers clause do not lose sleep over such proclamations. What concerns them are orders such as that Heritage Rivers initiative, which they see as usurping the authority of the people acting through their Congress. Since executive orders don't have to be debated under harsh scrutiny in the Congress (they are made a part of administrative law simply by

publication in the Federal Register) there is concern that serious usurpation might slide through without public debate. "There's never much fanfare surrounding many executive orders," admits Thierer. "They never get reported that well, and the president doesn't have to have a ceremony in the Rose Garden to announce them. They can be done in stealth fashion, and put on the books."

Doesn't this fly in the face of the checks and balances envisioned by the Founding Fathers?

"Absolutely," says Chenoweth. "And while President Clinton hasn't used a larger number of executive orders than other presidents, those that he has issued have been devastating to our balance of power. But that doesn't seem to stop this administration from trying to control all lawmaking."

Furthermore, "A lot of what is done they really don't spell out," says a House Republican staffer who watches executive orders. "You just have to wade through it."

Not that Congress is helpless in the face of presidential outrages and usurpations. "We shouldn't forget that Congress has the authority to pass a new law to replace any of this nonsense," the Heritage Foundation's Thierer says. But since any president faced with a challenge could veto legislation overturning his dictate, this may prove difficult. To override a veto takes a two-thirds vote in both houses—something very difficult to obtain, as now, when Congress is sharply divided on partisan lines.

But, notes James McClellan, a constitutional scholar at the Liberty Fund in Indianapolis, that doesn't excuse Congress from continually ceding power to the executive branch by passing laws which leave devilish details of administrative law to the president. In the

---

EXECUTIVE ORDERS 101

Simply put, an executive order is just what it sounds like: An order to the executive branch by the president to take action. All executive orders have been numbered since 1907, a total which now exceeds 13,000. Bill Clinton has issued 257 executive orders during his six years in office. While that total is comparable with the number President Reagan issued during eight years, it is minute compared to Franklin Roosevelt's whopping 5,322 executive orders in 12 years.

All executive orders must be revealed by publication in the weekly *Federal Register*, and also are available on the *Register*'s World Wide Web site at www.federalregisterdigest.gov. The White House keeps a searchable index of executive orders on its Website: www.whitehouse.gov.

case of President Clinton's controversial monument declaration in Utah, for example, the administration cited a turn-of-the-century law passed by Congress which granted the president authority to take "the smallest amount of land necessary" to protect environmental lands.

To Bill Clinton and Al Gore, this meant approval to seize control of 1.7 million acres with a simple announcement in the middle of a presidential election. Never mind that nearly 100 years ago in the original debate over the bill, notes a GOP staffer who has followed the controversy, Congress had no such large taking of land in mind. Because members couldn't agree on the appropriate amount, they left it up to the president, presuming that imprudence would be politically impractical. "It's a question of maybe whether Congress isn't putting limits on legislation that it should," says the staffer. "But it's a lot easier to pass legislation that is vague than specific."

"The real blame lies with Congress," McClellan insists. "They delegate all this authority, and unfortunately we're left with a Frankenstein monster."

It is a monster many worry has led to aggrandizement of the presidency—particularly in times of so-called "national emergency" in which, technically speaking, a Bill Clinton or future president legally could assume dictatorial power.

In fact, according to McDonald, thanks to a history of congressional passivity and a sense of opportunism by presidents as far back as Abraham Lincoln, we already may be vulnerable to such a usurpation. In his book on these matters, McDonald notes that a special Senate committee report issued in 1973 found declarations of national emergencies and executive orders still nominally in force from the time of Franklin Roosevelt that, combined with a growing list of powers delegated to the president by an uncautious Congress, "activated 470 provisions of federal law" during declared emergencies "which empowered the president, among other things, to 'seize property, organize and control the means of production, institute martial law, control all transportation and means of communication, and restrict travel.'" Supreme government control in the hands of the executive branch: Think of it, Mulder.

Reacting to these findings in the wake of the Watergate crisis, Democratic-controlled Congresses passed legislation in 1976 and again in 1985 which added provisions for Congress to terminate any presidentially declared state of emergency by joint resolution. However, no such resolution ever has been passed, nor are there imminent plans to do so.

But before anyone heads to the hills to join arms with the newest militia group, McDonald cautions that while stealthy dictatorial transfer of power to the president is possible theoretically, it isn't likely anytime soon. "I really don't think so in the present climate," he tells *Insight*, "because there simply is not enough trust in our government leaders today. In a sense, Lyndon Johnson and Richard Nixon did an awful lot of conducive work in this area. When you did find this happening was when there was a big sense of national unity, and a time of emergency and sense of urgency. This is not the national mood now."

Lincoln and Roosevelt, two presidents most cited for ignoring pesky constitutional limitations, faced authentic emergencies and acted with broad popular support (Lincoln to preserve the Union, Roosevelt to try to deal with the Great Depression and later to fight World War II). Even the X-Files' sinister FEMA cites benevolent plans for its dictatorship: to prevent aliens from colonizing and enslaving the planet.

But what about the authority of the judiciary to protect and defend the Constitution? In his book, McDonald describes Lincoln's clash with the federal courts when he suspended the writ of habeas corpus in border areas during the first year of the Civil War and ordered military commanders to arrest and imprison suspected Confederate sympathizers "without evidence, charges, or trial." After a federal circuit judge declared that any power to suspend habeas corpus was vested in Congress, Lincoln simply ignored the ruling. The courts could do nothing to resist a commander in chief during rebellion. Roosevelt also took advantage of a supportive public mood and reluctant legislative and judicial branches to exercise executive and emergency powers as a policy steamroller. For example, writes McDonald, FDR and his successor, Harry Truman, employed "far-reaching" executive orders throughout their terms, such as when "Roosevelt seized aviation plants, shipbuilding companies, a shell plant and nearly 4,000 coal companies in palpable violation of the Fifth Amendment's 'takings' clause." For a decade, not one executive order was declared invalid by the Supreme Court.

"You stop and think about what Harry Truman did," adds McDonald in a telephone interview. "He would go to Congress and say 'I want to do this, and if you don't do this I'm going to do it some other way.'"

The question is: Where in the Constitution is the president given the power to do it "some other way"? McClellan says some of the haziness has to do with the ambiguous guidelines the Constitution provides for presidents in Article II, which deals with the executive branch. "Article II is very general, very nebulous, in contrast to the section dealing with Congress. The powers of the president are in vague terms. And over the years this has meant more than the Framers ever intended."

That's what many Republicans thought in 1946 after they had captured both chambers of Congress. Wary (and weary) of their ordeal with FDR, a GOP-controlled Congress set out to curb some of the perceived abuses it had witnessed during four terms of a Democratic presidency, first adopting the 22nd Amendment to the Constitution, which limited presidents to two terms in office. Then, through an effort sponsored by Ohio GOP Sen. John Bricker, an amendment was proposed to limit the power of presidential executive orders and executive agreements. The effort fell one vote short of passage in 1954, when key Republican supporters changed their minds under pressure from President Dwight Eisenhower, a major cause of left-right conflict in the party for 25 years.

Now conservatives such as Chenoweth see the need to reexamine this important issue by proposing a constitutional amendment in the spirit of Sen. Bricker which she says would put into writing that "the Constitution is the highest law in the land rising above executive orders and treaties."

McDonald is more skeptical. "I think that it's the kind of thing people in Congress think would work," he says. "But I think presidents would find a way around it. The best check is "distrust" of potential usurpation, he adds. "If you've got politicians self-interested and jealous of their powers, then you might be able to check this. But if you don't, you're not."

There He Goes Again:

The Alternating Political Style of Bill Clinton

By Fred I. Greenstein, Princeton University

Some political leadership styles are of a piece. Jimmy Carter's is a case in point. Both in the comments he privately jotted on the margins of memos from his aides and in his public discourse, Carter exhibited a common concern for detail and insistence on the correctness of his own positions. Other styles are layered, as in that of Dwight Eisenhower, whose apolitical public demeanor concealed an analytically detached political sophisticate who obtained results by indirection (Greenstein 1982).

The political style of President Bill Clinton is neither unitary nor layered. It alternates. The tempest over whether Clinton was involved in a dalliance with a White House intern is a reminder of his tendency to oscillate between an uninhibited, anything-goes approach to leadership and a more measured operating mode in which he sets attainable goals and proceeds skillfully in his efforts to realize them.

The pattern is recurrent. After his election as governor of Arkansas in 1978, Clinton instituted a substantial increase in automobile licensing fees, peopled his administration with bearded political activists, and otherwise failed to conform to the political mores of his state. As a result, he was voted out of office two years later. He then spent the next two years stumping the state and promising to remedy his ways. He was returned to office, serving from 1983 to 1993 and establishing a reputation as a pragmatic and effective state executive (Maraniss 1995).

Similarly, the initial phase of the Clinton presidency was an exercise in excess. Having promised to "focus like a laser," Clinton hit Washington with a splatter of controversial initiatives—gays in the military, problematic cabinet nominations, and a controversial, closed-door health-care task force headed by his wife (Drew 1995; Johnson and Broder 1996; Woodward 1994). His public approval rating at the hundred-day mark set a record low for that point in a presidency. In the words of *Time*, his was an "amazing shrinking presidency."

But he then made an abrupt correction, signaling his willingness to adhere to the norms of the policy-making community. He further improved his performance when the Republicans took control of Congress in 1996, using his Capitol Hill adversaries as a foil to increase his own public support, and went on to become the fourth of the ten post-World War II chief executives to win reelection.

ANATOMY OF A POLITICAL STYLE

Underpinning Clinton's political style is a constellation of traits that vary in their ascendancy depending upon the circumstances in which he finds himself. The traits themselves are not unique, but their pattern is.[1]

1. Preoccupation with Policy

Clinton's most unusual quality is his deep absorption in public policy, particularly domestic policy. Most chief executives have broad programmatic aims, but, more so than any other president, Clinton is an aficionado of policy *qua* policy.

2. Political Passion

Clinton also is striking in the extent to which he is a political animal, although his passion for politics stands out less than his fascination with policy in a

From *PS: Political Science & Politics* (June 1998), pp. 179–181. Reprinted by permission from *PS: Political Science and Politics*. Copyright © 1998.

universe that includes Franklin Roosevelt, Lyndon Johnson, and Richard Nixon. As a compiler of reminiscences about him by citizens of his native state puts it:

> He had what seemed to be a compulsive need to meet people, to know them, to like them, to have them like him. These are the instincts of the calculating politician, but they long preceded Clinton's political impulses. Bill Clinton's is the case where a man's deepest human instinct perfectly matched, maybe even gave rise to, his most abiding ambition. (Dumas 1993, xvi)

3. Verbal Facility

The link between Clinton's policy preoccupation and his political proclivities is his capacity to pour out words. The record abounds with evidence of his ability to expatiate on his policies with modifications from audience to audience. He effortlessly spins out statements of prodigious complexity, as in this 101-word utterance on health care:

> The people who say that if I want to go to a four-year, phased-in competition model and that won't save any tax money on the deficit in the first four years, but will save huge tax money on the deficit in the next four years, miss the main point, which is that if we have a system now which begins to move health care costs down toward inflation, and therefore lowers health care as a percentage of the GNP in the years ahead, the main beneficiaries by factor of almost two to one will be in the private sector. (Clinton 1992)[2]

4. The Not-So-Great Communicator

But Clinton's astonishing fluency serves him badly. He finds it too easy to deluge the public with details and is less-than-adept at conveying the principles behind his programs. In this he is the antithesis of Ronald Reagan, who was notoriously lacking in information, but gifted at evoking larger themes.

5. Charm

In spite of being thin-skinned, Clinton has proved to be one of the more ingratiating occupants of the Oval Office. But his charm, like that of Franklin Roosevelt, can lead those who consult with him to believe he has accepted their views when he means only to acknowledge that he has heard them.

6. Dynamism and Good Cheer

Other elements in the amalgam are Clinton's preternatural optimism, energy, and ebullience. Even when he is deeply beleaguered, as in the controversies that bedeviled him during the 1992 New Hampshire primary and the Monica Lewinsky episode, Clinton has an ability to appear up-beat that also is reminiscent of FDR.

7. Lack of Self-Discipline

Then there is his lack of self-discipline and imperfect impulse control. Herein is a major source of his troubles, whether in the form of a tendency to overload the policy agenda, or to give excessively long speeches, or to be scandal-prone in his private life.

8. Insensitivity to Organization

Clinton's talents cry out for management, but he is insensitive to the need to back himself up with a well-ordered support system. He has acknowledged that he entered the presidency without attending closely to how to organize his White House (Nelson and Donovan 1993), and his initial team was short on political skill and Washington experience. Then his well-known learning curve manifested itself, and he took on such able, seasoned aides as David Gergen, Leon Panetta, and Michael McCurry.

9. Resilience and Capacity to Take Correction

Finally, there is his uncommon ability to rebound in the face of misfortune and his readiness to admit his own failings, qualities that account for the claim that he is incapable of sustained error.

THE TWO SYNTHESES

Under some circumstances, Clinton's attributes combine to contribute to his anything-goes approach to governance; under others, they converge in his more measured and effective style. His second mode often does not come into play until outside forces have constrained him. Thus, he was far more surefooted after the Republicans won control of Congress in 1994 than before, and he delivered a bravura State of the Union address in the midst of the media barrage about Ms. Lewinsky.

It is not clear why someone as intelligent and politically adept as Clinton should be so dependent on external correction. As is often pointed out, he is the step-son of an alcoholic; and the children of alcohol abusers exhibit a wide variety of behavioral difficulties (Kaufman and Pattison 1982; Cruse 1989). He also was raised by a doting mother, whose strong point was not setting limits, and his high aspirations in themselves are an invitation to overreaching himself.[3]

Clinton's outward characteristics seem to place him in James David Barber's active-positive character category, but he clearly has inner complexities that do not figure in Barber's classification (Barber 1992). More to the point may be the writings of Richard Neustadt (1960), which address the political requirements of presidential effectiveness. In addition to his formal powers, the president has two resources with which to accomplish his purposes, Neustadt argues.

One is his reputation in the policy-making community as a skilled, determined player and the other is the perception of other policymakers that he has the support of the public.

When he has his act together, Clinton can be impressively successful in meeting Neustadt's criteria, but there is no guarantee that he will not slip into his alternate mode. Stay tuned!

Fred I. Greenstein is professor of politics and director, Woodrow Wilson School Research Program in Leadership Studies at Princeton University.

NOTES

1. For an earlier attempt to take Clinton's measure, see Greenstein (1993–94).
2. It is less clear how good Clinton is at making the balanced judgments that are referred to by the term "common sense," or whether he thinks critically about the validity of the formulations he verbalizes with such ease.
3. For an examination of Clinton through a psychoanalytic prism, see Renshon (1996).

REFERENCES

Barber, J. D. 1992. *The Presidential Character: Predicting Performance in the White House.* 4th ed. Englewood Cliffs, NJ: Prentice Hall.

Clinton, W. J. 1992. "Excerpts from the Interview with President-Elect Clinton." *Wall Street Journal*, December 18.

Cruse, S. W. 1989. *Another Chance: Hope and Health for the Alcoholic Family.* Palo Alto, CA: Science and Behavior Books.

Drew, E. 1995. *On the Edge: The Clinton Presidency.* New York: Simon and Schuster.

Dumas, E. 1993. *The Clintons of Arkansas: An Introduction by Those Who Knew Them Best.* Fayetteville, AR: University of Arkansas Press.

Greenstein, F. I. 1982. *The Hidden-Hand Presidency: Eisenhower as Leader.* New York: Basic Books.

—. 1993-94. "The Presidential Leadership Style of Bill Clinton: An Early Appraisal." *Political Science Quarterly* 108 (Winter): 589–601.

Johnson, H., and D. Broder. 1996. *The System: American Politics at the Breaking Point.* Boston: Little, Brown.

Kaufman, E., and E. M. Pattison. 1982. "The Family and Alcoholism." In *Encyclopedic Handbook of Alcoholism*, ed. E. M. Pattison and E. Kaufman. New York: Gardner Press.

Maraniss, David. 1995. *First in His Class: The Biography of Bill Clinton.* New York: Simon and Schuster.

Nelson, J., and R. J. Donovan. 1993. "The Education of a President: After Six Months of Quiet Success and Loud Failure, Bill Clinton Talks About the Frustrating Process of Figuring Out His Job." *Los Angeles Times Magazine*, August 1.

Neustadt, R. E. 1960. *Presidential Power: The Politics of Leadership.* New York: Norton.

Renshon, S. A. 1996. *High Hopes: The Clinton Presidency and the Politics of Ambition.* New York: NYU Press.

Woodward, B. 1994. *The Agenda: Inside the Clinton White House.* New York: Simon and Schuster.

PART 9

The Bureaucracy

In many ways, the bureaucracy is the most important part of government. Congress and the president may have the more glamorous and visible job of deciding what the laws will be, but it is up to the bureaucracy to carry out those laws. Although bureaucrats tend to toil in obscurity, their power should not be underestimated. Bureaucrats are the "human face" of the government. The way people view government is greatly influenced by their interactions with government workers. To the extent that bureaucrats are helpful, honest, and efficient, respect for government grows. To the extent that they are inefficient or corrupt, respect for government is diminished.

Bureaucrats are much maligned. This is not a uniquely American phenomenon. Throughout history, bureaucrats have been portrayed as lazy workers who are more concerned with following proper procedure than in achieving results. But Americans may have greater distrust of the bureaucracy than most other nationalities, because of our emphasis on the free market system. We compare government workers with workers in the private sector and find government workers lacking.

Unhappiness with government has led to a movement toward privatization—handing over more of government's functions to private businesses. For example, several states now permit corporations to run private jails for profit. Privatization may deliver certain services at lower cost, but it presents its own problems. Government often has different goals than businesses do, goals that go beyond mere dollars and cents. As you read the following selections, think about the following questions: Does government do some things well? If so, which things? Which do you trust more to do the right thing—business or government?

The Fraud Fraud

By Michael Walzer

Defenders of privatization regularly refer to stories about waste and crime in the public sector. Indeed, there are a lot of stories, told by muckraking reporters or whistle-blowing civil servants—both groups standing in an old American tradition, though muckrakers once wrote about the private sector more often than they do today. In a way I feel comforted by these stories, even if I know in advance what they are going to say. Waste and crime go on—I can't do anything about that—but at least someone is watching.

But these periodic exposés serve a political agenda, with which I am less comfortable. Is it really true that there is more waste and crime in the public than the private sector? I doubt it. Waste and crime are significant costs for private business, but almost no one is doing the journalistic work (or the academic research) necessary to keep us informed about them. We do occasionally hear from private-sector whistle-blowers, chiefly on environmental, health, and safety issues—most recently, for example, in the tobacco industry. But rarely does anyone address the simple question: How much of the price that consumers pay for goods and services goes to cover the costs of waste and crime?

The question itself suggests the reason why it is so rarely answered. The costs are passed on to consumers, and those who pass them on don't want us to know their extent. The case is similar in the public sector, where officials don't want taxpayers to know about the money they routinely lose. The only difference is that news stories about governmental waste and fraud are far more frequent: public-sector officials are less successful than private-sector managers in repressing the information. The greatest benefit of the public sector is its openness to scrutiny and criticism.

So let's try to open up the question of crime and corruption in the private sector. (I'll leave waste aside for now, though its costs are probably greater.) Marketplace crime commonly comes in three forms (the categories are suggested in *Big Money Crime* by Kitty Calavita, Henry Pontell, and Robert Tillman): first, crimes against a company committed by its employees, contractors, clients, and customers; second, crimes against the public committed by a company through tax evasion, price fixing, or the violation of safety and environmental laws; and third, crimes against a company and the public committed by the company itself, as in the looting of savings and loan associations in the 1980s, where the criminal activity was based on the principle that "the best way to rob a bank is to own a bank." I shall pursue only the first of these, since it comes closest to the standard stories of fraud in government programs like Medicare and Medicaid. (It is, of course, mostly private-sector contractors who perpetrate these frauds.) But readers should be warned that the second and third kinds of criminal activity are far more costly; the savings and loan scandals cost taxpayers more than $150 billion.

It isn't easy for an amateur like me to find information on marketplace crime, but some facts and figures are available on the Internet, and with a little help from my friends, I went in search of them. The most likely sources, I was told, are the companies that sell protection against fraud; they regularly collect and distribute data about fraudulent activities.

One of these companies—KPMG Investigation and Security, Inc., headquartered in Amsterdam—publishes an international fraud survey, based on a canvass of business leaders in eighteen countries. Reported losses in the 1995 canvass exceeded $1 billion, but the survey concludes that "in view of . . . the reluctance or inability of many respondents to quantify their losses . . . this must be regarded as only the tip of the international fraud iceberg." Indeed, hard numbers are rare in the report; it is mostly perceptions and opinions that are quantified. Thus, 76 percent of American respondents described fraud as a major problem—making the United States one of the global "fraud hotspots."

The most common fraudulent activities are the obvious ones: kickbacks, company purchases for personal use, falsification of financial statements, misappropriation of cash (larceny and embezzlement), false representation, patent infringement, false invoices, and secret payments (bribes). The hardest hit sectors are also the obvious ones: insurance, financial services, and retail business. Again, quantification is difficult. A separate KPMG survey of airline fraud was unable to obtain meaningful data regarding the total cost of fraud. The only hard number that companies were willing to provide was the average "cost per single fraud occurrence," ranging from over $400,000 for kickbacks to $667 for cargo theft. No company revealed the number of cases from which these averages were calculated. The abuse of frequent flyer programs accounts for 28 percent of known "external fraud" (not the work of employees). But there is no account of how much this amounts to and no attempt to estimate the extent of unknown fraud.

All this is suggestive, if unsatisfying. And what it suggests is that there is a big story here, waiting for some stubborn and wily investigator. Given the debate about privatization (not only in the United States), fraud in the private sector is as much a matter of public interest and "need to know" as fraud in the public sector. Intelligent choices about public and private services can't be made without some sense of the relative losses to corrupt employees, contractors, clients, and customers in each one.

But doesn't the market give companies an incentive to reduce these costs? Obviously, KPMG and its likes would not be in business if there were no such incentives. And when the light of public debate illuminates some area of the private sector, like the health industry today, managers will work hard to reduce their losses—producing rules and regulations that rival those of governmental bureaucracies. On the other hand, the "reluctance or inability" of many companies to quantify their losses, the costs of protection, and the uncertainty of success, all militate against any major effort. And most often the light of publicity doesn't reach very far into the private sector. The lack of democratic openness and consumer awareness make it easy for companies to write off their losses and pass them on—so long as their competitors are doing the same thing. In effect, they agree to do the same thing, which is a perfectly legal form of collusion, well known also in government agencies.

Where are the losses to crime and corruption greater? It's hard to say. But the next time you hear politicians arguing for privatization, ask them if they know. Ask for hard numbers. After all, fraud is one of the more common forms of free enterprise, and, in a society as devoted to free enterprise as ours, its effects will be widely distributed: business entrepreneurs are unlikely to be outdone in fraudulent activity.

Crimes on Paper

A Reading for Critical Thinking

Filling out the wrong government form could cost you.

By James Bovard

As Hosep Bajakajian was preparing to fly back to his native Syria in 1994, U.S. customs officials at Los Angeles Airport detained him. They discovered that he and his wife were transporting $357,144 in cash—the profits from his two gas stations and money destined for Syrian relatives. Bajakajian had failed to fill out a Form 4790, as required by the Bank Secrecy Act of 1970. Travelers carrying more than $10,000 in cash into or out of the country must declare the money to Customs officials, or risk having it seized. Customs confiscated Bajakajian's cash, and he has been fighting ever since to get it back. His case is now before the Supreme Court.

Both a federal district and a federal appeals court have concluded that the money was honestly acquired. Bajakajian's only sin was failing to fill out the bureaucratic form. The fact that it was honest, hard-earned money, says the Customs Service, is "not relevant." At the oral hearings before the Supreme Court, the attorney for the Clinton administration said that any cash over $10,000 not reported on the Form 4790 is "dangerous money. We have a dangerous situation on our hands."

What happened to Hosep Bajakajian is just another example of the government's increasing fetish for paperwork. Each year, according to the Office of Management and Budget, citizens and businesses spend over 6.7 billion hours filling out forms for various federal agencies. These wasted hours are bad enough; more alarming, however, is the power government commandeers via endless reporting requirements. The more forms there are to complete, the more likely someone will make a mistake—and the more Damoclean swords the government has available with which to terrify its citizens.

Trivial paperwork violations have become a boom industry for federal prosecutors. In 1993 the federal government sued psychiatrist George Krizek for $81 million, charging that he had made false Medicare and Medicaid claims for his treatment of patients. Krizek was prosecuted under the False Claims Act, which states that a person can be found guilty of filing a fraudulent claim against the government (which carries triple damages and a $10,000 fine for each violation) if that person "acts in reckless disregard of the truth or falsity of the information" on which the claim is based. Federal Judge Stanley Sporkin estimated that Krizek had overcharged the government for $47,000 over a seven-year period. Krizek's lawyers said that the psychiatrist's sometimes imprecise billing (submitted by his Czech immigrant wife) also resulted in extensive undercharges to the government.

Yet, as a federal appeals court acknowledged, it was "undisputed that Dr. Krizek worked long hours on behalf of his patients, most of whom were elderly and poor. Many of Dr. Krizek's patients were afflicted with horribly severe psychiatric disorders and suffered simultaneously from other serious medical conditions." Medicare routinely refuses to compensate doctors for many of the services that they provide to its recipients, because of its own "deceitful" and "unfair" rules, the court panel noted. "Dr. Krizek," it decided, "is not public enemy number one. He is at worst, a psychiatrist with a small practice who keeps poor records. For the government to sue for more than eighty million dollars in damages against an elderly doctor and his wife is unseemly and not justified."

Of course, the federal government is exempt from the False Claims Act. While the feds increasingly claim a right to destroy paperwork violators financially, the government itself disrupts the lives of millions with its false claims. Each year the Internal Revenue Service sends out millions of deficiency notices with wrongful demands for additional payments and penalties. The agency knows that its system is wildly inaccurate. As *Worth* magazine reported, "According to a confidential agency report, only IRS demands for $25,000 or more are checked by humans for mistakes. IRS computers spit out bills charging lesser amounts with reckless abandon—and taxpayers often pay up without a peep."

Ben Lacy, a 74-year-old apple cider producer in Virginia, was faced with 24 years in jail and $2 million in fines after federal bureaucrats discovered *eight* errors in the thousands of lines of reports he was required to submit between 1991 and 1993 under the Clean Water Act. Assistant U. S. Attorney Nancy Spodick told reporters: "A lot of small companies are under the perception that the government shouldn't regulate them because they are small. I hope this serves to be a deterrent to companies big and small."

But the feds displayed a moral turpitude much worse than what they accused Lacy of. Federal prosecutors blocked a local environmental group from testifying that Lacy's operation in fact did no harm to the local stream—which was ostensibly why the Clean Water Act had been invoked in the first place. Worse yet, the government's key witness was a former Lacy employee who testified that Lacy had ordered his workers to falsify records and documents. The man later told a private investigator hired by Lacy's lawyers that he had lied on the stand—and had been encouraged to do so by the federal prosecutors. The feds, he said, had assured him that "it is very hard to convict someone of perjury."

Lacy received a second trial, and was convicted on one count of polluting a stream and seven counts of falsifying environmental records. He was fined $10,000 —far less than the more than $250,000 in legal expenses he had undergone to defend himself. Naturally, the prosecutors themselves faced no penalties from the Justice Department for possibly encouraging perjured testimony.

Incidentally, in November, after the U. S. Park Police effectively dumped fifty cases of confiscated beer into a tributary of the Potomac River, no charges were filed over what was a blatant violation of the Clean Water Act. A Park Police spokesman explained: "We didn't know. We were ignorant of it."

Another notorious case saw the feds try to torpedo an Arkansas company for not filing a form with the EPA regarding the disposal of its wastewater. In November 1992, a federal jury in Arkansas took less than an hour to acquit four corporate officials of Aviation Inc. of charges that they "conspired to knowingly transport hazardous waste without a manifest and knowingly discharged pollutants from a point source into waters of the United States without a permit."

The company operated an aircraft refinishing and maintenance business that used solvents to strip paint from aircraft. The federal government prosecuted the firm because the waste water it poured on the ground contained 0.0003 percent of the solvent methylene chloride, which the EPA labeled as hazardous. Decaffeinated coffee contains a higher percentage of methylene chloride than that. Neither the EPA nor the Justice Department bothered to conduct any tests to determine whether the wastewater was actually hazardous. But since the feds believed the company had violated the paperwork reporting requirement, they demanded their pound of flesh.

Federal agencies plant paperwork land mines with growing regularity. Consider the recent debate over airbag safety. For almost two decades, the National Highway Transportation Safety Administration deceived the American public regarding the risk of airbags—the auto "safety" devices activated by explosives built into car dashboards that hit people in the face at 200 miles per hour. Partly as a result of National Highway Transportation Safety Administration's suppression of evidence of airbag dangers, scores of children have been killed in grisly accidents, including a few decapitations. In November the agency announced that people could now apply for permission to deactivate their airbags—but only after they submitted an official form pleading medical necessity or some other extreme circumstance.

Because the feds will permit airbags to be deactivated only in exceptional cases, millions who wish to deactivate them won't be allowed to. If the feds decide that someone claiming medical necessity is lying, that individual could face perjury charges and up to five years in prison merely for trying to keep his family safe. Naturally, federal bureaucrats face no penalty for deceiving the public about airbags.

The airbag paperwork trap is a perfect example of how the government now exists: not to safeguard its citizens, but to expand the domain of its own power by destroying the lives of those who fail to cross their *t*'s or dot their *i*'s.

Trivial paperwork violations have become a boom industry for federal prosecutors.

James Bovard is the author of Lost Rights: The Destruction of American Liberty *(St. Martin's Press).*

Pandora's Box — American Style:

Government as a Cause of Problems

By Gerald F. Kreyche

In greek mythology, Pandora was sent to humans as punishment for Prometheus' stealing of fire from the gods. She was entrusted with a box containing all the ills that could beset the world and she opened it. All those ills escaped, but they were accompanied by hope. Now, every age and every culture has had its own Pandora's Box. In our country, it is the U.S. government which opened it.

Few question the bureaucracy's good intentions in trying to help society, but the road to hell is paved with such, as virtue driven to excess becomes a vice. To illustrate, let's document some ills that have resulted from the government's involvement in "doing good."

No one can deny that many minorities have been discriminated against everywhere in the world, and the 1960s saw a plethora of remedial legislation to correct this in the U.S. This noble endeavor has turned into an excess, and we are reaping the consequences today. Civil rights have become civil wrongs, and we are facing a strange brand of tyranny by the minorities.

Affirmative action, quota systems, diversity goals, preferential treatment, and set-asides—all are measures that, instead of unifying America by creating a level playing field (which is all Martin Luther King, Jr., wanted), now pit class against class, as white males are forced to the rear in the nation's march to "equality." Hiring and promotions to management must give minorities priority, and woe to the company that ignores this. Texaco and countless companies learned their lesson. The former reportedly agreed to give each black employee a 10% pay raise. Promised also were new management positions to be created for blacks. Pause for a moment and ask yourself how you would feel if you were a long-time white worker with Texaco. Fairness is one thing, but when the other guy's advance is at your expense, that's another—especially if his or her competence is below yours, as often is the case.

The government set the pattern here. Apparently, it believes the cure for discrimination is reverse discrimination. The nation seems to have decided on "political apartheid," namely that each ethnic group is a separate entity and not—as it really is—a part of mainstream America. (This bears similarity to the 19th-century policy error of recognizing Indian tribes as separate nations.) The government insists that each of those groups is entitled to jobs and privileges in proportion to their number. Never mind qualifications!

Recently, California passed a referendum prohibiting such discrimination in its colleges and state offices. On that occasion, a California university president let the cat out of the bag when he bemoaned that now he never could fill his diversity goals, a tacit admission that many minorities could not cut the mustard and so would be ineligible for admission to his institution.

By overemphasizing rights and privileges and understating duties and personal effort, the government has created a near-universal paranoia. Thriving on this are the Equal Employment Opportunity Commission, American Civil Liberties Union, National Organization of Women, and other advocacy organizations. Each celebrated case brings Jesse Jackson and other professional protesters out of the woodwork.

As a result of societal paranoia, lawyers are becoming more numerous and richer than ever. No case is too trivial to pursue, as there may be a pot of gold at the end of the rainbow. Prisoners are suing the state; kids are suing their parents; patients are suing their doctors; and teachers are suing their superiors. This has cowed nearly everyone from speaking out on anything. Moreover, it has forced doctors to practice expensive defensive medicine, performing more tests that otherwise would not be necessary.

The heavy hand of government not only warns of the danger of smoking, a legitimate concern, but for all intents and purposes is making every smoker a pariah in society. Increasingly, smoking is prohibited on airplanes, on the job, in restaurants, and in some cases in one's own home (the latter insisted upon by companies seeking to lower employee insurance rates). It reminds one of the ill-conceived 18th Amendment establishing Prohibition as the government continues to divide its citizens.

Pushing "inclusion" in the schools not only has hampered good teaching and destroyed discipline, but added burdens in the community. Special education classes no longer are sufficient and indeed are viewed as the old "separate but equal" problem and thus discriminatory. Everyone must suffer in order that the feelings of a few might not be hurt.

A Down's syndrome boy was denied a place on a Colorado high school football team, and the screams of protest could be heard to high heaven. The usual charge was hurled that his rights were violated. Similarly, a high school girl, largely confined to a wheelchair, was forced off a high school cheerleader squad because the squad said she required too much care. One feels sorry for these two, but as Pres. Jimmy Carter once declared, "Life is not fair."

Another ill was unleashed when the government thought it could change biology by declaring a war on sexual differences. The catch-all term, harassment, is the rubric under which it would make the U.S. a utopia. What are some of the results?

A seven-year-old boy kissed a girl at school and was said to be guilty of sexual harassment. In the Armed Forces, such harassment calls are coming in to hotlines by the thousands. In a climate where nearly everyone has lost their sense of morality, did anyone ever wonder what would happen when young men and women were put together in the same housing? To separate them, as does Israel, would have brought charges of discrimination.

See what you have done, Pandora!

Dr. Kreyche, American Thought Editor of USA Today, *is emeritus professor of philosophy DePaul University, Chicago, Ill.*

What Made the Government Grow

. . . and grow, and grow, from almost no employees to three million. Don't blame the welfare state, or the military; the truth is much more interesting.

By Bernard A. Weisberger

The tradition of distrusting government—almost any government— has such deep roots in the American past that a newcomer could justifiably think of the United States as a nation of a quarter of a billion near-anarchists. After all, it was Tom Paine, a major voice of the American Revolution, who declared that "government, even in its best state, is but a necessary evil; in its worst state, an intolerable one." Is Paine too radical for you? Try, then, a congressman in the First Congress: "[All] governments incline to despotism, as naturally as rivers run into the sea." Or President Jefferson, in his 1801 inaugural: A "wise and frugal government which shall restrain men from injuring one another . . . [and] leave them otherwise free to regulate their own pursuits is the very "sum of good government." Or our national sage, Emerson, some years later: "The less government we have, the better."

One could go on indefinitely netting sentiments like these from the mainstream of American discourse. Yet for a people who seem to be inherently skeptical of government, we have, after two centuries of national existence, an unbelievably generous amount of it. Even those of us who have friendly—or at least explanatory—words to say on behalf of "big government" can't deny the gargantuan size of the creature. A glance at the federal establishment alone, which usually provokes the loudest critical outcries, is sobering. A handy *Information Please Almanac* informs me that at the end of 1991 the total number of *civilian* federal employees, rounded off to the nearest thousand (a practice that we shall follow throughout this

excursion), was 3.103 million. Their payroll for the single month of October (likewise in round numbers) was $9.687 billion. State and local governments left those numbers in the shade; they employed 15.455 million workers and paid them, in the same month, more than $31 billion.

Before falling into apoplexy, however, antigovernment readers should recall that all these public employees, like those in private industry, return some of that money in tax payments and pump the rest of it into the economy through purchases and savings. All the same, a very natural curiosity arises about what on earth they all are doing.

A GUIDE TO THE GARGANTUAN

The official answer with respect to the national government is contained in *The United States Government Manual*, which is compiled annually by the Office of the Federal Register, a division of the National Archives and Records Administration. You can order the 1996–97 edition by mail from the Superintendent of Documents or buy it for thirty-six dollars at one of the bookstores maintained by the Government Printing Office in major cities. The text is available in electronic format, too, through the GPO's Electronic Information Dissemination Services. In print or in bytes, the *Manual* dissects and labels the working parts of the federal bureaucracy with dismaying thoroughness.

The 1994–95 edition, for example, is 917 pages thick, including 73 pages of appendices, 8 of which are devoted exclusively to listing the acronyms that

From *American Heritage* (September 1997), pp. 34–52. Reprinted by permission of *American Heritage* Magazine, a division of Forbes, Inc. © Forbes, Inc., September 1997.

speckle documents composed in bureaucratese. Even the most cursory and partial overview is somewhat numbing. Let us turn to a single agency of the legislative branch, the General Accounting Office.

The GAO's "fundamental" mission is defined as "supporting the Congress" through "a variety of services, the most prominent of which are audits and evaluations of Government programs and activities." Its chief official is the Comptroller General of the United States, who has a Deputy and a Special Assistant. Behind them stand five more Assistants, one each for Planning and Reporting, Operations, Policy, Quality Management, and Information-Management and Communications. Six more Assistants direct divisions, including General Government; Health, Education, and Human Services; National Security and International Affairs; and Program Evaluation and Methodology.

We have only begun. There is a General Counsel, and following him in the charts are thirteen Directors of Support Functions, whose dominions include the Civil Rights Office and the Office of Affirmative Action Plans, Congressional Relations, Counseling and Career Development, Internal Evaluation, and International Audit Organization Liaison. Each of these has a staff and employees whose total number goes unreported in the *Manual*.

It is not my purpose to pick on the GAO, which I choose largely because it was established in 1921, years before the contemporary welfare state. It should not be confused with the Congressional Budget Office, a relative newcomer, created in 1974. But it is a good example of how the system proliferates titles and appointments in its steady process of multiplying and rearranging tasks.

I needn't furnish many further excerpts from the *Manual* to make the point of bigness. The lightest skimming of its thousands of entries tells almost all. Under listings for the judicial branch, for instance, there is an Administrative Office of the United States Courts that has thirty-six directors, deputies, and chiefs of such divisions as "Accounting and Financial Systems," and "Relocation and Travel Management." The Executive branch has a "White House Office" that includes the President's Assistants, Deputy Assistants, and Special Assistants in areas that range from "Science and Technology" and "Environmental Affairs" to "News Analysis" and "Public Liaison." There are also, for the First Lady separately, a Chief of Staff, Press Secretary, and Director of Scheduling. In all, 126 such Executive-branch executives are listed, each naturally with support personnel of his or her own.

The fourteen Departments of the Cabinet account for about 425 pages of the *Manual*, and another 225 pages cover Independent Establishments and

Government Corporations, sixty strong. Some of these are frequent headliners—for example, the United States Postal Service, the Federal Communications Commission, NASA, and the CIA—while others are so specialized as to be almost unknown, such as the Federal Retirement Thrift Investment Board and the African Development Foundation.

To go inside some of these departments and agencies, old and new, is to swim in the multitudinous sea of responsibilities that the national government has assumed in the course of our history. Look at a single domain in the Department of Agriculture (USDA), which achieved cabinet status in 1889—say, that of the Under Secretary, Small Community and Rural Development. This functionary is the overlord of the Rural Electrification Administration, the Farmers Home Administration, and the Rural Development Administration, meaning that he or she is, among other things, in the electric-power, real estate, and banking businesses, since the Farmers Home Administration turns out to be an agency for guaranteeing loans to young and beginning farmers and to "limited-resource farmers" or those facing emergencies. Other Assistant Secretaries within the USDA (it's hard to resist the acronymic tug) supervise the regulation of packers and stockyards, the rendering of advice to consumers, the compilation of agricultural statistics and forecasts, the health inspection of plants and animals, the management of forests, and the conservation of soil. All these responsibilities have been gradually shoveled into the USDA hopper by congressional enactments over 135 years, so it is no wonder that there are so many.

A visitor called on the Secretary of War in 1796 and found no sentinel at the door and only two clerks scribbling. The State Department cannot have been much bigger.

But youthfulness as an agency is no barrier to growth either. Look at one single, randomly chosen page of subordinate agencies of the Department of the Air Force, which came into being only in the late 1940s: Frequency (i.e., radio frequency) Management; Historical Research; Inspection; Legal Services; Logistics Management; Management Engineering; Medical Operations; Medical Support; Military Personnel Center and Morale; Welfare; and Recreation and Services. Here, then, is the explanation for the inclusion on the federal payroll of hundreds and possibly thousands of historians, engineers, management specialists, doctors, lawyers, and entertainers serving only one branch of one subdepartment of the cabinet.

Enough. The point is surely made, and when one is confronted with these facts, it is easy to understand the urge to "re-invent" or even dismantle a governing apparatus so massive. But to do so with an instrument better than the indiscriminate hatchet, we must first understand how the creature grew to its present size from most modest beginnings.

A MULTITUDE OF NEW OFFICES

To illustrate just how modest, step back in time to President Washington's first administration. He had only four principal advisers, the Secretaries of State, War, and the Treasury, and the Attorney General. They managed their affairs with a bare minimum of support. A visiting French officer called on the Secretary of War in 1796 and found no sentinel at the door and only two clerks scribbling away while the Secretary himself was next door getting a shave. The State Department cannot have been much bigger; even four years later its Washington headquarters had only eight clerks and a messenger. Treasury was the swollen bureaucracy. It had 39 employees on the payroll at the end of 1789, but only twelve years later it had 78 officials and employees in Washington alone and 1,615 in the "field service," collecting duties and taxes and paying the government's bills.

Congress deliberately kept the departments on short rations. After all, hadn't the Declaration of Independence included in its charges against King George that he had "erected a multitude of New Offices and sent hither swarms of Officers to harass our People, and eat out their substance"? Even these modest administrative outlays troubled some state lawmakers. One from North Carolina, in 1790, deplored the "monstrous salaries given to the public officers," and another from Virginia condemned "giving [away] the honey from the hive, the marrow from the bones of the people."

Such outcries, however, did not impede the growth of the federal establishment—not even when the "Virginia Dynasty" of Thomas Jefferson and his supposedly frugal Democratic-Republican successors in the White House took control of the nation in 1801 and held it for the next twenty-four years. Some two-thirds of the way through that period, in 1816, the United States had already come to employ 4,837 civilians, 535 of whom worked in Washington. Of the total, 3,341—about two of every three—were employees of the Postal Department. The mail service, extending to hamlets scattered across the huge land area of the young Republic, would long continue to provide the largest share of federal jobs. The remaining 1,500-odd were probably concentrated in the Treasury Department. Its obligations had been swelled by the just ended War of 1812.

This last point seems obvious, and it brings us to a necessary pause for explanation. War is above all things irreconcilable with the ideal of frugal government. It is a shot of superhormones, jolting national authority and expenditures into adolescentlike spurts of growth that are never completely offset by later peacetime contraction. But we shall omit war from this accounting, especially since its effect both on the national debt and on governmental growth has been covered earlier in these pages (see "The Federal Debt," by John Steele Gordon, November 1995, and "The Warfare State," by Bruce D. Porter, July/August 1994).

A second obvious engine of growth is the simple fact of population increase. It is hardly a surprise that a nation of some 250 million (1990 census) should take more governing than one of approximately 4 million, the 1790 count. But a sixtyfold increase in the number of Americans does not explain a six-hundred-fold leap in the number of government employees serving them, from around 5,000 to more than 3 million. What is the historical explanation for the federal work force's multiplying ten times as fast as the populace?

Any attempt to answer that question poses another tough one: What do we measure as "big government"? The yardstick I've chosen here—namely, the changing head count of federal workers (ignoring all other levels of government)—is admittedly crude, is subject to maddening variations depending on sources and methods of computation, and overall may well deserve the scorn of statisticians. Without any detailed breakdown of what those workers have been doing at different times, it is hard to pinpoint where the need for them has been genuine and where not. But a history of each segment of the federal establishment is clearly beyond the scope of a short summary, and gross employment totals are at least an important indicator. Moreover, they do not have to be adjusted, like figures on national income and expenditure, for inflation. Even with this limitation to one index, it is hard to avoid stupefying lists of numbers, but I hope the patient reader will be rewarded with some understanding.

THE FRONTIER FACTOR

So how, then, did the federal government grow? First of all, in step with the pace of the nation's modernization. This wasn't a uniquely American process; during the nineteenth and twentieth centuries many nations experienced a relentless thrust toward administrative centralization and growth. But in the United States the first era of governmental expansion—roughly from

1830 to 1880—owed much to what *was* a special American experience, the opening of the frontier. By 1820, after a mere thirty-one years under the Constitution, the nation had already doubled its area, from some 890,000 square miles to approximately 1,790,000, thanks to the purchases of the Louisiana Territory in 1803 and of Florida in 1819. Not long after came an eight-year acquisition spree: Texas in 1845 and Oregon in 1846, the Mexican Cession in 1848, and the Gadsden Purchase of 1853—another almost 1,235,000 square miles in all. These additions created the continental United States (excluding Alaska, not bought until 1867) and swelled the public domain to more than a billion acres, many of them pristine wilderness, that had to be secured, protected, explored, and surveyed; later provided with law, postal services, and other official inducements to settlers; and finally conveyed to the states or to private owners. These were unmistakably government functions, and those who argue that the West was settled by individuals acting independently of government simply do not know what they are talking about. Moreover, government helped private capital create networks of roads, rails, navigable rivers, and canals ("internal improvements," in the political lexicon of the era), which were indispensable for integrating the new territories into the growing national economy.

That was one clear impetus toward an enlarged federal establishment. Two other strong economic trends were nudging in the same direction. One was a steady increase in foreign trade. American exports were valued at $74 million in 1830 and $853 million in 1880, while imports in the same period soared from $71 to $761 millions' worth. This threw extra demands upon the State Department's consular services and the Treasury's collectors, for even though the tariff rose and fell with changing political tides (generally low in the 1840s and 1850s and high from 1862 on), the sheer volume of the customs services' business followed a steady upward course. In addition, the rise of a manufacturing economy drew the government into greater participation in encouraging applied science, as a closer look at the growth of new bureaus shows.

But first, merely examine the overall figures. To repeat, the entire federal civilian work force of 1816—4,837—could have fitted comfortably into a present-day minor-league grandstand. Twenty-five years later, in 1841, it had not quite quadrupled, coming to just over 18,000, of whom 14,290 were in the Post Office. In 1851 the total was 26,274. In the next twenty years the number virtually doubled—51,020 in 1871—and then in ten years nearly doubled again, just cracking the 100,000 mark. For comparative

purposes, while the general population tripled (from approximately 17 million to 51 million) between 1841 and 1881, the number of federal employees increased five-and-a-half-fold.

It is possible to follow some of the individual streams feeding this swelling reservoir by taking note of the enlargement of the presidential cabinet. The major source was the Post Office; remember that in 1841 it carried on its rolls about 14,000 out of 18,000 federal civilian workers—about three out of every four. (Its share did not fall below half until 1917.) The Postmaster General was given cabinet rank in 1829, and the first holder of the job in its new dignity was William T. Barry. Until modern times it was not unusual for the P. M. G. to be the chairman or at least a major power broker of whichever party held the White House.

The Postmaster General's seat in the cabinet was the first new one in nearly thirty years—since the creation of the Department of the Navy in 1798. The next cabinet slot created was the somewhat broadly named Department of the Interior, in 1849, and it began as something of a catchall for the overflow of work that was swamping the older agencies. To begin with, Interior inherited the General Land Office from the Treasury. Treasury had already lavishly doled out acres of the public domain to the states (two million in 1836, for example); the states then used the land to fund schools, colleges, charitable undertakings, and transportation improvements. There were also direct federal grants for roads and canals, and millions of acres were sold each year: as few as a million and a quarter in 1829, as many as twenty million in 1836. Land sales, even at the extremely modest prices that the political power of the West demanded, accounted together with customs receipts for most of the national government's revenue.

After 1849 the Department of the Interior continued both the sales and donations at a quickening pace except in hard times. Grants to railroads (the idea being that they would sell the land to raise capital) rose from 3.75 million acres in 1851 to 41.5 million in 1865, when the first transcontinental line was in full construction. In 1862, with the passage of the Homestead Act, the nation theoretically abandoned selling land directly to individual families in favor of giving it away in 160-acre farmsteads. But even this overall process of rapidly privatizing much of the public domain, this unprecedented government handout of potentially income-producing property, required paperwork to accomplish. Not for nothing was the phrase *doing a land office business* invented to describe the kind of boom that kept the Department of the Interior busy and growing.

Interior also took over, from the Department of War, the management of Indian Affairs, with a growing list of administrative responsibilities. It relieved War of the Pension Department, an apparently minor shift in 1849 but with explosive workload results seventeen years later, when suddenly there were nearly two million Union veterans to deal with. It disencumbered the State Department of the Patent Office, which, considering that the number of applications filed per year rose from under 2,200 in 1850 to almost 40,000 forty years later, goes far toward explaining why the Secretary of the Interior complained in 1888 of having to keep up with "the accumulation of business by the rapid development of the country."

SCIENCE, INVENTION— AND GOVERNMENT

The patent office is a first-class reminder of another major boost in the number of federal jobholders, the involvement of the government in science and technology. The office had been lodged in the Department of State by Thomas Jefferson when he was Secretary, hardly a surprise given his own inventive bent. In fact, wherever science and learning were concerned, Jefferson managed to overcome his innate suspicion of government. In early meditations on federal support for postal roads, for example, he worried that contracts to build and maintain them would be a "source of boundless patronage" and "eternal scramble," but he badly wanted public support for the increase and diffusion of knowledge, and he soon learned that senators and representatives might be persuaded to open the public purse for science if a commercial motive could be invoked.

In getting an appropriation to finance the Lewis and Clark Expedition, Jefferson cited its potential usefulness in "extending the external commerce of the United States." In 1806, initial misgivings suspended, he proposed a constitutional amendment empowering the central government to open "new channels of communication" and support a "national establishment for education," a favored project of his. Nothing came of this, so the next year, when he sought an appropriation for a complete mapping of America's shorelines by a new agency, the Coast Survey (the head of which would be a European geographer and

mathematician, Ferdinand R. Hassler), he took care to stress the utility of the survey to "the lives of our seamen, the interests of our merchants, and the benefits to the revenue." Congress came through with an initial $50,000, but the progress languished in dry spells of funding and was still unfinished when Hassler died in 1843.

Yet by then the foundations had been laid for a surprising and generally unrecognized expansion of the federal role in science and invention, always justified by some presumable practical results. The Army's Corps of Topographical Engineers was authorized in 1824 to make surveys and plans for canals and roads and improve the navigation of rivers. Army expeditions made survey after survey of possible routes through the uncharted Rocky Mountains and Pacific West. Those of Lt. John C. Frémont made him a national hero, and in the 1850s no fewer than six possible routes for a transcontinental railroad were explored under Secretary of War Jefferson Davis. All these reconnoitering parties diligently collected masses of environmental and economic data—more than could be tolerated by some officials like Edward Bates, a future Attorney General, who groused that the reports of Davis's surveys "contain[ed] very little about the road, but [were] filled up mainly with a mass of learning on . . . *Geology, Ornithology, and ichthyology*, and many beautiful pictures of rocks, beasts, birds and fishes!"

Bates's kind of thinking supposedly shaped the so-called Jacksonian era of states' supremacy between 1830 and 1860. But while Jacksonianism did hinder the outlay of federal dollars on "pure" science, it did not prevent, for example, the dispatch of a United States Exploring Expedition under the Navy commander Charles Wilkes, which between 1838 and 1842 thoroughly mapped and described the weather, oceanic currents, peoples, plants, and animals of parts of the Antarctic and Pacific oceans and western South America—at a cost of more than $928,000. The United States Naval Observatory was completed in 1844, and in the following year the stalled coast survey was finally completed, a hydrographic survey of worldwide winds and tides was undertaken, and small naval expeditions by officers scientifically trained at Annapolis (established in 1845) began charting waters and harbors in places as unexpected as the Amazon, West Africa, and the Dead Sea. So much for America's supposed nineteenth-century isolation.

In 1843 Congress voted a modest amount for a demonstration of Samuel F. B. Morse's electric telegraph, a line between Baltimore and Washington. In the 1850s a special division was set up in the Patent Office to evaluate proposed new agricultural machinery. It also began to test new varieties of seed, feed,

The phrase doing a land-office business *was invented to describe the kind of boom that kept the Department of the Interior growing while the West was being settled.*

and fertilizer. Elevated to the status of an independent Bureau of Agriculture in 1862, it served as the nucleus of the Department of Agriculture in 1889. But that is getting ahead of the story.

The Navy's exploration and studies, the agricultural research, and the telegraph experiment could all be defended as having some ultimate commercial utility, but it was harder to see any crass objectives in the Smithsonian Institution, whose sole purpose from the moment its first director was chosen in 1846 was "the increase and diffusion of knowledge." Far more than a museum, the Smithsonian was active from its earliest days, spurring research in ethnology, mineralogy, and other branches of what we would now call human and earth sciences. It was part of a federal establishment that was growing during the industrialization of the 1840s and 1850s to take on responsibilities that were outside the will or capacity of the private associations praised by Tocqueville at the time as the backbone of American democracy.

"ACQUIRING HABITS OF LAVISH EXPENDITURE AND EXTRAVAGANCE"

Resistance to the trend was always manifest. Sen. Thomas Hart Benton thundered in 1826 that any increase in national public spending must have a fatal multiplying effect: "The actual increase of federal power and patronage . . . will be, not in the arithmetical ratio, but in geometrical progression." A Maine representative lamented ten years later that "every Government, like every individual, has a moral being . . . susceptible of acquiring habits of lavish expenditure and extravagance. . . . These habits, by a long course of perseverance, become incurable." Such complaints sound remarkably contemporary, but so do the words of the Ohio Canal Commissioners of 1825 arguing that tax money, not private investment, should improve the state's waterways. "Such works," said the commissioners, "should be considered with a view to the greatest possible accommodation to our citizens . . . public convenience is the paramount object: and a private company will look only to the best means for increasing their profits."

As the American growth process actually worked itself out, Benton's warning proved prophetic. Summary testimony to the trends we have been describing can be found in a glance at the *Official Registers of the United States* (the predecessors of *The United States Government Manual* of today) for 1829, 1861, and 1891. The first of them is a modest volume of 225 pages that lists by name all civil employees and military officers of the federal government. The Army list takes 22 of the 225 pages, the Navy even fewer, but Customs Collectors and Light House Superintendents

take up 41. There are 15 pages of Mail Contractors, and 5 of U.S. Consuls in places as scattered as Smyrna, "Hayti," and "Tuscany, Sardinia, *etc.*"

Thirty-two years later, on the eve of the Civil War, the volume has grown to 592 pages, 147 of them detailing post offices and postal contractors, while 85 pages go to Customs Collectors and other Treasury officials. The War and Navy Departments, even before hostilities have begun, claim 86 pages. The twelve-year-old Department of the Interior occupies 27, more than half of them devoted to the Land Office and the Indian Affairs section.

By 1891 it is ten years since federal civilian employment hit 100,000; another 57,000 such workers have been added, and the *Official Register* is now an encyclopedialike 990 pages long. The breakdown suggests the growing range and complexity of functions. It requires 18 pages to describe the various functionaries who assist the Fifty-second Congress, hungry for administrative help as congressional membership grows and the legislative agenda becomes more crowded. The Treasury Department needs 239 pages to list not only its collectors but the employees of the Mint, the Coast and Geodetic Survey (which it seems to have taken from the Navy), the Light-House Board, and the very busy Bureau of Immigration. The War Department takes up the same number of pages— 239—a good number of them listing employees of the Engineering Department, then actively engaged in flood control and internal-waterways improvement. The Post Office now requires a separate volume to list all its postmasters. The Department of the Interior takes up 147 pages of this 1891 *Register*. About a fifth of them list employees of the Commissioner of Pensions; another fifth are needed to cover the Census Office. Slightly over a quarter—40 pages—particularize the personnel of the Office of Indian Affairs.

There are some new arrivals in 1891. The Department of Justice, established in 1870 to give the Attorney General an organizational base, uses up only 7 pages, but Agriculture, finally made a cabinet department in 1889, already has more than 20 pages listing specialists scattered among divisions including Chemistry, Forestry, Vegetable Pathology, Economic Ornithology and Mammology, and Statistics. As a big-time employer the Department of Agriculture lags behind the Government Printing Office (a post–Civil War creation), which gets 34 pages, and the government of the District of Columbia, occupying 25, but is well ahead of two agencies less than ten years old: the Civil Service Commission (1 page) and the Interstate Commerce Commission (2 pages).

So there were fewer than 5,000 federal employees in 1816 and more than 155,000 seventy-five years later.

Multiplication with a vengeance: Such was the nineteenth century. What would the twentieth bring?

INTO THE TWENTIETH CENTURY

We all know the answer very well: more of the same. The federal civilian payroll reached 400,150 in 1912. Six years later, in 1918, it had more than doubled—to 854,500—a predictable result of our entry into World War I. Yet when the fighting ended and the Republicans restored the Republic to "normalcy," the number did not contract to pre-war levels, and in fact it never fell below half a million during the 1920s. In 1929 it was 579,559. To some extent this illustrates a truism that government agencies have a tendency to linger on well beyond their initial usefulness, thanks to political protectors and civil service tenure. But it is also evidence of the lasting effects of war itself.

Handling the legal and financial minutiae and aftereffects of demobilization, as well as taking care of veterans, provided more than adequate rationale for additions to the Treasury, Commerce, Interior, Justice, War, and Navy Departments. Similarly, during the post–Civil War decades, the volume of claims by the boys in blue made the Pension Office, according to its commissioner in 1891, "the largest executive bureau in the world," with a staff of 6,241. The much larger scale of the 1917–18 war's cleanup strained the Washington of the twenties at the seams. It was during that time that preparations went forward for realizing an earlier expansion plan, the construction of the massive Federal Triangle, the great complex of government office buildings that still stands between the White House and the Capitol.

> *There were fewer than 5,000 employees in 1816 and more than 155,000 seventy-five years later—multiplication with a vengence in the nineteenth century.*

But it was not merely the residue of wartime responsibilities that accounted for the enlarged national establishment under Harding and Coolidge. The same forces that had impelled the government to facilitate railroad and steamboat development in the previous century were still at work as the transportation and communications revolutions rolled on. Extra workers were needed to implement the Federal Aid Road Act of 1916, which allotted some $75 million to help states build highways (and was followed by another Federal Highway Act in 1921); likewise there had to be people to carry out the missions of the Federal Radio Commission, created in 1927 to allocate broadcast frequencies, and the Bureau of Commercial Aviation, set up in 1926 to systematize the licensing of planes and pilots on the fast-growing commercial air routes. The end purpose of several Congresses in assigning these responsibilities to Washington was to help business grow, and between 1921 and 1928 no one pushed harder for such benign intervention than the Secretary of Commerce, Herbert Hoover. The Department of Commerce itself, created in 1903, was the twentieth century's first addition to the cabinet.

"THE SAME OLD FIGHT WITH TOO MUCH GOVERNMENT"—1923

There is a natural tendency to assume that much of the government's enlargement at this time was brought on by the progressive movement, which swept the nation between 1901 and 1916, fostering an array of laws for the regulation of the economy and the improvement of public health and safety. Such new responsibilities undoubtedly swelled state payrolls, but in the federal government they present a fuzzier picture, in spite of complaints like those voiced by one Charles N. Fay in a 1923 volume that would doubtless still appeal to today's conservatives. Fay railed that Americans were facing "the same old fight with Too Much Government and Too Much Taxation [the capitalized words being the title of his book] that has scarred the history of every nation." He blamed the Granger movement (which attacked the railroads), William Jennings Bryan, "Progressivism, . . . Wall Street, the bankers, and the trusts, etc., and finally Woodrow Wilson's vague doctrine of 'The New Freedom.'" All were variants of "the Marxian attack on 'Capital.'"

A look at the figures for June 30, 1916, however, does not clearly support such a charge. Of some 438,000 civilian workers for the United States, just under 251,000, or about 57 percent, were still in the Post Office Department. The brand-new Federal Trade Commission, set up in 1914 to enforce antitrust law, had only 238 employees. The Department of Labor, separated from Commerce in 1913, had 2,504. The thirty-year-old Interstate Commerce Commission still had a payroll of just 2,243—far fewer than the 19,291 workers operating the recently opened Panama Canal. The preprogressive cabinet departments (other than the Post Office and Labor) were led in numbers by the War and Navy Departments, with 37,695 and 35,722 respectively. The Treasury employed between 30,000 and 31,000; then came Interior with 19,347, closely trailed by Agriculture at 18,736 and Commerce with 9,903. Justice had a mere 2,610 civil servants at its call.

It is true, of course, that many new "socialistic" tasks of government simply became lodged in traditional departments. Certainly the job of collecting the income tax after 1913 enlarged the Treasury Department; policing the purity of food and drugs under 1907 legislation added to the staff of the Department of Agriculture (a separate Food and Drug Administration did not come along until 1931); and conservation responsibilities increased Interior's payroll. At any rate, in the fifteen years between 1901 and 1916 total federal civilian employment rose from about 240,000 to 400,000, a 66 percent increase, and in the next fifteen years, when for most of the time the business of America was business, there was further growth to some 600,000. Between mid-1916 and the end of 1929 Treasury and Commerce increased ranks by approximately 70 percent, Agriculture by a third, and Labor by 88 percent. Interior, however, actually lost some 5,000 employees. The I.C.C. remained about the same; the F.T.C. grew, but only to 397 workers.

Pause for another breather now, and brace for the explosion as the historian confronts the New Deal, World War II, the Cold War, and the reshaping of the nation's economy and society from the 1960s to the present day—in all, sixty-four years of practically rocketlike acceleration in the size and power of the national government. Fully describing the changes would require a complete history of our times replete with statistical data. But perhaps we can pick our way among highlights and garner explanatory clues to our further progression toward accepting the monster—supergovernment—despite our proclaimed antistatist heritage. To begin with, an overview.

THREE MILLION BUREAUCRATS

In 1932, the final year of the Hoover Presidency, the federal civilian payroll stood at 605,496. As of June 30, 1940, the last year before the start of a military buildup, it was 1,042,420, a 72 percent jump in eight years. Starting from George Washington's first administration, it had taken 151 years to create a national government big enough to employ a million people. Under the stress of war, it took only two more to reach the second million (in fact 2.29 million) in 1942. After victory the number never fell below two million except briefly in 1950, before the start of the Korean War, which immediately shot it upward again. Seventeen years later, in 1967, the federal civilian work force was 3,002,461. That, too, was a wartime year (if in fact there is any year during the Cold War that can be considered peacetime), and any post-Vietnam shrinkage was small and short-lived. The totals hovered around 2.9 million from 1970 through 1984, and in 1985 again surged to more than three million, where they have remained at least through 1992, despite the Cold War's end in 1989. Even if 1967 is excluded as unusual and 1985 therefore taken as the benchmark, we still are confronted with a jump from a few hundred to one million government workers in 151 years, and from one million to three million in the following forty-five.

Any kind of detailed look will quickly show the impossibility of explaining these numbers without reference to the last fifty years of constant military readiness. We stipulated at the outset that war-related expansion would not be taken into account in explaining growth, yet since 1945 the line of demarcation between war and peace has been hard to find. All the same, it is worth a try. We can begin at any rate with an unambiguously domestic six-year boom in big government (1933–39) that goes under the label of the New Deal. Did the proliferation of the much defamed "alphabetical agencies" of the first two FDR administrations bring on the age of mega-administration and social engineering?

In 1939, despite all FDR's Depression-relief programs, more than half of the record-size work force was delivering the mail or manning the ramparts.

Yes, but with some qualifications. A breakdown of the 1939 federal payroll of 953,891 shows that the Post Office was still the biggest agency, with 291,114, followed by the War Department (even in its state of unreadiness), with 123,624, and the Department of the Navy, with 99,024. In short, more than half of that big work force was delivering the mail and manning the ramparts. Many Depression relief agencies had already disappeared (like the Agricultural Adjustment Administration and the National Recovery Administration, ruled unconstitutional) or been folded into the cabinet departments. Of those remaining, the Federal Works Agency, the shrinking remnant of the Works Progress Administration that occupied the unemployed with public-works projects, had 46,659 workers, but that was scarcely more than the 45,844 in the Department of the Interior. A pair of freestanding assistance programs, the Federal Security Agency (running the four-year-old Social Security Board) and the Federal Loan Agency, kept 40,713 people at work between them, but the long-established Department of Agriculture towered over these at 86,250. The most far-reaching example of government intervention into making over an entire region, the Tennessee Valley Authority, counted 14,597 employees, but the Panama Canal Department had more (16,505), and the Veterans'

Administration two and a half times as many (38,493). As for the regulatory authorities, the National Labor Relations Board had all of 874 civil servants at its beck; the Securities and Exchange Commission, 1,616; the Federal Communications Commission, only 624. For comparison, the Government Printing Office kept 5,874 men and women at work.

It appears on the one hand, then, that the growth was largely a continuation of long-term trends within the already established departments, which kept on doing on a larger scale what they had long been doing —mainly helping grease the wheels of a capitalist economy. On the other hand, many new or enlarged subdivisions of the Agriculture and Interior Departments, for example, were carrying out unprecedented programs of conservation, housing assistance, electrification, relocation, and other forms of state planning. After the massive shock of the Depression, the federal government was expected to concern itself as never before with the public welfare—with social security in a very general sense—and with doing for new beneficiaries some of the favors that it had long routinely done for Western settlers or businessmen seeking foreign markets. As Franklin D. Roosevelt put it in a speech shortly before the 1936 election, "*Of course* we will continue to seek to improve working conditions for the workers of America. . . . *Of course* we will continue to work for cheaper electricity in the homes and on the farms of America. . . . *Of course* we will continue our efforts in behalf of the farmers of America. . . . *Of course* we will continue our efforts for young men and women . . . for the crippled, for the blind, for the mothers, our insurance for the unemployed, our security for the aged. *Of course* we will continue to protect the consumer. . . ."

Shortly afterward a majority of voters in forty-six states registered their agreement by re-electing him. Perhaps it was because FDR's "we" referred to a government that he was always careful to call in his fireside chats "*your* government." It was Roosevelt's personification of government as trustworthy, friendly, and responsive to the most ordinary citizen that was revolutionary and that became the basis for a new American confidence—now lost—that a big and socially active national establishment was not necessarily, as Jefferson might have held, an evil in itself.

WAR BOTH HOT AND COLD

Americans had, of course, almost always accepted the necessity of a powerful government in times of war and international crisis, and it is impossible to underrate the influence of the embattled 1940s and 1950s on getting almost unopposed consent to an explosion in the size and distribution of the federal work force.

The figures for 1954, for example—a year in which Korea was just behind us, and Vietnam still far ahead —measure the impact of the preceding fifteen years. Well over two million people worked for the national government—2,407,676, to be precise— and half of them—1.208 million—for the Department of Defense, in charge of all the armed services since 1947. The Post Office did remain the second-largest federal employer, with just over 507,000, but the third was the Veterans' Administration, with a triple-digit staff of 178,857 tending to the veterans of three wars within the preceding thirty-nine years, though that mission also included the final phases of administering a mighty piece of social engineering, the GI Bill of Rights.

Social, economic, and defense-related purposes were in extricably tangled together. The biggest cabinet department after the Department of Defense was the Treasury, which kept 80,893 people busy writing all those checks for veterans and military contractors as well as for numerous other creditors of the United States—from bankers to dirt farmers and Social Security recipients. The IRS also accounted for much of Treasury's magnitude, reminding me of "Mr. Dooley's" comment on learning, in 1898, that the Spanish-American War was over. "Th' part that ye see in th' pitcher pa-apers is over," he mused, "but th' tax collector will continyoo his part iv th' war with relentless fury."

Old departments and agencies kept high staffing levels (by pre-war standards) in the 1950s in spite of the government's new emphases and priorities. In rounded figures Agriculture was 76,000 strong in 1954 and Commerce employed 42,000. The recently created Department of Health, Education, and Welfare, which absorbed many existing social service programs, was, with 35,000, near the bottom of the cabinet departments in size; the lowest rank was held by Labor with 5,129. Old regulatory offices, such as the Interstate Commerce Commission, Federal Trade Commission, Federal Power Commission, and Federal Communications Commission, had fewer than one or two thousand employees. New independent bodies charged with carrying out the propaganda and diplomatic side of the Cold War were not much bigger. The U. S. Information Agency employed 9,539; the Foreign Operations Administration, charged with foreign aid, 5,856. Even the scientific-research organizations with military overtones—heirs to such century-old bodies as the Coast and Geodetic Survey—were minor players. The National Advisory Committee for Aeronautics, the predecessor to NASA, had 7,161 operatives; the Atomic Energy Commission, 6,195. Many times that number of people were engaged merely in the sheer mechanics of keeping the government running. The General Services Administration had more than 26,000 employees, and almost 22,000 worked for Congress, more than double the number of twenty-five years earlier. If all these numbers are somewhat wearying, the lesson they teach is nonetheless plain. In 1954 the portion of government administering the welfare state was far less than the part concerned with national security.

WHO WANTS BIG GOVERNMENT?

Our fearful trip is nearly done—but increasingly difficult. Numbers get bigger, trends harder to define, and debate about the deep meaning of it all more contentious and partisan. Yet it may be possible to chance a few defensible generalizations without too many more thrashings in statistical thickets. To begin with, how and why did the total civilian work force of the federal government reach that threshold of three million around which it hovered steadily throughout the 1970s and 1980s?

There is a natural inclination to focus on the idealistic programs of the Kennedy and Johnson administrations, particularly LBJ's Great Society initiatives. In fact the Peace Corps *was* set up in 1961 and the Office of Economic Opportunity (headquarters of the war on poverty) in 1964, which also marked the birth of the Department of Housing and Urban Development and the passage of the Clean Air Act, prefiguring the birth of the Environmental Protection Agency two years after. And Medicare came along in 1965. These help account for the increase in the grand total of federal workers from 1960's 2,398,704 to that of 1970, 2,981,574—with that spike in 1967 to 3,002,461. But they do not stand alone. Military and economic developments were the primary purposes of two Eisenhower-era legacies—the Federal Aid Highway Act, also known as the Interstate and Defense Highway Act of 1956, and the National Aeronautics and Space Administration, authorized in 1958 to run the space race. A companion measure, the National Defense Education Act, put the government more deeply than ever into financing higher education.

Once embedded in the federal structure, these enterprises remained alive and often growing throughout the two decades after 1970, a period during which the Republicans controlled the White House for sixteen years, the Senate for six of those sixteen, but the House of Representatives for none at all. The turn to Washington for assistance took many forms, not all of them exclusively the design of liberals. The National Environmental Policy Act (1969); the Occupational Safety and Health Act (1970); the Consumer Product Safety, Water Pollution Control, and Equal Employment Opportunity Acts (1972); a Federal Energy Administration Act; and measures providing for important subsidies to mass transit and to school systems (1974)—all were passed on Nixon's watch, though sometimes over his objections or his veto. These acts put more power and personnel into the Department of Transportation, dating from 1966, and into two more cabinet departments created in the seventies, Energy (1977) and Education (1979), the latter bringing on the renaming of Health, Education, and Welfare as the Department of Health and Human Services. (The final department of the current fourteen-member cabinet, Veterans Affairs, was fashioned in 1988 under Ronald Reagan.) Nor can any recent history of the United States overlook the Employee Retirement Income Security Act of 1974, or the Toxic Substances Control Act, conferring fresh responsibilities on the FDA, or various laws mandating federal aid to local law enforcers.

The fact is, people did not truly want government "off their backs." They expected it to act in their behalf—though not necessarily that of others.

The message of the seventies, at least, and possibly of the eighties too, was that America's expectations of the federal government were still high, even though the rhetoric of the Great Society had been stilled. Whatever politicians might say, the "moderate" voters sent back congressional majorities to enlist Washington in keeping the air and water clean, the roads open, gas pumps flowing, retirement funds protected, workplaces safe, opportunities equal, the poor fed, students' noses in books, and businessmen's thumbs off the scale. Ripples of increase spread down the governmental chain; state and local government personnel boomed from 10.14 million in 1970 to 15.26 million in 1990.

The impact of the many new or expanded federal government ventures on the distribution of its employees resists easy description. Bear with me for one final flurry of numbers. A look at the statistics for 1976, the year of the bicentennial, shows a Defense Department still employing more than a million civilians, the United States Postal Service 675,653, and the Veterans' Administration nearly 222,313. The Treasury Department was 125,600 strong, having gained 33,079 workers in only the preceding six years. Health, Education, and Welfare counted 155,096 in its ranks, a big 43 percent jump over 1970. The Agriculture Department, in a nation with few farmers left, still had 128,052 employees, the Interior Department 81,844, and the Department of Justice nearly 54,000. HUD accounted for only 16,579.

A summation of the 1980s without fear, favor, or partisanship is also enlightening. At the end of the Reagan-Bush era—1992—there were 3.085 million federal toilers. More than 38,000 of them worked for Congress, and nearly 28,000 for the judiciary, nearly double as many as twelve years before. The Defense Department still led the cabinet with its 982,774 employees. Veterans Affairs (essentially the former VA) had 260,205 in its ranks, and the never resting Treasury Department now paid the salaries of almost 131,191. Health and Human Services stood at 155,662; Agriculture, still at a surprising 128,324. The Department of Justice had hugely expanded from 56,327 in 1980 to 96,927. Interior employed 85,260. The Department of Education, a favored target of conservatives, had only 5,113 workers. Of the independent agencies, the Environmental Protection Agency had 18,196 at work and was exceeded by NASA, with some 25,425, and by two bodies dating all the way back to New Deal days—the Federal Deposit Insurance Corporation, with 22,467, and the TVA, with 19,493, although the latter represented a major downsizing from the 1980 figure of 51,714. There were other shrinkages too, the General Services Administration having dropped since 1980 from about 37,654 to 20,770. Likewise, smaller agencies such as the U.S. International Development Cooperation Agency— that is, foreign aid—underwent reductions, but they had begun the decade of the eighties with fewer than 10,000, so their big layoffs represented small real numbers.

AND WHERE WILL IT EVER END?

Such cuts aside, the fundamental fact was that in 1990 the national government was still huge and still growing, albeit at a slackened pace. The reason was that for all the growing dissatisfaction with expensive bureaucracies, people did not truly want government "off their backs." They expected it to act in their behalf—though not necessarily that of others—in a variety of ways, and it did so in response to the same pressures that had led it in the 1800s to give away free homesteads, create land-grant colleges and agricultural experiment stations, erect naval observatories, and send consuls to foreign commercial centers.

A pair of political scientists wrote in 1990 that between 1964 and 1972 "a new age emerged [whose] most defining characteristic is an uneasy acceptance by liberals, moderates and even at times conservatives of a powerful national establishment." Ironically, they speculated, Ronald Reagan's personal appeal might have put a friendly face on it and thereby made it more acceptable even as he railed against it. In any case, they concluded, "Although big government may make all Americans queasy some of the time, it now makes only a tiny fragment nervous all of the time. With fewer and fewer exceptions, Americans have come to terms with a powerful central establishment. It may be telling that when they are informed that they have become quite comfortable 'living with leviathan,' most Americans today cannot begin to fathom what that means."

It is tempting to leave that as the final word, but it is impossible at close range to know if it really is. Following the election of 1992 (in which Ross Perot won 19 percent of the popular vote with stinging attacks on inept and bloated government), there came rumbles of a growing revolution, or perhaps a counterrevolution, and these culminated in the 1994 election of a Republican Congress swearing to cut the monster down to size. By January of 1996 President Clinton himself had apparently signed on with his declaration in the State of the Union message that "the era of big government is over." By then the "damn-the-government" outcry ranged from the extremes of right-wing militia revolutionaries to the modest promises of Vice President Gore to "re-invent" government.

But is there, in fact, a revival of the individualist philosophy of an Emerson or the praise of government frugality of a Jefferson cited at the beginning of this investigation? Are Americans willing to pay the price of a genuine and sweeping reduction in government? The 104th Congress, chosen in 1994, for all its promises to swing the ax, cut no important entitlement program with a large constituency—defense included. Its members, like everyone else, seemed uncertain of what the voters would do if they really kept their antigovernment promises.

"Canst thou draw out leviathan with a hook?" God asked of Job. Perhaps the question that the American people have yet to answer clearly is not only "Canst thou?" but "Wilt thou truly?"

Bernard A. Weisberger writes "In the News" in each issue of American Heritage.

PART 10

The Judiciary

Of the three branches of government, the judiciary is simultaneously the best understood and the least understood. It is the best understood branch because most of us, at some point or another, will have a first-hand encounter with the legal system. Whether it is the result of a traffic ticket, a divorce, a lawsuit, or some more serious matter, many of us will be called before the court at some point during our lives. (By contrast, it is far less likely that we will be called before a legislative committee or have the opportunity to meet the president or governor.) It is also the least understood branch of government, at least at the appellate level, because it is involved with extremely technical matters and toils largely out of the public eye. Whereas politicians seek the spotlight, judges shun it.

There is another difference between the judiciary and the other branches of government. Politicians are supposed to be biased—in fact, they are elected on the basis of their biases. Judges, on the other hand, are expected to strive for neutrality. We accept their decisions because we hope that they have reached those decisions after an intellectual, detached examination of the law.

But judges are only human. Try as they might (and some don't even try), it is extremely difficult if not impossible for many judges to completely shed their political and personal preferences when they step behind the bench. If judges were robots, then it wouldn't matter whether they were Democrats or Republicans. But it does matter. Judges may be less political than legislators or executives, but they are political nevertheless. As you read the following selections, keep in mind the very human, often political side of the judiciary.

Unrestrained:

A Reading for Critical Thinking

The Supreme Court May Be More Conservative, But It's as Activist as Ever

By Max Boot

In the conservative imagination, the Supreme Court's last term still glows brightly. Less than a year ago, the Court refused to grant President Clinton a stay in the Paula Jones case and threw out a challenge to the line-item veto. The Court also invalidated a large part of the Brady Act as an unconstitutional infringement on states' rights—the second major ruling since 1995 to reinvigorate federalism. And to cap things off, the Justices unanimously overturned two lower-court rulings permitting assisted suicide. The Right was triumphant, the Left despondent. "The era of liberal judicial activism," a noted liberal law professor lamented in the pages of the *New York Times*, "is long gone."

Would that it were. At best, the Rehnquist Court has done to judicial excess what Ronald Reagan did to federal spending: slowed its growth. Granted, the Court has given the Right a fair amount to cheer about—especially in its rulings breathing fresh life into the Takings Clause and the Tenth Amendment. But it has hardly adopted a consistent originalism, the doctrine that holds that judges should attempt to apply the law as it was understood when enacted instead of ruling according to their personal whims.

Just since 1995, the Rehnquist Court has overturned all state laws limiting the terms of congressmen; struck down Colorado's Amendment 2, which prohibited the passage of gay-rights laws; and forced the Virginia Military Institute and the Citadel to turn co-ed. Can anyone seriously claim that the Constitution has anything to say, one way or the other, about term limits, gay rights, or single-sex education? A Court that holds all-male education to be a violation of the Fourteenth Amendment's Equal Protection Clause could just as easily outlaw his-and-hers public restrooms on the grounds that they too are separate and unequal.

Why hasn't the Court mandated equal treatment in toilets as well as in military schools? Not because of any constitutional principle. The answer is pretty obvious: This would be a silly result. Some benighted observers might argue that the VMI opinion is equally silly—but that's not the view at the cocktail parties the Justices attend. The Rehnquist Court, like its immediate predecessors, is deciding cases on the basis not of neutral constitutional principles but of politics—a generally more conservative politics, but politics all the same.

The Court is no longer dominated by liberal extremists like William Brennan, Harry Blackmun, and Thurgood Marshall. The balance of power is now held by Anthony Kennedy and Sandra Day O'Connor. Hence outcomes are centrist, not liberal—but every bit as divorced from legal principle. As former Blackmun clerk Edward Lazarus writes of Kennedy and O'Connor in a new tell-all book "Both, in effect, hold constitutional interpretation hostage to their personal and often idiosyncratic views."

The case that best shows this judicial philosophy in action is *Planned Parenthood of Southeastern Pennsylvania* v. *Casey* (1992). The Court had appeared ready to overturn *Roe* v. *Wade*, an opinion that even many liberal legal scholars concede has little grounding in the Constitution. In a 1989 internal Court memo

From *National Review* (June 1, 1998), pp. 30, 32; excerpt from *Out of Order* (Basic Books, 1998). Reprinted by permission of Max Boot, author of *Out of Order*. Copyright © 1998, Max Boot.

Justice Kennedy had indicated his willingness to overturn *Roe*. But he and Justice O'Connor recoiled from the brink and joined David Souter, another faux Republican, in issuing a mealy-mouthed plurality opinion that desperately tried to tread a middle ground between the pro- and anti-*Roe* positions. The nub of the trio's position was that "to overrule under fire . . . would subvert the Court's legitimacy beyond any question." Maybe, but that's a political, not a legal, judgment.

What is the point of giving federal judges lifetime tenure if they're going to be as poll-driven as any congressman? The finger-to-the-wind method evident in *Casey* has infected recent Court decisions in other areas too—including some that count as political victories for the Right:

Punitive Damages: In *BMW* v. *Gore* (1996), the Court held that a $2-million punitive-damage award by an Alabama court had violated the Fourteenth Amendment's Due Process Clause. Both Clarence Thomas and Antonin Scalia dissented on the grounds that the majority was invoking the hoary old doctrine of "substantive due process"—the notion that the Due Process Clauses of the Fifth and Fourteenth Amendments guarantee certain substantive rights, not just a fair legal procedure before "life, liberty, or property" may be taken away. This empty vessel has traditionally been filled with whatever watery sentiments animated judicial activists of the day, producing discredited decisions ranging from *Dred Scott* v. *Sandford* (1857) to *Griswold* v. *Connecticut* (1965). Runaway punitive damages are a problem, but the Constitution doesn't solve it.

> *Once conservatives concede the principle that activism is OK, they're slitting their own throats, since it's unlikely that the courts will be dominated by conservative activists any time soon.*

Criminal Procedure: The Warren Court imposed upon all the states the exclusionary rule (*Mapp* v. *Ohio*, 1961) and the *Miranda* rule (1966). This means that confessions or evidence illegally obtained—with illegality defined by judges, not legislators, and often in unpredictable ways—cannot be admitted at trial. The Court has subsequently conceded that exclusion is not mandated by the Fourth Amendment. But it has refused simply to chuck out *Mapp* and *Miranda* and let criminal procedure once again become the province of the states. Instead, the Rehnquist Court

has sometimes strained logic and semantics in order to avoid excluding evidence when the result would be to let a heinous criminal walk free. The Justices have decided, for instance, that neither a dog sniff nor traipsing through somebody's "open fields" constitutes a "search." In other cases, the Justices have actually strengthened the Warren-era precedents; in 1997, for instance, the Court banned no-knock searches of drug safe houses even if the cops have a warrant.

All this has turned search-and-seizure law into what Yale's Akhil Amar calls a "mess" and an "embarrassment." The situation is best symbolized by federal judge Harold Baer Jr., who in 1996 refused to allow into evidence 80 pounds of drugs seized by police and then, after taking a political pounding, simply reversed his decision. Thanks to the Rehnquist Court's zigzag rulings, both decisions are equally grounded in precedent.

Reverse Discrimination: A bare bones majority of the Court, including Kennedy and O'Connor, appears committed to the view that the Fourteenth Amendment forbids nearly all racial preferences. This has produced a series of cases striking down government set-asides, racially gerrymandered congressional districts, and other programs designed to benefit minorities. Applying this doctrine, the U.S. Court of Appeals for the Fifth Circuit has banned the use of race in the admissions process at the University of Texas Law School.

Critics point out that the Fourteenth Amendment was meant to protect "civil," not political or social, rights—as those phrases were understood in 1868. This means that the Amendment was designed only to guarantee racial equality in contracts, property, and court access; neither voting nor public employment nor school admissions should be governed by the Equal Protection Clause. Therefore, goes the argument, conservative judges are guilty of judicial activism by applying equal-protection principles in these areas.

It is indeed hard to believe that the Fourteenth Amendment's ratifiers meant to abolish a racial spoils system in education when they were perfectly content to have segregated public schools in the District of Columbia. A constitutional amendment that allowed states to discriminate against blacks should certainly allow them to discriminate in favor of blacks. Certain affirmative-action policies may well run afoul of color-blind civil-rights statutes, but conservatives who invoke the *Constitution* to strike down these laws are as guilty of judicial activism as their liberal adversaries.

Assisted Suicide: The Court acted correctly in rejecting a right to assisted suicide, but its reasoning was troubling. Chief Justice William Rehnquist's majority opinion had to labor mightily—and not very convincingly—to distinguish the assisted-suicide decision from the Court's prior due-process rulings.

Stephen Reinhardt, the canny liberal judge who wrote the Ninth Circuit's assisted-suicide opinion, anchored this newfound right in the long line of abortion precedents. Quoting *Casey*, he declared, "Like the decision of whether or not to have an abortion, the decision how and when to die is one of 'the most intimate and personal choices a person may make in a lifetime,' a choice 'central to personal dignity and autonomy.' Indeed, the argument for assisted suicide as a constitutional right is stronger than the argument for abortion. After all, in the case of abortion, the rights of a third party are infringed upon, where as assisted suicide is (at least in theory) purely voluntary.

How does Rehnquist's majority opinion refute this logic? It doesn't. Here is the Chief Justice's key statement on this crucial subject: "That many of the rights and liberties protected by the Due Process Clause sound [*sic*] in personal autonomy does not warrant the sweeping conclusion that any and all important, intimate, and personal decisions are so protected, and *Casey* does not suggest otherwise." But this assertion, of course, provides no guidance for determining *which* "personal decisions" are protected: why abortion and not suicide? In Rehnquist's defense, it may be said that he has always voted against recognizing a right to abortion, but the Court majority—which favors abortion, but not assisted suicide—has some explaining to do.

What's the real difference between *Roe* and *Casey* on the one hand, and the assisted suicide cases on the other? It appears to be the differing climates of elite opinion surrounding those two issues. In 1973, the American Medical Association was on record as favoring a right to abortion—a fact of which Justice Blackmun took slavishly respectful note in *Roe*. In 1997, by contrast, the AMA opposed a right to physician-assisted suicide. In both cases the AMA is a pretty good proxy for other opinion leaders.

Conservatives may be tempted to accept all this, since, in many cases, the rulings are going their way. This is an alluring but shortsighted position. If conservatives concede the principle that activism is okay, they're slitting their own throats, since it is unlikely that the courts will be dominated by conservative activists in the foreseeable future.

The principled position is to say that political judgments should be left to voters and their elected representatives. The attempt by a handful of black-robed old coots isolated in Washington to craft national resolutions to contentious issues will always be doomed to failure.

Mr. Boot is the editorial features editor of the Wall Street Journal. *This article is adapted from the book* Out of Order *by Max Boot, to be published by Basic Books, a member of Perseus Books LLC. Copyright © 1998 by Max Boot.*

A Reading for Critical Thinking

The Ten Commandments and the Constitution

By Dennis Teti

The Supreme Court and Congress are on a collision course. Three times in the final week of its term, the high court struck down laws passed by overwhelming congressional majorities, championed by the president and defended by the Justice Department. This is historically unprecedented. Even during the last great confrontation between the branches in the 1930s, anti-New Deal justices never overturned so many federal statutes in so short a time.

Judicial resistance to popular rule through Congress is most starkly displayed in City of *Boerne* v. *Flores*, in which the court overturned the Religious Freedom Restoration Act (RFRA). Justices Kennedy, Stevens, and Ginsburg joined hands with Justices Scalia and Thomas and Chief Justice Rehnquist in the 6–3 ruling, which insisted that the court, not Congress, has "the final word" in interpreting the Constitution. Congress passed RFRA in 1993 at the behest of a large coalition of religious groups unhappy with a 1990 Supreme Court decision, *Employment Division* v. *Smith*. The court had sided in that case with the state of Oregon, which denied unemployment benefits to workers fired for using the hallucinogenic drug peyote. Because the workers used the drug for religious purposes, they claimed the state had violated their First Amendment right to freely exercise their religion. Both mainline and fringe religious groups worried that Smith would pave the way for local and state governments to violate their free-exercise rights, so they called on Congress for relief.

The oral arguments in *Boerne* made plain that the Supreme Court saw the case as a showdown with Congress. Anxious justices pressed the lawyers: Did lawmakers pass RFRA to express disagreement with Smith? And as hard as the justices pressed, the lawyers defending RFRA tried to reassure them that Congress wouldn't think of reversing the Supreme Court:

Q: [from the court]: Now, you admit, I suppose, that Congress cannot come in and overrule a decision of this Court it doesn't like by legislation. . . .

Counsel: Congress cannot overrule the Court.

Q: And there's some indication that this was what Congress was all about here. . . . If *Smith* were to come up again, I guess [RFRA] would be an effort by Congress to overturn that decision. . . .

Counsel: Overturn is shorthand, but yes, to achieve a different result on similar facts under the statute than we would achieve under the Constitution itself, that's correct, but that's no different from the Voting Rights Act or from Title VII. . . . You still get the final word on what the statute means.

The lawyers defending RFRA were of course in no position to meet this line of questioning with its proper response: Why shouldn't Congress try to correct or reverse the court? Congress is a co-equal branch of government, equally entitled to interpret the Constitution that governs all three branches. The Religious Freedom Restoration Act may not have been a wise response to a particular judicial decision. But the power Congress used to enact it is legitimate. Lawmakers employed their infrequently used authority to "enforce" the Fourteenth Amendment.

The Fourteenth Amendment's enforcement power unnerves judges, because, as RFRA shows, it can be invoked to challenge their decisions. And it has always unnerved judges. In overturning RFRA, the justices barked back to their 19th-century brethren on the high court who gutted Congress's enforcement power, overturning the national civil-rights statutes of Reconstruction, such as the 1871 Ku Klux Klan Act and the 1875 Civil Rights Act. (With no embarrassment, Justice Kennedy's opinion for the court in *Boerne* cited those long discredited decisions as precedents.) The modern civil-rights resolution restored Congress's enforcement power, and since the 1960s the court has sanctioned measures that depend on that power, including the Voting Rights Acts of 1965. With one insignificant exception, until the court's actions last month, every law enacted in this century under the Fourteenth Amendment's enforcement provisions has been upheld.

Congress's enforcement power also makes some conservatives uncomfortable because of its potential to expand the power of Washington. RFRA, which limited the powers of state governments, was controversial for that very reason. But there are other ways in which Congress can use its Fourteenth Amendment powers. In fact, it can reassert its right to these powers and at the same time resurrect federalism and popular self-government at the state and local levels against a nationalizing Supreme Court. And in the wake of *Boerne*, it should do so. Lawmakers can begin with a simple, unobjectionable proposal: legislation returning to the states the right to display the Ten Commandments on government-owned property.

In 1980 the Supreme Court found unconstitutional a Kentucky law requiring that the Ten Commandments be displayed in public schools. What's the harm? "If the posted copies of the Ten Commandments are to have any effect at all," said the court, "it will be to induce the school children to read, meditate upon, perhaps to venerate and obey, the Commandments." Many would applaud such an effect, but the justices saw it as a threat to the freedom of impressionable youth. No matter how desirable the Words of God might be as "a private devotion," the First Amendment doesn't allow them on government property, they maintained.

This anti-Ten Commandments policy returned to the news recently when Alabama judge Roy Moore posted the Commandments in his courtroom. Federal circuit judge Charles Price pronounced "Thou shalt not" and issued a restraining order. The dispute remains in the federal courts.

Meanwhile, on March 5, the House of Representatives passed a resolution 295–125 stating that it was the sense of the House that the Ten Commandments "set forth a code of moral conduct, observance of

which is universally acknowledged to promote respect for our system of laws and the good of society." The House resolution suggests there is a consensus across religious faiths that the Commandments should be publicly respected as the foundation of our constitutional principles. Two South Carolina counties have since enacted resolutions to post the Ten Commandments in their council rooms, and Congress is considering similar proposals for the Senate and House chambers.

Congress should not be deterred by the *Boerne* decision from moving beyond the expression of sentiments to actual legislation. It should legislate to enforce the people's right to recognize the Commandments in public. Yet, ironically, under a Constitution established to free man from oppression disguised as religion, many tremble before the high court as if it were a high priesthood. Civil libertarians who would never think of obeying ex cathedra decrees from Rome unhesitatingly declare there is no appealing a decision of the Supreme Court.

Both history and proper constitutional understanding teach a quite different lesson. It's true that the Constitution endows the three co-equal branches of government with different functions. Congress's responsibility is to enact laws; the president approves and enforces the laws made by Congress; the Supreme Court decides "cases" according to the laws made by Congress. But the Constitution does not grant any single branch power to interpret it in a way that the others must accept. On the contrary: Congress itself interprets the Constitution each time it passes a law, just as the chief executive does when he signs and administers those laws, and the justices do in each case they decide.

Since 1787 the Supreme Court has found some 139 national laws unconstitutional. Most of these judgments were of no great political moment. So Congress avoided provocation and did nothing. Occasionally, though, the lawmakers have challenged the court and have made the challenge stick. Here are a few examples:

In *Dred Scott* v. *Sandford* (1857), the Supreme Court declared that Congress could not ban slavery in U.S. territories. As president, Lincoln asked Congress to overrule the court, and in 1862 (three years before the Thirteenth Amendment) he signed a statute abolishing slavery throughout the territories.

After the court in 1918 overturned a federal child labor law, legislators responded by imposing an excise tax on the products of child labor. In 1922 the court rejected that measure as well. On a third try, Congress overrode both decisions by passing the Fair Labor Standards Act of 1938. In *U. S.* v. *Darby* (1941) the justices yielded and conceded Congress's power to regulate.

In 1959 the court ruled that the Fourteenth Amendment allowed states to require English literacy tests for voters. Congress, deciding the tests violated that amendment's equal protection clause, used its enforcement power to ban them. In *Katzenbach* v. *Morgan* (1966), the court backed off and set aside its earlier ruling.

The court in *Goldman* v. *Weinberger* (1986) upheld Air Force regulations prohibiting Orthodox Jews from wearing yarmulkes on duty. Congress enacted legislation overriding that holding and instructed the Air Force to permit the wearing of religious apparel in uniform.

Religious-liberty and other social-issue cases, of course, usually involve state, not federal, laws. Why are states and local communities controlled by restraints that apparently limit only the national government ("Congress shall make no law . . .")? Since 1925 the Supreme Court has read the Fourteenth Amendment to mean that the "liberty" mentioned in the due process clause brings state governments under the Bill of Rights. In other words, when state laws regarding religion and other social issues are overturned, the courts always assert that they violate the Fourteenth Amendment, not just the Bill of Rights.

For more than 60 years the courts have hung on this fragile constitutional thread their most controversial decisions—relating to school prayer, rights of the accused, judge-imposed taxes, obscenity and pornography, censorship, abortion, school busing, public assistance to religious schools, homosexual rights, and voter-passed referenda. That single thread is the claim that the Fourteenth Amendment prevents citizens from enacting state and community laws to protect America's culture and moral character.

The fragility of this theory as a judicial weapon became clear once Congress's enforcement power was restored to pass the Voting Rights Act of 1965. Under the Fourteenth Amendment's language, Congress has the same power to enforce not just equal-protection but due-process rights. That is the power the Supreme Court disputed in *Boerne*, but ultimately no one but Congress can say in what manner its power to enforce these rights should be used.

Indeed, by hanging its controversial decisions precisely on the Fourteenth Amendment, which includes a grant of authority to Congress, the Supreme Court invites Congress to intervene on the same terrain. And Congress should intervene, not to place new limits on states, but to restore self-government in states and local communities. The Ten Commandments issue is a perfect starter. Congress could pass a "federalism shield" law, declaring that the display of the Decalogue on state and local government-owned property is among the liberties protected under the Fourteenth Amendment's due-process "liberties." The statute would explicitly recognize the reserved right of the people under the Tenth Amendment to govern themselves by declaring that the states may use their "police powers" to regulate these displays. This would restore the traditional right to acknowledge the Commandments in public life that people enjoyed until the Supreme Court abridged it in 1980.

Would Bill Clinton sign such a measure? It's difficult to imagine him standing against a popular law to respect the Ten Commandments. The tougher question is whether the Supreme Court would sustain it. Of course the ink wouldn't be dry before the ACLU hauled this law into court. Consider, however, what the modern Supreme Court has already said about Congress's enforcement power:

In 1966, the court in *U.S.* v. *Price* recognized that Congress's enforcement power is so broad that it "embraces all of the rights and privileges secured to citizens by all of the Constitution and *all* of the laws of the United States."

In 1970 Justices Stewart and Blackmun and Chief Justice Burger swept earlier decisions aside in reference to Congress's superior fact-finding ability. "Congress," they wrote in Oregon v. Mitchell, "may paint with a much broader brush than may this Court, which must confine itself to the judicial function of deciding individual cases and controversies upon individual records. The findings that Congress made when it enacted the Voting Rights Act of 1965 would have supported a nationwide ban on literacy tests."

In the 1980 case of *Fullilove* v. *Klutznick*, Burger and Justices White and Powell said, "Correctly viewed, Sec. 5 [of the Fourteenth Amendment] is a positive grant of legislative power authorizing Congress to exercise its discretion in determining whether and what legislation is needed to secure the guarantees of the Fourteenth Amendment."

Some court-watchers argue that the justices will strike down any law that disputes their holdings, and the overturning of the Religious Freedom Restoration Act implies as much. But except during the 1930s, the justices have usually been less willing to make war on the national legislature than to cross swords with the states.

And there's good reason for the court to be more wary of Congress than of state legislatures. The states, after all, can't raise or reduce the number of justices on the court; Congress can. The states can't change the court's jurisdiction; Congress can. The states can't make and unmake the federal court system; Congress can. The states can't impeach federal judges; Congress can.

Conservative critics of the Supreme Court should neither despair at its decisions nor propose amendments that can only weaken people's loyalty to our constitutional heritage. There is nothing wrong with our Constitution that time, patience, and political acumen can't correct.

The way to win a showdown with the court is first to wage one. If Congress enacts a simple Ten Commandments bill and the high court voids it, Congress can respond by passing more far-reaching measures. "Federalism shield" laws speeding up state criminal trials or restoring "moment of silence" rights to public schools come to mind. The Supreme Court might need a little time to get the message before it acquiesces in the resurrection of self-government. But over time the nation's elected legislature is inexorable—if it is willing to fight.

Dennis Teti is research director for the Tricentennial Foundation for America and adjunct professor of political science at Hillsdale College.

We the 50 Peoples

State constitutionalism
challenges the federal judicial leviathan.

By Brian Doherty

Hawaii recently panicked the nation when a state judge there declared that prohibiting same-sex marriages violated the Hawaii constitution's equal protection clause. The decision is being appealed to Hawaii's Supreme Court, which previously sent the case back to the circuit court, demanding that the state must meet a strict burden of proof for the necessity of denying same-sex marriage rights. When the rest of the country caught wind of the Hawaii Supreme Court's willingness to overthrow the same-sex marriage ban, the reaction was swift and sure: Congress passed and President Clinton signed a law that allows other states not to honor the marriages, in contradiction to the Constitution's "full faith and credit" clause.

When you think Constitution, you probably imagine the Supremes, those nine contentious, berobed guys and gals in their august Washington halls. But such brethren aren't just in D.C. Every state has its own set, interpreting its own constitution. While the federal Constitution guarantees a certain minimum protection of citizens' rights, that's just a floor. States can set a higher ceiling. Hawaii's Supreme Court caused a ruckus, but its decision to expand a right beyond the federal standard is as American as outrageous tort lawsuits.

Hawaii isn't the only state thumbing its nose at federal courts. After a half century of moribundity, in which federal courts were the arena for most fights over citizens' rights, state courts are more and more establishing higher ceilings for what *they* see as citizens' rights. What state courts call "rights" can stretch from freedom from police searches to the right to state money for abortions—so these decisions are often controversial. As state courts are changing the lives of specific litigants *and* developing new legal biospheres

for their states, they also face charges of playing politics instead of the disinterested judge.

The new wave of state constitutionalism isn't just abstract judicial ideology—it has real effects in the lives of real people:

- A Maryland citizen won't lose his farm for having a couple of pounds of marijuana in his backyard barbecue.
- People in Kentucky, Michigan, and Texas can engage in oral or anal sex in the privacy of their home, without fearing jail time.
- Cops in New York and Montana can't search your entire property up to your house's door looking for probable cause for arrest, even though the "open fields" search doctrine embraced by the U. S. Supreme Court allows that.
- An arrested suspect in Pennsylvania doesn't have to worry about cops searching his car without a warrant, and a passenger in a car whose driver was arrested doesn't have to let a cop rummage through her purse.
- Judges in Texas can't impose gag orders that prohibit discussing a lawsuit outside a courtroom, despite federal permission for those restrictions under some circumstances.

Of course, if you disagree with the policy decisions inherent in such judicial rulings, the whole movement can seem like politics sailing under a judicial flag of convenience. Such accusations are perhaps inevitable in legal debates, which are matters of rhetoric and persuasion, not mathematical precision. Most people who praise or condemn judicial federalism, suggests University of Chicago law professor Richard Epstein, do so

From *Reason* Magazine (March 1997), pp. 48–50. Reprinted with permission. Copyright © 1997 by the Reason Foundation, 3415 S. Sepulveda Blvd, Suite 400, Los Angeles, CA 90034. www.reason.com

because of the results they believe it's likely to produce. "There's no one thing you can say about this trend," says Epstein. "Most objections to the practice [of expanding rights beyond federal standards] are to the substantive decision, not the diffusion of authority."

The fact that state courts have been disagreeing with the feds more and more is a sign, Epstein surmises, of a deeper loss of legitimacy and splintering of thought in legal philosophy and practice, and in intellectual culture at large. "I'm amazed at how much the degree of disagreement in the law has changed since I was in law school," Epstein says. "In 1970 the disagreement was over 30 degrees [of the legal philosophical spectrum], now it's over 180 degrees." As cultural and philosophical divisions widen, Epstein says, institutions like the Supreme Court have a harder time maintaining a broad legitimacy.

State constitutions preceded the federal Constitution; its Bill of Rights was largely modeled after already existing state bills of rights. In America's early days, state courts guarded their prerogatives jealously, and until the 1920s federal courts didn't enforce the Bill of Rights on the states at all. During the '60s, the Warren Court stepped up such federal enforcement aggressively. Federal courts usurped most bill-of-rights action.

Law arises from the arguments lawyers make—and when civil liberties action was in the federal courts, that's where lawyers flocked. The go-to-the-feds mindset arose from the civil rights battles of the '50s and '60s, says Timothy Lynch of the Cato Institute, who writes about and cheers growing state constitutional activism. "Back then the attitude was, 'They're battling Jim Crow down South. The state courts are stagnant backwaters. The action is in the federal courts, that's where we can get results.' It's been hard for lawyers to break out of that mindset."

Thomas B. Stoddard of the Lambda Legal Defense Fund, a gay rights legal activist group, told *National Journal* in 1991, "If I had my druthers, I would rather go to the Supreme Court and liberate every single state in the union." But the federal Supreme Court's *Bowers* v. *Hardwick* decision in 1986 upheld a Georgia sodomy law—and by implication any other state's sodomy law.

So Lambda is now pursuing cases against sodomy laws in state courts on state constitutional grounds, with some successes. "State courts recognize that their state constitutions provide greater security for individual rights than does the federal Constitution in many cases—specifically when it comes to privacy and equal protection," says Lambda staff attorney Suzanne Goldberg. "So we've chosen the states as a deliberate strategy."

The federal Supreme Court's rights juggernaut slowed down in the late '70s and early '80s. With the Rehnquist Court in full swing, liberal former Supreme Court Justice William Brennan declared a renaissance in state constitutionalism in a speech in November 1986. By 1991, legal scholar Ronald L. K. Collins had counted 750 decisions where state supreme courts, relying on their own state constitutions, extended citizens' rights beyond federal Supreme Court precedent.

After a half century of moribundity, state courts are more and more establishing higher ceilings for what they see as citizens' rights. What state courts call "rights" stretches from freedom from police searches to the right to state money for abortions.

Jennifer Freisen, a professor at Loyola Law School in Los Angeles and author of *The State Constitutional Law: Litigating Individual Rights, Claims and Defenses*, says state constitutionalism "is still resurging. It's so heavy I can hardly keep up with it." Freisen has compiled more than 1,200 pages of decisions where state courts have consulted their own constitutions to reach conclusions about citizens' rights different from the federal Supreme Court's decisions under similar circumstances.

State constitutions still don't enjoy much respect. James A. Gardner of the Western New England School of Law argued in a 1992 *Michigan Law Review* article that we shouldn't even consider state constitutions "constitutions" in the same sense as the federal one.

Unlike the federal document, state constitutions aren't streamlined, long-lasting edifices. America has had 146 different state constitutions; 31 states have had two or more constitutions, and 18 have had four or more. And as of 1985, America's state constitutions had been amended more than 5,000 times.

The average state constitution is four times as long as the federal one, and some are eight times as long. And they are often larded with material that seems more the stuff of statute—or humor—than of the sacred compact binding a people into political unity. Louisiana amended its constitution to make Huey Long's birthday a state holiday. Texas's constitution declares that banks may use automated teller machines. The width of ski trails in state parks is a constitutional matter in New York.

State court judges themselves don't treat their constitutions with much respect, Gardner found. He argues that "contrary to the claims of New Federalism, state constitutional law today is a vast wasteland of confusing, conflicting, and essentially unintelligible pronouncements." Gardner sampled 1,208 state supreme court decisions from 1990 and found that in only 21 percent of the cases did the court even attempt to address state constitutional issues.

The new state constitutionalism may not yet have matured into a coherent judicial philosophy. Still, state courts have made a batch of decisions in the past decade expanding different constitutional rights beyond federal standards. Search-and-seizure cases have been busy arenas for state court activism; states such as Hawaii, Pennsylvania, New York, and Arizona have explicitly prohibited various kinds of police searches and seizures that have been countenanced by the federal Supreme Court.

New York has been a leader in expanding Fourth Amendment rights, but not everyone is cheering. Peter Reinharz, a prosecutor with New York City's Family Court Division, publicly excoriated his state's decisions regarding search and seizure in a recent issue of *City Journal*. Like most critics of the new state constitutionalism, Reinharz doesn't attack the *concept* of state courts relying on their state constitutions for independent reasoning, but he does question the judges' policy wisdom.

"I've been a prosecutor for 15 years," Reinharz says. "There's not one cop on patrol who can explain to me what the four tiers [established by New York courts to test proper searches] are about. You can't design tests that can't be interpreted by the people to whom they must apply."

Reinharz complains that the relevant language in the state and federal constitutions regarding protection from searches is absolutely identical, so no textual reason exists for departing from federal Supreme Court precedent. Cato's Lynch says he frequently encounters such arguments. "It's like people view it as somehow impolite to tell the Supreme Court, 'Sorry, but we reject your reading.'"

State constitution watcher Jennifer Freisen adds, "I don't believe the U.S. Supreme Court is infallible. I don't worship them. They could be wrong. If a [state court] decision is based on decent legal reasoning, there's no reason to fetishize the Supreme Court, to fetishize centralized power."

Explicit *differences* in the language of similar federal and state rights guarantees often have a role in the new state constitutionalism as well, as with the right to bear arms. Twenty-two state constitutions explicitly say you can use guns for personal defense, and 20 weapons laws have been overturned based on state constitutional guarantees, dating back to 1822. "In a lot of cases, state constitutions aren't monkeyed up with 'militia' clauses," says Stephen Halbrook, an activist lawyer and gun rights scholar who has argued many gun rights cases in both state and federal courts.

"A lot have phrases like 'defense of self and state.' The first gun control law in American history was in Kentucky, and the state court promptly overturned it."

Today, after a recent series of disappointing decisions in such states as Ohio, Oregon, and Colorado upholding weapons bans that Halbrook thinks clearly violate their state constitutional weapons rights guarantees, he's no longer so sure that state courts are any better than federal ones on gun rights.

Along with being tougher on government intrusions on citizens' liberties, state courts have also ex-

Twenty-two state constitutions explicitly say you can use guns for personal defense, and 20 weapons laws have been overturned based on state constitutional guarantees, dating back to 1822.

tended some "rights" that are in fact obligations for others—insisting that their state governments are constitutionally required to be more generous with tax dollars. Despite a federal Supreme Court decision to the contrary, the states of Minnesota, California, Montana, and New Mexico have decided that it would be positively unconstitutional to limit public funding for abortions.

That state courts are making decisions relying on their own constitutions, their own text, their own history, and their own judgment is an encouraging sign that political power in the United States doesn't have to be calcified in a central leviathan. While federalism leaves room for the multiplication of error, the more states realize they don't have to obey the federal government, in judicial precedent or other areas, the more room to maneuver the American citizen has—the more room for social and legal experimentation and evolution.

Even James Gardner, one of the fiercest academic critics of the state courts' legal reasoning, recognizes the new state constitutionalism's potential value. "Despite their shoddy methods, I came to the conclusion that I don't think states need any other reason to depart from Supreme Court precedent than that they think the Supreme Court was wrong," Gardner says. "We don't have a state and federal government to provide different polities with different values and to constitutionalize them. It's to provide two different avenues of protection for rights that we as Americans have decided we have."

Brian Doherty (BMDoherty@aol.com) is assistant editor of REASON.

PART II

U.S. Foreign Policy

For decades, the defining feature of U.S. foreign policy was the Cold War. The world was a dangerous place, but it was also a relatively well-ordered one. The end of the Cold War was rightly greeted with jubilation, but it did not mean that the world had become any less perilous. If anything, U.S. foreign policy may have become more difficult, as threats to national security became more decentralized and harder to predict.

Now that America is the world's only remaining superpower, more than ever the world looks to it for leadership. During the past few years alone, America has been called upon to broker or secure peace in Yugoslavia, Haiti, Somalia, Northern Ireland, the Middle East, and in other far-flung locations. Nuclear tensions between India and Pakistan have escalated. Rogue nations such as Iraq and North Korea direct their hostility toward the United States. The World Trade Center in New York and American embassies in Kenya and Tanzania have been bombed, possibly signaling a stepped-up campaign of terror against U.S. interests at home and abroad. Economic chaos in Russia threatens to destabilize the fragile democracy that has emerged there. And the list goes on.

Many questions face U.S. policymakers. For example, should the military be reduced? Should government revenues previously spent on the military be redeployed for domestic needs? Or should the size of the military be increased? Should we pursue anti-ballistic missile technology, or is that technology too expensive and unreliable? Are economic sanctions an effective way of securing the cooperation of foreign nations? How will we deal with the threat of biological, chemical, or nuclear terrorism? Should the United States seek to achieve its national security goals unilaterally, or should it work within the framework of existing multinational organizations such as the United Nations? The following selections address some of the challenges the United States faces on the world stage in the next century.

A Reading for Critical Thinking

The Trade Weapon, and Other Myths

By Michael Ledeen

Saddam Hussein's recent act of bravado—barring American observers from sites believed to be used for the production of weapons of mass destruction—was not an isolated event, but part of a growing challenge to our use of trade sanctions to punish regimes we do not like. The resistance to American policy is not restricted to such rogue regimes as Iraq; even before Saddam's slap in the face of the United States and the United Nations, many of our European allies, Arab leaders, and our "friends" in Moscow had indicated their desire to weaken or even lift trade sanctions on Iraq, and this attitude is spreading to the other three countries against which we have organized embargoes: Iran, Cuba, and Libya.

• Despite our call for a multinational embargo on Tehran's mullahcracy, Total (France) and Gazprom (Russia) have signed a big oil and gas deal with Iran.

• The mid-December Islamic conference in Tehran —attended even by such allies as Saudi Arabia and Egypt—was a clear rejection by Muslim nations of the Clinton administration's "dual containment" policy.

• Over a year ago China signed an agreement to develop oil fields in southern Iraq (Italy, France, Russia and Ukraine have similar deals), and has sold, *inter alia*, missiles, warships, fighter aircraft, and chemical agents to Iran—where the Chinese are also building two nuclear power reactors.

• Italy, traditionally most attentive to Washington's concerns, has announced its intention to normalize relations with Libya, where, despite our impassioned pleas to the contrary, South African President Nelson Mandela recently paid two visits, and publicly denounced our embargo policy. Egypt has announced it is negotiating with Qaddafi for the construction of a pipeline from Libya.

The pattern extends to our own backyard: the European Union has passed legislation forbidding European corporations to comply with the American embargo against Cuba, and has threatened to punish any American company that brings suit against Europeans doing business on Castro's island. Several Canadian companies are active investors in Cuba, and recently a South Korean delegation participated in a trade show in Havana. So strong is the international opposition to our policies that, in an early November U. N. vote, only Israel and Kazakhstan voted with us in favor of the Cuban embargo.

The leaders of the rogue regimes have been quick to exploit the criticism of American policy, and Saddam was no doubt encouraged by the open splits on sanctions to defy the U. S. Events proved him right: despite dark warnings about dire consequences, the toughest proposal from Washington was to restrict travel by top Iraqis. This was a cheap enough price for Saddam to pay for halting the on-site inspections, which enabled him to save some of his capacity to manufacture weapons of mass destruction. And now we hear a rising chorus calling for easing the sanctions.

Such a vast international consensus against the embargoes suggests that there is something fundamentally wrong with our strategy. The advocates of sanctions argue that their critics are driven by greed: there are profits to be made by trading with the rogue nations. There is merit to the claim, but it is far from a complete explanation of the campaign against sanctions. No doubt there are businessmen and politicians who regret the loss of business during the embargoes, but they would not be nearly so outspoken if the embargoes had plainly succeeded. The policy is under attack primarily because it has failed to accomplish its principal objectives: weaken the rogue regimes, and eventually bring them down. The rogues are still there, and none of them seems to have been significantly weakened by sanctions.

Whenever the U. S. has a problem with another country it likes to impose trade sanctions on it. They're a great weapon to use against friends, but for all intents useless against regimes that hate us anyway. There's also a tendency to think that sanctions relieve us of the need to defend freedom in oppressed countries — or to assume that trade by itself can bring freedom.

Embargo supporters have only one recent success to point to: South Africa, where most everyone, from Nelson Mandela to the apologists for apartheid, agrees that the moral and economic isolation of the country encouraged the National Party to end white minority rule and turn the country over to the black majority. But South Africa was not a rogue regime, whatever its internal evils. Unlike Cuba, Libya, Iran, and Iraq, South Africa was not at war with the West and did not support terrorist attacks against us and our allies. Above all, the South African government was sufficiently sensitive to civilized international opinion to reform itself once it had been sufficiently stigmatized by nations with which it wished to associate. The rogue regimes do not wish to associate with us, they are not in the least inclined to internal reform, and they are not sensitive to criticism; they expect and even welcome our attacks.

Indeed, there is an impressive and growing body of opinion—including many who might have been expected to embrace sanctions—that economic embargoes not only fail to bring down evil regimes, but they punish the people of the target nations instead of the ruling tyrants, and may even backfire and rally the people around the regime. In Cuba, for example, economic misery has increased since our embargo began to bite following the fall of the Soviet Empire, but there is no sign of either intensified resistance to the regime or greater willingness by Castro and his henchmen to reform the system. The critics argue that we

are only impoverishing the Cuban people, without improving their chances for freedom. Similarly in Iraq, the embargo cuts deepest against the neediest Iraqis, and no less a personage than Hillary Rodham Clinton has gone out of her way to stipulate that the U.S. will not punish Iraqi children for the sins of their fathers: food and powdered milk flow freely into the country.

The view that sanctions are counterproductive is often reinforced by the claim that a contrary policy—wide-open trade—is more likely to weaken the tyrants and spread democracy. The advocates of "Most Favored Nation" status for China repeatedly made this case during the debate last summer. Thus, Jeane Kirkpatrick, Jack Kemp, Lamar Alexander, Steve Forbes, and Donald Rumsfeld: "There is more freedom in the [Chinese] economic realm than in any other. Trade can help maintain that freedom, and help expand that freedom to other realms. . ." Thus, House Majority Leader Dick Armey: "Freedom to trade is the great subversive and liberating force in human history."

The most grandiose claims for the revolutionary political effects of commerce are silly. Many tyrannies—like Saudi Arabia, China, and Zaire, to take just three—have long had vigorous international trade, but show little inclination to expand their citizens' freedoms, and in many cases the profits, or hefty commissions therefrom, have gone straight into the pockets of the repressive elites. We had considerable commerce with the Soviet Union, but no serious adult thinks that East-West trade hastened the fall of Communism by enriching Soviet citizens and demonstrating the advantages of freedom. Quite the opposite; the economic *failure* of the Soviet Empire was a major factor in its collapse, and that failure was neither accelerated nor prevented by our trade policies. Insofar as the collapse of the Soviet Empire had economic causes, they were rather the consequence of the irremediable faults of the Communist system itself.

But if some of the claims on behalf of free trade are wildly overstated, recent history provides some examples to support the belief that economic success may encourage a peaceful transition from dictatorship to democracy. The two cases most often cited to support this claim are Taiwan and South Korea. Both have democratized in recent years, albeit in very different ways: Taiwan's ruling elite announced it would withdraw from all top governmental positions, and imposed a democratic system from the top down. In South Korea, democracy resulted from challenges to the system from below, ultimately toppling the old regime. In each case, the transition to democracy coincided with spectacular increases in living standards, and the new wealth created in Taiwan and South Korea was closely linked to trade: exports to the advanced industrial countries generated a lot of capital.

But wealth alone does not drive the passion for democracy. If it did, the oil-rich Middle Eastern countries, along with Nigeria and Angola, would be flourishing democracies instead of corrupt tyrannies. The relationship between economic success and political freedom is far more complicated than the models offered either by the advocates of free trade or of economic sanctions. What are we to do with Spain, the first country to effect a peaceful transition from dictatorship to democracy? Generalissimo Francisco Franco knew that once he died, Spain would do away with his authoritarian regime and move toward democracy. He believed that the transition would be successful, at least in part because a moderately successful middle class had been created during his rule, and that middle class—in Spain, as elsewhere, the truly revolutionary force of modern history—wanted a greater share of political power. But, unlike the Asian "tigers" of Taiwan and South Korea, Spain's transition to democracy can hardly be explained by the effects of commerce, for Spain was treated much as South Africa under apartheid: stigmatized, sanctioned, and condemned throughout much of the world. Like South Africa, Spain (and Chile and Portugal, similarly) moved toward democracy after being subjected to widespread embargoes and international censure.

Some countries democratized after a period of sanctions, while others democratized after a period of extensive trade and economic expansion. There is no common economic denominator. Nor is there a clear causal relationship between democracy and the adoption of free-market economic institutions. The latter preceded the former in the recent Asian cases, while political freedoms came first in Central and Eastern Europe, as they had a generation earlier in Japan and Germany, where the basic rules of democracy were imposed by occupying armies. The common denominator is freedom: once freedom was introduced, either in the economic or the political system, the people pushed for its expansion.

The key element in the fall of the oppressive regimes is not economic, but political: the people and the rulers lost faith in the old methods, and undertook to change them. South Africa, Taiwan, South Korea, Spain, and Portugal all wanted to be part of the Western world. The democratization of South Africa and the European satellites was a return to the fold of civilized societies living under the rule of law, while the Taiwanese and South Koreans came to understand that democracy was an integral part of the most successful societies, and they wanted to join the club. Sometimes the leaders of the old regime initiated the

political transformation, while in others the changes were instituted by the former victims. In most cases, the transition was guided by exceptional leaders like King Juan Carlos in Spain and the son of Chiang Kai-Shek in Taiwan. The same holds true for countries like Poland (Lech Walesa) and Czechoslovakia (Vaclav Havel) and even the Soviet Union, where Mikhail Gorbachev came to understand that the Communist system he inherited needed drastic overhaul. That he never intended to destroy Communism is a tribute to the potency of the political forces he unwittingly unleashed, and points us in the right direction to understand what needs to be done with the rogue regimes.

The rogue regimes do not wish to associate with us, they aren't inclined to internal reform, and they're not sensitive to criticism. They expect and even welcome our attacks.

The critics of sanctions are right, at least up to a point: there is no reason to believe that sanctions, in and of themselves, will bring down tyrants and encourage freedom. On the other hand, the advocates of free trade as the engine of democracy are also wrong. The decisive element is the political will to change the regime, either by the leaders, or by sufficiently powerful opponents. And, insofar as American foreign policy is concerned, there is an important difference between friendly and hostile tyrants: we have considerable political leverage over friendly countries, but precious little over enemies.

The advocates of sanctions do not make the important distinction between friends and enemies, perhaps because they believe, as do so many Americans, that all people are fundamentally the same, and that the methods that work in our society will work in others as well. Sanctions do work in America, as witness the considerable success of domestic boycotts, against grapes and lettuce, or investments in unpopular causes, or the wrong sort of motion pictures. In like manner, nations that share our values can be swayed by sanctions. Even friendly tyrants, like the shah of Iran, Ferdinand Marcos of the Philippines, or Chile's General Augusto Pinochet, can be pressured to grant political concessions to their domestic opponents. In such cases, the usual bag of diplomatic tools, the carrots and sticks so appetizing to Foggy Bottom, can have significant effect. Not so with tyrants who hate us and everything we stand for.

Neither sanctions nor free trade will bring down a tyrannical regime with the will and power to maintain itself against all domestic challengers. No matter how great the misery of the Cuban people, Castro will survive so long as he is willing and able to kill anyone who tries to bring him down. Nor would the political situation change if Cuba were flooded with investors and tourists, and the standard of living of the Cuban people rose dramatically. Stalin's power was not seriously threatened by the economic ravages of the thirties, nor were his successors undermined by the economic successes of the 1950's. The Soviet dictatorship rested on the systematic use of terror, as do those in Cuba, Syria, Libya, Iran, and Iraq today. If we want to bring down the rogue states, we will have to use power against those regimes, as we did against the Soviet Union. The military defeat of the Red Army in Afghanistan, and the setbacks suffered by Soviet proxy forces in Grenada and Angola, were at least as important as economic failure, as was Ronald Reagan's outspoken denunciation of the evils of the Soviet Empire, broadcast relentlessly beyond the Iron Curtain by the radio transmitters of the West, and published in myriad newspapers, magazines, and *samizdat* during the years of oppression.

Both the claims for embargoes and for wide-open free trade are excuses for the lack of serious policy designed to bring down the rogue regimes, or, at a minimum, to protect ourselves from the fulfillment of the rogues' evil intentions. There are no hard and fast rules for such policy, but they often include: support for opposition movements and leaders, covert action to subvert the regime, the use of military and/or paramilitary forces against various targets, and an outspoken determination by our own national leaders to directly challenge the rogues.

We have had ample opportunity to do this in Iraq, but we have repeatedly declined to act. The first, and by far the best opportunity was the Gulf War, but we stopped short of finishing the job. The second chance came in the late summer of 1996, when Saddam invaded the "no fly" zone we had established in northern Iraq. He invaded in order to crush Iraqi opponents whom we had supported, but we stood by as they were decimated. Clinton ordered our armed forces to lob a few cruise missiles at meaningless targets from a safe distance, but Saddam's victory was manifest. The third opportunity was Saddam's frontal challenge to the United States last fall, and we dithered ourselves into prolonged talks which only elevated Saddam's status to that of legitimate interlocutor.

Saddam's affront to the United States is a serious matter, because it was taken in order to enhance Iraq's military power. The ostensible point of our policy is to prevent Iraq from rebuilding its frightening military machine, but our weak reaction enabled him to preserve and perhaps even to expand his ability to wage war. As in the Gulf War, and again when Iraq smashed its opponents in the north, we failed to use power to destroy an enemy, or to prevent him from growing stronger. This is a grave error, and we must hope against hope that we will not have to pay a terrible price for it. The one encouraging note so far is that some of those Americans who participated in the unfortunate decision to end the Gulf War without bringing down Saddam's regime now insist that Clinton see the error of their ways, and carry out a serious policy.

Unlike the Asian "tigers," Spain's transition to democracy can hardly be explained by the effects of commerce, for Spain was treated much as South Africa under apartheid.

If and when we do get serious, there is one element of trade embargoes that should be embraced: the prevention of rogues like Saddam from increasing their military power. It would seem self-evident that we want to maintain the greatest possible margin of military superiority against all enemies, actual and potential; deterrence does work. It follows that we should not sell advanced military technology to dangerous countries, or to countries that resell the technology to rogues or potential enemies, and we must also do everything in our power to prevent other countries from doing it as well. We know how to do this, having used such an embargo to deadly effect against the Soviet Union. By the end of the Cold War our military power was so clearly superior to theirs that they were afraid to lash out against us. This highly successful strategy—truly one of the great accomplishments of the Reagan administration—was discarded, in part by the Bush administration, and then, with reckless abandon, by Clinton, particularly in the case of the People's Republic of China. Our China policy is the extreme case of the "free trade solves all problems" school.

During the Clinton presidency we have provided the Chinese with some of our best military technology, much of it at bargain-basement prices. We have sold them the crucial "hot section" technology that gives modern aircraft engines their special thrust, thereby ensuring that the next generation of Chinese fighter aircraft will have the world's best engines. We have sold them enormous quantities of supercomputers, the central nervous system of modern warfare. In the past two years alone, the Clinton administration approved the sale of forty-six supercomputers, which is more than those currently in use in the Pentagon, the military services, and the intelligence community combined. This will enormously help the Chinese design advanced weapons, including weapons of mass destruction, as well as aircraft and missiles, and it will provide them with a quantum jump in their ability to encrypt their own communications and decipher ours. We have permitted them to purchase advanced machine tools to build wing spans for fighter planes, the manufacturing know-how for the Global Positioning System (which they can use to give their missiles lethal accuracy), and small jet engines (for cruise missiles), as well as laboratories for testing "stealth" technology. And this is only a part of a long list.

To be sure, China is not an enemy today, and we all hope it will not become one. Deng Xiaoping's decision to liberalize the Chinese economy may eventually have political consequences. One of the lessons of the fall of the Soviet Empire is that the desire for freedom is not easily divisible into limited areas of human activity. Gorbachev seemed to believe he could grant political freedom while maintaining economic control; the Chinese gerontarchs, and the likes of Singapore's Lee Kwan Yew sound as if they believe they can grant economic freedom while maintaining political control. But freedom is not so easily contained. Having achieved limited freedom, the human impulse is to seek more of it. Gorbachev's failure suggests that the Chinese may face the awesome choice of granting political power to larger segments of the population—thereby risking profound political upheaval—or clamping down on the economic freedom that has so enriched the nation in recent years. The Chinese know all about this explosive dilemma, and their leaders are quick to warn the Chinese people that they are not about to permit a replay of the Soviet debacle. No one is so prescient as to be able to confidently predict the outcome of such a crisis, and until the issue is decided we must be on our guard. China may become an enemy, and if that happens we do not want the Chinese to have the best weapons we can design. This issue is an integral part of any serious policy toward the rogue nations. China provides them considerable support, and there are grounds to fear that this is not merely a quest for financial gain. While Forbes, Kemp et. al. have said that "there is no new Cold War, and China is not a new Cold War enemy," a recent Chinese military "study document" says the opposite, and blames us for it: "A new Cold War has begun against the socialist state," conducted by "hostile Western nations." After analyzing our performance in the Gulf War, the Chinese leaders have called for the creation of a modern army capable of winning a "high-tech" war, in which we are the obvious target.

It is folly to provide them with the means to carry out this mission, and to strengthen the rogues with advanced Western technology.

Providing China with the wherewithal to become an effective threat to us, and thereby strengthening the rogue nations whose hostile intentions are beyond doubt, is the truly criminal act of Bill Clinton's presidency. Yet it has been carried out with hardly a voice of protest from the Congress, the press, and the intelligentsia, all of whom bear considerable responsibility for it. Even the China "hawks," who rightly criticize Clinton for going easy on the bloody regime of Jiang Zemin, and who steadfastly denounce the repression and murder of Chinese democrats, female infants, and religious believers, have failed to demand an end to this folly, and to put together a multinational embargo on future sales. Instead of dealing with the serious matters of military and political power, our national debate has been hung up on the pseudo-issue of embargoes vs. free trade. The latest symptom of this collective insanity comes from the Pentagon, where Secretary of Defense William Cohen is busily dismantling the one organization in the U. S. government with the skills, the institutional memory, and the independence of spirit required to enforce high tech controls: the Defense Technology Security Agency.

But even if we manage to slow the growth of Chinese military power, we will want to use political weapons to encourage the democratization of the People's Republic. Prospects are not as dim as might be imagined. As the *Washington Post*'s Keith Richburg recently observed, even as the economic success of countries as diverse as Taiwan, Indonesia, Malaysia, and South Korea is threatened by the Asian financial debacle, the demands for freedom and democracy are steadily growing. And the remedies for the Asian epidemic, "more transparency in decision-making, opening of markets, less corruption and cronyism," all work for a further, and deeper, democratization of Asian societies. These remedies are primarily political, not economic, and they come at a moment of economic weakness, when the people are losing faith in the capacities of the old regime.

It is only a matter of time before the Chinese people come to doubt the capacities of the oppressive Communist gerontocracy, and we must encourage them, and their leaders, to doubt and ultimately change it. When the moment of truth comes, the two crucial factors will be our own military power (which must be so great that the leaders of the old regime dare not challenge it, even to save themselves from ruin) and our political resolve (for if we are seen to be unwilling to fight for our own cause, our military strength will be discounted).

Here again, Bill Clinton's repeated failures in Iraq have dangerous global consequences. If we cannot deal with a tiny country in the Middle East, if we permit Saddam Hussein to crush a fledgling democratic movement in Iraq, why should the tyrannical rulers of a billion and more souls in China take us seriously?

MICHAEL LEDEEN, foreign editor of TAS, *holds the Freedom Chair at the American Enterprise Institute and is the author most recently of* Freedom Betrayed: How America Led a Global Democratic Revolution, Won the Cold War, and Walked Away *(AEI Press).*

Dollar
Diplomacy Returns

By Lawrence F. Kaplan

It has long been a truism of international politics that the best guarantor of peace is democracy; whatever quarrels they may have with one another, democratic nations do not resort to war to resolve them. But this fundamental understanding has lately been undergoing a profound revision. According to the new wisdom, it is not the political organization of a society but rather its economic orientation that counts, and specifically the degree of its integration into the emerging global economy. The revised version has been neatly summarized by one of its major boosters, the *New York Times* columnist Thomas L. Friedman: "No two countries that both have a McDonald's have fought a war against each other."

The new commercialist understanding, far from remaining only the property of pundits, has in fact been enshrined in official policy. In its name, the Clinton administration has undertaken a major shift in the priorities of American diplomacy. "The days when we could afford to subordinate our economic interests to foreign-policy or defense concerns are long past," declared former U.S. trade representative Mickey Kantor. What the United States must do, in the words of former Under Secretary of Commerce Jeffrey Garten, is "use all its foreign-policy levers to achieve commercial goals." And the President himself has pledged to place "our economic competitiveness at the heart of our foreign policy."

It has been decades since this line of thinking—that the chief business of America in the world should be not politics but business—has been taken seriously. Throughout the cold war (leftist critics to the contrary

notwithstanding) commercial interests played a much smaller role in American foreign policy than did the imperatives of strategy and ideology. This was true from the late 1940's, when President Truman angered American industrialists by instituting export controls against the Soviet block, all the way through to the time of President Reagan, who wielded economic sanctions against the Soviet Union, Poland, and Libya over the protestations of the U.S. Chamber of Commerce.

The Clinton White House characterizes its own approach to foreign affairs as "pragmatic neo-Wilsonianism," but Woodrow Wilson, as it happens entered office with the explicit intention of putting an end to the "dollar diplomacy" of the Taft administration. In international affairs, the true inclinations of the Clintonites bear a much closer resemblance to the policies of Harding, Coolidge, and Hoover—and, like theirs, the new policy comes clothed in high-minded rhetoric. According to the President, focusing on trade not only makes good economic sense but actually helps the United States to realize the traditional objectives of its foreign policy. Specifically, the new dollar diplomacy is said to accomplish three things: enhance international security and lessen the likelihood of conflict; promote democracy; and ensure American primacy on the global scene.

As to the first of these, a White House spokesman has said that commerce, by "knit[ting] together the countries whose livelihoods depend upon each other," ends by "creating a direct stake in peace and stability." It was in line with this belief, indeed, that the entire foreign-policy establishment was overhauled during the first Clinton term. The Commerce Department, from a newly established "war room," was charged with spearheading trade missions across the globe; the Defense Department installed trade desks at the Pentagon; the intelligence community shifted resources to accommodate administration demands for commercial intelligence; and within the White House, a National Economic Council was created as a counterweight to the National Security Council, itself increasingly focused on economic matters.

Unfortunately, the logic of the administration's new approach was soon revealed to have things exactly backward. Thus, during the first Clinton term, the White House held America's military relationship with a key ally—Japan—hostage to a dispute over car parts, even as it encouraged trade and investment agreements with real or potential adversaries like Syria, North Korea, and China. In neither case did American diplomacy conduce to stability or cooperation. When tensions escalated on the Korean peninsula early in 1994, irked Japanese officials suggested that in the event of a conflict there, the United States should not look to Japan for support. As for ongoing American efforts to influence the behavior of our adversaries, trade, if anything, has proved less of a help than a burden, creating an interest in maintaining the status quo and inhibiting our ability to use power for political ends.

For a clear example of how an aggressive economism can corrupt the broader ends of American foreign policy, one need look no farther than our regime of export controls. Early in his first term, the President declared a "national emergency" to deal with the threat of weapons proliferation. But even as he spoke, his administration was striving to dismantle COCOM, the multilateral organization that had monitored high-tech exports during the cold war. At the urging of industry, the President then abolished most restrictions on the sale of computer, telecommunications, satellite, and even nuclear technology.

Within a year of the 1995 decision to deregulate the export of supercomputers—sophisticated devices whose uses include the design of advanced weapons systems and the simulation of atomic explosions—Russia's ministry of atomic energy had acquired four of them for the country's premier nuclear-weapons laboratory. Soon it was reported that one of the 47 supercomputers sold to China over the previous eighteen months had surfaced at a military-research institute. At the very moment Congress was responding to these sales by voting to reinstate controls, the President lifted the ban on selling American nuclear reactors to China; it was, he explained, a confidence-building measure. But how much the Chinese need their confidence

bolstered by American dual-use technology may be gleaned from a 1997 CIA report, according to which they are now the world's "most significant supplier of weapons of mass destruction and related goods and technology."

Is it really necessary to point out that, even in an era of globalization, commercial ties are properly an effect, not a cause, of political stability? In the serene conviction that things are the other way around, the White House has been recklessly testing a proposition that has been found wanting over and over again in this century: the theory that trade and war are incompatible. The European flirtation with this idea in the period prior to World War I ended decisively at the Marne. In its American version, the idea enjoyed a vogue in the 1920's before being put to rest by the ensuing decades of Depression, war, and East-West conflict. It is alarming to see it being touted again, as if nothing has been learned, and nothing remembered.

The second tenet of the Clinton White House is that open markets promote democracy and political freedom. In the words of National Security Adviser Samuel Berger, "the fellow travelers of the new global economy—computers and modems, faxes and photocopiers, increased contacts and binding contracts—carry with them the seeds of [political] change."

The link between free markets and political liberalization—another staple of an earlier period—may or may not prove valid in the long run. But there have been, and remain, numerous capitalist states with authoritarian political systems. For every Britain there existed a Wilhelmine Germany; for every Taiwan or South Korea, a Malaysia and an Indonesia. As no less an apostle of economism than Milton Friedman has acknowledged, "It is clearly possible to have economic arrangements that are fundamentally capitalist and political arrangements that are not free."

In this area, too, the United States has become caught in a bind of its own devising. For one thing, the notion that we can achieve democratization by chasing free markets has inevitably led us to turn a blind eye to flagrant abuses of human rights in countries where we happen to want to do business. Our relations with the Republic of Sudan are an example. Sudan's links to terrorism, and the war it has been conducting against its own Christian population, have earned it a place on the State Department list of rogue states with which American companies are, theoretically, prohibited from doing business. Last year, however, when a U.S. petroleum corporation complained to the White House that a lucrative deal with the Sudanese government was being held up by the 1996 Anti-Terrorism Act, the President's response was to exempt Sudan from the act's provisions. Business first; democracy later.

Then, too, the subordination of political principle to the expansion of economic ties leads to the justified impression of American hypocrisy. In the name of our ostensible commitment to political liberty, we have maintained sanctions against some relatively weak states of marginal commercial significance like Burma and Cuba; in the meantime, we have actively promoted trade with nations like China that boast no less abysmal human-rights records but large markets. As the French newspaper *Le Monde* noted in an editorial, "The Chinese case destroys the American pretension to universality on human rights."

The point is well taken. When it is driven by commercial imperatives, the international conduct of the United States becomes indistinguishable from that of a frankly cynical country like France. By definition, the primary aim of commercial diplomacy is not liberty but prosperity—a fine and important thing, but hardly a cause for which Americans should ever be asked to fight and die.

Finally, the Clinton administration offers an argument from self-interest: as the era of geo-politics has given way to the era of geo-economics, we are told, commercial diplomacy has become the means for achieving and maintaining American global primacy. In the view of Mickey Kantor, support for free trade "is about assuring the world that the United States will continue to be the world leader in this new era of interdependence."

The "realist" case for commercial diplomacy, however, is the weakest justification of all. Although the President has spoken confidently of our ability to "harness the global economy to the benefit of all of our people," it is no easy task for any government to "harness" an interdependent world. To be sure, the White House has occasionally flirted with openly mercantilist policies—organizing trade missions for American corporations, engaging in commercial brinkmanship with trading partners. Yet while government sponsorship has helped to secure international contracts for a select number of industries, these contracts make up only a tiny fraction of overseas American investment. In turn, the percentage of international transactions that is accounted for by trade and direct investment has been rapidly diminishing.

The real medium of globalization is finance. The monetary mass circumnavigating the globe, and turning over at a daily rate of $1.2 trillion, represents fifteen times the value of international trade. In this vital sector, neither the U.S. nor any other nation can act as a "world leader." To the contrary, just as monetary flows have assumed a central role in the international economy, the ability of the state to regulate these flows has all but evaporated.

It is a fanciful and dangerous conceit to imagine that a nation can command an arena shaped by non-state actors in much the same manner that it wields political or military power. "The United States has to send a signal to our allies," the President said recently, "that we know we are in a new world, and it's a world in which we are interdependent." If so, multinational firms are merely heeding the President's own message when they ignore the threat of U.S. sanctions and invest in Burma, Iran, and numerous other rogue states. Sanctions and embargoes, after all, run counter to the logic of interdependence, which leads to the elimination of trade barriers, not the erection of new ones.

In the game of trade, nations gain more by cooperating than by competing for power. The game of politics is otherwise—a fact obscured by the President's affinity for describing the global economy in terms of national competition. But American bond traders are not Marines, and the market cannot be relied on to bolster the aims of the state. To the contrary, if left unchecked it can just as easily subvert them.

The defects of commercial diplomacy—its lack of strategic underpinnings, its tenuous moral legitimacy, its disjunction from anything resembling a truly national interest—have been apparent for decades. Security, political liberty, and national preeminence are not secondary goals, nor can they be achieved by means of sheer acquisitiveness. To pretend otherwise is to engage in an act of willful amnesia and hubris for which, some day, a suitably high price may be exacted.

Lawrence F. Kaplan is a fellow in strategic studies at the Paul H. Nitze School of Advanced International Studies in Washington, D.C.

Bits, Bytes, and Diplomacy

A Reading for Critical Thinking

By Walter B. Wriston

THE THIRD TECHNOLOGICAL REVOLUTION

An American historian once opined, "Peace is the mastery of great forces; it is not the solution of a problem."[1] Great new forces are at work in the world, and if we are to master them, the beginning of wisdom is to recognize that the world is changing dramatically and at unprecedented speed. We are in the midst of a revolution. A revolution by definition causes old power structures to crumble and new ones to rise. The catalyst—but not the cause has always been technological change. Now, as in revolutions past, technology is profoundly affecting the sovereignty of governments, the world economy, and military strategy.

We are now living in the midst of the third great revolution in history; When the principle of the lever was applied to make a plow, the agricultural revolution was born, and the power of nomadic tribal chiefs declined. When centuries later, men substituted the power of water, steam, and electricity for animal muscle, the Industrial Revolution was born. Both of these massive changes took centuries to unfold. Each caused a shift in the power structure. Today, the marriage of computers and telecommunications has ushered in the Information Age, which is as different from the Industrial Age as that period was from the Agricultural Age. Information technology has demolished time and distance. Instead of validating Orwell's vision of Big Brother watching the citizen, the third revolution enables the citizen to watch Big Brother. And so the virus of freedom, for which there is no

antidote, is spread by electronic networks to the four corners of the earth.

History is strewn with wonderful inventions. Most of them were designed to solve specific problems: the wheel to move things, engines to supply power, clocks and compasses to tell time and direction. The inventions that made possible the information revolution were different. They changed the way we solve problems. When Johann Gutenberg pioneered movable type in Europe in 1436, and when Intel designed the integrated circuit in the 1970s, the way we record, store, access, and peruse knowledge made quantum leaps forward and affected not only how we do our jobs, but what we do.

These two events were just as important as they sound. Gutenberg broke the monopoly of the monks who copied manuscripts by hand and guarded them jealously. They understood that knowledge was power and sometimes chained books to the shelves. In *The Discoverers*, Daniel Boorstin cites a 12th-century manuscript inscription: "This book belongs to the monastery of St. Mary of Robert's Bridge, who ever shall steal it from this house, or mutilate it let him be forever cursed. Amen." Contrast that mindset with the ability of a researcher anywhere in the world with a computer and a modem to tap into the entire database of the Library of Congress, the Bibliotheque de France, or the British Library. In today's parlance, this change constitutes a paradigm shift.

George Gilder explains that "the key to paradigm shifts is the collapse of formerly pivotal scarcities, the

From *Foreign Affairs* (September/October 1997, Vol. 76, No. 5), pp. 172–182. Reprinted by permission of *Foreign Affairs*. Copyright © 1997 by the Council on Foreign Relations, Inc.

rise of new forms of abundance, and the onset of new scarcities. Successful innovators use these new forms of abundance to redress the emergent shortages."[2] The enormous use of timber for railroad ties and trestles as American railroads pushed west caused Theodore Roosevelt to declare a national shortage of timber, which was soon replaced by an abundance of concrete, iron, and steel. Shortly thereafter, electricity and steam power overcame looming shortages of labor and materials. The recent alleged shortage of broadcast frequencies caused electronic engineers to expand the spectrum's useful frequencies. This cycle has continued throughout history. In the three pillars of the order that resulted from the Industrial Revolution—national sovereignty, national economies, and military power—the information revolution has increased the power of individuals and outmoded old hierarchies.

A GLOBAL VILLAGE

Sovereignty, the power of a nation to stop others from interfering in its internal affairs, is rapidly eroding. When Woodrow Wilson went to Paris to negotiate the Treaty of Versailles, he ordered his postmaster-general to assume control over all transatlantic cable lines in order to censor the news from Europe. Today no one and no nation can block the flow of information across national borders.

During the Persian Gulf War, Saddam Hussein proposed what was viewed in Washington as a phony peace settlement. President Bush had to convey that judgment to the 26 nations in the coalition. As Marlin Fitzwater, former White House Press Secretary, remembers, the "quickest and most effective way was CNN, because all countries in the world had it and were watching it on a real-time basis . . . and 20 minutes after we got the proposal . . . I went on national television . . . to tell the 26 members . . . that the war was continuing." In this and many other instances, the elite foreign policy establishment and its government-to-government communications were bypassed. No highly trained foreign service officer meticulously drafted a note, no secretary of state signed it, and no American ambassadors called on foreign ministers to deliver the message. The United States entrusted a vital diplomatic message to a private television company seen by the whole world. Wilson's strategy was to control the flow of information by fiat, while Bush realized that since he could not beat the world information free market, he had better join it.

Today special interest groups of all kinds, from terrorists to human rights activists, bypass government-based communications channels. In *The News Media in National and International Conflicts*, Andrew Arno explains that when relations sour between two countries "it is often more a matter of strained relations between centers of interest than whole countries." We have seen these forces at work from South Africa to Korea as one pressure group after another steps around national governments to further its own crusade.

The convergence of computers and telecommunications has made us into a global community, ready or not. For the first time in history, rich and poor, north and south, east and west, city and countryside are linked in a global electronic network of shared images in real time. Ideas move across borders as if they did not exist. Indeed, time zones are becoming more important than borders.

The convergence of computers and telecommunications has made us into a global community.

Small villages are known as efficient marketplaces of ideas. A village quickly shares news of any innovation, and if anyone gets a raise or new privileges, everyone similarly situated will soon be pressing for the same. And why not? These people are just like me, the villagers say. Why should I not have what they have? The Internet carries conversations between millions of people without regard to gender, race, or color. The impact of the global conversation, like that of a village conversation, is enormous—and it is multiplied many times.

A global village will have global customs. Denying people human rights or democratic freedoms no longer means denying them an abstraction they have never experienced, but violating the established customs of the village. It hardly matters that only a minority of the world's people enjoy such freedoms or the prosperity that goes with them; these are now the benchmarks. More and more people around the globe are demanding more say in their own destiny. Once people are convinced that this is possible, an enormous burden of proof falls on those who would deny them.

The global conversation puts pressure on sovereign governments that over time will influence political processes all over the world. The information revolution is thus profoundly threatening to the power structures of the world, and with good reason. In Prague in 1988 the first protesters in the streets looked into CNN cameras and chanted at the riot police, "The world sees you." And it did. It was an anomaly of history that other Eastern Europeans watched the revolution on CNN relayed by a Russian satellite and mustered the courage to rebel against their own sovereigns. All this has confirmed Abraham Lincoln's sentiment, expressed on his way to his first inauguration, that the American Declaration of Independence "gave liberty not alone to the people of this country, but hope to all the world, for all future time." At the time Lincoln spoke, his words were heard by only a handful of people. It is a testament to his prescience that changes he could not have imagined have brought his words, and freedom itself, to unprecedented portions of humanity.

A NEW SOURCE OF WEALTH

The flood of real-time data has also transformed the international economy. The depth of the global market renders economic theory based on national markets suspect. In the world's financial markets, sovereign governments have lost the ability to influence the price others will pay for their currency on anything but a momentary basis. When I started in the banking business, the total foreign exchange market in New York was only about $50 million. If the Federal Reserve called Citibank or Chase and instructed them to sell $10 million, an order that size could move the market. Today, the market is $1 trillion, and central bank intervention in foreign exchange becomes an expensive exercise in futility. The market is a giant voting machine that records in real time the judgment of traders all over the world about American diplomatic, fiscal, and monetary policies. It has created an information standard that is far more rapid and draconian than the gold standard ever was. Moments after a president announces a policy in the Rose Garden, the market's judgment is reflected in the price of the dollar.

Information technology has also produced a new source of wealth that is not material; it is information—knowledge applied to work to create value. When we apply knowledge to ongoing tasks, we increase productivity. When we apply it to new tasks, we create innovation. The pursuit of wealth is now largely the pursuit of information and its application to the means of production. The rules, customs, skills, and talents necessary to uncover, capture, produce, preserve, and exploit information are now humankind's most important. The competition for the best information has replaced the competition for the best farmland or coal fields. In fact, the appetite to annex territory has already attenuated, and major powers have withdrawn from previously occupied territories.

The new economic powerhouses are masters not of huge material resources, but of ideas and technology. The way the market values companies is instructive: it now places a higher value on intellectual capital than on hard assets like bricks and mortar. Microsoft, with only a relatively small amount of fixed assets, now has a market capitalization well in excess of Ford, General Motors, and Chrysler combined, all of which have huge bases. The powerful economies of Singapore and Hong Kong, countries with virtually no physical assets, demonstrate the growing irrelevance of territory to wealth. This shift requires a different management structure and mindset, and affects not only individual companies, but entire nations.

The new economic powerhouses are masters of ideas and technology.

The changing perception of what constitutes an asset poses huge problems in expanding or even maintaining the power of government. Unlike land or industrial plants, information resources are not bound to geography or easily taxed and controlled by governments. In an economy that consists largely of information products, the government's power to tax and regulate erodes rapidly. Our laws and systems of measurement are becoming artifacts of another age. Bill Gates, with the skills to write and market a complex software system that can produce $1 billion of revenue, can walk past a customs officer anywhere in the world with nothing of "value" to declare, but his wife might have to pay duty on her new ring. Bad data produces bad decisions and leaves us puzzled as to why old policies no longer work. The measures of the industrial society, which count the number of railroad brakemen but do not record the number of computer programmers, highlight a growing problem in setting policy. As DNA research reveals more precise understandings about the way a living organism functions than gross observations of developed biological structures, so we need more precise measures of how nations and companies function in our new environment.

INFORMATION DOMINANCE

These changes affect not only the civilian production machine on which our economic strength rests, but also our military capabilities. In science, there used to be two ways to proceed: the first was to construct a theory, and the second was to conduct a physical experiment. Today we have a third: computer simulation. In the Persian Gulf War, for example, young, basically inexperienced Americans defeated Iraq's feared Republican Guards. A retired colonel asked one commander: "How do you account for your dramatic success, when not a single officer or man in your entire outfit ever had combat experience?" "But we were experienced," said the commander. "We had fought such engagements six times before in complete battle simulation at the National Training Center and in Germany."[3] The U. S. military today is a spectacular example of the replacement of physical assets by information. Information, to be sure, has often made the difference between victory and defeat. Where is the enemy located? How many troops are involved? How are they armed? What is new is the ease and accuracy with which such questions can be answered.

Military intelligence has become much more complex and even has a new name: "information dominance." Today Apache helicopters flying over Bosnia upload detailed pictures of action on the ground to a satellite, record them with a video camera, or beam them directly to local headquarters. Videos taken from the air verify the Dayton accords. Major General William Nash observed that in Bosnia, "We don't have arguments. We hand them pictures, and they move their tanks." This is a long way from 1943, when analysts were hunting through the stacks of the Library of Congress for maps and photographs of possible German targets for Allied bombers since few, if any, were available in the War Department. Today even the ground troops on patrol are equipped with night vision goggles and use a hand-held Global Positioning System device to pinpoint their exact position from satellites. Because the soil is strewn with mines, knowing exactly where you are is a matter of life and death even when there is no fighting. Mines that have been located by an airborne mine detection system are exploded by remotely controlled drone Panther tanks. And so in the military as in civilian life, information in all its forms is replacing hard assets.

Reliance on information technology also has dangerous downsides. The American information infrastructure, in the words of the recent *Report of the Defense Science Board Task Force on Information Warfare*, is "vulnerable to attack" and "creates a tunnel of vulnerability previously unrealized in the history of conflict." Rogue states and groups can conduct information warfare even though they do not command a large military establishment. Today we are witnessing guerrilla warfare, ethnic conflicts, and active terrorist groups. As the Task Force notes:

> Offensive information warfare is attractive to many because it is cheap in relation to the cost of developing, maintaining, and using advanced military capabilities. It may cost little to suborn an insider, create false information, manipulate information, or launch malicious logic-based weapons against an information system connected to the globally shared telecommunications infrastructure. The latter is particularly attractive; the latest information on how to exploit many of the design attributes and security flaws of commercial computer software is freely available on the Internet.

Adversaries, both real and potential, have a lot to work with since the Department of Defense has over two million computers, over 10,000 local-area networks, and over 100 long-distance networks that coordinate and implement every element of its missions, from weapons design to battlefield management. During the calendar year 1995, up to 200,000 intrusions may have been made into the DOD's unclassified computers. These intruders "have modified, stolen and destroyed data and software and shut down computers and networks." Effective diplomacy at critical junctures in any age is backed by the knowledge that if all else fails, military force can be used to attain national goals.

Therefore, vulnerability to an attack on information infrastructure is attracting the attention of a presidential commission and numerous task forces. But with about 90 percent of our military traffic moving over public computer networks, it is increasingly hard to tell the military from the civilian infrastructure. The bureaucratic distinctions between intelligence and law enforcement, between permitted surveillance at home and abroad, may be unsuited for information warfare. There are no borders in cyberspace to mandate these distinctions. The smallest nation, terrorist group, or drug cartel could hire a computer programmer to plant a Trojan horse virus in software, take down a vital network, or cause a missile to misfire. Voltaire said: "God is always for the big battalions." In this new world he may be wrong. The United States' increasing reliance on massive networks may make it more, not less vulnerable.

It may even be unclear what constitutes an act of war. If U. S. satellites suddenly go blind and the telephone network on the eastern seaboard goes down, it is possible that the United States could not even identify the enemy. Its strategic stockpile of weapons would be of little use. There would be no big factory to bomb—only a person somewhere writing software. The possibility of an electronic Pearl Harbor has sparked a debate on how to counter the threat. The Commission on Critical Infrastructure Protection established by President Clinton's executive order is a step in the right direction and has been described in Senate testimony "as the equivalent of the Manhattan Project." It will work at the crossroads of the First Amendment and national security, at the vortex of personal privacy through encryption and the National Security Agency's desire to breach it, and at the frontier of what Sun Tzu two millennia ago described as "vanquishing the enemy without fighting."

VIRTUAL LEADERSHIP

We live in revolutionary times, as did the Founding Fathers. They exhibited a keen interest in technology

—provision for copyright and patent protection was written into the Constitution itself. This provision was implemented by an act of Congress in 1790 creating a patent board consisting of the secretary of state, the secretary of war, and the attorney general. It was a prestigious group: Thomas Jefferson, Henry Knox, and Edmund Randolph. That board is long gone and the schism between the diplomat and the scientist has grown wider at the very time it is becoming more and more important that the two understand each other. Because so much change in the current revolution is driven by technology, our task in mastering these new forces is made more complex by the difficulty of communicating across disciplines. Diplomats, trained in the humanities, often tend to validate C. P. Snow's famous lecture on "Two Cultures," in which he argued that scientists and humanists are ignorant of each other's knowledge and are content to stay that way. Many diplomatic historians have minimized or even ignored the impact of scientific discoveries on the course of history, preferring instead to follow the great man theory or look for the historical tides that carry the world along. Indeed, the indexes of many standard texts on diplomatic history do not even include the words "technology" or "economics."

An expert is a person with great knowledge about a legacy system— indeed there are no experts on the future. Henry Kissinger observed in *Diplomacy* that "most foreign policies that history has marked highly, in whatever country, have been originated by leaders who were opposed by experts. It is, after all, the responsibility of the expert to operate the familiar and that of the leader to transcend it." During World War I, an aide-de-camp to British Field Marshal Douglas Haig, after seeing a tank demonstration, commented, "The idea that cavalry will be replaced by these iron coaches is absurd. It is little short of treasonous." In the United States, the ridicule and court-martial of Brigadier General Billy Mitchell, when he postulated the importance of air power by offering to sink a battleship, is instructive. Secretary of War Newton D. Baker thought so little of the idea that he was "willing to stand on the bridge of a battleship while that nitwit tries to hit it from the air." Indeed this recurring phenomenon was encapsulated in Arthur Clarke's First Law, cited in his *Profiles of the Future*: "When a distinguished but elderly scientist states that something is possible he is almost certainly right. When he states that something is impossible, he is very probably wrong." In the case of U.S. national security, a refusal to take note of real change in the world is a recipe for disaster.

The new technology will not go away—it will only get better in accordance with Moore's law, which postulates that microchips will double in density and speed every 18 months. Bandwidth will grow even faster. The third technological revolution has brought about immense global prosperity. Contrary to the doomsayers who postulated that the world would run out of resources by the year 2000, it is difficult to find a single commodity that is worth more in real terms today than it was ten years ago. Knowledge, once an ornament displayed by the rich and powerful at conferences, now combines with management skills to produce wealth. The vast increase of knowledge has brought with it a huge increase in the ability to manipulate matter, increasing its value by the power of the mind and generating new products and substances unknown in nature and undreamed of only a few years ago. In the past, when the method of creating wealth changed, old power structures lost influence, new ones arose, and every facet of society was affected. As we can already see the beginning of that process in this revolution, one can postulate that in the next few decades the attraction and management of intellectual capital will determine which institutions and nations will survive and prosper, and which will not.

But despite all of the advances of science and the ways in which it is changing the world, science does not remake the human mind or alter the power of the human spirit. There is still no substitute for courage and leadership in confronting the new problems and opportunities that our world presents. What has changed dramatically is the amount of information available to our policymakers. One hopes that the data processed by the minds of trained diplomats will produce real knowledge, and with enough experience, wisdom. Wisdom has always been in short supply, but it will be sorely needed in the days and years ahead, because in the words of former President Richard Nixon, "Only people can solve problems people create."

NOTES

1. Henry M. Wriston, *Prepare for Peace*, New York: Harper & Bros., 1941, P. 237.
2. George Gilder, "Over the Paradigm Cliff," *ASAP*, February 1997, p. 29.
3. Kevin Kelly, *Out of Control: The Rise of a Neo-Biological Civilization*, Reading, MA: Addison-Wesley, 1994, p. 246.

Walter B. Wriston, former Chairman and Chief Executive Officer of Citicorp/Citibank, served as Chairman of the Economic Policy Advisory Board in the Reagan Administration.

PART 12

Working with the
World Wide Web

In this part, you will find the following:

- WebLinks: A Directory of Annotated Web Sites
- How to Cite a Web Site
- Web Journal
- Web Site Evaluation Form
- Reading Review Form

For each Web site listed in the directory, you have been provided with a site **name,** site **address** (or Universal Resource Locator), and a brief **description** of what can be found at each site. Each site has been numbered for easy reference and referral, and the sites are listed alphabetically by site name.

Before accessing these Web sites, you may want to review **Readings 1–3** at the front of the book. They contain useful background information on the technology of the Web and how to make the most of your time online. You may also want to review the **Quick Reference Guide to Topics/Readings/Web Sites,** which coordinates readings with Web sites.

The Web Site Evaluation Form can be used in any of a number of ways. Use the questions on the form to guide your work on a Web site. Or ask your professor if you can fill out the Web Site Evaluation Form and turn it in for extra credit in your course. The Web Journal can be used as your personal address book for making notes about sites you have visited. You can record your reactions to a site and briefly note what you find.

WebLinks:
A Directory of Annotated Web Sites

[For your convenience, the **Quick Reference Guide to Topics/Readings/World Wide Web Sites** at the front of the book correlates the readings in the book with Web sites from the directory that follows. Also, please review the description of *Updates to WebLinks (http://www.morton-pub.com/updates/updates.stml)* that appears in the front of the book in the section **A Note from the Publisher** for additional information about Web sites.]

A

Affirmative Action Special Report   No. 1

http://www.washingtonpost.com/wp-srv/politics/special/affirm/affirm.htm

This site is maintained by the *Washington Post* and features an extensive collection of articles chronicling various developments in the ongoing controversy over affirmative action. It is uncomplicated to surf through and provides a background and history about affirmative action as well as links to other sources.

Amendments Never Ratified for the U. S. Constitution   No. 2

http://www.law.emory.edu/pub-cgi/print_hit_bold.pl/FEDERAL/usconst/notamend.html

The text and history of six amendments that were proposed but not ratified are presented. Links are included to text-only sites detailing the United States Constitution and ratified amendments.

American Civil Liberties Union   No. 3

http://www.aclu.org

This exhaustive page from the American Civil Liberties Union (ACLU) contains news about civil liberties in the courts, in Congress, in the executive branch and in the states. A search engine allows for open-ended or more restrictive exploration within the site. The ACLU's position on virtually every civil liberties issue imaginable is included.

American Politics   No. 4

http://www.sfsu.edu/~polisci/amer.html

San Francisco State University provides a starting point for researching many subjects within American politics. No text is included: however, a variety of links lead to useful information.

American Voter: Rate Your Rep   No. 5

http://voter.cq.com/cq_rate.htm

This site allows you to compare the votes cast by a representative with your own beliefs, based on your answers to 10 questions. The site, sponsored by *Congressional Quarterly*, features the opportunity to search for votes cast by elected official, subject matter and/or within a specific time period. Press information on the bills and issues, and links to the latest key votes in the House of Representatives and Senate, are included.

Americans Talk Issues Foundation   No. 6

http://www.auburn.edu/tann/ati/

This site of the Teledemocracy Action News + Network (TAN+N) outlines the Americans Talk Issues Foundation's innovative polling method, deliberative polling. This scientific random-sample method is explained, and tests to validate the methods and results are included. It is an interesting site that compares the elements and advantages of deliberative polling to the elements and disadvantages of conventional polling.

Americans United for Affirmative Action   No. 7

http://www.auaa.org/

Cofounded by the son of Martin Luther King, Jr., Americans United for Affirmative Action (AUAA) fights to retain affirmative action. The site contains news about developments in affirmative action, arguments in favor of it, information about civil rights in general, and links to related sites.

Anti-Stadium   No. 8

http://www.resonator.com/stad/s_issues.htm

This forum against stadium construction is presented by Grassroots Against Government Mandated Entertainment (GAGME). The site contains an incredible amount of information about stadium construction nationwide, and includes links to essays, articles, and other sources opposing such construction.

Apologizing for Slavery: History in the News No. 9
🌐 http://www.hurleyweb.com/hns/slavery.shtml

This brief, text-only page reviews the debate about apologizing for slavery and puts it into an historical context. Written by a history teacher, this page is part of a larger Web site, *History in the News (http://www.h-net.msu.edu/~hns/)*, which was founded in 1996 to "improve the public's understanding of current events by setting these events in their historical contexts."

APSANet: The American Political Science Association On-Line No. 10
http://www.apsanet.org

Maintained by the American Political Science Association (APSA), a professional society, this site is easy to navigate and contains lots of useful, timely materials. Links provide bridges to association information, details on how and where to access volumes of *American Political Science Review* online, and connections to *PSonline* where special features and articles on current subjects from the APSA journal of record, *PS: Political Science and Politics*, can be found.

Are New Stadiums Worth the Cost? No. 11
🌐 http://www.brook.edu/pub/review/summer97/noll.htm

This excerpt from a book by two economics professors concludes that new stadiums are not worth the cost. It is provided on the Web by The Brookings Institution, an organization that functions as an independent analyst and critic. Details on the complete text are available.

The Articles of Confederation— The U. S. Constitution Online No. 12
🌐 http://www.usconstitution.net/articles.html

The Articles of Confederation (the Preamble, all the Articles, the conclusion, and the list of signatories) are available at this site. These pages are part of a larger, comprehensive site devoted to all things regarding the U. S. Constitution.

B

Ballparks No. 13
🌐 http://www.ballparks.com/

A site for sports lovers. Much information about baseball, football, basketball and hockey stadiums is provided. Pictures are included. No politics here—just an ode to the majesty of stadiums.

C

California State University, Los Angeles: Department of Political Science No. 14
🌐 http://www.calstatela.edu/dept/pol_sci/index.htm

A general overview of what political scientists do is featured on this page from California State University. The site is a good source for understanding the field, getting ideas for topics to study further, and acquiring career information.

Campaign Finance Information Center No. 15
🌐 http://www.campaignfinance.org/

The Campaign Finance Information Center (CFIC) site includes a very extensive collection of articles and databases about campaign finance, and access to the newsletter, *CFIC Tracker*. Although the site is intended for journalists, there is plenty of information for anyone interested in the subject. Links to Freedom of Information sites and other sources of political contribution data are available.

CAPWEB: The Internet Guide to the U. S. Congress No. 16
🌐 http://www.capweb.net/classic/index.morph

This easily navigable page is full of useful, informative details about all facets of government. Topics relating to the Senate, the House, and all three branches of government are broken down into subgroups for quick selection. News from Capitol Hill is also included.

A Catalog of New U. S. Unilateral Economic Sanctions for Foreign Policy Purposes 1993–96 No. 17
🌐 http://usaengage.org/studies/nam.html

USA*ENGAGE, representing American business and agriculture, presents a report from the National Association of Manufacturers (NAM) that outlines all economic sanctions the United States has imposed on other nations in the time period indicated and why manufacturers oppose such sanctions. Detail is provided on measures adopted to promote the following objectives: human rights and democratization, anti-terrorism, nuclear non-proliferation, political stability, anti-narcotics, worker rights/use of prison labor, and environmental protection. Press releases, news clippings, related studies, and recommendations for future policy reforms are included. Links to sites on international trade and other issues are available.

Celebration: A Town Is Born No. 18
🌐 http://homearts.com/cl/decorate/57celfl.htm

Hearst Communications posts this essay about the Disney community, Celebration, FL. A description of the town, pictures and a "virtual walking tour" are available.

Center for the Defense of Free Enterprise No. 19
🌐 http://www.eskimo.com/%7Earnold/index.html

The Center for the Defense of Free Enterprise argues that economic development should take precedence over government regulation and environmental protection. They advocate "wise use" of nature rather than "preservation without use."

The Center for Deliberative Polling No. 20
🌐 http://www.la.utexas.edu/research/delpol/cdpindex.html

The University of Texas conducted an experiment very much like that described in Reading 19, "Democracy in Texas." The site contains news and announcements about deliberative polling events. Videos of past polls are available. Statistical data on poll results before and after deliberation is included. The page links to related sites.

Center for the Study of Federalism — No. 21

● http://www.temple.edu/federalism/

The International Association of Centers for Federal Studies (IACFS), established to promote the study and understanding of federal principles and patterns, maintains this site. Abstracts from *Publius: The Journal of Federalism* are available. Many links to similar sites are provided.

China's Most Favored Nation Trade Status — No. 22

● http://policy.com/issuewk/97/0623/index.html

Policy.com presents this searchable public policy resource site. Lots of information is provided on the following topics: economic statistics, human rights facts, most favored nation legislation details and impact on foreign policy. The debate between supporters and opposers is featured. Links to related sources are available.

Christian Coalition — No. 23

● http://www.cc.org/

This is the official site of the conservative interest group. It features legislative updates, news releases, and articles from the organization's publication *Religious Rights Watch* and *Christian American*. A "scorecard" of how members of Congress vote on religious and family issues is also provided. Audio files of the Christian Coalition's weekly television show is available through RealAudio™. Links to related federal, voter education, and pro-family pages are included.

Citizens Against Government Waste — No. 24

● http://www.govt-waste.org/

Citizens Against Government Waste is devoted to exposing projects that lead to waste, fraud, and abuse in government. Essays outlining specific concerns, a press release archive, and other reports are included. Information on the voting records of members of Congress, and suggested budget cuts with detailed explanations and realized savings are featured.

Citizens Against Government Waste: Pork Patrol — No. 25

● http://www. govt-waste.org/porkpatrol.htm

The searchable site from Citizens Against Government Waste (CAGW) lists what the organization considers to be the 302 most wasteful projects in 1998. A roster of 1998 Oinker Award winners, a state-by-state ranking of pork dollars per capita, and related press releases are also featured.

Citizens for Leaders with Ethics and Accountability Now/Stadiums — No. 26

● http://www.clean.org/welfare/stadiums/

Maintained by the Citizens for Leaders with Ethics and Accountability Now (CLEAN), this page features a fantastic list of links to information about sports stadiums. Many of the available articles center on stadium issues in Seattle, WA, including a lease agreement between the city and the Seattle Mariners.

The Civil Rights Project — No. 27

● http://www.law.harvard.edu/groups/civilrights/

This five-year project at Harvard University addresses issues of racial justice through conferences and academic research. This Web page is mainly an overview of the project. Links to many civil rights sites are available.

The Committee to Impeach the President — No. 28

● http://www.impeachclinton.org/

The Clinton Investigative Commission (CIC) maintains this site, which contains some of President William Clinton's alleged misdeeds. Outlines of impeachment grounds and procedures, excerpts from President Richard Nixon's impeachment, and details of the House Judiciary Constitution Subcommittee Hearing on Impeachment are featured. Links to the Starr Report and Clinton's testimony are available.

Common Cause — No. 29

● http://www.commoncause.org/

Common Cause is a non-partisan lobbying group that promotes ethics in government. Although the organization is working towards ethics reform, civil rights, and accountability in government, the site focuses mainly on campaign finance reform. Significant amounts of searchable information, current and archived news releases, and an online survey are available. Links to other government reform sites are included.

The Complete Internet Researcher: Excerpt on the Accuracy of Internet Resources — No. 30

● http://www.aallnet.org/products/crab/blackman.htm

The American Association of Law Libraries presents this excerpt from Josh Blackman's *How to Use the Internet for Legal Research*. The advantages and pitfalls of doing research on the Web are explored. Detailed articles are available on how to determine if material is complete and accurate, how information errors occur, skills for using the Internet and search engines, and more. This exhaustive site includes links to related sources.

Congressional Quarterly: Campaign Finance — No. 31

● http://cnn.com/ALLPOLITICS/1997/04/09/cq/campaign.finance/index.html

This searchable site provides a collection of information about campaign finance, including a history of campaign finance legislation and a discussion of Supreme Court decisions relating to the issue. A glossary of terms and survey results from informal, online polls are included. Archives of articles from *Congressional Quarterly* are available at this CNN/Time ALLPOLITICS page.

Constitution Finder — No. 32

● http://www.richmond.edu/~jpjones/confinder/

The University of Richmond presents this links-only page. An alphabetical index to constitutions, amendments, charters and related documents can be searched by nation or state.

The Constitution of the United States — No. 33

● http://www.access.gpo.gov/congress/senate/constitution/toc.html

This online copy of the Constitution, sponsored by the United States Senate, includes historical notes, text of the Constitution and amendments, details of proposed amendments, and extensive annotations to relevant court cases, statutes and commentary. Annotations are provided by the Library of Congress.

Contract with America — No. 34

● http://speakernews.house.gov/contract.htm

This site contains the text of the key Republican document when the Republicans swept to power in 1994. A link leads to a Republican page promoting their issues.

C-Span   No. 35

🌐 http://www. c-span.org/

This searchable site from the non-commercial cable network has extensive information on Congress and other branches of government. Plenty of informative details on governmental issues of all kinds are provided. Visitors can watch C-Span live online and view videos of selected past events with RealPlayer™.

D

Democratic Leadership Council   No. 36

🌐 http://www.dlcppi.org/

The Democratic Leadership Council (DLC), cofounded by William Clinton, shares its site with the Progressive Policy Institute (PPI). The page is the home for moderate Democrats and contains news, DLC positions and briefings, and the texts of speeches by DLC members. Access to archives of DLC publications, *The New Democrat* and *The DLC Update*, are available.

Democratic National Committee   No. 37

🌐 http://www.democrats.org/index.html

This is the official site of the national Democratic Party. The page contains press releases, current briefings and news archives. Democratic positions on issues and the contrasting Republican agenda are featured. Links to the Democratic Party at the state and county level are included.

Directory of Federalism Links   No. 38

🌐 http://www.infidels.org/~nap/index.federalism.html

Roughly 30 links to essays and sites relating to federalism topics or issues are found on this page. No text is available.

E

The Economist OnLine   No. 39

🌐 http://www.economist.com

The Economist is a British news weekly that provides good coverage of worldwide current events, politics, and economics. At this site you can get a summary of the world's main events at *Politics This Week*. Should you choose to subscribe to the site, you can also access an archive of articles.

Electronic Privacy Information Center   No. 40

🌐 http://epic.org/

This searchable site is presented by the Electronic Privacy Information Center (EPIC). Articles on privacy protection and censorship, information on online privacy, images of declassified government documents, and access to *The Epic Alert* newsletter are available. Links to related sites are included.

Electronic Resources for Political Scientists   No. 41

🌐 http://www.cc.columbia.edu/cu/polisci/resources. page/technimain.html

Columbia University's Department of Political Science provides links to a variety of resources in American politics, comparative politics, international relations, political theory and methodology. Access to political science journals is also available.

Ethics in the News   No. 42

🌐 http://www.lobbyistdirectory.com/ethxnews.htm

The Council for Ethics in Legislative Advocacy (CELA) presents this site that highlights ethical violations by lobbyists. It contains an extensive collection of articles about shady practices and lobbying industry ethics organized by state. A copy of an ethics pledge for self-regulation endorsed by CELA and links to a national directory of lobbyists is included.

F

Fairness and Accuracy in Reporting   No. 43

🌐 http://www.fair.org/

Is the media liberal? Fairness and Accuracy in Reporting (FAIR) doesn't think so. It argues that the media has a conservative bias. The searchable site details what's wrong with the news, illustrates alleged stereotypes, presents current news, analyzes the treatment of international news and evaluates media outlets.

Families Against Mandatory Minimums   No. 44

🌐 http://www.famm.org/home.htm

Families Against Mandatory Minimums (FAMM) takes the position that mandatory minimum sentences for drug possession send people to jail for too long and are mostly used against minorities. The site contains a history of mandatory minimum sentences and features a chart outlining federal minimums. Descriptions of some case studies of mandatory sentences, *The FAMM-gram* newsletter, and links to legal resources are included.

Family Research Council   No. 45

🌐 http://www. frc.org/frc/home.html

This searchable site is provided by the conservative, religious-interest group Family Research Council. It features news releases, reports, and information about education, drugs, the military, family issues, and abortion from a Christian perspective. Current news is available on RealAudio™. Articles from the organization's publications, including *Perspective, Family Policy and Washington Watch*, can be accessed online. Loads of links to related pages are included.

Federal Emergency Management Agency   No. 46

🌐 http://www.fema.gov/

This extremely thorough site is maintained by the Federal Emergency Management Agency (FEMA). It provides up-to-date details on pending and recent natural disasters and the federal government's response to them. Information on every emergency and solution imaginable is featured. An alphabetical index makes searching by topic simple and quick. Hundreds of related sites can be accessed under the Global Emergency Management System (GEMS) page.

Federal Gang Violence Act   No. 47

🌐 http://www.senate.gov/member/ca/feinstein/ general/gangs.html

This site contains the text of and information about the federal anti-gang legislation introduced by Senator Orrin Hatch (R-UT) and Senator Dianne Feinstein (D-CA). Press releases on gangs and gang legislation are available for review. The page is sponsored by Senator Dianne Feinstein.

The Federal Reserve System   No. 48

🌐 http://woodrow.mpls.frb.fed.us/info/sys/index.html

An overview of the history and purpose of the Federal Reserve System is presented at this site, which features a search function. Essays on related topics, articles on banking issues and access to publications are available. Economic data and statistics are provided. Links to other sources are included.

The Federal Web Locator   No. 49

🌐 http://www.law.vill.edu/Fed-Agency/fedwebloc.html

Provided by the Center for Information Law and Policy, this site offers "one-stop shopping" for information on the federal government. The search function is easy to use to quickly find topics of interest. Links are available to most government offices and agencies, non-governmental federally related organizations and international sites for associations such as the United Nations and the World Bank.

The Federalist Papers   No. 50

🌐 http://www.jim.com/jamesd/federal.ist/index.htm

From the site: "The Federalist Papers were first published on October 27, 1787, in the New York newspapers to defend and promote the ratification of the new U. S. Constitution." This site contains all 85 of the Federalist Papers, which are indexed by number. An easily searchable primary source site.

The Federalist Society for Law and Public Studies   No. 51

🌐 http://www.fed-soc.org/

A conservative legal group, The Federalist Society believes that judges should interpret the Constitution as the Framers thought it was meant in 1787. Their site contains selected articles that support or explain their beliefs, perspectives on current cases and features written on issues pertaining to the American Bar Association. Links to chapter Web pages at universities around the nation are available.

Foreign Affairs   No. 52

🌐 http://www.foreignaffairs.org/

Easy to search site contains documents on foreign relations, and summaries and full text of articles from the *Foreign Affairs* journal. Links connect to over 75 related sites.

Freshman Learn to Love Pork Barrel   No. 53

🌐 http://search.nando.net/newsroom/nao/nc/070696/nc02_13949.html

This text-only site features an article about how some freshman members of Congress vow to slash government waste but end up following predecessors into the pork-barrel spending trap. The document was originally published in *The News & Observer* of Raleigh, NC.

G

The Gallup Poll   No. 54

🌐 http://www.gallup.com

America's leading polling organization, Gallup, presents this searchable site. A wealth of information is provided including an in-depth outline on the types of research performed, how polls are conducted and the results of the latest public opinion polls. Details as to how polling 1,000 people can yield accurate results are illustrated. Public releases, special reports and archived articles are also available.

The Guardian of Liberalism: America, Cigars, and Arthur M. Schlesinger, Jr.   No. 55

🌐 http://www.cigaraficionado.com/Cigar/Aficionado/Archives/199509/fc995.html

This site contains a profile of historian Arthur Schlesinger that was published in an issue of *Cigar Aficionado*. No links are provided.

H

Houghton Mifflin Documents Collection/ American Government   No. 56

🌐 http://www.hmco.com/cgi-bin/college/polisci/amgov/doc_collection/bin/amgov

Houghton Mifflin offers this page as a reference tool that corresponds by chapter topic to textbooks on American government. The site can be searched by subject to find links to Web pages relating to political science.

House of Representatives   No. 57

🌐 http://www.house.gov/

The official site of the House of Representatives contains information on members of the House and how to contact them, roll call votes since 1990, information on committees, the House schedule and current issues brought to the floor. Details on bills and resolutions being considered are presented. Links are provided to related governmental and educational pages.

I

Inaugural Addresses of the Presidents of the United States   No. 58

🌐 http://www.cc.columbia.edu/acis/bartleby/inaugural/

This Web page contains the text of every presidential inaugural address from George Washington to President William Clinton. Initial commentary provides a quick background on the president and/or the day of inauguration, helping to set the tone for the speech. The site is sponsored by Columbia University's Bartleby Library.

The Independent Counsel Law   No. 59

🌐 http://www.law.cornell.edu/uscode/28/ch40.html

The text of the actual law that authorized the appointment of independent counsels is featured at this site. The text-only page is a service of the Legal Information Institute (LII).

Index to the Anti-Federalist Papers   No. 60

🌐 http://www.wepin.com/articles/afp/index.html

Historical essays on why the Constitution should not have been ratified are included among similar topics at this site maintained by the West El Paso Information Network (WEPIN). This libertarian organization supports the idea of sovereign individuals, believing that government should be subservient to the individuals it serves.

The Internet Public Library/Ready Reference Collection   No. 61

🌐 http://www.ipl.org/ref/RR/

This searchable site provides an overview on many political science topics. Subjects can be narrowed down by category for more specific details. Links to other sites are available.

L

Latino National Political Survey No. 62

🌐 http://www.iprnet.org/IPR/library.html#LNPS

Sponsored by the Institute for Puerto Rican Policy (IPR), this site allows you to download the results of the largest privately funded household survey of United States Latino political attitudes and behavior. Although conducted in 1989–90, making the material somewhat dated, variables include cultural and linguistic characteristics, political values, public policy perspectives and ethnic attitudes. The page is text-only with downloadable files containing the introduction, questionnaires used and data collected.

Latino Voters Break the Trend No. 63

🌐 http://www.citizenparticipation.org/html/f96gonzalez.html

This essay, posted on a page from the Founders' Committee for Citizen Participation, discusses increased Latino turnout in the 1996 election. The article, written by Antonio Gonzalez, president of the Southwest Voter Registration Education Project and the Southwest Voter Research Institute, is strictly text. However, the site is searchable and has links to other pages dealing with citizen participation.

Legal Information Institute No. 64

🌐 http://supct.law.cornell.edu/supct/index.html

The Legal Information Institute (LII) "offers Supreme Court opinions under the auspices of Project Hermes, the court's electronic dissemination project." The site is searchable and includes an alphabetical list of historic cases. Information on 580 of the most important decisions of the court as well as archived opinions of the court since 1990 are featured. Details on the Supreme Court calendar and a schedule of oral arguments can be found. Links to similar sites are included.

M

Media Research Center No. 65

🌐 http://www.mrc.org/

The Media Research Center (MRC) is a conservative media watchdog group dedicated to exposing liberal bias in the press. Their site contains regular news updates, special reports or reviews on the media and its subjects, a compilation of outrageous and humorous media quotes, and information from MRC's news and entertainment divisions. Access to articles from the center's publications, *MediaNomics* and *MediaWatch*, are available. Links are included to Conservative News Service, Parents Television Council, and Conservative Communications Center.

Morrison v. Olson No. 66

🌐 http://caselaw.findlaw.com/scripts/getcase.pl?court=US&vol=487&invol=654

Text of the Supreme Court case in which the Court upheld the constitutionality of the Independent Counsel Law is available on this page. Justice Scalia's dissent is particularly interesting. The site, which is primarily text, includes the opportunity to search other cases.

"Most Favored Nation Status for China Promotes Freedom" No. 67

🌐 http://majoritywhip.house.gov/china970624MFN.asp

This site contains the speech given by Representative Tom DeLay (R-TX) on June 24, 1997, arguing that China should retain Most Favored Nation status. Text only; no links are available.

N

The Nation: Digital Edition No. 68

🌐 http://www.thenation.com/home.htm

Founded in 1865, *The Nation* is a weekly magazine that provides a forum for discussion of political and social issues. The Nation Digital Edition electronically provides selected articles and essays from the issues and includes a searchable archive. RadioNation, a weekly radio show, is available with RealAudio™.

National Abortion and Reproductive Rights Action League No. 69

🌐 http://www.naral.org

This searchable site is hosted by the leading pro-choice organization, National Abortion and Reproductive Rights Action League (NARAL). The page includes information on abortion and reproductive health issues, news releases and factsheets providing a quick look at reproductive health, and the real-life stories of women and families who faced reproductive issues. Details on federal initiatives and the text of the *Roe v. Wade* decision are included. Links to related articles and sites.

National Association for the Advancement of Colored People No. 70

🌐 http://www.naacp.org/

The official site of the National Association for the Advancement of Colored People (NAACP) contains news and press releases about civil rights and activities. Issue alerts and links to similar sites are included.

National Association of Latino Elected Officials No. 71

🌐 http://www.naleo.org/

The National Association of Latino Elected Officials (NALEO) is devoted to increasing political participation among the Latino community. Their site contains press releases and related newsclips, and information on the National Hispanic Leadership Agenda. The Web page is somewhat limited, but continues to grow.

National Center for Policy Analysis/Privatization No. 72

🌐 http://www.public-policy.org/%7Encpa/pd/private/privat.html

This site presents an argument in favor of privatization from the National Center for Policy Analysis (NCPA). Essays in support of privatizing many currently government-run industries and examples of privatization worldwide are included. Articles on successful privatization as well as articles outlining deterrents to privatization are also available.

National Center for State Courts No. 73

🌐 http://www.ncsc.dni.us/

This site from the National Center for State Courts (NCSC) is searchable, and contains details and statistics on state court administrations. Current news and links to similar pages are available.

National Conference of State Legislatures — No. 74

🌐 http://www.ncsl.org/

This searchable site features information about state legislatures, state legislative policies, and relations between federal and state governments. Links are provided to related pages. The site is maintained by the National Conference of State Legislatures (NCSL).

National Governors Association — No. 75

🌐 http://www.nga.org/

This comprehensive site from the National Governors Association (NGA) furnishes information on specific states and governors as well as general detail on the position of governor. Key state issues are outlined. Press releases, issues papers, supported policies and links to related sites are available.

National Institute on Drug Abuse — No. 76

🌐 http://www.nida.nih.gov/NIDAHome.html

The National Institute on Drug Abuse (NIDA) is part of the National Institutes of Health. This organization fights to reduce the use of legal and illegal drugs. Their searchable site features a large quantity of information on the physiological, psychological and economic damage that can occur with drug abuse. Reports, congressional testimonies, media advisories and articles from the newsletter *NIDA Notes* are available. Research reports on addictions, therapies, and preventions are included. Links to related sites are provided.

National Issues Convention — No. 77

🌐 http://www.pbs.org/nic

The Public Broadcasting System sponsored this "experiment in democracy." The site explores deliberative democracy and presents the results of a deliberative poll. Links to other election-related sites are furnished.

National Organization for Women — No. 78

🌐 http://now.org/

Hosted by the National Organization for Women (NOW), this site analyzes key issues including reproductive rights, affirmative action, electoral politics and women in the military. Press releases and updates on issues relating to women's rights are presented. Articles from *National NOW Times* and links to related sites are available.

National Political Index — No. 79

🌐 http://www.politicalindex.com/

One of the most comprehensive lists of links to political sites available on the Internet. Over 3,500 Web pages are indexed with new sites continually added.

National Right to Life — No. 80

🌐 http://www.nrlc.org/

The leading pro-life group, National Right to Life (NRL), sponsors this searchable site that includes information on abortion, euthanasia and the Will to Live project. News on abortion legislation, records of how members of Congress have voted on abortion bills and press releases are included.

National Taxpayers Union and National Taxpayers Union Foundation — No. 81

🌐 http://www.ntu.org/

The National Taxpayers Union (NTU) and National Taxpayers Union Foundation (NTUF) are dedicated to reducing taxes. Their site outlines congressional office expenses and includes a chart of the biggest and smallest spenders. Press releases and news articles on government expenditures and campaign finance reform are available. Issues important to taxpayers—IRS reform, congressional pay and perks, constitutional agenda—are presented. Newsletter articles from NTU's *Dollars & Sense* and NTUF's *Capital Ideas*, and links to similar sites are included.

National Voting Rights Institute — No. 82

🌐 http://world.std.com/%7Envri

The National Voting Rights Institute challenges the use of private money in public elections. Their mostly text-based site contains articles on legal developments regarding the role of wealth in elections, a review of the most expensive campaigns and races, and profiles of campaign funds by representative. The opportunity to search for donors to candidates' funds and a report providing insight on why donors give are available.

National Youth Gang Center — No. 83

🌐 http://www.iir.com/nygc/#Legislation

The National Youth Gang Center (NYGC) was developed by the Office of Juvenile Justice and Delinquency Prevention. The page is primarily text and includes a search engine for finding gang-related laws by state or by subject matter, and information on prevention programs. The National Youth Gang Survey Program Summary is also available to download.

The NES Guide to Public Opinion and Electoral Behavior — No. 84

🌐 http://www.umich.edu/%7Enes/nesguide/nesguide.htm

The National Election Studies (NES) provides tables and graphs illustrating public opinion, electoral behavior and political choice since 1952. The data is divided into nine topics including social and religious characteristics, ideological self-evaluation, public opinion on public policy issues and evaluation of candidates. A great deal of statistical data is available. An overview of the study process, reports and newsletters are also featured.

North American Free Trade Agreement — No. 85

🌐 http://the-tech.mit.edu/Bulletins/nafta.html

This site contains the full text of the landmark trade agreement by Canada, Mexico, and the United States. Text only; no links are available.

O

The Oklahoma City Bombing Trial Transcripts — No. 86

🌐 http://www.courttv.com/casefiles/oklahoma/transcripts/

Sponsored by Court TV, this all-text Web page contains verbatim transcripts from every day of the Timothy McVeigh trial. McVeigh was convicted of bombing the federal building in Oklahoma City.

Once Upon a Time In Arkansas   No. 87

🌐 http://www.pbs.org/wgbh/pages/frontline/shows/arkansas/

The PBS series Frontline presents this text-only site about the Whitewater land deal. Exhaustive coverage provides thorough understanding of Whitewater.

P

Pew Center for Civic Journalism   No. 88

🌐 http://www.pewcenter.org/

This searchable site is presented by the Pew Center for Civic Journalism, an organization dedicated to improving journalism to help "stimulate citizen involvement in community issues." The page contains a description of current projects, press releases and speeches on supported issues, and articles from the newsletter *Civic Catalyst*. Links to related sites are included.

Political Points   No. 89

🌐 http://www.nytimes.com/library/politics/polpoints.html

The *New York Times* sponsors this page that contains hundreds of links to sites in the following categories: The Government, Parties and Persuasions, General Guides, and Political Media and Commentary. Access to materials is provided to members only; registration is currently free of charge.

Political Science Resources   No. 90

🌐 http://sun3.lib.uci.edu/~dtsang/pol.htm

The University of California, Irvine provides an exhaustive list of links to international organizations, nonprofit entities, governmental offices, online informational clearinghouse and more. Coverage of nearly every political science issue is available.

Political Science and Sociology Online Publications   No. 91

🌐 http://osiris.colorado.edu/polsci/res/pubs.html

The University of Colorado at Boulder provides this site that features links to national and international publications. Journals, magazines, news sources, and publishers that present political science content are included.

Political Science Virtual Library   No. 92

🌐 http://www.lib.uconn.edu/polisci/index.html

Links and downloadable files relating to political science are provided. Sites from associations and research institutions, journals, online libraries, and universities are included. The University of Connecticut sponsors this page.

The Pork Barrel Objection   No. 93

🌐 http://epn.org/prospect/11/11kelm.html

This text-only site provides an essay by an author who argues that pork barreling is a good thing. The article was originally published in a 1992 issue of *The American Prospect*.

Preservation, Mixed Use and Urban Vitality   No. 94

🌐 http://www.dnai.com/%7Ekvetcher/MixedUse.html

An essay by architect Jonathan Cohen on how the design of cities contributes to quality of life is featured on this all-text page. A brief history of urban planning is included.

Presidents of the United States   No. 95

🌐 http://www.ipl.org/ref/POTUS/

The Internet Public Library provides a thorough look at every president of the United States. Searches can be conducted by name or subject matter. Backgrounds, election results, cabinet members and notable events are some of the topics covered for each president. Links to biographies, historical documents, audio files, and related sites are included.

The Privacy Forum   No. 96

🌐 http://www.vortex.com/privacy.html

This searchable site contains an extensive collection of documents on privacy. Special reports on current topics and the *Privacy Forum Digest*, including searchable archives, are also available. Audio information can be accessed with RealPlayer or Streamworks. Questions and concerns on privacy or technology can be submitted for a private response. The page is sponsored by several major computer and software companies.

Proposition 209   No. 97

🌐 http://vote96.ss.ca.gov/Vote96.html/BP/209.htm

The full, official text of Proposition 209, the California Civil Rights Initiative that banned affirmative action in California, and an analysis of the proposition are provided at this site. Maintained by the California Secretary of State.

The Public Opinion Laboratory   No. 98

🌐 http://felix.iupui.edu/pol/

The Public Opinion Laboratory is run jointly by Indiana University and Purdue University. This site presents the results of some of their surveys as well as a list of current research. Links to other research sites and related pages.

R

Religious Freedom Restoration Act of 1993   No. 99

🌐 http://www.welcomehome.org/rainbow/nfs-regs/rfra-act.html

The full text of the Religious Freedom Restoration Act of 1993 is presented on this page. The act, which was passed with overwhelming bipartisan support, attempted to reverse a Supreme Court decision and provide greater protection for religious liberties. The law was declared unconstitutional in 1997.

Republican National Committee   No. 100

🌐 http://www.rnc.org/

The official site of the national Republican Party contains explanations of the GOP's positions on issues, memos to Republican leaders, information on political strategies and details on other matters. Articles from *Rising Tide* magazine are also included. Audio and video of GOP events is available with RealPlayer. The site is searchable, presents a lot of information and is easy to navigate.

Reviewing the Revolution   No. 101

🌐 http://www.heritage.org/congress/

This essay makes the case that the first session of the 104th Congress under GOP rule was a success. The conclusion was written by the Heritage Foundation, a conservative think-tank. Text only; no links are available.

The Roadhog Info Trough   No. 102

🌐 http://www.suv.org/

Documented information presented at this site argues that sport utility vehicles cost more to operate, are less safe, and are more destructive of the environment than cars. Environmental advocate Friends of the Earth sponsors this page. Links are provided.

Rocky Mountain Media Watch   No. 103

🌐 http://www.bigmedia.org/

This site presents evidence to back up the Rocky Mountain Media Watch (RMMW) belief that local news is too sensationalistic and profit-driven, and has "abandoned public interest." Press releases, articles and reports documenting their assertion are featured. Information on petitions requesting the FCC deny licenses to certain stations and explanations as to why they should be denied are included.

Roll Call Online   No. 104

🌐 http://www.rollcall.com

Roll Call is one of the best sources of insider news about Congress. This site, which is updated twice a week, contains news, commentary, analysis, and policy briefings.

Roper Center for Public Opinion Research   No. 105

🌐 http://www.ropercenter.uconn.edu/

The Roper Center studies public opinion and "maintains the world's largest archive of public opinion data." Over 60 years of commercial and academic research materials from more than 100 countries is available from the center. Their site includes polling data on a multitude of topics, an overview of surveys conducted worldwide, articles from *The Public Perspective* and a searchable survey archive.

S

School Violence and the Legal Rights of Students   No. 106

🌐 http://eric-Web.tc.columbia.edu/monographs/uds107/school_contents.html

This text-only site contains articles on the rights of students while attending school and the violence that can occur there. Detailed material provides information on preventing violence in schools and describes the factors to becoming a perpetrator or becoming a victim. Problems stemming from gang activity and long term solutions are outlined.

Search Executive Orders   No. 107

🌐 http://www.pub.whitehouse.gov/search/executive-orders.html

Maintained by the White House, this database can be searched for all executive orders since January 20, 1993. Access to White House publications is also provided.

Social Security Privatization   No. 108

🌐 http://www.socialsecurity.org/

This site from The Cato Institute presents the argument that Social Security should be privatized. Text of congressional testimony, and articles and papers by various authors in support of the idea are featured. Speeches and interviews can be heard with RealPlayer. A calculator that presumes how much money could be gained by privatization and the text of a signed petition to reform social security into an investment-based system are included.

Speech to the American Law Institute   No. 109

🌐 http://gos.sbc.edu/g/ginsburg.html

This text-only site contains a speech by Ruth Bader Ginsburg regarding Supreme Court procedures. The page is sponsored by Gifts of Speech (GOS), an organization striving to preserve speeches made by influential women.

The Sport Utility Vehicle Anti-Fan Club   No. 110

🌐 http://www.howard.net/ban-suvs.htm

This site presents an extensive, comprehensive and fairly well documented discussion on the environmental and safety concerns regarding sport utility vehicles. The information is presented in a fun way using graphics to emphasize points. A chart illustrating air pollution substances, sources and effects, and a lot of links are available.

The Starr Report   No. 111

🌐 http://icreport.house.gov/

This page is one of many that features the Starr Report on President William Clinton's relationship with Monica Lewinsky. The text is organized by chapter and posted by the House of Representatives.

State Constitutions   No. 112

🌐 http://www.louisville.edu/library/ekstrom/govpubs/goodsources/history/constitution/stateconstitution.html

A directory of State Constitutions and other related information from the library at the University of Louisville. Comprehensive and searchable.

States News   No. 113

🌐 http://www.statesnews.org/

Updated each weekday, The Council of State Governments (CSG) provides news about state governments and policy issues, and details on CSG's support of public policies. The opportunity to select a subject and browse through previous state legislation discussion forums is available. Many links to current articles from news sources around the nation and other related sites are included.

STAT-USA/Internet   No. 114

🌐 http://www.stat-usa.gov/stat-usa.html

The United States Department of Commerce provides information from the federal government on the business, economic and trade communities. The searchable State of Nation files furnish economic data by business or industry category. Some files are accessible only to subscribers.

Supreme Court Justices of the United States   No. 115

🌐 http://www2.cybernex.net/%7Evanalst/supreme.html

Pictures and biographies of the current justices and all chief justices are featured. Links to related sites are included.

T

Tax Foundation   No. 116

🌐 http://www.taxfoundation.org/index.html

The Tax Foundation monitors federal, state and local fiscal issues. Their page presents information on median incomes, tax reform, tax policy updates and commentary on fiscal issues. The Tax Bites page provides articles, including charts, on a variety of tax-related issues.

Thomas/Legislative Information on the Internet No. 117

🌐 http://thomas.loc.gov/home/thomas2.html

This site is an easy-to-use, searchable database of all Congressional statutes and bills since 1973. It features reviews of public law, roll call votes, committee reports and the opportunity to search and review documents of the Congressional Record. Learn about floor activities in the House of Representatives and Senate as well as more about the legislative process from articles on the subject. The page is sponsored by the Library of Congress.

To Form a More Perfect Union No. 118

🌐 http://lcweb2.loc.gov/ammem/bdsds/bdexhome.html

The Library of Congress presents this site that outlines the history of the Continental Congress and Constitutional Convention. Text only; no links are available.

Top 10 Dumbest Reasons to Build a New Stadium No. 119

🌐 http://www.echonyc.com/%7Eneild/fieldofschemes/top10.html

This amusing site from the authors of the book *Field of Schemes* includes news and information about cities "where sports swindles are underway." Links to related news sources are included.

U

Ultimate Guide to Sport Utility Vehicles No. 120

🌐 http://www.popsci.com/suv_site/

Popular Science magazine hosts this site that provides information on nearly every sport utility vehicle sold in North America. The report is based on tests conducted by the journal. Information on how the models were tested, and a part-by-part explanation of what 4WD means and how it works is detailed. A review, a rating, statistical information, insurance claim histories and costs are presented for each vehicle. Links to related sources are available.

United Nations No. 121

🌐 http://www.un.org

The official site of the United Nations (U.N.) contains a searchable document index, daily news updates, the history of the U.N. and descriptions of U.N. departments and offices. A listing of member states, information about U.N. reform, and details on speeches and resolutions are available. Five major U.N. missions are outlined: peace and security, international law, economic and social development, human rights and humanitarian affairs. The site is available in English, French, Russian, and Spanish. Links to related sites are included.

U. S. Back's Off Sanctions, Seeing Poor Effect Abroad No. 122

🌐 http://www.mtholyoke.edu/acad/intrel/nosanc.htm

A reprint of a July 1998 *New York Times* article by Eric Schmitt that reports trade sanctions have been ineffective is featured at this site. The article is strictly text, although links to other articles on foreign policy and globalization are available.

The U. S. Constitution Online No. 123

🌐 http://www.usconstitution.net

A comprehensive, well-maintained, easily searchable, and reliable site for primary documents and links to other online resources regarding the U. S. Constitution. Covers *Constitutional FAQs*, in-depth discussions on *Constitutional Topics*, information on *Amending the Constitution*, as well as *Constitution-related links* and *Other Constitutional resources*.

U. S. State Constitutions and Web Sites No. 124

🌐 http://www.constitution.org/cons/uscons.htm

With one or two exceptions for states that are not yet online, this site contains an easy point-and-click directory of all state constitutions as well as "commentaries on the state constitutions that point out their strengths and deficiencies from the viewpoint of constitutional principles."

U. S. State Department No. 125

🌐 http://www.state.gov/

This searchable site contains news about the latest developments in foreign policy and details on foreign policy issues. Thorough information on foreign policy, travelling abroad and living overseas is available. Data on the Secretary of State's office and links to embassies in foreign countries and other related sites are included.

The United States Constitution No. 126

🌐 http://www.house.gov/Constitution/Constitution.html

The full text of the supreme law of the land is featured on this page. The amendments are also available.

United States Constitution Search No. 127

🌐 http://www.law.emory.edu/FEDERAL.usconser.html

The opportunity to search the Constitution by specific word(s) is provided. The site is sponsored by Emory University.

United States Information Agency No. 128

🌐 http://www.usia.gov/

The United States Information Agency (USIA) is an "independent foreign affairs agency" that "supports U. S. foreign policy and national interests abroad." Their Web page details various issues and programs: the Fullbright program, citizen exchanges, au pair program and public diplomacy. Data on foreign press centers in the United States and information resource centers is also presented. New releases and a few links are available.

United States Senate No. 129

🌐 http://www.senate.gov

The official page of the upper chamber of Congress provides information on legislative activities, committees and individual senators. A history of the Senate and its procedures, statistics about the Senate and details on upcoming Senate activity is available. The site is searchable and contains links.

University of Houston Libraries/Political Science Sites No. 130

🌐 http://info.lib.uh.edu/politics/polsci.htm

Links to numerous sites relating to political science and American politics are featured. No text available.

V

Voter's Guide to Judicial Elections   No. 131
🌐 http://www.ca.lwv.org/lwvc.files/judic/

This site contains information about judicial elections in California, but much of the detail is applicable to judicial elections elsewhere. The page is sponsored by the League of Women Voters.

Voting Rights Act Clarification   No. 132
🌐 http://www.usdoj.gov/crt/voting/clarify3.htm

These pages are part of the larger U. S. Department of Justice site (http://www.usdoj.gov). Here the Department of Justice addresses a rumor about the Voting Rights Act that has been circulating around the country for some time and has been especially virulent on the Internet. The rumor is completely false, and the DOJ clarifies the law and dispels the rumor.

W

War on Black People   No. 133
🌐 http://www.drcnet.org/guide1-96/waron.html

This text-only site features an essay that discusses the racial implications of the fact that possession of crack is punished far more severely than possession of cocaine. Presented by the Drug Reform Coordination Network (DRCNet), the Internet source for drug policy reform.

Waste in Your State   No. 134
🌐 http://www.taxpayer.net/TCS/States/stateindex.html

A searchable list of wasteful federal spending in 35 states and the District of Columbia is available on this page. Sponsored by Taxpayers for Common Sense (TCS), the site also features press releases, reports, information on projects supported by TCS and letters addressed to Capitol Hill. An outline of TCS victories that saved taxpayers money and an online copy of *The Waste Basket*, a weekly bulletin on government spending, are included. This informative site also contains links to related pages.

Western Connecticut State University Department of Social Sciences/WCSU List: Political Science Internet Resources   No. 135
🌐 http://www.wcsu.ctstateu.edu/socialsci/polscres.html

This page features links to related sources of information on political science. The site is presented by Western Connecticut State University.

The White House   No. 136
🌐 http://www.whitehouse/gov/WH/Welcome.html

The White House homepage features a searchable index of archived documents, the history of the building and a virtual tour. Recent presidential initiatives, press briefings, executive orders and the text of radio addresses are included. Information on the president, vice president and their families is featured. Links are available to related sites.

Why Americans Hate the Media   No. 137
🌐 http://www.theatlantic.com/atlantic/issues/96feb/
media/media.htm

The title says it all. This informative article by James Fallows appeared in the February 1996 issue of *Atantic Monthly*. Comments made by the author can be heard with RealAudio. Links to related sources are included.

Women in Politics   No. 138
🌐 http://www.glue.umd.edu/%7Ecliswp/

The University of Maryland presents the history of women in politics and information on the Equal Rights Amendment. Details on suffrage, women's roles throughout history and a timeline of women in politics are included. Links to similar sites are available.

Woodrow Wilson: Repudiation of "Dollar Diplomacy"   No. 139
🌐 http://www.mtholyoke.edu/acad/intrel/ww83.htm

The short speech given by former President Woodrow Wilson arguing that the United States should help China economically is contained on this text-only site. The speech was originally published in the *American Journal of International Law*.

The World Bank   No. 140
🌐 http://www.worldbank.org

Comprehensive (if slow-loading) site on the World Bank—what it is, what it does, who "owns" it, and a complete explication of its mission: "loans, advice, and an array of customized resources to more than 100 developing countries and countries in transition." Additionally, this site is a good source for global economic data.

How to Cite a Web Site

Although a standard has not yet been developed for referencing on-line information, guidelines are in progress. The *MLA Handbook* and the *Publication Manual for the American Psychological Association* don't have full guidelines in their fourth editions, though electronic references can credit the author and enable readers to access the material. Many legitimate sources and references are on the Web, but some sites are advertisements and others have questionable validity.

Before citing from the World Wide Web (WWW), the following questions should be considered: Will the data be available to the reader or will the site quickly disappear? Is the data widely accessible or available only on a limited basis, e.g., a campus local network? In general, if both print and electronic forms of material are the same, the print form is preferred, though this may change as electronic forms become more available to researchers and libraries.

Electronic correspondence including E-mail, conversations via electronic discussion groups, and bulletin boards are cited as "personal communication" in the text according to the American Psychological Association. World Wide Web data files are cited in the text as author and date or, if no author is available, by the title of the file or home page. In the reference list, Web sites are cited by title of the data file, year, month, day, title of browser, address. An example is

"Prevention Primer" (1996, July 17.) National Clearinghouse for Alcohol and Drug Information. World Wide Web: http://www.health.org.

Important note: Before citing anything from the Internet and/or World Wide Web, be aware that much of what you may find may not be valid. For example, a recent study conducted by Davison and Guan found that, after accessing 167 nutrition-related documents, 45 percent of these provided information that was not consistent with one or more of established dietary guidelines and included advertisements recommending supplements, herbal remedies, weight-loss products, and specific diets. Internet resources continue to expand rapidly and nutrition professionals and students need to develop strategies to address inconsistent or questionable dietary information available through this technology. (Source: "The Quality of Dietary Information on the World Wide Web," *Journal of the Canadian Dietetics Association*, Winter 1996.)

For further information on citing from the Web, see the following:

In Print

American Psychological Association. (1995.) *Publication Manual of the American Psychological Association, 4th ed.* Washington DC: American Psychological Association.

Gibaldi, J. (1995.) *Handbook for writers of research papers 4th ed.* NY: Modern Language Association of America.

Online

MLA on the Web

⊕ http://www.mla.org/

This is the site of the Modern Language Association. Here you will find guidelines on MLA documentation style. Click on *Citing Sources from the World Wide Web* and you will reach an easy-to-understand explanation on how to cite sources from the Web. A must-visit site. Text only, no links, but clear and authoritative examplesprovided.

Classroom Connect: How to Cite Internet Resources

⊕ http://www.classroom.net/classroom/CitingNet Resources.html

Although written for K–12 educators, this site offers a good, clear "how-to" guide for referencing online sources in bibliographies. Some links to other sites.

How to Cite Information from the Internet and the World Wide Web

⊕ http://www.apa.org/journals/webref.htm

This brief page from the American Psychological Association explains the APA's recommendations for citing Web materials. Text only, no links.

Name _____

Course # _____ Section _____

Date _____ Soc. Sec. # _____

Web Journal

Journal Notes

http:// _____ Topic _____

_____

_____

_____

_____

_____

_____

_____

Web Journal

Journal Notes

http:// _____ Topic _____

_____

_____

_____

_____

_____

_____

_____

ReadingsPLUS with WebLinks

ReadingsPLUS Web Site Evaluation Form

Student Name _____

Date _____ Soc. Sec. # or Student I.D. # _____

Course Name & Number _____ Instructor Name _____

Web Site Name: _____

Site Number (if applicable) _____

Site Address/URL _____

Briefly describe your online experience. Were you able to access the site?

Identify the Source / Who runs site. Who is the person or what is the organization behind the site?

Is the site links-intensive or content-intensive? Or is it a combination of text and links to other sites?

Provide a brief overview of site. What resources and subjects or types of material are covered?

How would you rate the quality of content? Was the information useful to you? If yes, how so? If not, why not?

How would you rate the quality of the site's graphics and its navigability/ease-of-use?

When was the site last updated?

What does this site offer compared to other sources of information used in this course?

ReadingsPLUS Web Site Evaluation Form

Student Name _____

Date _____ Soc. Sec. # or Student I.D. # _____

Course Name & Number _____ Instructor Name _____

Web Site Name: _____

Site Number (if applicable) _____

Site Address/URL _____

Briefly describe your online experience. Were you able to access the site?

Identify the Source / Who runs site. Who is the person or what is the organization behind the site?

Is the site links-intensive or content-intensive? Or is it a combination of text and links to other sites?

Provide a brief overview of site. What resources and subjects or types of material are covered?

How would you rate the quality of content? Was the information useful to you? If yes, how so? If not, why not?

How would you rate the quality of the site's graphics and its navigability/ease-of-use?

When was the site last updated?

What does this site offer compared to other sources of information used in this course?

ReadingsPLUS Reading Review Form

Student Name _____

Date _____ Soc. Sec. # or Student I.D. # _____

Course Name & Number _____ Instructor Name _____

Reading Number: _____ Reading Title: _____

_____

Reading Summary
Describe the central idea or argument of this reading.

Key Terms
List two or three key terms used in the reading and briefly define them.

Compare and Contrast Information
Select one question from the following three questions and answer it.

(1) How does the information in this reading compare to what has been presented in class on this topic, or in your textbook (if you're using one)? For example, does it support or does it contradict what you have previously learned?

(2) How does the information in this reading compare to information you've encountered on this topic at a related Web site?

(3) How has this reading influenced or changed your opinion on the topic?

Index

Abortion, 134, 136–137, 183, 186, 188, 190
Activism, 181
Affirmative action, 56–57, 75, 167
Air Force, 186
Alcoholics Anonymous, 62
Alfred P. Murrah Federal Building, 12
Allegheny Institute for Public Policy, 48
America OnLine, 53
American diplomacy, 198
American Indians, 56
American Medical Association, 134
American Revolution, 169
American Spectator, 21, 24
Amistad, 64
Andrew Jackson Memorial and Museum, 39
Anne Morrow Lindbergh, 16
Anti-federalist movement, 53
Anti-poverty policy, 44
Anti-tax activists, 48
Anti-tobacco legislation, 109
Anti-abortion, 136
Armed Forces, 168
Article IV, 14
Articles of Confederation, 13, 130
Asiagate, 99
Assisted suicide, 182–183
Atomic bomb, 20
Authoritarianism, 19
AzScam, 39

Baby boomers, 103
Bankruptcy, 108
Benoit, Gary, 140
Big Brother, 35, 201
Bill of Rights, 13, 15, 149, 186, 189
Bolshevism, 16
Boot, Max, 181
Bovard, James, 165
Bradley, Jennifer, 146
Brady Bill, 12
Brent H. Bake, 99
Bribery, 38
Bureaucracy, 50
Bush Administration, 21
Business Week, 42

Campaign spending,107
Campaigns, 106, 112
Candals, 94
Capitalism,18, 20
Capitalist society, 35
Carney, Eliza Newlin, 50

Cass R. Sunstein, 149
Catch-22, 24
Celebration, Florida, 28–37
Censorship, 186
Chinagate, 38
Cigarette industry, 108
City-states,, 133
Civil liberties, 67, 70–71
Civil rights, 67, 87, 167
Civil Rights Act, 15, 58, 170
Civil rights reform, 131
Civil servant, 163
Civil War, 15, 124, 174
Civil-service tests, 56
Clean Water Act, 166
Clinton, Hillary, 82
Clinton, William, 16, 21, 42, 61, 66–69, 75, 80–83, 156–157, 160
CNN, 202
Code civil, 15
Cohen, Richard M., 102
Cohn, Jonathan, 124
Cold war, 94, 176, 196, 198
Commercial diplomacy, 200
Communism, 94, 193
Community, 30, 37
Computer revolution, 18
Conflicts of interest, 118
Congress, 50, 140
Constitutionalism, 190
Consumers, 163
Copyright, 205
Corruption, 38
Counterdevolution, 50
Crimes, 165
Criminal procedure, 182
Critical reading strategies, 2
Customs service, 165
Cyberdemocracy, 18
Cyberspace, 18, 26, 66

D.A.R.E., 156
Dallas, 46
Davidson, Zoë, 117
Deadbeat dads, 68
Declaration of Independence, 131, 171
Declaration of the Rights of Man, 15
Democracy, 16–20, 36, 103, 105–106, 129, 153, 193–194, 199
Democratic Party, 75, 78, 112, 132
Department of Justice, 151
Desegregation, 131
Devolution,43–44, 50
Dictatorship, 155, 193
Diplomacy, 199, 201

Discretionary funds, 39
Discrimination, 56
Disney, 28, 34, 36
  Disneymania, 34
  Walt, 30, 31
  Walt Disney Imagineering, 30, 35
  Walt Disney World 28, 31
Domestic policy, 130
Donations, 120
Drug abuse, 63
Drug addiction, 68
Drug policy, 61
Drug war, 59, 61
Drunk driving, 50
  laws, 54
Due Process Clause, 183

Economies, 202
Economy, 84, 87, 94, 203
  world, 201
Education, 44–45
Elections, 105–106
Electronic town hall, 18
Embargo, 196
Embargo policy, 192
Embargoes, 195
Embezzlement, 164
Environmental Protection Agency (EPA), 151, 166
Epcot, 30
Executive order, 155
Executive orders, 157
Experimental Prototype Community of Tomorrow (EPCOT), 30

Fanaticism, 19
Fascism, 16, 17
Federal budget, 126
Federal Bureau of Investigation (FBI), 21, 154
Federal employees, 169, 172
Federal government, 45
Federal grants, 43
Federal land management, 155
Federal Trade Commission (FTC), 26
Federalism, 51, 53–54, 181, 186, 188
Federalist Papers, The, 18, 141
Fifteenth Amendment, 14
Filegate, 21, 38
Filibuster, 131
Filibustering, 129
Finis Welch, 56
First Amendment, 13, 24
First Amendment, 71
Fletcher, George P,. 12
Foreign affairs, 130

Foreign policy, 191, 194, 198–199
Fornigate, 38
Founding Fathers, 12, 43, 128, 130, 140, 142, 146, 155
Fourteenth Amendment, 15, 58, 182, 184–186
Fourth Amendment, 22
Fraud, 163
Free enterprise, 164
Free speech, 107
Free trade, 195
Free-market, 194
Freedman, Samuel G., 59
freedom, 193, 196
Fully Informed Jury Association (FIJA), 13
Fundraising, 120

Gang Reporting Evaluation and Tracking (GREAT), 73
Gates, Bill, 203
Geraldo, 21
Gettysburg Address, 131
Glazer, Nathan, 56
Global community, 202
Global economy, 198, 199–200
Global Positioning System, 204
Global village, 202
Globalization, 20, 199–200
Globalized economy, 18
Golway, Terry, 68
Gore, Al, 25–26
Government employee, 171
Grants, 39
Great Depression, 16, 157
Great Society, 178
Guerrilla warfare, 204
Gulf War, 195, 202–203

Hancock, John, 22
Hardcastle, Valerie Gray, 2
Harriet Tubman, 64
Harvard University, 42
Health care regulation, 38
Health reform, 83
Hispanics, 56
Hood, John, 38
Human rights, 19, 199–200, 202

Immigrants, 56
Impeachment, 85, 109, 150, 154
Imperialism, 19
Independent counsel, 151, 153
Independent Counsel Act, 149–150, 152, 154
Industrial Revolution, 17, 202
Information, 202–205
Information revolution, 202
Information warfare, 204

Insurance, 120
Intact dilation and extraction, 134
Intact dilation and extractions, 138
International security, 198
Internet, 51, 54, 202
Internet Resources, 4
Internet Tax Freedom Act, 53
Interstate commerce, 141, 145
Iron Curtain, 195
Internal Revenue Service (IRS), 150, 166, 177
Islamic fundamentalism, 19
Isolationism, 130

Journalism, 90, 91, 92, 93, 95, 96, 97, 98, 102, 103, 163
Judicial activists, 182
Justice Department, 26, 52

Kaiser Family Foundation, 42
Kaminer, Wendy, 66
Kaplan, Lawrence F., 198
Kaplan, Sheila, 117
Kickbacks, 164
Klein, Joe, 134
Korean War, 176
Ku Klux Klan Act, 185

Lake, Matt, 6
Land use, 52
Larceny,164
Late-term abortion, 135
Late-term-abortion, 137
Law enforcement, 41, 204
    drunk-driving, 54
Ledeen, Michael, 192
Legislation, 184
Lewinsky, Monica, 21, 23–24, 66, 81–82, 101, 108, 149, 153, 160
Liberties, 186
Liberty, 186
Library of Congress, 201
Lind, Michael, 129
Lobbying, 109–110, 112
Lobbyists, 111–115, 117
Locke Foundation, 39, 40–41
Los Angeles Times, 73

Maharidge, Dale, 75
Mahtesian, Charles, 46
Marijuana, 188
Mark Silverstein, 73
Marxism, 20
MCI Communications Corporation, 53
McVeigh, Timothy, 12–15
Media, 99, 152
Medicaid, 163
Medicare, 43, 128, 163, 165
Megan's law, 25
Megastates, 133
Microsoft Corporation, 26, 53, 203
Microstate, 132–133
Militarism, 16
Military, 16, 83, 84, 202
    strategy, 201
    strength, 196
    technology, 195
Minorities, 70, 73, 167
Miranda rule, 23, 182

Mobsters, 39
Monarchy, 106
Monicagate,100
Motion picture industry, 114

Narcotics Anonymous, 62
Nazis, 16, 130, 138
NBC News, 42
Neo-Rotarian, 28
Neotraditional, 32–33
Neotraditionalism, 31
New Deal, 15, 23, 176, 184
New Federalism, 50
New Urbanist projects, 32
Nichols, Terry, 13
1964 Civil Rights Act, 67
1996 Telecommunications Act, 52
Nixon, 50, 85, 205
Nobel Peace Prize, 84

Packwood, Bob, 22–24, 38
Pandora's Box, 167
Paparazzi, 25, 26, 96
Partial birth, 135
Partial-birth abortion, 136
Partial-birth-abortion, 134, 137, 138
Patent protection, 205
Patriotism, 132
Peace, 198
Pentagon, 196
Peoples Liberation Army, 99
Perjury, 24, 149
Personal bankruptcies, 68
Policy on Internet Sexual Harassment, 66
Policymakers, 161
Political apartheid, 167
Political favors, 117
Political style, 159
Pork, 39, 124, 126, 127, 128
    pork-barrel spending, 41, 124, 125, 128
    pork-busters, 125, 127, 128
Pornography, 186
Prejudice, 56
Price fixing,163
Princess Diana, 25, 26, 100
Private property rights, 155
Professional sports, 47
Prohibition,143, 168
Property management, 36
Public Broadcasting System, 79, 99
public servant, 153
public service, 90
Public Utility Commission (PUC), 79
Public works, 47, 124
Punitive damages, 182

Reagan, 50, 52
Reedy Creek Improvement District, 31
Reformists, 120
Rehnquist Court, 181–182, 189
Rehnquist, William, 12
Religion, 184
Religious freedom, 12
Religious fundamentalism, 19
Republican Party, 112
Reverse discrimination, 182
Richmond, Elizabeth B., 4

Roe v. Wade, 134, 136, 139, 181
Rosen, Jeffrey, 21
Rotarians, 28, 29, 37

Saddam Hussein, 197, 202
Same-sex marriage, 188
Scandal, 38, 39, 81–83, 103, 106, 150, 152–153
Schlesinger, Jr., Arthur, 16
Search and seizure, 182, 190
Search engines, 6, 8, 10
Secret Service, 149
Siegal, Nina, 70
Self-government, 16, 105
Sexual harassment, 168
Sexual orientation, 156
Sexual promiscuity, 107
Single-sex education, 181
Slavery, 64, 65, 131, 185
Smoking,168
Social Security, 43, 84, 94, 176, 177
Sons of Liberty, 22
Sovereignty, 201, 202
Soviets, 26
Spamming,115
Sport utility vehicle, 68–69
Stadiums 47–48
    soccer stadium, 46
    Three Rivers Stadium, 46
    Trans World Dome, 47
State corruption, 38
Suffrage, 129, 131
Supercomputers, 199
Supreme Court, 52, 57, 184, 186
Surplus funds, 39
Surveillance, 204

Tax, 43, 52, 186, 203
    evasion 163
    hikes 47
    incentives 45
    law 111
    sales tax 46, 53
Taxpayers, 163
Teen pregnancy, 68
Telecommunications, 53, 115
Telecommunications Act of 1996, 93
Tenth Amendment, 42, 53
Terrorists, 193, 202, 204
Teti, Dennis, 184
Thirteenth Amendment, 15, 185
Thirteenth Amendments, 14
Thomas Jefferson, 34
Thurber, James, 24
Tim Graham, 99
Tobacco industry, 116, 120, 163
Tocqueville, 17, 35, 37, 174
Tripp, Linda, 23, 26
Tyranny, 53

Underground Railroad, 64
Utopia, 30

Veto, 156
Video Privacy Protection Act, 25
Vietnam, 103, 176–177
Violence, 107

Waco, Texas, 14
Wall Street, 91
Walt Disney Imagineering, 30, 35

Walt Disney World, 28, 31
Walzer, Michael, 163
War on drug, 60
Watergate,85, 100, 103, 150, 153, 154, 157
Watergate Babies,115
Weisberger, Bernard A., 169
Welfare, 44, 141, 142
Welfare reform, 42, 44
Welfare state, 140, 143, 170, 178
Whitewater, 38, 85, 149
Wilkes, John, 22–23, 24, 26
Wolf, Naomi, 64
Women's movement, 56
World economy, 201
World War I, 175
World War II, 16, 48, 84, 157, 176
World Wide Web, 26

Young Turks, 115

Zaller, John R., 81